T0181372

Lecture Notes in Information Systems and Organisation

Volume 18

Leonardo Caporarello · Fabrizio Cesaroni
Raphael Giesecke · Michele Missikoff
Editors

Digitally Supported Innovation

A Multi-Disciplinary View on Enterprise,
Public Sector and User Innovation

 Springer

Editors
Leonardo Caporarello
Department of Management and Technology
Bocconi University
Milan
Italy

Fabrizio Cesaroni
Department of Economics
University of Messina
Messina
Italy

Raphael Giesecke
School of Science
Aalto University
Espoo
Finland

Michele Missikoff
Institute of Sciences and Technologies
   of Cognition
Rome
Italy

ISSN 2195-4968   ISSN 2195-4976   (electronic)
Lecture Notes in Information Systems and Organisation
ISBN 978-3-319-40264-2   ISBN 978-3-319-40265-9   (eBook)
DOI 10.1007/978-3-319-40265-9

Library of Congress Control Number: 2016942018

Printed on acid-free paper

This Springer imprint is published by Springer Nature
The registered company is Springer International Publishing AG Switzerland

Contents

Introduction by the Editors

Leonardo Caporarello, Fabrizio Cesaroni, Raphael Giesecke and Michele Missikoff

Abstract Innovation is a key goal of most organisations, and digitalisation through information and communications technology (ICT) is a key support means. The variety of ICT based innovation is striking, as is its current impact on most of the world's gross product. In this book we aim to map out a broad overview of ICT supported innovation on practical, evidence based context level, as well as on theoretical, and methodological levels. Consequentially, we present multi-disciplinary views on organisational innovation in enterprises and the public sector, as well as the ubiquitous, social media based user innovation. The studies included in this book will thus guide both innovation scholars as well as industrial practitioners—and innovators at large—in their present and future innovation studies and undertakings. In detail, we include innovation in knowledge work and human-computer interaction; innovation of and in socio-technical systems; and user based innovation in public services vs. innovation in social media use. Our contexts include innovative mobile solutions as well as factories of the future, with a focus on 3D and 4D printing.

L. Caporarello (✉)
Department of Management and Technology, Bocconi University,
Via Roentgen 1, 20136 Milan, Italy
e-mail: leonardo.caporarello@unibocconi.it

F. Cesaroni
Department of Economics, University of Messina,
Piazza Pugliatti 1, 98122 Messina, Italy
e-mail: fabrizio.cesaroni@unime.it

R. Giesecke
School of Science, Aalto University, P.O. Box 15500, 00076 Aalto, Finland
e-mail: Raphael.Giesecke@aalto.fi

M. Missikoff
CNR, Inst. of Sc. and Techn. of Cognition, Via S. Martino Della Battaglia 44,
00185 Rome, Italy
e-mail: michele.missikoff@iasi.cnr.it

© Springer International Publishing Switzerland 2016
L. Caporarello et al. (eds.), *Digitally Supported Innovation*,
Lecture Notes in Information Systems and Organisation 18,
DOI 10.1007/978-3-319-40265-9_1

1 Digitalisation as Enabler for Innovating and Innovations

Innovation is regarded as a key lever to relaunch the EU socio-economic system. In particular SMEs—who represent 98 % of the enterprises active in the European production system [1]—need to systematically address innovation as part of their everyday business. Likewise, large organisations, be they private or public, aim for investing in innovative activity to improve products and services in order to create, reinforce and sustain their competitive advantage.

Innovation spans over a vast cultural territory—from the arts to the area of systematic, multidiscipline research and application, based on various focused disciplines: from organisation and management science to ICT, from creativity to psychology and sociology, from marketing and industrial engineering and management to education and learning. According to the *Open Innovation Strategy and Policy Group* [2, 3], innovation activities to date need to be based on:

- integrated collaboration,
- co-created, shared value,
- cultivated innovation ecosystems,
- unleashed exponential technologies, and
- extraordinarily rapid adoption.

Consequently, in order to be ready for the new challenges facing the future of innovation, enterprises need to rethink their culture and organisation. They have also to promote the adoption and effective use of advanced information and communications technologies (ICT). In fact, due to its role of enabler, being at the same time a strategic infrastructure, ICT plays a central role in innovation, considering the rich panorama of methods, tools, platforms, and in general, solutions that are on offer.

This book addresses various issues related to the role of ICT in promoting and supporting enterprise innovation. In particular, the aim is to provide an account of the opportunities that advanced ICT solutions offer to improve the innovation capability of (complex) organisations, with a focus on networked SMEs. Innovation is a very wide and articulated notion, more and more beyond its noteworthy relevance from the economic and social perspective. The reason lies in the enormous benefits that innovation can produce for the productive and social system. In that respect, innovation also represents a vast scientific and cultural area of investigation.

This book acknowledges this pervasive nature of innovation and presents a variety of papers that investigate the use of ICT methods and tools in the context of innovation initiatives. However, even when leaving out innovation *unrelated to ICT*, what remains is still a wide area of investigation. In addition, the ICT sector (in its different declinations: theory, methodologies, implementations, applications, etc.) is so vast that the interplay between innovation and ICT represents an extremely rich area of research and experimentation. Therefore, carrying out an innovation project is not a simple job, and nowadays it is even harder than in the past, since globalisation poses unprecedented challenges. Consequently, innovation requires new, open, collaborative approaches.

From the organisational point of view, we deal with socio-technical systems operating within networks of enterprises, which need to achieve the necessary coordination and synergy in a distributed, multi-actor decisional and operational context. Therefore, managing an innovation project requires approaches, methods and tools inherently different from what is used in 'traditional' project management. It is necessary to deeply rethink existing tools and methods. Moreover, at the same time, new tools and methods need to be developed. We need to revisit and reshape our culture and experience in ICT to be prepared to the advent of the new breed of socio-technical systems, aimed at supporting innovation in networked enterprises. Whereas 'enterprises' in this context stands for all kinds of organisations—we a focus on SMEs, but also including large highly decentralised corporations and even public institutions.

One of the most modern and flexible ICT-based solutions available to enterprises are collaborative content management the platform. To date, there are a number of dedicated ICT platforms that address specific phases or problems inherent to innovation projects. From idea management (such as *IdeaScale* or *Innocentive*) to collaboration platforms (such as *BSCW* or *Slack*), to content (e.g., *Drupal*, *Alfresco*) and knowledge management (e.g., *Poolparty*, *Ontorion*), to collaborative decision-making (e.g., *Fingertip*, *Review19*). However, despite the large number of *specialised* platforms and tools, there is a lack of *integrated* software environments capable of supporting innovation in its full lifecycle, in the context of networked enterprises. In addition, the impact of other, less-focussed, technologies, from mobile computing to agent systems, from cloud computing to service systems, need to be revisited to explore their impact on innovation projects.

With all these different aspects of innovation as such, and innovation related ICT in mind we need a conceptual clarification of the interplay between ICT and innovation. Consequently, we start with introducing three main dimensions: innovation *by*, *with*, and *in* ICT (Fig. 1).

Innovating *by using* ICT—This dimension regards ICT as an enabler during the innovation process. It encompasses innovation in any possible industrial sector, where innovative ICT solutions are adopted as a means in the design, development, production or distribution, of goods and services. For instance, when using CAD and a 3D printer to produce a customised chair, made to order exactly in the colour, shape and size required by the customer. Note that in this dimension the final product can be a 'traditional' one (as simple as a chair) and low-tech (without embedded technology), but it needs advanced ICT solutions in order to be competitive in the market.

Innovation *with* ICT—This dimension regards ICT as an enabler of the actual product or service. In detail, we aim at understanding the high potential that new ICT solutions have when adopted to be an integral part of new goods and/or services innovation. For instance, Airbnb or Uber (founded 2008 and 2009, respectively) could not be conceived 10 years ago, when Internet and smart mobile devices where not systematically used by the majority of the world's active

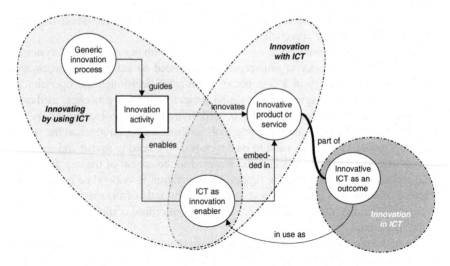

Fig. 1 The three dimensions of innovation in, with, and by using ICT

population. Embedding advanced ICT solutions in an innovative product, process, or service is the most relevant frontier of enterprise innovation today. The same is true for new organisational models that are based on collaboration platforms and shared knowledge systems.

Innovation *in* ICT—This dimension concerns innovation initiatives that target ICT as such. They aim directly at new ICT methods, tools, components and devices to be introduced in the market. Today, ICT represents one of the most dynamic research and industrial areas. In addition, as suggested in this book, ICT represents the most relevant technology in terms of its pervasiveness and impact on the further socio-economic systems.

The three dimensions of innovations guide us in structuring this book. In the first two parts, we examine ICT enablers in use—at first (Part I) in a context of organisational capabilities and processes, and as enablers for novel business models. In Part II we investigate specific ICT enablers in use for innovation within specific business processes, such as service development or manufacturing.

In Part III we focus on the experiences enterprise have gathered when implementing innovative ICT enablers. Such implementations can encompass two dimensions: we start with innovating by using ICT, and end with innovations with ICT.

In Part IV the focus is on the third dimension, innovating ICT solutions as such. This part extends from innovative digital services and cloud applications towards digital operating systems, architectures towards ICT hardware platforms.

2 Part I: Innovative ICT Enablers in Use on Organisational Level

The growing sophistication of ICT and the possibility it shows to easily connect distant objects and actors, to share knowledge, and to facilitate complex relationships among a plethora of agents, offers to enterprises a powerful means for developing innovations. It is those innovations, that may provide higher value to customers and a stronger competitive advantage compared to traditional solutions. To exploit such potentialities associated to ICT, however, firms are often required to evolve from traditional forms of doing business. Both the relationships with customers and the relationships with suppliers and partners have to be reshaped, often with the final goal of facilitating the active involvement of external agents in internal processes. In turn, new business models have to be conceptualised, designed and pursued.

The four chapters composing Part I of the book deal exactly with these issues. Specifically, Chap. 2 and 3 focus on the role of customers, and explore how ICT solutions may help enterprises to favour user participation and to collect promising ideas for new products and services directly from the enterprise's customer base. Chapter 4 discusses the different business models that enterprises should adopt depending on the role they play within the ICT ecosystem. Finally, Chap. 5 explores how enterprises may take advantage of the rich informative context represented by the Deep Web, which enterprises may exploit by engaging in proper competitive intelligence activities.

3 Part II: Specific ICT Enablers in Use for Innovation

The second part of the volume deals with the idea that ICT represents a powerful tool that may support enterprises in their innovative effort. With respect to traditional design tools, ICT opens up novel possibilities of innovation development through the gathering of information that allow a fine-tuned analysis of the socio-technical system and, in general, of complex real environments. By exploiting these possibilities, enterprises can better connect with their customers, in order to deliver better-suited products and services. They can also adopt more efficient manufacturing processes (for instance, by employing 3D and 4D manufacturing methods), in order to reduce lead time and development costs. Overall, processes of new product and service development become more efficient, thus enhancing the enterprises' capability to gain a sustainable competitive advantage.

In the seven chapters composing Part II we discuss all these aspects. Specifically, the first focus area of this part is in the design and development processes. Chapter 6 elaborates on novel design techniques based on Augmented Reality (AR), whereas Chap. 7 investigates programming contexts in software development. Chapters 8 and 9 are set within the development process as well, both addressing socio-technical systems from a human-computer interaction perspective. All four Chap. 6–9, thus address the important area of innovation in knowledge work. Then, Chap. 10 extends the service development process from enterprises to the public sector through studying co-creation processes of public services based on citizen engagement via social media. Finally, the two last Chaps. 11 and 12 are embedded in the factories of the future context, with a focus on 3D and 4D printing in manufacturing. Chapter 11 examines the fast changing automotive supply chain with a focus on 3D printing, whereas Chap. 12 investigates 4D printing as an emerging technology in use.

4 Part III: Implementing Innovative ICT Enablers

The first two parts of the volume are focused on innovation and manufacturing processes. Following, part 3 shows practical examples of how ICT can be integrated and combined with other technologies in order to provide innovative, information-based services. Due to its pervasiveness, ICT can in fact be considered a general purpose technology [4], whose benefits may spread over a wide range of application domains. Through ICT solutions, enterprises can increase the knowledge content of their products, thus including functionalities that better satisfy consumers' needs in ways that often are non-invasive for customers. Such possibilities represent a potential advantage for enterprises especially in knowledge-intensive sectors, such as utilities, retailing, healthcare and business-to-business services, as the examples reported in this part of the volume will demonstrate.

Specifically, Chap. 13 discusses the case of a utility company that made use of ICT solutions to effectively manage over time its application portfolio. Chapter 14 presents the case of a large retailing company and its attempt to reach inventory management improvements in the retail stores by exploiting the possibilities offered by ICT solutions. Chapter 15 focuses on the healthcare sector and shows how ICT can be employed by healthcare organisations to provide services in a widespread territory by limiting invasive (negative) effects and by promoting cooperative exploitation of information between individuals and communities. Chapter 16 pays attention to the sector of software development (in a business-to-business context) and proposes new solutions that software developers may use to raise their productivity. Finally, Chap. 17 focuses on the transport sector and discusses how ICT enables the development of a new model of public transportation through the diffusion of shared solutions.

5 Part IV: Innovating Novel ICT Solutions

The last part of the volume concentrates on innovations in ICT and pursues two complementary goals. On the one hand, it aims at showing how the ICT trajectory is evolving over time, and how the performance and efficiency of ICT solutions is constantly improving. On the other hand, it aims at offering some examples of the different directions of evolution of the ICT trajectory. Like other technological trajectories, technology dynamics of ICT are cumulative [5, 6] and future evolutionary patterns are strictly linked to development efforts that enterprises and research organisations have been promoting in the past and in the present time. Analysing which aspects of ICT are capturing the attention of researchers thus provides useful indications of possible outcomes that may be expected in the near future.

Part IV of the volume explores some of these directions and shows which specific aspects are currently attracting the attention of enterprises operating in the ICT sector (that is, software developers and IT applications providers). Chapters 18 and 19 focus on operating systems and discuss which software developments may be introduced to enhance the functionality of operating systems and the interaction between interface elements and the sensors' layer. Chapter 20 then explores the case of cloud computing and discusses the importance of storage systems as a key factor to ensure sustainability in data centres devoted to provide cloud services. Data centres are also the focus of Chap. 21. In this case, however, the attention is posed on power consumption of IT infrastructures and how it is affected by the distribution of computational activity among IT machines. A solution is thus proposed to reorganise the computational process in order to significatively reduce the impact on power consumption. Finally, Chap. 22 describes an innovative solution that may be adopted by providers of cloud computing infrastructures to customise both application and the analysis of benchmarking data in monitoring activities.

References

1. Eurostat: European business—facts and figures. Online publication. http://ec.europa.eu/eurostat/statistics-explained/index.php/European_business_facts_and_figures (2016)
2. OISPG, European Commission: Open Innovation, Directorate-General for the Information Society and Media, Luxembourg: Publications Office of the European Union. http://files.openinnovation-platform.eu/policydocs/open_innovation_2012.pdf (2012)
3. Chesbrough, H.: *Open Innovation: The New Imperative for Creating and Profiting from Technology.* Harvard Business School Press (2003)
4. Helpman, E.: General Purpose Technologies and Economic Growth. The MIT Press, Cambridge, MA (1998)
5. Dosi, G.: Technological paradigms and technological trajectories: a suggested interpretation of the determinants and directions of technical change. Res. Policy **11**(3), 147–162 (1982)
6. Zollo, M., Winter, S.G.: Deliberate learning and the evolution of dynamic capabilities. Organ. Sci. **13**(3), 339–351 (2002)

Part I
Innovative ICT Enablers in Use on Organisational Level

Empowering IT Organizations' Capabilities of Emerging Technology Integration Through User Participation in Innovations Based on IT

Nabil Georges Badr

Abstract To innovate their business models companies often rely on emerging technologies in IT. Disruption introduced by emerging IT affects the stability of the IT services, and the ability of IT organizations to sustain the continuity of services required by the business. Thus, IT organizations are perceived as a hindrance rather than an enabler to innovation. Through a systematic review of the literature, this paper shows that "user participation" writings focus mostly on the "client" of the technology and overlooks the capabilities needed to empower IT organizations capabilities to integrate innovations in IT. Through in-depth case studies in IT services companies, the research learns what mechanisms of user participation in IT innovation would enhance or improve these capabilities. Relating to the IT capabilities of exploitation and exploration, the results recommend some practices of collaboration and user participation that could enable IT organizations' to more effectively integrate emerging technology in IT.

Keywords IT organizational capabilities · Consequences of adoption · Consequences of IT diffusion · Obstacles to integration · IT learning capabilities · Emerging IT integration

1 Introduction

Information Technology establishes a foundation for strategic innovations in business processes [1], sets up modular components aligned with standard business processes [2], and provides the basis for development and implementation of present and future business applications for a competitive edge [3, 4]. Emerging technologies in IT (EIT) are those technologies at the *"earlier stages of their lifecycles and have been adopted by less than 20 % of their target population"* (Gartner IT Glossary). IT innovations in form of emerging technologies in IT such

N.G. Badr (✉)
Grenoble Graduate School of Business, Grenoble, France
e-mail: nabil.badr@alumni.grenoble-em.com

© Springer International Publishing Switzerland 2016
L. Caporarello et al. (eds.), *Digitally Supported Innovation*,
Lecture Notes in Information Systems and Organisation 18,
DOI 10.1007/978-3-319-40265-9_2

as cloud computing, communication, collaboration, social networking, mobile, and search engine tools continue to play an integral role in supporting corporate innovation [5–7].

Companies are in the process of implementing emerging technologies in IT, however, they are at varying stages of implementation. Innovations based on IT depend greatly on the combination of the technology, the organization's technical expertise, and the organization's ability to make effective use of the new capabilities [8]. Disruption introduced by emerging IT affects the stability of the IT services, and challenges the ability of IT organizations to sustain the continuity of services required for business continuity [9]. Challenges in operationalizing this innovation (i.e. *advancing new technology from the lab to operations*) affect the ability of IT organizations to implement and support these technologies. Sometimes insurmountable these challenges leave the firm incapable to incorporate emerging information technologies into their business model. Effectively, in practitioner circles, "*IT organizations are perceived as a hindrance rather than an enabler to innovation (Cap Gemini 2014)*".

What mechanisms should IT organizations reinforce with their customers in order to hone their capabilities in the integration of emerging IT?

2   Background

Research on innovation supports innovative characteristics of emerging IT [10–14] and the disruption introduced into the IS operation [15, 16]. The literature on antecedents to innovation diffusion connected adoption characteristics such as ease of use and usefulness [17], maturity [18], and rapid change of the technology [19] to the success of the diffusion process. Factors such as managerial influences in encouraging adoption [20], mandating its use [21] or offering choice for differing levels of use [22] by organizations as a whole or by individuals that are willing to adopt technologies were addressed. Some theories considered particular adoption contexts such as propagating institutions that may have an effect on lowering the knowledge barriers of adoption [23]. Key tools and skillsets required for adoption and diffusion were explored [24].

In an advanced stage of the adoption process, researchers argue that diffusion theories should be tailored to specific classes of technologies [25] and task-technology compatibility [26]. Costs, perceived risks [27] and the likely payoffs [28] were also represented, that may affect the outcome, in success or failure to implement innovation in a way that generates net benefits [25]. Contextual factors were identified affecting IT implementation such as project and resources, end user participation, organizational structure and commitment, IT and CIO competency, and complementary investments [29]. Recent research showed that early investments in resource in an ERP project might positively affect the adoption process of the application [30]. Other mechanisms that foster an innovative culture in organizations are likely to facilitate the introduction, adoption and diffusion of innovations with a resulting effect on firm performance [31].

2.1 IT/IS Integration

In closer relation to the organizational resources, leadership, and attributes, IS integration is the outcome of the technology implementation [32]. Integration in IT is considered the sum of technology and organizational elements [33] participating in the technology diffusion process. Literature streams on IT implementation and integration found elements relating people, process, technology and knowledge assets as obstacles for the implementation of enterprise wide systems [34], specifically, in key activities of change management, prioritization, resource allocation and stakeholders' involvement [35]. IT assessment and introduction models were recommended to address barriers to technology integration [10] identifying the role of IS function in different stages of integration, discussing operational efficiency and contribution to business formulation [36] without assessing the impact on these activities on IT organizations engaged in implementing the technology.

Later research tackled organizational issues related to change in the transition from core technologies [37] and mechanisms for organizations to cope with such change [19]. A plethora of technology selection models focused on success factors [38–41] and systems quality [42] of an information system implementation, were introduced. Still, no linkages were found on the potential collaborative mechanisms that IT organizations in IT services could use with their customers to deliver the related IT services and successfully integrate innovation.

2.2 User Involvement in IT Integration

The literature on "user involvement" in IS/IT is copious: Antecedents and consequences of adoption and diffusion have been linked to user involvement in IT [43–45] and user resistance is seen as an inherent phenomenon in IT implementations [46, 47]. Reasons for this resistance could be many. To list a few, the extant literature discusses influences of power and politics [48], perceived threat [49], misuse [50], or external and internal influences [51], levels of sophistication of the infrastructure [52], user satisfaction [44], or organizational readiness [34]. Khoo [53] found that the maintenance of IT innovations imposed a toll on the user's as in the case of upgrades and continued development. The implementations of IT innovation were qualified as problematic "frequently costly and time-consuming" [54, p. 77].

On the other hand, researchers showed interest in modeling factors that influence "user acceptance" of technology [17] or how the IT organization is or is not promoting adoption [55]. Among factors affecting "user acceptance", concerns of technical compatibility, technical complexity, and relative advantage (perceived need) were deemed important [26]. In more recent publications, data privacy was a major concern for Bradford and Florin [46] in their study of accounting software implementation; similarly, with Crum et al. [56] in the case of electronic data interchange solutions. Angst and Agarwal [57] agreed. Kuo [58] showed that personal factors of gender, age, educational background, influence technology readiness, and Lee et al. [59] introduced factors of simplicity and consistency, however as antecedents to the functions of the business. This stream in the literature focused on the "*clients*" of the technology integration efforts overlooking what capabilities IT organizations needed to cultivate in order to accomplish their objectives. The next section reviews extant literature for some guidance for IT organization to manage consequences of IT integration in order to ensure success.

2.3   IT Organizational Capabilities

Studies have outlined details on the role of IS function in different stages of integration [36] discussing operational efficiency and contribution to business formulation without assessing the impact on these activities on IT organizations. Little mention was found on managing the consequences on IT organizations of integrating uncertain investments in IT.

IT organizations commonly participate in the decision making [60, 61] for emerging IT integration. Involved at the scanning phase of the innovation process [61], IT organizations identify emerging technologies that could contribute to innovation strategies [60]. Then, they engage their resources and capabilities in the implementation and support of IT solutions [31, 34, 58, 59]. Largely, IT organizational capabilities have received a fair share of attention in various context. IS research on resource based views (RBV) delineates resources as physical capital (e.g. *property, plant,* etc....), human capital (e.g. *people, experience, relationships,* etc....), and organizational capital (e.g. *organizational structure and processes,* etc....) in the seminal work of Barney [62]. IT capability was conceived as the ability to enhance competitive agility by delivering IT-based products, services, and business applications increasing the firm's capacity [63] and building sustainable competitive advantages [64]. Closer to the technology implementation function, IT capability was described as the ability to diffuse or support a wide variety of hardware and software [65].

Other references to IT capability, include the ability to respond to change [63] and mobilize IT-based resources [66] in an industry leadership position [67]; and the ability to effectively use IT tools and information to model, measure, and control business [66]. Competencies are built by combining such resources and capabilities [68] leading to the ability "*to conceive, implement, and exploit valuable IT applications*" [69, p. 491]. Recent empirical studies [70, 71] showed that firms or business units with stronger **exploration and exploitation capabilities** outperform others. Though both capabilities could be conceived as theories for learning [71], exploration capabilities are aimed at discovering new possibilities for innovation while capabilities of exploitation are intended to invest old knowledge [72] to realize operational effectiveness.

For the background of this research, **exploitation capabilities** are operational level capabilities that reflect an ability to perform routine and required activities [73] within the IT function. These capabilities include fundamental processes of operation with the required key resources such as applications, information, infrastructure and people [74]. On the other hand, the absorptive capacity [75] of IT organizations was tied to improving decision making process leading to a decision to invest in EIT. Thus, **exploration capabilities** are centered on (1) learning capability, including the notion of absorptive capacity [75], and (2) innovation capability [76]. These exploration capabilities rely on information acquisition and transformation to collective knowledge assets [31, 77].

Related to technology innovation, diffusion patterns and the presence of large assimilation gap [25] were linked to factors of innovation mindfulness [78] and technical efficiency [79] of organizations. The literature on innovation capability of an organization emphasized an organizational structure and leadership that motivates creativity [80] and idea generation. For instance, this could be realized through an internal collaboration led by distributed innovation groups on the enterprise level [60]. A reward system to drive innovative behavior and encourage creativity [14] with the appointment of innovation champions [81] and employment diversity [82] were touted as encouragement for innovative and incremental development activities.

Thus, the literature presents mechanisms that foster an innovative culture in organizations which facilitate the introduction, adoption and diffusion of innovations showing a resulting effect on firm performance [28] and consequences of technology integration initiatives. Nevertheless, the literature lacks guidance on how IT organization could hone their capabilities in order to drive these initiatives and none of the reviewed literature addressed potential methods used by IT organizations to engage their customer in such innovation process. Learnings from the two cases presented in this paper, would be a welcome addition to topical concepts in academic research and a valuable guidance in practice for IT organizations to engage their internal and external customers in the integration process of emerging IT.

3 Methodology

This research explores major challenges to IT organizations and mechanisms that these organizations employ with their customers in order to hone their capability in emerging IT integration. This exploratory research into practice takes the form of qualitative case studies [83, 84]. In line with similar work in IS case study research using two cases for a comparative study [85–91].

3.1 Site Selection

The two sites in this study are IT service companies. IT organizations in these companies have two customers [92]: IT is not only a cornerstone for the internal business model with internal users of the company, but also the core business in providing customer facing services. This puts an added burden on the IT organization to stretch the abilities and cover users' issues internal and external to the company context with a persisting conundrum of providing a reliable service to existing customers or creating new customer through innovation [93].

The two in-depth case explorations are conducted on location with IT organizations in Telecom **Company A**, and in application hosting services **Company B**, selected purposefully [94] for this research (Table 1). The sites are analogous in their IT organizational setting with a centralized IT management [95] and a collective decision making [96], the IT organization in both companies performed similar duties and shared comparable responsibilities in managing and maintaining IT services supporting both internal and customer facing services. Both companies are IT services companies providing IT services for Lebanon and the MENA (*Middle East and North Africa region*). The similarities in the sites selected could reinforce the findings by adding depth into the discovery; similarities to note are of industry context [97], culture [98], and international presence [99], with IT a centralized management model [95] and a collective decision making [96].

Table 1 Summary for the two site case study

	Company A	Company B
Company background	Leading internet services provider and hosting solutions, established in 1995 (130 + employees)	Hosting and cloud services, re-established in 2006 (42 employees)
IT organization	15 members managing security credentials, internal moves and changes; planning of new technology deployment; internal and external customers	12 employees in charge of planning, implementation and support of internal infrastructure with a service desk attending to escalated customer calls
Emerging IT integration objectives	Streamlined business processes, partners, resources in order to introduce new network features to existing customers	Enabled them to position services in a niche market with added value to their existing and new customers
Risk mitigation measures	Clear definition of risks on IT and the business to leverage company resources and accomplish the business objectives	Informed on the challenges and risks, customers participated in creating the solution to mitigate the risks
Realized value	Extended their network delivering 3G/4G services to subscribers	Provide a turnkey IT solution based on software as a service (SAAS)

These sites also present complementarities that may shed a light on some cross case observations further enriching the empirical study. The sites differ in organization size [100] and maturity [101]. Though both companies were chosen to have similar characteristics in culture [98] and international presence [99], in the preliminary exploration, these sites have presented variances into their approaches such as involving customers [102, 103] in the process of integrating EIT into **Company B**'s customer facing and internal operations [11].

3.2 Data Collection

Data collection activities (Dec 13, 2012–April 3, 2013) combined interviews and brainstorming sessions [104]. Focus group workshops [105] were conducted due to the nature of the topic that requires stimulation and interaction. These workshops recorded all the participants' input while probing for details; where possible, using illustrative examples [94] to help establish neutrality in the process. In total data collection involved 15 informants chosen from the two companies. Interviews were conducted with the managers in charge of IT, operations, sales and general Managers at each company. Focus group participants were managers and members of customer support teams, IT administration, Infrastructure design and implementation teams and the project management office. The interviews were in two waves, before and after the focus group exercise in a form of member checking [106] in order to assess the usefulness of the study. Secondary data sources (presentation manual, user's manuals, tools and web sites) were reviewed for information on company and IT organizational structure (construct validity).

3.3 Data Analysis

Case summaries and cross-case comparison were compiled in a tabular summary [107], in the form of interview transcripts directly after the field activities [108], including field notes from observations and relevant exhibits (e.g. organizational structures). The timely and detailed transcripts heightened the accuracy of what was reported, supporting the descriptive validity [109]. Nevertheless, the study's reliability is reinforced through the use of a case study protocol, the consistent review of the data, observations, and discussions and a systematic case study methodology [110]. The analysis investigated data correlation through a predefined coding system [111] in order to organize these data and provide a means to introduce the interpretations [112]. Grounded in the literature review, a step by step coding technique [113] was applied to the interview transcripts [114], and relevant concepts are identified. 'Key Points' for the coding are shown in Table 2 as potential effects of the mechanisms employed on the IT capabilities grouped under categories

Table 2 Key point codes

Capability of IT	Potential effect (key point)
Exploitation capabilities	Enhance operational level capabilities
	Reduce the risk at the customer end
	Enhance support capability
Learning capability	Improve learning capability (acquire and disseminate knowledge)
Innovation capabilities	Drive more business opportunities and add value with an enhanced ability of IT to participate in delivering the vision internally
	Bolster innovation capabilities (new ideas for new products)

of exploitation, learning and innovation capability. Following the coding exercise, data analysis was completed by category and organized in relevance to the research question (see Appendix).

4 Findings

Obstacles to integrating innovations were extant in the empirical data. These obstacles include a plethora of user resistance issues reportedly caused by the level of sophistication, potential effect on stability of services, architectural implications, and system interaction with existing systems. This came with no surprise.

Findings from the empirical data exhibit a few interesting concepts (Table 3). Findings are represented as a set of mechanisms employed with their reported potential effect on the IT organizational capabilities. Mechanisms that IT organizations applied in collaboration with internal and external customers were connected to capabilities of exploitation, learning and innovation.

5 Discussion

The informants revealed mechanisms of user participation that IT organizations applied in collaboration with the internal and external customers. **Company A** found "*a lot of reluctance imminent from the customer which inhibited the ability of the company to deploy their new services*". To convert a risk averse customer, both companies reported having to engage in a collaborative exchange of knowledge with their respective customers. These mechanisms were stated to present an effect of risk reduction at the customer end thus reducing user reluctance to innovation integration.

Spears and Barki [45] reinforced the importance of the users' awareness of risks [13], **Company B** included their internal (users) and external customers in the assessment of risk which helped prepare the organization for the integration of EIT. With risk averse customers, **Company B** "*established a collaborative exchange of*

Table 3 Findings from empirical analysis—mechanisms applied

	Mechanisms that IT organizations applied	Potential effect
IT exploitation capability	Align internal deployments with external customer needs	Enhance operational level capabilities
	Customers drive implementation standards	
	Project deployment in phases	
	Collaboration to encourage the customer to accept the technology (workshops subject matter experts)	Reduce the risk at the customer end
	Engage in education to convert risk averse customer	
IT learning capability	Collaboration between internal and external facing IT	Improve learning capability (acquire and disseminate knowledge—external user/customer)
	External facing IT teams collaborate with customers	
	Include customer in the definition, testing and validation of new products and services	
	Establish training plans/training for customers	
	Employee training and knowledge building programs	Improve learning capability (acquire and disseminate knowledge—internal user)
	Employees involved in the deployment of the projects	
	Deploy knowledge management systems to manage customer issues (lessons learned extracted from support ticket database)	
	Establish technology champions to transition knowledge	
IT innovation capability	Engage IT team in consultancy services to customer.	Ability to participate in delivering the vision internally
	IT team scouts for opportunities at the customers' base. (Drive more business opportunities/add value)	
	Collaborate with customer to define new product strategies (co-creation) and consult customers evaluation of new technologies	Bolster innovation capabilities (new ideas for new products)

knowledge and engaged in an education process to help them get over the risky nature of the technology." They performed *"joint assessments with the customer resources and mapped the risks directly to customer expectations."*

5.1   Enhancing Exploitation Capability

In order to enhance their capability to deploy the solution, **Company A** *assigned a subject matter expert to drive knowledge transfer to the customer through learning workshops conducted at customers* explained the director of IT. **Company A** also employed a *"phased approach to transition the new technology into production"*. They had to *"iteratively realign their internal customer's (user) expectations to reduce the customization of the system"*. Conversely, **Company B** *"adjusted their internal platforms to meet the external customer needs"*. Later in the project life-cycle, **Company B** *"conducted customer sponsored testing and implementations to gain the customer perspective on the required continuity parameters"*. At the same time they *"involved their employees in the deployment of the project"*, which helped them incrementally acquire the knowledge required for the support phases of the project [115].

5.2   Improving Learning Capability

"User participation" in IS provides valuable business knowledge [42]. The findings indicate that IT organization's learning capabilities were enhanced by acquiring and disseminate knowledge with the internal and external customer. The Director of IT **Company A** specified that *"the products that do require some customization warrant the involvement with the customer in the definition, testing and validation of these products and services"*. A collaboration that enriched the individual skills of the participants (IT organization and customer). The degree of tacit-ness of newly acquired knowledge [116] necessitated richer organizational information processing mechanisms. The transfer of knowledge to internal customers at **Company A** (i.e. employees of the company) was accomplished through user training sessions. This helped **Company A** to *"overcome users' resistance to adopting the new BPM platform and eased the task on the IT organization"*. Training sessions were carried in-house.

Meanwhile, **Company B** assigned technology champions to transition knowledge and encourage the dissemination of information among the team. *"As a result our ability to set SLAs with our customers and meet them is much improved"* specifies the General Manager. The project manager of **Company B** added explaining how they involved the employees, as *their internal customers*, in the deployment of hosting projects. The IT organization established *"biweekly knowledge sharing sessions with internal customers (employees) in order to discover the challenges and help reduce adoption issues"*. Users' manuals stored were in an online database. Extending outside the boundaries of the firm, *"training plans tailored for the customer empowered the IT organization to become more effective"* in supporting the customer base.

Company B included *knowledge management systems* in their toolset as part of their knowledge sharing strategy [117]. Knowledge management systems consolidated the acquired knowledge into an information base on internal and external customers.

"The customer support team focuses on the customer. The infrastructure team plays the role of second level support. The IT support team meets with the IT infrastructure team regularly to review the customer issues, build the knowledge base and solicit the collaboration of ideas across the technical team internal and external. Knowledge transfer tactics between the teams were applied"; explicated the Customer Support Manager. These usually *"involve the sorting and categorization of information with knowledge management systems in order to leave time for the internal functionality empowering the front lines. Through communication between these teams, the internal team is aware of the customer issues"*.

The IT organization used this convergence of information to participate in delivering the vision internally with an enthusiasm to contribute input. Such knowledge management and transfer capabilities [77] continue to build on the organizational knowledge [118] to improve the operational/functional competences of the IT organization [119] by combining the knowledge of the customer facing and the internal IT teams: *"Everyone participates in generating the strategy for the company. Customer support managers are intimate with customer issues and bring back customer success stories and share them with their IT internal counterparts"* said the IT infrastructure Manager at **Company B**. The IT director of **Company A** had a similar argument stating that *"the learning and the correlation of the effect of internal outages on the customer services and inversely, may serve as lessons learned for the potential impacts of internal IT changes on customer services"*.

Thus, in both sites of the study, internal and external facing IT teams collaborated incessantly with their customers and among each other. Their accumulated experience increased the levels of knowledge [118]. This learning capability of experimentation [75], and the interaction with the external environment [120] were shown by research studies to positively associate with the introduction of novel product innovations in firms.

5.3   Bolstering Innovation Capability

As part of their approach to drive revenue from innovation integration, **Company B** sends their IT team scouts for opportunities at the customers' base. This gets the IT organization to gain an intimacy with the customers' strategy. They then collaborate with the customer's IT organization to define new product strategies and engage in the evaluation of new technologies: *"Our IT team scouts for opportunities at the customers' base and brings forth recommendations to drive more business out of the market share"*. *"This has given us a way to earn the first seat at the table when our customers begin to consider their strategic plans"*. *(Deputy GM/Operations Director B)*. This practice unlocks the prospect for some customers to push the business to offer the services provided by a certain technology. The IT organization is then motivated to scan for emerging technologies and evaluate them. The opportunity to lead the host company's innovation strategy through this external exposure and collaboration enabled IT to bring forth recommendations to drive more business through the innovation of the products and service platform: "*Some of our customers impose technology changes on us, for example disaster recovery sites are being implemented to serve our customer requests even before our suppliers can drive this change in their ranks. So the customer is then pushing us and we push our suppliers*" *(General Manager—Company B)*. Insight from the literature supports a form of co-creation [121] to exploit the tacit knowledge of the customer (Davis et al. 2009) into the delivery of the new services bringing forth a value proposition to the company internally and a greater competitive value [112].

6 Conclusion

"*User participation*" is not a novel notion in the context of IT integration. Nevertheless, the findings from this study extend related theory in suggesting mechanisms that emphasize the advantages of *user participation* in the context of IT organizational capability in IT services. Customers (internal & external) are included in the early stages of the deployment with an education process to convert the risk averse. Such collaboration would encourage the customer to accept the technology thus enhancing the exploitation capability of IT. Knowledge is acquired and disseminated through a network of internally and externally focused IT teams that transition the knowledge from the field to the operation and propagate it inversely. Knowledge management systems are deployed to manage customer issues while IT teams collaborate with customer to define new product strategies and consult with their customers in the evaluation of new technologies in a form of co-creation that is bound to add value.

On the other hand, IT services companies face a compound challenge of supporting the needs of internal and external customers [89]: (1) building and maintaining the IT infrastructure essential for their business and (2) designing and deploying IT applications and services for their customers. Issues of prioritization and risk are abound as an outage on an internal system could hinder the ability of the company to serve its internal and external customer, at the same time. This requires an ambidexterity in the IT organization that has maintain the uptime and SLAs of the services deployed for the internal and external customers via close communication with the support teams facing the external customer. Externally, IT organizations then strive to get closer and collaborate with their external customers as well. In spite of the advantages of value creation through customer learning, issues of costs, customer readiness, degree of involvement and skills challenge such collaboration. Yet, this practice unlocks the prospect for some customers of the business to drive the business strategy to offer the services provided by a certain technology.

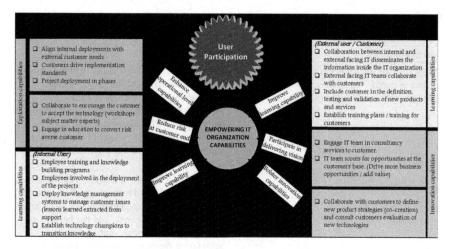

Fig. 1 Mechanisms of user participation to empower IT organizations capability

Thus, our study adds value to research as it treats a systemic issue in IT organizations of companies in the IT industry: These organizations are often asked to be the internal IT provider for the internal customers (i.e. employees) and external solutions and service providers for IT clients (i.e. customers). Presenting guidance through mechanisms that would empower IT organizations (Fig. 1), these findings may prove as lessons in practice for such organizations.

7 Limitations

Academics support the strengths of case study research "*as a comprehensive research strategy, specifically with regards to business research*" [122, p. 92]. Publications argue the extent of case study research generalizability [123, 124], though Tellis [125] affirms the inherent selectiveness of the case study research that focuses on one or two unexamined issues fundamental to understand the phenomena. Although the research has reached its aim, some unavoidable limitations can be noted. A potential limitation arises here in the setting of the centralized IT. Today's working practices are hybrid between telecommuting workforce, distributed or centralized. This may change the outcome in some of the concepts that require collaborative activities that may be hindered by differing types of organizations. Furthermore, IT links to culture and cultural contexts have been prevalent in the literature [126] affecting the organization's approach to collaboration, communication and risk management [127]. It is also important to note the inherent bias in the choice of the sites for the case study. The choice to focus on one industry, the IT services industry. Nevertheless, data from these paradigmatic [128] cases are

Table 4 Coded Concepts

IT exploitation capability	
Mechanisms	Empirical evidence
Align internal deployments with external customer needs—customers drive implementation standards (SLA)	Director of IT (A): "We had to iteratively align the implementation of the project to their expectations; often realigning their expectations to reduce the customization of the system". "This allowed our IT team to proceed with a better vision of the outcome and made sure that the changes on the system are controlled"
	Deputy GM/Operations Director (B): "The deployment of cloud technology allowed us to leverage our internal platforms and align it with our customer needs, and the benefits of an integrated technical solution based on automating the internal business process"
Project deployment in phases	Director of IT(A): "In order to keep the continuity of the services, the new technology must be transitioned into operation in a phased approach with a vigilant monitoring effort to maintain the services to our customers"
	Deputy GM/Operations Director (B): "We conducted customer sponsored testing and implementations to gain the customer perspective on the required continuity parameters, and involved their employees in the deployment of the project"
Engage in an education process to convert risk averse customer	General Manager (B): "With risk averse customers, we establish a collaborative exchange of knowledge and engage in an education process to help them get over the risky nature of the technology" […] "we performed joint assessment with the customer resources and map the risks directly to customer expectations"

(continued)

Table 4 (continued)

IT exploitation capability	
Mechanisms	Empirical evidence
Collaboration to encourage the customer to accept the technology (workshops subject matter experts)	IT Director (A): "We see a lot of reluctance in the IT teams of our customers. Our IT organization (especially in the latest project for a local bank), assigned a subject matter expert to conduct workshops at our customers and get them to understand the technology, get confident in it, then we were able to sell it to them. The IT team felt empowered to participate in the sale. That was a great team effort"
Collaboration between internal and external facing IT teams	Customer Support Manager (B): "The IT support team meets with the IT infrastructure team regularly to review the customer issues, build the knowledge base and solicit the collaboration of ideas across the technical team internal and external"
	Customer Support Manager (B): "The customer support team focuses on the customer. The infrastructure team plays the role of second level support. Knowledge transfer tactics between the teams were applied"
External facing IT teams collaborate with the customer	IT Infrastructure Manager (B): "Everyone participates in generating the strategy for the company. Customer support managers are intimate with customer issues and bring back customer success stories and share them with their IT internal counterparts"
Include the customer in the definition, testing and validation	Director of IT (A): "The products that do require some customization warrant the involvement with the customer in the definition, testing and validation of these products and services"
Establish training plans and perform training with the customer	Deputy GM/Operations Director (B): "Training plans (external and internal) for customer support makes them more effective"
Employee training and knowledge building programs	Deputy GM/Operations Director (B): "Extensive employee training and knowledge building programs were implemented"
	IT Support Manager (A): "To overcome the users' resistance to adopting the new BPM platform, we performed many user training sessions and developed easy to use users' manuals"
	Customer Support Manager (B): "We have setup a database of training materials that reduced costs of training and labs for the training activities to be carried in-house"...

(continued)

Table 4 (continued)

IT exploitation capability	
Mechanisms	Empirical evidence
Employees involved in the deployment of the projects	PMO (B): "Our employees are our internal customers; we involve them in the deployment of the projects in order to gain knowledge on adoption issues that might be applied to our external customers. We establish regular (biweekly) knowledge sharing session for the knowledge transfer"
Deploy knowledge management systems to manage customer issues	Director of IT (A): "The learning and the correlation of the effect of internal outages on the customer services and inversely, may serve as lessons learned for the potential impacts of internal IT changes on customer services"
	Customer Support Manager (B): "Most of our data collected from support calls are analyzed then disseminated among the remaining IT teams in a knowledge base in the form of lessons learned. They involve the sorting and categorization of information with knowledge management systems in order to leave time for the internal functionality empowering the front lines. Through communication between these teams, the internal team is aware of the customer issues"
Establish technology champions to transition knowledge	General Manager (B): "The champion usually leads working groups based on the projects at hand. This facilitates the transition of knowledge and encourage the dissemination of information among the team. This was very fruitful in the cloud project. Our ability to set SLAs with our customers and meet them is much improved"
IT team scouts for opportunities at the customers' base.	Deputy GM/Operations Director (B): "Our IT team scouts for opportunities at the customers' base and brings forth recommendation to drive more business out of the market share". "This has given us a way to earn the first seat at the table when our customers begin to consider their strategic plans"

(continued)

Table 4 (continued)

IT exploitation capability	
Mechanisms	Empirical evidence
Collaborate with customer to define new product strategies (co-creation) and consult customers evaluation of new technologies	Deputy GM/Operations Director (B): "Among our peers, we are distinguished by the fact that we know all our customers on a personal level even internationally. We have built 1:1 relationships with each one of them. Familiarity with cloud customers established a confidence for hosting services and opening the door for doing business"
	Deputy GM/Operations Director (B): "Our customers are consulted in our process of evaluating technologies and sometimes have a say in preferring one over another"
	General Manager (B): "Our customers bring to us concerns and drive our business strategy. We then go to the IT team and leverage the knowledge to build our services"
	General Manager (B): "This is a two way subject: (1) some of our customers impose technology changes on us, for example disaster recovery sites are being implemented to serve our customer requests even before our suppliers can drive this change in their ranks. So the customer is then pushing us and we push our suppliers"

suitable to support a conceptual insight on the scope of mechanisms that might enable the IT organization to successfully integrate innovation in collaboration with two customers, internal and external.

References

1. McKay, D.T., Brockway, D.W.: Building IT infrastructure for the 1990s. Stage by Stage **9** (3), 1–11 (1989)
2. Duncan, N.B.: Capturing flexibility of information technology infrastructure: a study of resource characteristics and their measure. J. Manag. Inf. Syst. **12**(2), 37–57 (1995)
3. Davenport, T., Linder, J.: Information management infrastructure: the new competitive weapon. In: Proceedings of the Twenty Seventh Hawaii International Conference on System Sciences. IV, pp. 885–896 (1994)
4. Weill, P.: The role and value of information technology infrastructure: some empirical observations. In: Banker, R., Kaufman, R., Mahood, M.A. (eds.) Strategic Information Technology Management: Perspectives on Organizational Growth and Competitive Advantage, pp. 547–572. Idea Group Publishing, Middleton, PA (1993)
5. Carlo, J.L., Lyytinen, K., Rose, G.M.: Internet computing as a disruptive information technology innovation: the role of strong order effects. Inf. Syst. J. **21**(1), 91–122 (2011)

6. Carlo, J., Lyytinen, K., Rose, G.M.: A knowledge-based model of radical Innovation in small software firms. MIS Q. **36**(3), 865–A10 (2012)
7. Fitzgerald, M.: Inside renault's digital factory. MIT Sloan Manag. Rev. 1–4 (2014)
8. Peppard, J., Ward, J.: Unlocking sustained business value from IT investments. Calif. Manag. Rev. **48**(1), 52–70 (2005)
9. Arduini, F., Morabito, V.: Business continuity and the banking industry. Commun. ACM **53** (3), 121–125 (2010)
10. Huff, S.L., Munro, M.C.: Information technology assessment and adoption. MIS Q. 327–340 (1985)
11. Swanson, E.B.: Information systems innovations among organizations. Manage. Sci. **40**(9), 1069–1092 (1994)
12. Agarwal, R., Prasad, J.: The role of innovation characteristics and perceived voluntariness in the acceptance of information technologies. Decis. Sci. **28**(3), 557–582 (1997)
13. Buyya, R., Shin Yeo, C., Venugopal, S., Broberg, J., Brandic, I.: Cloud computing and emerging it platforms: vision, hype, and reality for delivering computing as the 5th utility. Future Gen. Comput. Syst. **25**(6), 599–616 (2009)
14. Saleh, S.D., Wang, C.K.: The management of innovation: strategy, structure, and organizational climate. IEEE Trans. Eng. Manag. **40**, 13–21 (1993)
15. Bower, J.L., Christensen, C.M.: Disruptive technologies: catching the wave. Harvard Bus. Rev. (1995)
16. Bhattacherjee, A.: Management of emerging technologies: experiences and lessons learned at US West. Case Stud.: Inf. Manag. **33**(5), 263–272 (1998)
17. Davis, F.: Perceived usefulness, perceived ease of use, and user acceptance of information technology. MIS Q. **13**(3), 319–340 (1989)
18. O'Leary, D.E.: The impact of gartner's maturity curve, adoption curve, strategic technologies on information systems research, with applications to artificial intelligence, ERP, BPM, and RFID. J. Emerg. Technol. Account. American Accounting Association. 6 (2009)
19. Benamati, J., Lederer, A.L.: Managing the impact of rapid IT change. Inf. Resour. Manag. J. **23**(1), 1–16 (2010)
20. Leonard-Barton, D.: Implementation as mutual adaptation of technology and organization. Res. Policy **17**(5), 251–267 (1988)
21. Moore, G.C., Benbasat, I.: Development of an instrument to measure the perceptions of adopting an information technology innovation. Inf. Syst. Res. **2**(3), 192–222 (1991)
22. Bayer, J., Melone, N.: A critique of diffusion theory as a managerial framework for understanding adoption of software engineering innovations. J. Syst. Softw. **9**(2), 161–166 (1989)
23. Swanson, E.B., Ramiller, N.C.: The organizing vision in information systems innovation. Organ. Sci. **8**(5), 458–474 (1997)
24. Bunker, D., Kautz, K., Anhtuan, A.: An exploration of information systems adoption: tools and skills as cultural artefacts—the case of a management information system. J. Inf. Technol. **23**(2), 71–78 (2008)
25. Fichman, R.G., Kemerer, C.F.: The illusory diffusion of innovation: an examination of assimilation gaps. Inf. Syst. Res. **10**(3) (1999)
26. Cooper, R.B., Zmud, R.W.: Information technology implementation research: a technological diffusion approach. Manag. Sci. **36**(2), 123–139 (1990)
27. Johnston, A.C., Warkentin, M.: Fear appeals and information security behaviors: an empirical study. MIS Q. **34**(3), 549–566 (2010)
28. Devaraj, S., Kohli, R.: Information technology payoff in the health-care industry: a longitudinal study. J. Manag. Inf. Syst. **16**(4), 41–67 (2000)
29. Shin, N., Edington, B.H.: An integrative framework for contextual factors affecting information technology implementation. J. Inf. Technol. Theory Appl. **8**(4), 21–38 (2007)
30. Bernroider, E.W.N.: Effective ERP adoption processes: the role of project activators and resource investments. Eur. J. Inf. Syst. **22**(2), 235–250 (2013)

31. Uzkurt, C., Kumar, R., Kimzan, H.S., Eminoglu, G.: Role of innovation in the relationship between organizational culture and firm performance. Eur. J. Innov. Manage. **16**(1), 92–117 (2013)
32. Hasselbring, W.: Information system integration. Commun. ACM **43**(6), 33–38 (2000)
33. Gattiker, T.F., Goodhue, D.L.: What happens after ERP implementation: understanding the impact of inter-dependence and differentiation on plant-level outcomes. MIS Q. **29**(3), 559–585 (2005)
34. Legris, P., Collerette, P.: A roadmap for IT project implementation: integrating stakeholders and change management issues. Project Manag. J. **37**(5), 64–75 (2006)
35. Garcıa-Sanchez, N., Perez-Bernal, L.: Determination of critical success factors in implementing an ERP system: a field study in mexican enterprises. view from practice. Inf. Technol. Dev. **13** (3), 293–309 (2007)
36. King, W., Teo, T.S.H.: Integration between business planning and information systems planning: validating a stage hypothesis. Dec. Sci. **28**(2), 279–308 (1997)
37. Taylor, A., Helfat, C.E.: Organizational linkages for surviving technological change: complementary assets, middle management, and ambidexterity. Organ. Sci. **20**(4), 718–739 (2009)
38. Ghosh, S., Skibniewski, J.S.: Enterprise resource planning systems implementation as a complex project: a conceptual framework. J. Bus. Econ. Manage. **11**(4), 533–549 (2010)
39. Lawson-Body, A., Willoughby, L., Mukankusi, L., Logossah, K.: The critical success factors for public sector CRM implementations. J. Comput. Inf. Syst. **52**(2), 42–50 (2011)
40. Nazor, I., Fertalj, K., Kalpic, D.: Prediction model for characteristics of implementation of information systems in small and medium enterprises. Int. J. Innov. Manage. Technol. **3**(6), 740 (2012)
41. Dwivedi, Y.K., Wastell, D., Laumer, S., Henriksen, H.Z., Myers, M.D., Bunker, D., Srivastava, S.C.: Research on information systems failures and successes: status update and future directions. Inf. Syst. Frontiers **17**(1), 143–157 (2015)
42. Santa, R., Scavarda, A., Fang, Z., Skoko, H.: Managing the operational effectiveness in services using technological innovation. Int. J. e-Bus. Manag. **5**(1), 16–32 (2011)
43. Ives, B., Olson, M.H.: User involvement and MIS success: a review or research. Manag. Sci. **30**(5) (1984)
44. DeLone, W.H., McLean, E.R.: The DeLone and McLean model of information systems success: a ten-year update. J. Manag. Inf. Syst. **19**(4), 9–30 (2003)
45. Spears, J.L., Barki, H.: User participation in information systems security risk management. MIS Q. **34**(3), 503–A5 (2010)
46. Bradford, M., Florin, J.: Examining the role of innovation diffusion factors on the implementation success of enterprise resource planning systems. Int. J. Account. Inf. Syst. **4**(3), 205–222 (2003)
47. Lapointe, L., Rivard, S.: A multilevel model of resistance to information technology implementation. MIS Q. **29**(3), 461–491 (2005)
48. Markus, M.L.: Power, politics, and MIS implementation. Commun. ACM **26**(6), 430–444 (1983)
49. Joshi, K.A.: Model of users' perspective on change: the case of information systems technology implementation. MIS Q. **15**(2), 229–240 (1991)
50. Marakas, G.M., Hornik, S.: Passive resistance misuse: overt support and covert recalcitrance in is implementation. Eur. J. Inf. Syst. **5**(3), 208–220 (1996)
51. Martinko, M.J., Henry, J.W., Zmud, R.W.: An attributional explanation of individual resistance to the introduction of information technologies in the workplace. Behav. Inf. Technol. **15**(5), 313–330 (1996)
52. Armstrong, C.P., Sambamurthy, V.: Information technology assimilation in firms: the influence of senior leadership and IT infrastructures. Inf. Syst. Res. **10**(4), 304–327 (1999)
53. Khoo, H.M., Robey, D., Rao, S.V.: An exploratory study of the impacts of upgrading packaged software: a stakeholder perspective. J. Inf. Technol. **26**, 153–169 (2011)

54. Swanson, E.B.: The manager's guide to IT innovation waves. MIT Sloan Manag. Rev. 55–83 (2012)
55. Rai, A., Patnayakuni, R.A.: Structural model for case adoption behavior. J. Manag. Inf. Syst. **13**(2), 205–234 (1996)
56. Crum, M.R., Premkumar, G., Ramamurthy, K.: An assessment of motor carrier adoption, use, and satisfaction with EDI. Transp. J. **35**(4), 44–57 (1996)
57. Angst, C.M., Agarwal, R.: Adoption of electronic health records in the presence of privacy concerns: the elaboration likelihood model and individual persuasion. MIS Q. **33**(2), 339–370 (2009)
58. Kuo, T.: The antecedents of customer relationship in e-banking industry. J. Comput. Inf. Syst. **51**(3), 57–66 (2011)
59. Lee, J., Lee, D., Moon, J., Park, M.: Factors affecting the perceived usability of the mobile web portal services: comparing simplicity with consistency. Inf. Technol. Manag. **14**(1), 43–57 (2013)
60. Cash, J.I., Earl, M.J., Morison, R.: Teaming up to crack innovation and enterprise integration. Harvard Bus. Rev. **86**(11), 90–100 (2008)
61. Peppard, J., Edwards, C., Lambert, R.: Clarifying the ambiguous role of the CIO. MIS Q. Executive **10**(1), 31–44 (2011)
62. Barney, J.B.: Firm resources and sustained competitive advantage. J. Manag. **17**(1), 99–120 (1991)
63. Clark, C.E., Cavanaugh, N.C., Brown, C.V., Sambamurthy, V.V.: Building change-readiness capabilities in the IS organization: insights from the bell atlantic experience. MIS Q. **21**(4), 425–455 (1997)
64. Bhatt, G.D., Grover, V.: Types of information technology capabilities and their role in competitive advantage: an empirical study. J. Manag. Inf. Syst. **22**(2), 253–277 (2005)
65. Byrd, T.A., Turner, E.D.: An exploratory analysis of the information technology infrastructure flexibility construct. J. Manag. Inf. Syst. **17**(1), 167–208 (2000)
66. Bharadwaj, A.S.: A Resource-based perspective on information technology capability and firm performance: an empirical investigation. MIS Q. **24**(1) (2000)
67. Teo, T.S.H., King, W.R.: Integration between business planning and information systems planning: an evolutionary-contingency perspective. J. Manag. Inf. Syst. **14**(1), 185–214 (1997)
68. Grant, R.M.: The resource-based theory of competitive advantage: Implications for strategy formulation. Calif. Manag. Rev. **33**(3), 114–135 (1991)
69. Mata, F.J., Fuerst, W.L., Barney, J.B.: Information technology and sustained competitive advantage: a resource-based analysis. MIS Q. **19**(4), 487 (1995)
70. Gibson, C., Birkinshaw, J.: The antecedents, consequences, and mediating role of organizational ambidexterity. Acad. Manag. J. **47**(2), 209–226 (2004)
71. He, Z.L., Wong, P.K.: Exploration versus exploitation: an empirical test of the ambidexterity hypothesis. Organ. Sci. **15**, 481–494 (2004)
72. March, J.G.: Exploration and exploitation in organizational learning. Organ. Sci. **2**(1), 71–87 (1991)
73. Collis, D.J.: Research note: how valuable are organizational capabilities? Strateg. Manag. J. **15**, 143–152 (1994)
74. Broadbent, M., Weill, P., St. Clair, D.: The implications of information technology infrastructure for business process redesign. MIS Q. **23**(2), 159–182 (1999)
75. Cohen, W.M., Levinthal, D.: Absorptive capacity: a new perspective on learning and innovation. Adm. Sci. Q. **35**, 128–152 (1990)
76. Lawson, B., Samson, D.: Developing innovation capability in organizations: a dynamic capabilities approach. Int. J. Innov. Manag. **5**(3), 377–400 (2001)
77. Alavi, M., Leidner, D.: Review: knowledge management systems: conceptual foundation and research issues. MIS Q. **25**(1), 107–136 (2001)

78. Swanson, E.B., Ramiller, N.C.: Innovating mindfully with information technology. MIS Q. **28**(4), 553–583 (2004)
79. Abrahamson, E.: Managerial fads and fashions: the diffusion and rejection of innovations. Acad. Manag. Rev. **16**(3), 586–612 (1991)
80. Mumford, M.D., Licuanan, B.: Leading for innovation: conclusions, issues, and directions. Leadersh. Quart. **15**, 163–171 (2004)
81. Tidd, J., Bessant, J., Pavitt, K.: Managing Innovation: Integrating Technological, Market and Organisational Change, 3rd edn. (2005)
82. Crawford, J,. Leonard, L.N.K., Jones, K.: J. Inf. Syst. Technol. Manag.: JISTEM **10**(3), 483–502 (2013)
83. Eisenhardt, K.M.: Building theories from case study research. Acad. Manag. Rev. **14**(4), 532–550 (1989)
84. Eisenhardt, K.M., Graebner, M.E.: Theory Building from cases: opportunities and challenges. Acad. Manag. J. **50**(1), 25–32 (2007)
85. Goodhue, D.L., Thompson, R.L.: Task-technology fit and individual performance. MIS Q. **19**(2), 213–236 (1995)
86. Palaniswamy, R., Frank, T.G.: ORACLE ERP and network computing architecture: implementation and performance. Inf. Syst. Manag. **19**(2), 53 (2002)
87. Newman, M., Zhao, Y.: The process of enterprise resource planning implementation and business process re-engineering: tales from two chinese small and medium-sized enterprises. Inf. Syst. J. **18**(4), 405–426 (2008)
88. Van Der Zee, J.M., de Jong, B.: Alignment is not enough: integrating business and information technology management with the balanced business scorecard. J. Manage. Inf. Syst. **16**(2), 137–156 (1999)
89. Miozzo, M., Grimshaw, D.: Capabilities of large services outsourcing firms: the outsourcing plus staff transfer model in EDS and IBM. Ind. Corp. Change **20**(3), 909–940 (2011)
90. Chau, M., Xu, J.: Business intelligence in blogs: understanding consumer interactions and communities. MIS Q. **36**(4), 1189–1216 (2012)
91. Conforto, E., Amaral, D.: Evaluating an agile method for planning and controlling innovative projects. Project Manag. J. **41**(2), 73–80 (2010)
92. Keel, A.J., Orr, M.A., Hernandez, R.R., Patrocinio, E.A., Bouchard, J.: From a technology-oriented to a service-oriented approach to IT management. IBM Syst. J. **46**(3), 549–564 (2007)
93. Berthon, P., Hulbert, J.M., Pitt, L.F.: To serve or create? strategic orientations toward customers and innovation. Calif. Manag. Rev. **42**(1), 37–58 (1999)
94. Patton, M.Q.: Qualitative Evaluation and Research Methods, 2nd edn. Sage Publications, Newbury Park, CA (1990)
95. Damanpour, F.: Organizational innovation: a meta-analysis of effects of determinants and moderators. Acad. Manag. J. **3483**, 555–590 (1991)
96. Rogers, E.M.: Diffusion of Innovations. Free Press, New York (1962)
97. Miles, R.E., Snow, C.C., Miles, G.: The Future.org. Long Range Plan **33**(3), 300–321 (2000)
98. Kwon, T.H.A.: Diffusion of innovation approach to MIS infusion: conceptualization, methodology, and management strategies. In: Proceedings of the Tenth International Conference on Information Systems, pp. 139–146. Copenhagen, Denmark (1990)
99. Zmud, R.W.: Diffusion of modern software practices: influence of centralization and formalization. Manag. Sci. **28**(12), 1421–1431 (1982)
100. Fichman, R.G., Kemerer, C.F.: The assimilation of software process innovations: an organizational learning perspective. Manag. Sci. **43**(10), 1345–1363 (1997)
101. Grover, V., Goslar, M.D.: The initiation, adoption, and implementation of telecommunications technologies in U.S. organizations. J. Manag. Inf. Syst. **10**(1), 141–163 (1993)

102. Johansson, J., Malmström, M., Chroneer, D., Styven, M., Engström, A., Bergvall-Kåreborn, B.: Business models at work in the mobile service sector. I-Business **4**(1), 84–92 (2012)
103. Willcocks, L., Feeny, D., Olson, N.: Implementing core IS capabilities: Feeny-Willcocks IT governance and management framework revisited. Eur. Manag. J. **24**(1), 28–37 (2006)
104. Hargadon, A.B., Sutton, R.I.: Technology brokering and innovation in a product development firm. Adm. Sci. Q. **42**, 716–749 (1997)
105. Stewart, D.W., Shamdasani, P.N., Rook, D.W.: Focus Groups: Theory and Practice. Sage Publications, Thousand Oaks, CA (2007)
106. Lincoln, Y.S., Guba, E.G.: Naturalistic Inquiry, pp. 313–316. Sage, Newbury Park, CA (1985)
107. Creswell, J.W.: Qualitative Inquiry and Research Design: Choosing Among Five Traditions. Sage, Thousand Oaks, CA (1998)
108. Glaser, B.G., Strauss A.: The Discovery of Grounded Theory: Strategies for Qualitative Research. Chicago, IL: Aldine Publishing Co. The seminal work in grounded theory. (1967)
109. Maxwell, J.A.: Understanding and validity in qualitative research. Harvard Educ. Rev. **62**(3), 279–300 (1992)
110. Yin, R.K.: Case Study Research: Design and Methods, 4th edn. Sage, Newbury Park, CA (2009)
111. Miles, M., Huberman, A.M.: Qualitative Data Analysis: A Sourcebook of New Methods. Sage Publications, Newbury Park, CA (1991)
112. Strauss, A., Corbin, J.: Basics of Qualitative Research. Sage Publications, Newbury Park, CA (1990)
113. Allan, G.: A critique of using grounded theory as a research method. Electron. J. Bus. Res. Meth. **2**(1), 1–10 (2003)
114. Douglas, D.: Inductive theory generation: a grounded approach to business inquiry. Electron. J. Bus. Res. Meth. **2**(1), (2003)
115. Somers, T., Nelson, K.: The impact of critical success factors across the stages of enterprise resource planning implementations. In: Proceedings of the 34th Hawaii International Conference on System Sciences (2001)
116. Subramaniam, M., Venkatraman, N.: Determinants of transnational new product development capability: testing the influence of transferring and deploying tacit overseas knowledge. Strateg. Manag. J. **22**, 359–378 (2001)
117. McLaughlin, S.: Defining a process for developing responsive knowledge pathways. Knowl. Process Manag. **17**(4), 155–167 (2010)
118. Jansen, J.J., Van den Bosch, F.A.J., Volberda, H.W.: Managing potential and realized absorptive capacity: how do organizational antecedents matter? Acad. Manag. J. **48**(6), 999–1015 (2005)
119. Easterby-Smith, M., Prieto, I.M.: Dynamic capabilities and knowledge management: an integrative role for learning? Br. J. Manag. **19**(3), 235–249 (2008)
120. Varis, M., Littunen, H.: Types of innovation, sources of information and performance in entrepreneurial SMEs. Eur. J. Innov. Manag. **13**(2), 128–154 (2010)
121. Chesbrough, H.: Open Services Innovation: Rethinking your Business to Grow and Compete in a New Era, 1st edn. Published by Jossey-Bass (2011)
122. Zivkovic, J.: Strengths and weaknesses of business research methodologies: two disparate case studies. Bus. Stud. J. **4**(2), 91–99 (2012)
123. Stake, R.: The Art of Case Research. Sage Publications, Newbury Park, CA (1995)
124. Lee, A.S., Baskerville, R.L.: Conceptualizing generalizability: new contributions and a reply. MIS Q. **36**(3), 749–761 (2012)
125. Tellis, W.: Application of a case study methodology. Qual. Report, **3**(3) (1997)
126. Leidner, D.E., Kayworth, T.: Review: a review of culture in information systems research: toward a theory of information technology culture conflict. MIS Q. **30**(2), 357–399 (2006)

127. Martinsons, M.G., Davison, R., Martinsons, V.: How Culture influences IT-enabled organizational change and information systems. Commun. ACM **52**(4), 118–123 (2009)
128. Flyvbjerg, B.: Five misunderstandings about case-study research. In: Seale, C., Gobo, G., Gubrium, J.F., Silverman, D. (eds.) Qualitative Research Practice, pp. 420–434. Sage, London and Thousand Oaks, CA (2004)
129. Roberts, N., Grover, V.: Leveraging information technology infrastructure to facilitate a firm's customer agility and competitive activity: an empirical investigation. J. Manag. Inf. Syst. **28**(4), 231–270 (2012)

How and for What Purposes Global Food Brands Use Online Contests: Entertainment or Innovation?

Silvia Massa and Stefania Testa

Abstract Based on an overview of 90 contests in the food sector this paper aims at reaching a better understanding of the many drivers pushing companies to launch contests, and thus suggesting a possible classification of the contest types. The emerged contests types are the following: entertainment (pure entertainment; surveying; talent scouting) and ideation (product; sustainability; advertising). Entertainment, in its broad definition, results to be the main purpose. Surprisingly, only a few contests were classifiable as "ideation/sustainability", in contrast with several authors who claim that increasingly, companies recognize innovation contests as instruments for alerting attention towards today's most urgent sustainability issues and for mastering them.

Keywords Online contest · Innovation strategy · Innovation management

1 Introduction

Online contests have recently emerged as a widely used innovation practice [1] and therefore they have become a growing research field for management scholars. For online contest, we mean a web-based competition of participants who use their skills, experiences and creativity to provide a contribution to a particular challenge defined by an organizer. Despite their growing popularity, the field is still heterogeneous and needs to be better-structured [2] also in regard to terminology and possible contest purposes. For example, [2] identifies three main purposes: marketing; sustainability; ideation. Other authors [1] identify three purposes, as well: education (development of skills), innovation and sustainability. [3] includes also recruitment among the possible purposes of contests.

S. Massa (✉) · S. Testa
University of Genoa, Genoa, Italy
e-mail: silvia.massa@unige.it

S. Testa
e-mail: stefania.testa@unige.it

© Springer International Publishing Switzerland 2016   35
L. Caporarello et al. (eds.), *Digitally Supported Innovation*,
Lecture Notes in Information Systems and Organisation 18,
DOI 10.1007/978-3-319-40265-9_3

It is worth noting that, despite the economic relevance of the food sector worldwide and the fact that food companies are among those that primarily make use of contests [4], in the entire set of academic literature on online contests that we reviewed we hardly found papers dealing with contests in this sector. For example, [2] considered a set of 65 online contests, selected in order to represent a large variety of industries, but apparently, none is in the food sector. Also [1] reviewed 201 publications about contests in a large variety of sectors (among which automobile; energy; fashion; information and communication technology; jewelry; leisure and entertainment; lighting; software; sports etc.) but they hardly mention food and beverage sector. There are some studies that deal with open innovation in the food sector [5] and with the use of social media to foster innovation with customers in the same sector [6] but they are not focused on contests.

This is surprising because the food sector is characterized by some peculiarities, which, in our opinion, make contests interesting tools to be thoroughly investigated. Food industry, more than other industries, needs rapid adaptation to new scenarios [7], innovative problem solving [8, 9] and special attention to a huge variety of consumer needs [10]. Contests may help in coping with all these issues, by providing a direct, rapid and trustworthy external cooperation channel. Furthermore, considering the phenomenon from the consumer perspective, food is more accessible/understandable to people than technology [11], for example. People love to eat [11], and food is supposed to have a strong emotional content [12]. All these elements may have a positive effect on consumer motivation to participate in contests.

Therefore, for the reasons mentioned above, this paper aims at enriching our knowledge about this relevant and peculiar phenomenon. In particular the research question, which is the focus here, is: How and for what purposes do global food brands use online contests? In order to answer such a question the 15 best global food brands[1] have been investigated.

This article unfolds as follows. The next section presents the research design and methodological approach adopted. In the third section, the empirical findings are presented. Finally, we discuss results and their implications for practice and suggestions for further research.

2 Research Methodology

We selected food brands included in the 2013 BusinessWeek/Interbrand Best Global Brands ranking. This ranking includes the 100 most valuable brands in the world from all business fields. This study's sample includes 15 food brands: Coca-Cola, Pepsi, Kellogg's, Budweiser, Nescafè, Heinz, Danone, Nestlè,

---

[1]Those included in the world's 100 most valuable brands as measured by BusinessWeek/Interbrand's "Best Global Brands 2013".

Smirnoff, Sprite, Johnnie Walker, Moet & Chandon, Corona Extra, Heineken, and Jack Daniels. We identified the online contests that the above-mentioned brands organized in the time-span[2] 2006–2014 (see Appendix). For each of the 90 online contests identified, we collected several data useful to understand how and for what purposes the contests have been organized. In order to understand how the contests have been organized the following variables have been considered: on which kind of media contests have been organized; the type of task required; the complexity of the elaboration (e.g. idea, prototype, solution etc.); the target group that was invited to participate; the time length of the contests; the type of reward; the type of evaluation (e.g. jury, peer review etc.) as well as community functionalities and tools provided by the organizers (e.g. discussion forum, chat, toolkits and so forth) [3]. We gathered data by studying the online contests (data available on the websites where contests have been launched) but it is worth noting that not always all data were available for contests already closed. Secondary data (website documents and interviews about the investigated online contests) were collected too. A query in an internet search engine was executed which contained company and brand name and the keyword 'contest' or the title of the contest in order to collect comments, feedbacks from participants and organizers. Sometimes the term "contest" is used to identify sweepstakes, a form of lottery tied to products sold. These cases have been excluded from the sample. Because of the explorative nature of this study, quantitative advanced methods for analyzing data were not used.

3 Findings

The examination of the 90 contests organized by the sampled companies led to the identification of the purpose categories shown in Fig. 1. We identified two main broad purposes that we called: entertainment and ideation.

In the entertainment category, the following three sub-categories have been identified: pure entertainment, entertainment/surveying and entertainment/talent scouting.

In the pure entertainment group, contests that aim uniquely at producing entertainment and enjoyment among customers are included. Therefore, they can be considered an add-on to traditional marketing strategy [13].

In the entertainment/surveying group, contests that aim at discovering information on customer daily life, habits and preferences while entertaining them, are included. As it is often stressed in the literature [14, 15], to acquire information from customers and potential customers about their preferences, requirements, and needs is a prerequisite for successful new product development.

---

[2]The time-span of the empirical research was not a priori decided. The first online contest of the considered brands that we found on the Web is the "1st Creative Challenge in China" by PepsiCo that dates back to 2006.

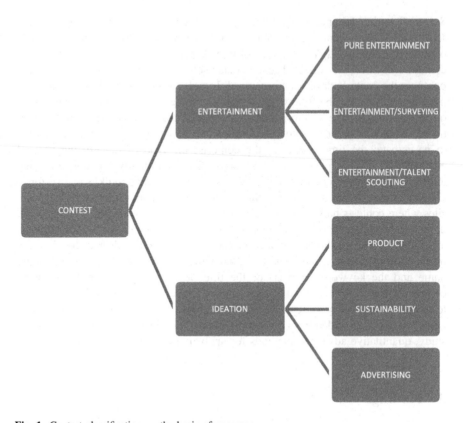

Fig. 1 Contest classification on the basis of purposes

In the entertainment/talent scouting group, contests that aim at discovering talents among customers while entertaining them, are included. To our knowledge, there are no references in the literature explicitly referring to this issue.

In the ideation broad category, the following three sub-categories have been identified: product, sustainability and advertising.

In the product category, contests that are traditionally described in current literature are included i.e. those contests that aim at collecting innovative ideas and solutions for company products and services [16–18].

In the sustainability category, contests that aim at fostering social innovation, i.e. new ideas that work to meet pressing unmet needs and improve people lives [19], are included.

In the advertising category, contests that aim at collecting ideas to inspire marketing actions are included. To our knowledge, also in this case, there are no references in the literature explicitly referring to this type of contests.

Considering the whole set of contests, 33 % of the total number (30 on 90) focused on the research of ideas for new or improved products, whereas the remaining 67 % (60 on 90) focused on entertainment.

Fig. 2 Contest classification by purpose sub-categories

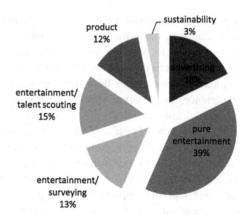

Figure 2 shows the classification of the contests according to the sub-categories emerged by the empirical analysis, which describe the relative goals at a further level of detail.

The main purpose of the sampled food companies is to entertain customers. In this category, pure entertainment contests and contests aimed at talent scouting prevail. Ideation contests are equally distributed between contests aimed at searching ideas for new/improved products/services and searching ideas for marketing actions. Less common are contests aimed at searching ideas for sustainability, even though they have been proved to positively affect brand image, at least in the short time, as the Pepsi Refresh contest (2010) demonstrates [20]. In fact, by means of such a contest the company repositioned the brand from a Super Bowl advertising icon to a catalyst for ideas to refresh the world. Unfortunately, several marketing errors were made, above all a scarce focus and brand relevance, and after 2 years the program was closed (for an in-depth reflection on this failure see e.g. http://adage.com/article/viewpoint/a-teaching-moment-professors-evaluate-pepsi-refresh-project/237629/, accessed on 15th June, 2015).

In the following we examine in more details the previously mentioned categories, as emerged from the empirical investigation.

3.1 Entertainment

Online contests that have consumer entertainment as their primary purpose frequently leave the food sector to enter different fields, such as that of music, where consumers are supposed to find amusement, but also appreciation of their talent.

Thus, the term entertainment assumes, in this context, several meanings. Based on the collected empirical evidence, we have identified three main sub-meanings that correspond to relevant purpose refinements: pure entertainment, entertainment/surveying and entertainment/talent scouting.

Pure Entertainment In the case of online contests with the purpose of pure entertainment, the firm, indeed, use online contests as a marketing initiative, as a different way to promote itself by entertaining consumers and involving them in recreational activities connected with the brand. Since the seminal paper [21], the marketing literature has been developing the concept of offering an entertainment experience, far removed from theatres and amusement parks, as a response to a precise customer need.

For example, Pepsi's "Dance for a chance" contest asked fans to watch Beyoncé's latest Pepsi commercial and to submit videos that show their best Beyoncé moves by performing her dance sequence from the ad. Fans who submitted a 10 s dance video clip themed after Pepsi's latest TV commercial featuring Beyoncé had the opportunity to appear in a unique "super fan" music video choreographed by Beyonce's choreographer. In addition, the eight grand prize-winners had the opportunity to meet Beyoncé in New York as Pepsi's guests.

A second example regards Corona Extra beer brand that gave "everybody a chance to truly escape from the routine". The purpose of this contest was to encourage users to access an application on Facebook social network, which aimed at finding out users' opinions of the possibility of dropping it all to run a beach bar. Participants had to state why they wanted to change their summer plans and why they deserved to win the prize, and therefore manage the Corona/Coronita Beach Bar. After an interview with the Jury, finalists and the winner were chosen.

Entertainment/Surveying In the case of online contests with a purpose that we called "entertainment/surveying", the firm couples the purpose of customer entertainment with that of obtaining free information on daily life and consumer behavior of participants.

For example, with the '60+ Challenge' Heineken was looking for insightful and actionable information regarding the lives of today's 60–70 year-olds. The aim was to understand how this generation lives, what their preferences and inclinations are and if these have changed since hitting this age. Participants could submit pictures, short films or written documents.

A second example regards Danone's probiotic' yogurt-type drink Actimel (also known as DanActive in the United States and Canada). The contest's brief asked participants to tell a story that comes from daily life of how Actimel gives them the "inner strength" that can help them doing small things that can lead to the great big things that matter. Format accepted for contributions were: video, animation, pictures, sketches, storyboards, any visual medium that would allow participants to express their story, and for viewers/readers to understand it easily.

Entertainment/Talent Scouting In the case of online contests with a purpose that we called "entertainment/scouting", the firm couples the purpose of customer entertainment with that of talent scouting, i.e. to give the possibility to anyone who possesses an artistic skill to give herself a challenge to realize her dream. The firm assumes the role of talent scout, thus gaining popularity and image, such as, for example, Corona Extra beer company with Movida Corona Contest for both DJ and vocalist. Participants had to create their profile and upload their session to the platform. The winners of each national final had the opportunity to represent their country in the international grand finale in Pacha Ibiza, one of the world's most famous nightclub. Now in its 13th year, the international Movida Corona DJ competition is considered as the perfect platform for up-and-coming DJs to launch their careers.

A second example is Heineken Jammin' Festival Contest. Heineken Jammin' Festival is a large live rock festival in Venice, Italy featuring international and Italian rock acts. It started in mid-June 1998 at the Imola Autodrome and has attracted attendances of more than 100,000 over the course of the three-day event. For the tenth anniversary of the festival in 2007, the location changed to Mestre, Parco San Giuliano and the festival was preceded by a contest to select four Italian emerging bands that would have performed at the show. A jury composed by members of Rock TV, a digital channel entirely dedicated to rock music, together with the votes of online supporters declared the winners.

3.2 Ideation

Product Among this kind of online contests we include contests aimed at collecting ideas for new or improved products/services. They can ask for new features (e.g. a new receipt, new/added ingredients, new flavors, etc.), new packaging, new ways of consuming the product, changes to make the product more convenient or more environmental-friendly, arriving to require a complete new product concept.

For example, Danone, with the contest "Infuse Silhouettes Yogurt's Packaging with Kindness and Diversity", asked customers to create two packaging designs that celebrate the creamy taste of its Silhouette yogurt, the first building on the idea of kindness and the second on the idea of diversity. The contributors were invited to download the current packaging in order to modify it, respecting some rules (e.g. the use of color Purple, the need to include Silhouette logo and Danone logo, etc.). The contest lasted 13 days and, after a month, the results were published. The jury selected 3 winners from the 28 participants coming from 13 countries. Jury's prizes reflected the brand decision to acquire the intellectual property rights of the entries and amounted to €3000,00 for the first prize, €1500,00 for the second and €500, 00 for the third. The proposals were not published neither during nor after the contest. Instead, the names of the winners, their brief profiles and comments were published on the contest page.

Smirnoff with "Can you create the next new and exciting Smirnoff Ice® flavor?" contest asked people to imagine an "exciting, original, great-tasting new flavor variant for Smirnoff Ice".

Participants were asked to submit an idea for a different flavor option with a name and a broad description of ingredients and taste. Moreover, it was required to bring to life the occasion, who would drink it and how those people would feel through pictures and words. The contest aimed to reward originality in the flavor idea and name as well as the great ingredient tasting. Moreover, the overall concept proposed was required to fit in the "Smirnoff Ice® world". The contest lasted 17 days and, after a month, the results were published. The jury selected 3 winners from the 39 participants coming from 13 countries. Jury's prizes amounted to €3500,00 for the first prize, €1500,00 for the second and €600, 00 for the third. The proposals were not published neither during nor after the contest, apart from the names of the winning entries. As in the previous case, the names of the winners, their brief profiles and comments were published on the contest page.

Sustainability Among this kind of online contests, we include contests aimed at promoting sustainability: such contests may look at new ideas to combat climate change, to master challenges of demographic changes and humanitarian issues ("greater good application" according to [3]). In this group is included for example the already mentioned Pepsi Refresh contest (2010) which awarded $20 million in grants to individuals, businesses and non-profit organizations that promoted new ideas that could have a positive impact on their community, state, or the whole United States. Among the ideas that secured grants there were 108 schools, 68 parks and playgrounds, 20 children's homes, shelters and affordable houses. The rules of the project stated that the first 1,000 ideas proposed online each month could be considered for a share of $1.3 million available. The first month of launch, it took less than a week for reaching the threshold and the site stopped accepting ideas. Customers could choose their preferred idea by voting using codes printed on Pepsi Sodas. During the Gulf Disaster (2010) an additional $1.3 million was committed to projects for communities in the areas which were adversely affected by the disaster. Projects ranging from providing mental health services for oil disaster victims, to building seafood farms to help employ displaced workers, to creating shelters for animals that lost their homes were funded. As already reported, in 2012 Pepsi abandoned the Refresh Project. Another contest, which may be classified in this group, is Heineken "Sustainable packaging challenge" (2012) ("corporate challenge application" according to [3]). Heineken used its dedicated Web site IdeasBrewery.com (launched in 2012) to host this contest. Heineken was looking at sustainable packaging from three different angles: materials, transportation, and behavioral change that might stimulate more consumers to return bottles for recycling. The contest got about 150 entries. The winner proposed an innovative device designed to motivate consumers to return/recycle bottles. His "The Heineken $1000 bottle" idea turns beer pong into a recycling game: customers scan their bottles when they return them for prizes that are randomly assigned to the bar code on certain bottles. The winner won 10,000 $ and was invited to Amsterdam and work collaboratively with Heineken experts to develop his idea further.

Advertising Among this kind of online contests, we include contests aimed at addressing new or difficult markets (e.g. in terms of geographic areas, demographic or social segments etc.) through the creation of appropriate advertising campaigns. Convincing ideas for new commercials, slogans, posters etc. are collected.

For example, Danone launched the contest "Create a TV ad for Danone yoghurt!". The aim of the contest was to convince Egyptian families, especially adults, to enjoy Danone plain set spoonable yoghurt all year round. In fact, the contest's "context" section explains that in Egyptian consumers' minds, it is mostly eaten during the month of Ramadan. The relationship between Ramadan and yoghurt is mostly "cultural" and is based on the belief that yoghurt is helping digestion and soothes the stomach during a month where heavy eating is prevalent to compensate for the fasting of the day. Thus, the TV ad submitted should be an emotionally engaging and humorous story to catch Egyptian families' interest and make them realize that plain yoghurt is tasty, healthy and fun to eat all year long. To this purpose a 30 s animation or video was required that could be used as a TV commercial in Egypt. First prize was USD 5,000, second prize USD 3,000, third prize USD 2,000. Submissions were not published neither during nor after the contest.

Jack Daniel's launched a contest to introduce a lighter and sweeter version of Jack Daniel's to young adults through a poster. The idea was to offer a new drinking taste profile for young people who like what Jack Daniel's stands for but want to enjoy it on their own terms. The suggestion was to create something engaging and compelling to build a connection between young adults, who are fun freedom seekers, and the new drink, respecting the brand personality and the legendary figure of Jack Daniel. Jury's prizes amounted to €5000, 00 for the first prize, €3000, 00 for the second and €1000, 00 for the third. Submissions were not published neither during nor after the contest.

4 Discussion and Preliminary Conclusions

Based on an overview of 90 cases, we aimed at reaching a better understanding of how and for what purposes worldwide top food brands organize their online contests. Entertainment, in its broad definition, results to be the main purpose. In particular, we tried to distinguish subcategories able to more precisely identify brands' drivers. For example, we deemed relevant to introduce the clusters of "entertainment/talent scouting" and "ideation/advertising" that so far did not receive any emphasis in the academic literature despite their relevance in practice. As regards the former, to our knowledge there is no paper dealing with this topic. As regard the latter, several authors already underlined that the advent of social media has challenged companies as sole creators of marketing messages and contents (see e.g. [22, 23]) but, to our knowledge, they mainly refer to spontaneous actions of customers (e.g. peer recommendations, words of mouth, reviews found in blogs or forums) and not to firm-driven actions of customers (e.g. proposals generated for ad hoc contests), with a few exceptions. [24] provides a tutorial on how to drive advertising creation endeavors of customers toward long-term marketing objectives but they do not explicitly focus on contests.

Surprisingly, only a few contests were classifiable as "ideation/sustainability", in contrast with several authors (see e.g. [25–29]) who claim that increasingly, companies recognize innovation contests as instruments for alerting attention towards today's most urgent sustainability issues and for mastering them.

The brands examined tap into the crowd's creativity in different manners: by using a dedicated crowdsourcing vendor by setting up a dedicated website to run contests, by using their existing social media channels to involve fans.

Commercial crowdsourcing platforms comprise a network of creative users (from amateurs to professional designers or filmmakers) who compete in projects sponsored by different brands. The role of these platforms is to transform the business objective into a compelling creative brief, to broadcast this brief on the platform, to moderate and curate incoming submissions and to take care of intellectual property transfer. The brands in our sample have been using a variety of crowdsourcing platforms, among which Eyeka is the most adopted (about 36 % of the whole sample). Eyeka provides its customers with high level community functionalities and supporting tools for creatives. Eyeka adopts three alternative policies in terms of protection of the entries, depending on the type of contest. At the end of the upload period, entries can be publicly displayed on the platform, they can be commented by the other contributors (i.e. creators who have at least one entry accepted in the contest) or they can be visible only to the brand. In Ideation contests the standard is that submissions are confidential, such as in the case of Smirnoff Ice or Jack Daniel's on Eyeka. The case is different for Entertainment contests. These tend to be more open: normally the social platform used allows for commenting and voting each other submissions and virality on social networks is welcomed.

As regards the support offered to creatives, Eyeka provides them with a list of resources to be used to create entries with the relevant conditions of use. Sometimes toolkits are provided to help the development of the creative contribution (see e.g. Silhouette Packaging, by Danone, that provided the creatives with the blank packaging to be modified).

In our sample, a common alternative to commercial crowdsourcing platforms is publishing the contest on proprietary platforms, i.e. websites that can provide community functionalities, support tools, connection to company social networks etc. The main difference is that the proprietary platform is entirely dedicated to the contest and is managed by the brand itself. This choice allows the brands to make peculiar choices, for example in terms of protection of the submissions, as well as to communicate more directly with the users. This is the case, for example, of Heineken Sustainable Packaging Challenge that was hosted by the proprietary platform ideasbrewery.com. This platform allowed and foster the sharing of ideas, their commenting and public appreciating. This is a peculiar choice for contests of ideation, where normally confidentiality is required, based on the assumption that if the process is open and transparent other potential idea submitters could be inspired (see the interview to Heineken Innovation Program Manager Ellen Bark-Lindhout, available online at http://www.packworld.com/package-design/strategy/heineken-finds-package-designs-through-crowdsourcing, accessed on 12th June 2015).

Recently, the platform Ideasbrewery evolved into the new innovation portal Heineken Innovation Brewhouse, through which the brand invites creative minds around the world to share their ideas on a continuous basis.

The third alternative that we observed in our sample is to engage creatives by means of social media, such as Facebook, Twitter, Instagram, Pinterest or more specific ones such as Mixcloud, i.e. an online music streaming service that allows for the listening and distribution of radio shows, DJ mixes and podcasts, which are crowdsourced by its registered users. For example Movida Corona Contest was hosted on Mixcloud, where entrants were encouraged to show an ability to promote themselves by the tools available and other social media platforms. In this case, of course, confidentiality is not an issue.

As regards the classification proposed for the contests, it is worth noting that boundaries among clusters are rather blurred and the purpose of a contest may be twofold and cross different boundaries.

The next step of our research will be to identify specific design and management factors for each category and provide a set of guidelines according to the company's strategic goals. It will be worthwhile to conduct interviews with some of the organizers of the examined contests in order to assess the validity of our future findings and collect data about contests' performances. In fact, a major concern in the literature is a lack of measurable success criteria for online contests. Furthermore, the current classification should be considered preliminary and it could be revised to probably further sharpen the identified groups.

Appendix

Brand	Contest title
Budweiser	Budweiser's simple Facebook cover photo contest draws buzz
Budweiser	Budweiser's clydesdale home delivery holiday contest
Coca Cola	Show us the last time you did something for the first time
Coca Cola	Diventa l'inviato speciale di Radio DJ e vola a Londra
Coca Cola	Interpreting Coca Cola as an energizing refreshment
Coca Cola	Dispel myths about Coca Cola, through a refreshing video
Corona Extra	Movida Corona 2013
Corona Extra	Movida Corona 2012
Corona Extra	Movida Corona 2011
Corona Extra	Movida Corona 2010
Corona Extra	Movida Corona 2009
Corona Extra	Corona beach bar
Corona Extra	Concorso MTV days: vinci un trattamento da re
Danone	Help young moms have a serene first year with their baby
Danone	Engage and empower pregnant women with an essential app from Aptamil

(continued)

(continued)

Brand	Contest title
Danone	Actimel happy belly: show us a happy belly looks like
Danone	La tua pancia sorride
Danone	Show us why it is your favourite yogurt
Danone	Show us your morning routine with Actimel helps you get ready and prepared for a great day
Danone	When you feel good inside, how does it show on the outside?
Danone	Share Danette's pleasures!
Danone	Can you bring Dino the dinosaur to life?
Danone	Infuse silhouettes yogurt's packaging with kindness and diversity
Danone	Create a tv ad for Danone yogurt
Danone	importance of eating good food
Danone	Have fun with yogurt, 365 days of the year
Danone	Give us a peep of your pleasurable eating personality
Danone	Take a smell step to win big with Actimel
Danone	Design a pack for Vitasnella, the women's yogurt
Danone	Show us how you can enjoy more of life with Actimel
Heineken	The 60+ ideas challenge
Heineken	Take a photo of 60+ life style
Heineken	Your future bottle remix challenge
Heineken	Heineken future bottle design challenge 2013
Heineken	Light up the dark with a new Heineken contest
Heineken	Heineken engagement bring the best out of the 'Heineken man' in an instant, in a bar
Heineken	Heineken unlock legend
Heineken	Heineken Jammin festival contest 2012
Heineken	Heineken ideas brewery
Heineken	Heineken ideas brewery global draught beer challenge
Heineken	The sustainable packaging challenge
Heineken	Heineken limited edition design contest
Heineken	Heineken Jammin festival contest 2011
Heineken	Heineken Jammin festival contest 2010
Heineken	Heineken Jammin festival contest 2009
Heineken	Heineken Jammin festival contest 2008
Heineken	Heineken Jammin festival contest 2007
Heineken	Invent a new Heineken experience
Heineken	Make Strongbow gold cider the must have drink in a bar
Heinz	Heinz wholesome memories contest
Jack Daniel's	Toast at the troops
Jack Daniel's	Is the thought that counts
Jack Daniel's	Introduce a lighter version of Jack Daniel's to young adults

(continued)

(continued)

Brand	Contest title
Jack Daniel's	Jack Daniel's independence project
Kellogg's	Bring to life how Kellogg's helps give kids a better start to the day
Kellogg's	Unleash your urge for new krave milk chocolate
Moet & Chandon	Moet moment campaign
Nescafè	Turn coffee into a hip, sought-after Chinese new year gift
Nescafè	Dazzle us with your new concept for the ideal cup of coffee
Nescafè	Reinvent instant coffee, café style
Nescafè	Euro design contest
Nestlè	Celebrate women's drive to better themselves everyday
Pepsi	Pepsi twist
Pepsi	Pepsi taste
Pepsi	Dance for a chance
Pepsi	Pepsi football anthem
Pepsi	Half time
Pepsi	Change the game
Pepsi	Taj Mahal 2011
Pepsi	2nd Pepsi Co 10
Pepsi	The coke challenge
Pepsi	2012 Pepsi calendar
Pepsi	5th crash the Superbowl
Pepsi	Goa India 2010
Pepsi	Refresh project
Pepsi	Shangai festival 2010
Pepsi	Rome 2010
Pepsi	Pepsi films, refresh your world in 60 s
Pepsi	Dorito's king of ads
Pepsi	Pepsi Co 10
Pepsi	4th creative challenge in China
Pepsi	London film festival
Pepsi	3rd creative challenge in China
Pepsi	2nd creative challenge in China
Pepsi	1st creative challenge in China
Smirnoff	Mofilm Texas 2013 video contest
Smirnoff	Can you create the next new and exciting Smirnoff ice flavors?
Smirnoff	The Smirnoff nightlife exchange project
Smirnoff	The Smirnoff nightlife exchange contest
Sprite	2014 Sprite films program

References

1. Adamczyk, S., Bullinger, A.C., Möslein, K.M.: Innovation contests: a review, classification and outlook. Creativity Innov. Manag. **21**(4), 335–360 (2012)
2. Hallerstede, S.H., Bullinger, A.C.: Do you know where you go? A taxonomy of online innovation contests. In: Proceedings of the XXI ISPIM Conference (2010
3. Haller, J.B., Bullinger, A.C., Möslein, K.M.: Innovation contests. Bus. Inf. Syst. Eng. **3**(2), 103–106 (2011)
4. Roth, Y.: The state of crowdsourcing in 2015. https://en.eyeka.com/resources/analyst-reports (2015)
5. Bigliardi, B., Galati, F.: Models of adoption of open innovation within the food industry. Trends Food Sci. Technol. **30**, 16–26 (2013)
6. Martini, A., Massa, S., Testa, S.: Customer co-creation projects and social media: the case of Barilla of Italy. Bus. Horiz. **57**(3), 425–434 (2014)
7. Rabbinge, R.; Linnemann, A.: European food systems in a changing world. Euro. Sci. Found. (2009)
8. O'Reilly, S., Haines, M., Arfini, F.: Food SME networks: process and governance—the case of Parma ham. J. Chain Network Sci. **3**(1), 21–32 (2003)
9. McCorriston, S.: Why should imperfect competition matter to agricultural economists? Eur. Rev. Agric. Econ. **29**, 349–371 (2002)
10. Kjaernes, U., Harvey, M., Warde, A.: Trust in Food: A Comparative and Institutional Analysis. Palgrave Macmillan, London (2007)
11. Henchion, M.: The speciality food sector. http://www.teagasc.ie/ (2014)
12. Manniche, J., Testa, S.: Knowledge bases in worlds of production: the case of the food industry. Ind. Innov. **17**(3), 263–284 (2010)
13. Zichermann, G., Linder, J.: Game-Based Marketing: Inspire Customer Loyalty through Rewards, Challenges and contests. Wiley and Sons, NJ (2010)
14. Katila, R., Ahuja, G.: Something old, something new: a longitudinal study of search behaviour and new product introduction. Acad. Manag. J. **45**, 1183–1194 (2002)
15. Urban, G.: Don't Just Relate—Advocate: A Blueprint for Profit in the Era of Customer Power. Pearson, Upper Saddle River, NJ (2005)
16. Walter T, Back, A.: Towards measuring crowdsourcing success: an empirical study on effects of external factors in online idea contest. In: Proceedings of Mediterranean Conference on Information Systems (MCIS), pp. 1–12
17. den Besten, M.: Using social media to sample ideas: lessons from a Slate-Twitter contest. J. Syst. Inf. Technol. **14**(2), 123–130 (2012)
18. Montgomery, K.C., Chester, J.: Interactive food and beverage marketing: targeting adolescents in the digital age. J. Adolesc. Health **45**(3), 18–29 (2009)
19. Bilgram, V.: Performances assessment of co creation initiatives: a conceptual framework for measuring the value of idea contests. In: Brem, A., Viardo, E. (eds.) Evolution of Innovation Management: Trends in an International Context, Palgrave Macmillan UK, pp. 32–51 (2013)
20. Mulgan, G., Tucker, S., Ali, R. Sanders, B.: Social Innovation: What it is, why it matters and how it can be accelerated. http://eureka.bodleian.ox.ac.uk/761/ (2007)
21. Wiederhold, B.: Who gets funding? let the people decide. Cyberpsychology Behav. Soc. Networking **14**(7–8), 409–410 (2011)
22. Pine, B.J., Gilmore, J.H.: Welcome to the experience economy. Harvard Bus. Rev. **76**, 97–105 (1998)
23. Cova, B., Dalli, D.: Working consumers: the next step in marketing theory? Mark. Theory **9**(3), 315–339 (2009)
24. Hautz, J., Füller, J., Hutter, K., Thürridl, C.: Let users generate your video ads? the impact of video source and quality on consumers' perceptions and intended behaviors. J. Interact. Mark. **28**(1), 1–15 (2014)

25. Mirvis, P. H., Hurley, S. T., MacArthur, A.: Transforming executives into corporate diplomats: The power of global pro bono service. Organ. Dyn. **43**(3), 235–245 (2014)
26. Adamczyk, S., Hansen, E.G. Reichwald, R.: Measuring sustainability by environmental innovativeness: results from action research at a multinational corporation in Germany. Paper presented at the International Conference and Doctoral Consortium on Evaluation Metrics of Corporate Social and Environmental Responsibility, 8–10 June, 2009, Lyon (2009)
27. Arnold, M. Ramakrishnan, S.: Combat climate change—do open innovation methods help? Paper presented at the 16th International Conference of the Greening of Industry Network, Aalborg (2009)
28. Adler, J.H.: Eyes on climate prizes: rewarding energy innovation to achieve climate stabilization. Harvard Environ. Law Rev. **35**, 1–45 (2011)
29. Hansen, E.G.H., Bullinger, A.C., Reichwald, R.: Sustainability innovation contests: evaluating contributions with an eco impact-innovativeness typology. Int. J. Innovation Sustainable Dev. **5**, 221–245 (2011)

Future Internet: Cloud-Based Open Business Models

Fabrizio Cesaroni, Tindara Abbate and Massimo Villari

Abstract Cloud-based technological solutions are expected to play a key role in the near future due to their pervasiveness and the possibility they show to spur processes of economic growth by increasing efficiency and favoring differentiated business applications. However, in order to exploit such possibilities, firms need to define and adopt appropriate business models. By analyzing the case of an EU cloud platform, we discuss which business models can be adopted by different actors involved in the development and usage of cloud-based platforms. We show that such platforms represent general purpose technologies, which allow new forms of division of labor among technology suppliers and technology users, with positive returns for both types of actors.

Keywords General purpose technology · Cloud · Open business model · FIWARE

1 Introduction

The recent advent of cloud-based solutions has represented an important technological breakthrough, whose benefits will be fully revealed and realized only in the next future. Cloud technology is expected to generate a strong impact on the organization of firms' activities and operations, on the relationships among various agents (both firms and public institutions), and eventually on the way in which citizens (customers) behave and interact among them within the society. For this

F. Cesaroni · T. Abbate (✉)
Department of Economics, University of Messina, Messina, Italy
e-mail: tindara.abbate@unime.it

F. Cesaroni
e-mail: fabrizio.cesaroni@unime.it

M. Villari
Department of Engineering, University of Messina, Messina, Italy
e-mail: massimo.villari@unime.it

© Springer International Publishing Switzerland 2016
L. Caporarello et al. (eds.), *Digitally Supported Innovation*,
Lecture Notes in Information Systems and Organisation 18,
DOI 10.1007/978-3-319-40265-9_4

reason, a growing number of firms and governments have started to invest heavily in the development of such technologies, in order to obtain a leading position that might guarantee in the future the exploitation of a sustainable competitive advantage.

Apart from the development of superior technological capabilities in the field of cloud computing, however, the possibility to fully exploit the technology and benefit from it depends on the firms' ability to pursue a business model (that is, to organize all the activities, from value proposition to value delivery) [1, 2] that perfectly fits its inner characteristics and totally exploits its specific features. Indeed, similarly to past technological breakthroughs (e.g., the advent of electricity or, more recently, that of biotechnologies), which have been studied by historicists of technology [3], new technological paradigms often impose firms to think at a different organization of labor and at a different way of designing value propositions. In the case of cloud computing, a similar process is, therefore, to be expected.

Accordingly, this study addresses the following research question: which business models might be pursued by firms to benefit from the advantages offered by cloud-computing?

In order to address this research question, we analyze the practical case of FIWARE, a recently funded EU initiative, which has seen the involvement of different actors (from large IT operators to small software developers) with the objective of developing a cloud-based, IT-based platform for potential business purposes. By studying the case of FIWARE, we thus explore the features that cloud-based open business models should have. In doing so, we adopt the perspective of both large firms involved in the development of the IT platform, and small software operators involved in the development of subsequent applications.

In the next section, we start by providing a theoretical framework needed to address the empirical analysis. In Sect. 3 we explain the methodological approach we have followed to perform the analysis, whose results are shown in Sect. 4. Finally, Sect. 5 concludes the paper by discussing the managerial and theoretical implications of our study.

2   Theoretical Background

During the last decades, prior research on Open Innovation [4] has clearly shown that firms may benefit from collaborations with external partners by allowing the in-flow of external technologies and technological competences. In fact, external technologies may be integrated with the internal technological base in order to generate new products and services and thus enhance the firm's ability to create value. This process of technology in-flow may be undertaken along the entire process of innovation development, since the initial stages of basic research, to the latter stages of product and service design.

Apart from internal strategic considerations, firms' possibility to exploit an Open Innovation approach may only be limited by two conditions: (i) the lack of adequate absorptive capacities [5, 6]; and, (ii) the difficulty to set-up strong appropriability mechanisms that protect partners' intellectual property from uncontrolled deployment by third parties [7]. As for the former, firms thus need to invest in both scientific and technological research that allow them to monitor the external technological environment, identify the owners of complementary technological skills and competences, integrate external technological knowledge with the internal knowledge base, and eventually convert the potentialities offered by external technologies into actual products and services capable of generating a competitive advantage. As for the latter, firms both need to protect their technologies with patents and other forms of intellectual property rights, and to negotiate with potential partners the allocation of property rights on exchanged technologies.

Only once these two conditions are met and difficulties associated to their implementation overcome, firms may take full advantage of collaborations with external technology suppliers. Traditionally, firms that have undertaken such an approach have pursued an open business model [1, 2, 8] characterized by a strict control over the core elements of the technology to be embedded into innovative products and services, while external technology acquisitions have been limited to marginal and complementary technological components, often customized by the external supplier for the benefits of the potential technology user. In other words, technologies and technological knowledge exchanged in innovative collaboration processes are often specialized and (co-)developed ad-hoc to solve contextual problems.

However, when technologies object of exchange are General Purpose Technologies (GPTs), as in the case of IT platforms analyzed in this study, different forms of open business model may be pursued by partners, with advantages for both technology suppliers and technology users. Indeed, as prior research has shown [9, 10], GPTs allow a different configuration of division of labor at the industry level and a different organization of the innovative process. A simple comparison between the business models based on Specialized Technologies (STs) with respect to business models focused on GPTs allows to fully get the sense of the advantages provided by GPTs. As shown in Fig. 1a, in the case of an ST setting, the external technology is developed to fully respond to the potential user's application needs and to be fully integrated into its internal knowledge base. In this situation, the development costs of the specialized (that is, customized) external technology are totally incurred in by the technology supplier, while the technology user only incurs in the indirect costs of developing an absorptive capacity and of securing internal intellectual assets. Adaptations costs of external technology to internal needs, albeit not absent, can be supposed to be limited, given the fact that it is the technology supplier mainly in charge of providing a technological solution that fits context-dependent conditions.

By contrast, in the case of a GPT setting (Fig. 1b), the technological solution developed by the technology supplier does not respond to any specific (context-dependent) application condition, but is intended to satisfy a large number of possible application needs, not necessarily closely related one to the other. Indeed, the more general the technology is, the larger the number of application domains that can be served by the same GPT. In this case, albeit an ST solution implies a customization effort, the cost to develop a GPT is likely to be higher than that of an ST, provided that it requires to overcome the limited context-dependent

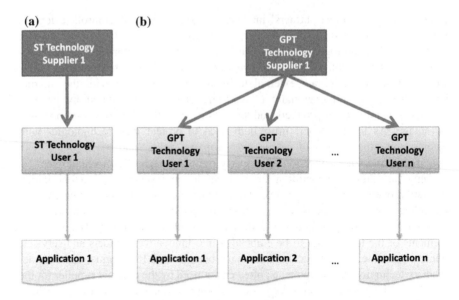

Fig. 1 ST versus GPT user-supplier interaction. **a** Specialized technology (ST). **b** General Purpose Technology (GPT)

conditions of a narrow application domain. Furthermore, the development of GPTs is often associated to the development of ad-hoc toolkits [11], which the technology supplier provides to users in order to facilitate the adaptation of the GPT to their local conditions.

Provided that such toolkits avoid adaptation costs to be excessively high for the users, both technology suppliers and technology users may benefit from a GPT setting: with respect to an ST setting, technology suppliers may more than compensate the extra costs of generalization of the technology by selling it to a larger number of customers (application domains); and technology users may benefit from a more stable technology, which has been already applied to other technological domains, without incurring in excessive adaptation costs.

As it will be discussed below, IT platforms represent a perfect example of GPTs that allow the implementation of such open business models. The advantages for both the developers of the IT platform (GPT) and the users of the same platform will be highlighted.

3 Research Design

The objective of this research is that of analyzing which business models can be effectively pursued by firms to benefit from the advantages offered by cloud-computing. To achieve this objective we performed a descriptive-interpretative qualitative research [12], aiming to provide a useful description, explanation and interpretation of the phenomenon under investigation. We have chosen this research method because its purpose is to examine a phenomenon that is occurring at a specific place and time, including the conditions, practices, structures and relationships that exist, processes that are going on, or trends that are evident [13]. Therefore, we carried out an Internet search to find and select a successful project, focused on cloud-computing and characterized by the involvement and participation of multiple actors with different roles, competences and objectives. To identify a potential case study, we referred to the European cloud platform oriented "to advance Europe's competitiveness in Future Internet technologies and to support the emergence of Future Internet-enhanced applications of public and social relevance" (http://www. ec.europa.eu). In turn, we selected the FIWARE platform for different reasons: (i) it is an EC project that is included in the Future Internet Private Public Partnership (FI-PPP) program, oriented to improve the effectiveness of business processes and infrastructures supporting applications in relevant areas such as transport, health, and energy; (ii) it can be used by a range actors—large firms, small-medium enterprises, public administrations, software houses, etc.—to validate innovative technologies in the context of smart applications and to prove their ability to support user driven innovation schemes; and, (iii) finally, it facilitates the interactions and collaborations between business and academics.

Then, we proceeded to an accurate data gathering about FIWARE by using different types of materials, methods and investigators [14]. Firstly, we conducted preliminary desk research to identify and acquire data and information that already existed in documents, internal reports, dossiers, and articles in order to obtain a good understanding of the FIWARE, as a suitable open platform. We also examined the descriptive material and other documents available on the European website. Second, we performed field research through different rounds of in-depth interviews with academic developers of FIWARE [15] in order to explore specific aspects related to this open platform, such as its main characteristics, reference architectures, principal functionalities, applications and services offered, potential development and etc. The interviews were conducted in March 2015, and each interview lasted approximately 2 h, following the traditional methodological pre-scriptions on data collection through personal interviews [16].

In addition, we organized two meetings—using Skype technology—with eight different key actors of the FIREWARE platform: FIWARE core developers (Telefonica-Spain, IBM-Israel and Engineering-Italy), FIWARE utilizers (SMEs and SPs), like AwayTeam-Israel, Détente Consulting-Romania, DH-Lab-Italy and city hall of Messina and Bari. The aim was to generate enough in-depth material to understand the following aspects: the role of each organization into FIWARE platform, its relationships with other participants, and its objectives. The meetings were organized in March and April 2015 and lasted approximately many hours.

The data and information obtained by interviews and meetings were transcribed, codified and analyzed using text mining and lexical analysis. For validating our qualitative analysis, we presented the results to the respondents in order to obtain their feedback and corrections [17]. The results of this case analysis are reported in the next section.

4 FIWARE Architecture and Philosophy

Nowadays, Cloud computing, Big Data, and Internet of Things (IoT) are enabling key technologies for the Internet of the Future. In this context, the European Commission (EC) envisioned the possibility to foster the wide adoption of such systems, in total openness, avoiding vendor lock-in and simplifying the composition of new services. In addition, the EC understood the need to find the right compromise between academic and industrial fields. To this end, the EC has started the Future Internet Private Public Partnership (FI-PPP) program that has brought to the delivery of a new complex European cloud platform, named FIWARE. The aim of FIWARE is to yield an open standard platform and an open, sustainable, global ecosystem. As it is possible to see in Fig. 2, the FIWARE Reference Architecture includes a set of general-purpose platform functions (Building Blocks), available through APIs, called Generic Enablers (GEs). GEs gather advanced and middleware interfaces to networks and devices, advanced web-based user interfaces, application/services ecosystems and delivery networks, cloud hosting, data/context management, IoT service enablement, and security (see the number from 1 to 7 in Fig. 2). FIWARE considers GE Open Specifications (that are public and royalty-free) and their implementations (GEi). There might be multiple compliant GEi(s) of each GE open specification. At least, there is one open source reference implementation of FIWARE GEs (FIWARE GEri(s)) with a well-known open source license.

4.1 The FIWARE EcoSystem

The FIWARE Ecosystem is shown in Fig. 3 (see [19]). Starting from the left part of the picture, in FIWARE, a common and well-known GEs repository is defined (that is the static part of FIWARE). The different geometric shapes of each GE remark the possibility offered by FIWARE of hosting and executing (see the RunTime Environment—RT of it, which is the dynamic part) any type of GE. Below the repository there is the platform itself that is a composition of more federated platforms that can easily interact each other thanks to the XIFI agreement (see [20]). In the picture each RT shaped cradle shows how more platforms are able to host GEs in different contexts/companies. Indeed, GEs can be seamless moved from RT shaped cradle to another and vice versa (see the dashed-lines). FIWARE allows this, thanks to the openness of its platform and APIs. Here Users, SMEs (Small and Medium-sized Enterprises, named also Local Players), SPs (Service Providers) and

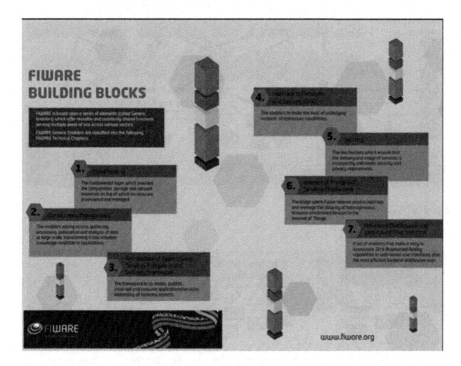

Fig. 2 FIWARE building blocks [18]

IoTs can interact through the Internet with the same kind of platforms and protocols, for different purposes but in a same way. FI-LAB Front-End in the picture depicts this common abstraction for interacting with FIWARE. To this FIWARE is representing a Standard de Facto of future complex systems, at least in Europe, where clouds and IoTs need to be used in any scenario as eHealth, Smart Cities and so on. Figure 3, inside the shaped cradle also shows a few rectangular small elements labeled SE. They represent the Specific Enabler developed by each company. Companies can make their businesses developing customized SPs able to satisfy needs of Users and SMEs and for connecting new IoTs and devices.

4.2   Business Domains in FIWARE EcoSystem

Figure 4 shows four different shaped cradle systems identifying four business IT companies (Big Players), named: (A), (B), (C) and (D). Each RunTime Environment (RT) is able to execute any Generic Enabler of FIWARE (see triangle, pentagon, exagon, etc., shapes), however the portfolio of Specific Enablers (see rectangular shapes) for each companies is different each other. The portfolio of SPs

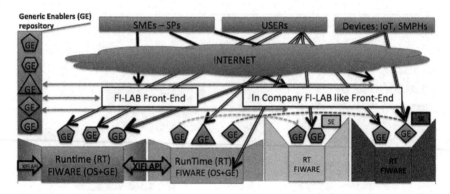

Fig. 3 FIWARE ecosystem

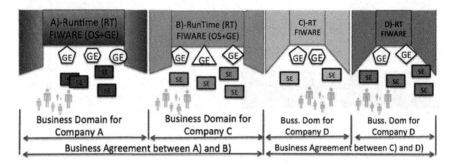

Fig. 4 FIWARE business domains

along with their users' customizations represents the compelling offerings of each company. Hence, business scenarios might be differentiated in terms of number of GEs, SEs and customizations.

4.3 Identifying Business Models of Participants to the FIWARE Initiative

The FIWARE ecosystem depicted so far reveals that different agents participate in the co-development of the initiative, playing different roles, contributing with specific resources and competences, pursuing different goals, and being subject to different motivations. Within this complexity of roles and resources, we could however identify a few common patterns that we characterized in terms of different business models adopted by the different categories of actors. Specifically, we could identify two main business models.

A first typology of business model is adopted by those Big Players (that is, large IT operators) that play a key role in the development of the system and in the definition of its inner characteristics. To such actors (that are responsible for the different GEs) it is demanded the relevant task of providing and developing the technological knowledge, skills and competences that are needed to make the system work. This task implies a relevant effort, both in terms of financial and human resources and technological capabilities. In principle, these actors do not participate in the development of downstream applications, and therefore the returns for their effort mainly arise from the licensing of the (usage of the) open platform to downstream operators. In this sense, such large firms mainly act as external technology suppliers, which indirectly benefit of the returns that technology users will generate through specific applications in different business domains. Provided that the FIWARE platform is expected to be applied in a broad variety of business domains (and, therefore, it can be considered a GPT), the total returns for the platform developers will correspond to the sum of the marginal returns of the application of the platform to each domain. In turn, in order to maximize the expected total returns, the platform developers have incentives to make the FIWARE technology as general as possible and its usage as simple as possible (that is, with limited adaptation costs) for the downstream users.

By contrast, an alternative typology of business model is adopted by those actors of the FIWARE ecosystem represented by downstream application developers (which are responsible of SEs, according to the terminology of FIWARE). In most cases, such actors are small and local software developers that are expected to design and develop applications to solve the contextual needs of specific groups of customers. These smaller, downstream software developers are therefore adopting an open business model. On the one side, the business model is open upward, to let the inflow of technology (the FIWARE platform) from large technology developers. On the other side, the business model is open downward, to let final customers participate in the co-development of the specialized application. In turn, the amount of value created through this business model results from the difference between the (high) value offered to final customers for the specialized and customized solutions, and the (low) cost of technology acquisition from upstream suppliers.

Moreover, our analysis also allowed to identify a few cases in which upstream system developers took also a stake in downstream operations, by acting as a specialized application developers. In these cases firms benefit of their double role, being both suppliers of GPT solutions and developers of downstream business applications. Is so doing, they exploit also the additional advantage of possessing a perfect knowledge of the functioning of the platform, thus reducing even more the costs of its adaptation to local needs.

5   Discussion and Conclusions

The analysis of the FIWARE case has clearly shown how the development of an IT platform that exploits the possibilities offered by cloud computing can provide advantages to different types of organizations and public institutions. Our analysis revealed that the various actors that participate at the development and usage of the platform adopt GPT-based business models that confer to them a potential competitive advantage. Therefore, it results important to discuss under which conditions such business models may offer a benefit with respect to more traditional (non GPT-based) business models.

As far as the first typology of cloud-based business models adopted by the Big Players is concerned, we saw that the more general the upstream technology (i.e., the GEs embedded into the FIWARE platform) is, and the simpler is its usage for downstream application developers, the higher the incentives for the Big Players are, since they may distribute their technological developments to a larger share of potential users. As such, this situation is quite different from traditional approaches adopted by firms in the IT sector, which were used to develop specialized technologies for each application domain and gain returns from the proprietary exploitation of the same technologies. By contrast, the division of innovative labor among the various actors involved in the FIWARE ecosystem and implied by the technology represents a new model of industry organization. Within this new cloud-based model, the large firms acting as technology developers are therefore required to pursue a business model in which the value proposition is mainly defined by the offering of a general purpose technology to a diversified plethora of downstream users that may adopt the technology in contexts that are unknown *ex-ante* to the original developers.

As for the second typology of business model (adopted by downstream operators responsible of specific SEs), what makes it more or less advantageous with respect to traditional business models is the existence of two independent conditions: (1) the upstream platform (the GEs) has to be general enough to be easily and cheaply applied to differentiated business domains, which mainly depends on how the upstream system developers have designed it; and, (2) the amount of absorptive capacities [5, 6] possessed by the downstream software developer, and therefore its experience, know-how and technological competences, along with its ability to understand and respond to the (latent) needs of final customers. If both conditions are satisfied, that is, if upstream operators have made the platform general enough and if downstream operators are in possess of adequate absorptive capacities, then the cost of technology adaptation that downstream software developer have to incur into apply the GPT to the specific application need is expected to be lower than the cost that the same software developer should incur to totally develop the application in-house, if the GPT platform (FIWARE) were not present. As such, in the presence of an industry structure organized around a cloud-based GPT, also downstream operators have incentives to adopt an open business model.

Finally, it is worth noticing that also governments may benefit from the development of cloud-based platforms such as FIWARE. The advantage to them is not obviously economical in nature. Rather, as in the case of the European Commission that has partly funded FIWARE, governments are often required to spend public financial resources under the form of research grants to promote the development costs of the platform. The grant may also cover the whole amount of financial resources needed to the full development of the platform, thus leaving it open and freely available to downstream operators. Nevertheless, the social benefits of similar technologies are expected to overcome the share of public funds devoted to their development, mainly because the existence of the technology and the possibility for downstream users to benefit from it should favor its application to various business domains thus boosting the economy. In this respect, platforms such as FIWARE represent physical infrastructures available to many actors. And, as other general purpose technologies, such infrastructures are expected to become engines for economic growth [9].

References

1. Teece, D.J.: Business models, business strategy and innovation. Long Range Plann. **43**(2), 172–194 (2010)
2. Zott, C., Amit, R.: Business model design: an activity system perspective. Long Range Plann. **43**(2), 216–226 (2010)
3. Rosenberg, N.: Perspectives on Technology. M.E. Sharpe, Armond (New York) (1976)
4. Chesbrough, H.W.: Open Innovation: The New Imperative for Creating and Profiting from Technology. Harvard Business School Press, Boston, MA (2003)
5. Cohen, W.M., Levinthal, D.A.: Absorptive-capacity: a new perspective on learning and innovation. Adm. Sci. Q. **35**, 128–152 (1990)
6. Zahra, S.A., George, G.: Absorptive capacity: a review, reconceptualization, and extension. Acad. Manag. Rev. **27**, 185–203 (2002)
7. Cohen, W.M., Nelson, R.R., Walsh, J.: Protecting their Intellectual Assets: Appropriability Conditions and Why Us Manufacturing Firms Patent (or not). National Bureau of Economic Research (NBER), Cambridge, MA (2000)
8. Chesbrough, H.W.: Open Business Models: How to Thrive in the New Innovation Landscape. Harvard Business School Press, Boston, MA (2006)
9. Helpman, E.: General Purpose Technologies and Economic Growth. The MIT Press, Cambridge, MA (1998)
10. Gambardella, A., McGahan, A.M.: Business-Model Innovation: General Purpose Technologies and Their Implications for Industry Structure. Long Range Plann. **43**, 262–271 (2010)
11. Von Hippel, E., Katz, R.: Shifting innovation to users via toolkits. Manag. Sci. **48**, 821–833 (2002)
12. Denzin, N.K., Lincoln, Y.S.: Handbook of Qualitative Research, 2nd edn. Sage Publication Inc., Thousand Oaks, London, New Delhi (2000)
13. Strauss, A., Corbin, J.: Basics of Qualitative Research: Techniques and Procedures for Developing Grounded Theory, 2nd edn. Sage, Thousand Oaks, CA (1998)
14. Denzin, N.K.: The Research Act: A Theoretical Introduction to Sociological Methods. McGraw-Hill, New York (1978)

Potential Benefits of the Deep Web for SMEs

Andreea-Roxanna Obreja, Penny Hart and Peter Bednar

Abstract While its size and complexity make it a powerful knowledge source, the Deep Web also has a wide variety of offerings that can be adapted to meet business needs such as: competitive intelligence, cross-enterprise collaboration, techno-elitism and innovative technology solutions. Additionally, elements associated with higher risks in terms of trading and security such as onion routing start finding their place in the current business environment. This paper outlines the potential of the Deep Web as a SME business tool by reviewing a set of benefits and risks associated with its content, tools and technologies. The study gives an account of the academic and practitioner literature on concepts, benefits and risks. Their applicability in the real business world is discussed as an outcome of interviews conducted with various SME representatives. The technology gap is highly visible in this field, with some businesses at the forefront of the Deep Web exploitation for years and others which have no knowledge of it. Data has been gathered from previous academic and practitioner publications, a number of small and medium enterprises and academics with interest in the field in order to provide a brief account of the socio-technical world surrounding the Deep Web. The limitations observed during the primary research stage show that company confidence in the Deep Web is at an early stage. This paper aims to provide an initial review of its potential role within the business world and the risks that companies are vulnerable to both as Deep Web users and sources of Deep Web data.

A.-R. Obreja (✉) · P. Hart · P. Bednar
School of Computing, University of Portsmouth, Portsmouth, UK
e-mail: andreea-roxana.obreja@myport.ac.uk

P. Hart
e-mail: penny.hart@port.ac.uk

P. Bednar
e-mail: peter.bednar@port.ac.uk

P. Bednar
Department of Informatics, Lund University, Lund, Sweden

© Springer International Publishing Switzerland 2016
L. Caporarello et al. (eds.), *Digitally Supported Innovation*,
Lecture Notes in Information Systems and Organisation 18,
DOI 10.1007/978-3-319-40265-9_5

Keywords Deep web · Invisible web · Hidden web · Dark web · Dark-Net · SMEs · Socio-technical analysis · Systems practice · Business applications · Business informatics · Organizational change

1 Introduction

The Deep Web is not a new concept but rather a part of the World Wide Web that has grown exponentially over the last few years. Also illustrated as "invisible Web" or "hidden Web", the recurring characteristic is that its content is "invisible" to conventional search engines and it comprises of a *"collection of executable Web pages which have no program-oriented interfaces or service descriptions like WSDL"* [1].

Although rather difficult to quantify, the World Wide Web hosts significantly more data than what traditional search engines and web browsers can render. Examples include pages deliberately excluded from search engine algorithms by their owners and dynamically-generated pages of little value beyond single use or contents of searchable databases [2]. The part of the Web typically searchable by the traditional search engines is defined as Surface Web, while the rest represents the Deep Web. A simple example would be plane tickets prices: when searching for the best price of a ticket, a search engine like Google will display a number of suggested airlines or travel agents (from the Surface Web) but to actually see the prices, a user would have to fill in an online form on the airline's or agent's website and retrieve data from a database that typically lies within the Deep Web, therefore exploring both in the same transaction. Similar examples include finding a product on the eBay or Amazon databases. Because the details of the product are constantly updated (price, dispatch point, reviews etc.) they are pulled from a database rather than stored on a static, indexable page. This means that once the user is searching for a product, the data is retrieved from the database as a result of a query and assembled instantly [3]. Every interaction with the search interface is monitored and recorded as data about the user that he/she will not have access to (part of the Deep Web) but will shape the results of subsequent searches. Consequently, the average Web users access the Deep Web on a daily basis without necessarily knowing it under this name. However, the Deep Web hosts a sum of resources apart from databases that can be queried by filling in a simple web form. These resources are sometimes discarded by traditional search engines or deliberately made more difficult to access but they are quite valuable in certain contexts which is discussed in more detail in the next sections.

The media's accounts of the Deep Web have centered on its role as a freedom of speech facilitator on one hand and enabler of illicit activities such as drug dealing, on the other [4]. Although the terms 'Deep Web' and 'Dark Web' were used interchangeably, adding a negative stigma to the entire Deep Web and ignoring its benefits, the publicity it brought prompted some businesses to exploit its advantages including access to more data and novelty for marketing. The dark web represents a collection of websites that are publicly visible, that cannot be found using search engines and where it is very difficult to trace their owners [5]. The difference, discussed and agreed with the primary respondents of the study, is that Dark Websites are generally used for illegal activities such as drug and arms dealing.

The study focuses on the business potential of the Deep Web. The research questions included: the businesses' view and interpretation of the Deep Web, the challenges they have met in exploring or using it for business activities and the business needs and concerns associated to the concept. The knowledge derived, discussed and generated by this study applies to small and medium enterprises which by definition have less than 250 workers, a maximum of 40 million euro annual turnover and a maximum 27 million euro annual balance-sheet total [6, p. 262].

This paper is structured as follows. Section 1 introduces Deep Web concepts and delimitates its data from what lies within the Surface Web or the Dark Web. Section 2 defines the Deep Web and briefly accounts for its business background. Section 3 provides a brief overview of the research that has been undertaken. The outcomes of researching the business potential of the Deep Web for SMEs are discussed in detail in Sect 4. In Sect. 5 a distinction is made between company policies and individual business practices in relation to Deep Web data. Finally, conclusive re-marks are presented in Sect. 6.

2 Deep Web Background

The Deep Web's origins date back to 1996 in a paper titled "Hiding Routing Information" presented at a workshop in Cambridge, England [7]. The initial definition of the Deep Web suggests that *"surface Web content is persistent on static pages discoverable by search engines through crawling, while Deep Web content is only presented dynamically in response to a direct request"* [8, p. 2]. More recent publications illustrate Deep Web content as a far more significant amount (compared to the Surface Web) of data hidden behind the query forms of searchable databases [9, p. 94]. In this study, dynamically-generated pages, non-indexable by standard search engines, including ones that have been cited on static Surface Web pages have been classified as Deep Web content.

Dynamically created content is typically built up from existing content in databases which can belong to governmental institutions, education establishment, online-based companies and many others. This content is typically retrieved through online forms that generate queries. While Deep Web content can be made visible to search engines if cited on static pages, traditional crawlers are unable to crawl and index dynamic content [10, pp. 118–120]. Bergman [8, p. 3], later on supported by Fraire [11] argues that it is impossible to completely "scrub" large Deep Web sites for all content in this manner because of what it would mean. In plain language, for example, queries into a database would need to exhaust all the combinations of answers which can be used when filling in an online form.

Surface Websites	Surface Web-accessible Deep Web search engines	Freely available protocol for un-indexed web content	Commercial software for Deep Web database research
Web forms– amazon.com, booking.com etc. Information cited on the Surface web	Biznar.com CompletePlanet data.gov mednar.com worldwidescience.org	TOR .onion addresses .i2p	Explorit – Deep Web Technologies Deep Web Harvester - BrightPlanet

Fig. 1 Deep web access points

The current content creation rate for the Web makes it rather difficult to quantify its size. Devine et al. [12, p. 16] estimates that Google indexes 26.5 billion public web pages whereas the Invisible Web would include 300 + billion database driven pages, which would make the surface content less than 10 % of the Invisible Web. More recent papers estimate the searchable content at the significantly lower percentage of 0.03 % [13, pp. 44–45]. The practitioners provide an estimation of the size of the Deep Web alone of 92,000 TB spread across 550 billion pages [14, p. 9].

Figure 1 summarises various Deep Web access points depending on their online availability. The first one is the most resource-consuming and grants access to databases belonging to various organisations that lie within the Deep Web and can be queried by filling in individual web forms to retrieve publicly-available or subscription-based data. The second and most accessible one is by utilising third-party tools such as Base–German from Bielefield, Biznar from Deep Web technologies or more industry-focused search portals like data.gov, mednar.com or worldwidescience.org [12]. The third is by using the TOR protocol to access .onion websites and discover the more in-depth non-indexed information straight from the source [15]. The fourth one is using commercial applications which are able to "scrub" through a large number of databases (but not the entire Deep Web) to provide meaningful search results. The techniques employed include federated search or Deep Web harvesting, which basically imply that the customer decides which databases are of interest and then the service provider creates a single search facility able to look at all those data sources [3]. Examples of companies providing Deep Web search applications are Deep Web Technologies and BrightPlanet.

2.1 Business Background

Similarly to the World Wide Web, the Deep Web has attracted both producers and consumers of data. The consumers who advertise the use of the Deep Web to prove the extent of their research and the depth of the information they can provide are represented by intelligence and research companies which can be private investigators, companies providing background checks or suppliers of insurance companies,. Examples include: i-Sight and 3i-MIND (www.i-sight.com, http://www.3i-mind.com).

A couple of examples of companies for which the Deep Web represents the "selling product" are Deep Web Technologies and Bright Planet. Deep Web Technologies, a US based company has been at the forefront of utilizing the Deep Web as a research area for businesses and academic bodies. BrightPlanet claims to have pioneered harvesting of Big Data from the Deep Web and advertises its products as the fastest, more powerful tools to create new intelligence.

The case studies on the BrightPlanet website provide an insight into a different type of consumer, companies acquiring Deep Web solutions. Examples include pharmaceutical companies that fight against fraud and counterfeiting and can use the Deep Web to identify their fraudulent competitors or HR Staffing companies who might want to improve their data sets [16]. As appealing as these Deep Web resources are presented in the marketing materials of the solutions providers, they come at a price. In most cases, as the representative of the software provider company D confirmed, the end-user (customer) is responsible for accessing and using the data. With no specific legislation in place, in UK, these activities are regulated by the Data Protection Act [Data protection act of 1998, 20] which clearly states that:

the data can only be used for the purpose for which it has been collected.

One element of concern that has attracted various ethical debates is data aggregation. Similarly to the Surface Web, Deep Web data can be aggregated and given new meanings for purposes that were not originally intended [17]. Putting together public government databases such as electoral rolls with freely available social media data could lead to disclosing private information that an individual does not want under public scrutiny. This supports the extremely high level of cautiousness that companies should employ when using Deep Web data but also why they should be aware of the types of data that competitors, for example, might find on the Deep Web.

3 Method and Findings

3.1 Initial Research

The research for this study included both primary and secondary sources. A brief literature review was performed in order to provide a link between some examples of Deep Web resources and their applicability in the SME business activities followed by a reflection on legal and ethical aspects. The aim of the primary research was to analyse the SMES' awareness of Deep Web concepts and to evaluate how they could benefit/are already benefiting from using the Deep Web for business purposes. The conceptual framework focused on the attention that the Deep Web has received so far and the tools that have been created to explore the vastness of it. As previously mentioned, these tools are sometimes presented as Deep Web solutions because they scrub the Deep Web for data and render it into meaningful search results include freely available search engines such as BASE or commercially available software such as Explorit marketed by the US-based company Deep Web Technologies. From a business point of view, this translated into 'there are a number of Deep Web solutions available on the market, but do they really solve a problem or fulfill the SME's needs?'

In order to assess the benefits and issues around the business use of the Deep Web, a preliminary review of companies that advertise the use of the Deep Web online was conducted. A basic search of the terms 'Deep Web' and 'business' pointed to several companies, including SMEs in the intelligence gathering sector, which claim that they use the Deep Web for comprehensive investigations. Six of them were invited to take part in this study or briefly share their experience using the Deep Web for business purposes but none of them provided a formal refusal or a reply. The reasons for their reluctance to disclose this kind of information can only be speculated upon. Apart from a guaranteed confidentiality specific to their activity sector or protection from potential competitors, there might be a connection to the blurry regulatory framework surrounding the Deep Web. The absence of Deep Web business specific legislation in EU and US, where those companies are registered, demonstrates that the technology is relatively new and both businesses and regulatory bodies are in the exploratory phase.

3.2   Primary Research Selection Criteria

The selection of business research subjects was based on two criteria: (a) the company's experience of online data research and (b) their previous evaluation of the Deep Web for business purposes. SMEs which are based or sell their services in the UK across various industries and which have intermediate knowledge of new technologies and the Surface Web (i.e. have used various search engines or online monitoring and analytics tools to collect data about their market segment, customers or competitors but do not have dedicated resources for extensive online data gathering) were invited to take part in the study. Contact was established through the authors' professional network or personal contacts. The only company using the Deep Web as a business tool ceased communication after the initial interview and briefing. It is owned by an entrepreneur with academic background, it uses the Deep Web for accident investigation and from now on it will be called company C. The reluctance of companies who are already using the Deep Web to share data about its business advantages contributed towards the refinement of the study aim, reducing it to the business potential of the Deep Web. Consequently, contact was established with a co-founder of an Analytics and Big Data SME which is creating value for its partners exchanging useful information generated by analytic software and sensors (Company A). A similar experience was shared by a web-design student start-up (Company B). Company F is also currently building e-commerce applications and plan to increase their market share of cutting-edge technology mobile applications.

Level of interest	Experience with the Deep Web	Identifier	Company/Individual description
Low	None	Company G	Delivering personalised software solutions mostly to publicly-funded organisations
	None	Company F	Currently building e-commerce applications and planning to increase their market share of cutting-edge technology mobile applications.
	None	Approximately 7 other business representatives	Interests in innovation and Deep Web as competitive advantage Interests in intellectual property protection online
Intermediate	Evaluated it as a potential business tool	Company A	Currently building Business Analytics solutions Interest in Open Data and knowledge gathering
	Evaluated it as a potential business tool	Company B	Web development start-up Interest in cutting-edge technology
High	Used as business tool	Company C	Accident investigation
	Listed as main business activity	Company D	Deep Web search solutions provider
	Listed as main business activity	Company E	Commercialising Deep Web harvesting tools
	Academic expertise	Darknet lecturer	General opinion: Deep Web has little business value and poses too many risks for companies
	Academic expertise	PhD Student	TOR Network expertise

Fig. 2 Primary research subjects

To anchor the potential business needs that the Deep Web could meet in the real business world, a software provider specialized in mining the Deep Web, referred to as Company D was invited to take part in the study. Company E which is commercialising Deep Web harvesting tools has also been contacted but the company representative specified that he does not participate in interviews anymore. Preliminary results of the study were discussed with businesses at an academic conference which are listed under Low interest in Fig. 2.

Due to the fact that the secondary research revealed inconclusive data on the Deep Web limitation from the Surface Web and security requirements when accessing it, the authors have used their professional network to invite academics, a lecturer specialising in Cyber-security and the Darknet and a PhD student, both with previous experience in the Darknet and Tor network concepts to add their contribution to the paper.

The table in Fig. 2 describes the primary research subjects according to their willingness to invest in a Deep Web business strategy as it was expressed at the beginning of the interviews stage of the primary research. The level of interest is based on the company's experience of the Deep Web, the results of evaluating or using it as a business tool and its ranking on their priority list both from a knowledge-gaining and resource allocation point of view. It is also an indicator of their engagement in Deep Web research activities prior to this study. A low interest means they have just heard about the Deep Web and would not be willing to resources to pursue their interest at the moment whereas high means resources have been already invested and the Deep Web is a major interest in their professional life.

3.3   Method

A flexible primary research design strategy was employed because of the novelty of the concept (business value of the Deep Web) and was motivated by the exploratory character of the research questions, which strongly demanded a qualitative research and analysis. In this project, coding and memoing were used to record and interpret the responses from interviews. Other principles included establishing trust, refining interview questions between sessions and conducting each interview systematically but giving the interviewee a fair opportunity to lead the discussion within the interviewer's parameters.

The initial data collection also included Freedom of Information Requests sent to various UK Governmental Departments. The FOI Requests were sent to: Companies House UK; Department for Business, Innovation and Skills; Ministry of Justice and the Information Commissioner's Office. Their general purpose was to assess if and how various regulatory committees in the UK are positioning themselves in relation to the Deep Web in a business context. A secondary goal was to review the UK bills that could cover aspects of the Deep Web usage for business purposes. The Freedom of Information Requests received a generic answer: "*We do not hold any information regarding which pieces of legislation cover the use of the Deep Web by UK businesses*". Additionally, with respect to the legislation regulated by the ICO, including the Data Protection Act 1998 and the FOIA, the same principles apply to the Deep Web as much as they would apply to any other part of the Web.

Pre-determined categories of questions were used for interviews in order to avoid bias. The general analysis themes emerged from the data during coding and bias was avoided at all times during the interviews and analysis stage. Thematic coding was used to analyse the data obtained through two sets of interviews and one focus group with the business representatives. Questions were refined as interviews went by and a preliminary analysis was done after each interview stage. The goal was to create themes and for each theme, categories of ideas. At this point, comments and personal reflections were added to the categories. The next step was to identify patterns, similar phrases and which categories needed to be expanded through subsequent interviews. After conducting all the planned interviews, the patterns were used to focus the analysis further and led to a second literature review.

4   Findings

As mentioned in the introduction, this study aims to provide a balanced account of the potential benefits of using the Deep Web for business purposes and the risks associated with them. Access to more data was deemed as top priority and strongest argument in researching the Deep Web by the business respondents. The two applied examples below were selected to explain that what one enterprise perceives

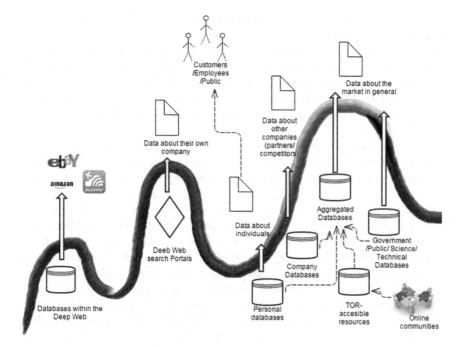

Fig. 3 An example of deep web exploration path for an SME

as a benefit can easily become a liability and can be translated into another organisation's major security concern when it comes to exploiting the wide offering of Deep Web data.

Figure 3 presents the type of data that an SME might encounter while exploring the Deep Web. This example path is not based on what a specific company interviewed for the paper might have encountered but rather on a synthesis of Deep Web resources available. The elements identified along the way are not registered in chronological order. The upper part of the path refers broadly to types of data while the lower one describes various databases that the data might be pulled from. For the purpose of the paper, the databases mentioned above are assumed to be publicly available or subscription-based that the company has been granted access to; databases protected behind firewalls are beyond the scope of this discussion. The Deep Web search portals can be freely available applications such as BASE or commercial ones. Personal databases are created by individuals and made public either through the Surface Web or the Deep Web (might also be accessed through TOR). Science and technical databases can belong to academic institutions. Online communities are the technical, elitist communities previously referred to in this paper.

Applied Example 1: Companies achieving competitive advantage through extensive Deep Web data gathering.

Businesses, regardless of their dimension/number of employees, have understood that 'there are more needles in more haystacks than ever' [18, pp. 27–31] and only by performing extensive searches and including all the sources available, they can grasp relevant information.

Both companies and individuals presented in Fig. 2 under Intermediate and High level of interest started their reviews of the Deep Web by stating that it can provide access to massive amounts of data. The second aspect that all business representatives agreed was that in this day and ages, they need access to all the data that they can get and they cannot simply afford to discard a data source before checking its value themselves.

The discussions on Deep Web data revealed three recurring points of interest for the business respondents: real-time data, competitive intelligence and data that has been made available through the Deep Web about the representatives' own companies.

The stigma created by the media and the risks associated with accessing the Deep Web via the TOR protocol for example led to a debate on what the Deep Web can offer which the Surface Web cannot. The software provider representative made a strong argument by enumerating the following: access to real-time data collected through sensors, multi-lingual searches in a global market where plurilingualism is an imperative need and availability of market monitoring systems and timely notifications for real-time competitive intelligence. Only company A deemed real-time data as a priority while multi-lingual searches for various Deep Web databases was seen as a promising feature for all the companies involved in the study, given the fact that the global market is an existing and future vital business target. Having access to constant monitoring systems and timely notifications of changes in the market which can be provided through commercial Deep Web harvesting applications could be beneficial to the SMEs involved in the study. The business representatives agreed that the size of their companies facilitates flexibility and fairly easy refinement of business strategies.

Mentioning market conditions triggered the participants to debate competitive intelligence. Monitoring the competitors' activity is essential both for SMEs and larger companies. While large corporations allocate massive budgets to competitive intelligence, SMEs do not have the necessary resources to compete with that. Consequently, they are the major beneficiaries of many databases which might be freely available on the Deep Web. The disadvantage of it is that even though information might be publicly available on the Deep Web, issues of liability might arise for businesses which use it if it is later proven to have been either collected through illegitimate actions or collated for an illegitimate purpose. This also ties to the second applied example: competitive intelligence gathered on the Deep web can be a significant threat for companies who are unaware of how much of their data is accessible through Deep Web tools.

Apart from data that cannot be accessed at all through traditional search engines (e.g. un-indexed databases), a Deep Web search can be quicker and more comprehensive compared to a Surface Web one enabling resource-savings. The potential service consumers were fairly blunt when referring to financial costs and benefits associated with the use of the Deep Web. Company A's experience of a few years ago was that there had been no predictable resource of investment for their business and the costs had outbalanced the benefits they have expected, massive amounts of data freely available through a fairly-easy to learn tool. However, they were in the course of reviewing the Deep Web as a business tool again as a result of this study and expected more positive outcomes.

Other Deep Web features discussed in the competitive advantage context were: its marketing potential and the TOR-facilitated anonymity. The novelty of the Deep Web attracted media attention increasing its visibility both within and outside the technical community contributing towards its advertising potential. A brief mention of the Deep Web as a business tool can bring more publicity and customer interest. However, for those who take issue with it (e.g. technology sceptics, privacy advocates), it might be a drawback regardless of whether they are potential customers or partners. As the primary research respondents demonstrated with their experience, for most individuals, the media stigma of the Deep Web will be a motivation to research it and form their own opinions of it, before judging it from a business enhancement prospective. The fact that TOR can provide a secure and untraceable exploration of the Web, including .onion addresses did not appeal to potential service consumers. SMEs are struggling to enhance their visibility and fortify their reputation. The business respondents strongly argued that their company policy was strictly built around openness and transparency, making their own anonymity less important. Anonymity and untraceability of digital footprint is discussed in the second applied example from a data protection point of view.

There are a number of risks associated with accessing the Deep Web and later on using data gathered from Deep Web sources. First of all, companies interviewed for this study considered that they would not need a higher level of protection when accessing the Deep Web compared to the surface Web. In reality, this might not be the case. The PhD student interviewed during the primary research stage of the project outlined that additional security is needed when exploring the Deep Web using TOR. In his view, exit node attacks such as harvesting username and passwords, or attacking binaries are much easier to conduct when accessing TOR.

As previously mentioned, in terms of liability for the data gathered, the Deep Web technology provider emphasised that the responsibility for using Deep Web technology to search various datasources falls mostly on end users or customers. Apart from ensuring that they are authorised to access a certain data source, they are liable for how the data is subsequently user or processed.

Apart from provenance, the quality of data is to be considered. Accessing a Deep Web community is not as straightforward as accessing the Surface Web and therefore requires additional technical skills. The affiliation to a Deep Web community is based on a culture of technical-elitism. This has the potential to facilitate a better identification of niche technology needs and consequently, the creation of ingenious products. A follow-up correlation that can be derived and analysed is the integration of these products in the Internet-of-things. Relying on crowd-sourced recommendations rather than a search engine, the quality of the Deep Web data sources depends on the perspective of the user. However, the Deep Web is a larger part of the entire Web (compared to the Surface Web) because of the amount of data sources available and the fact that they include a massive volume of scientific and technical databases.

The Freedom of Information requests demonstrated that the UK Government is yet to target the Deep Web through a specific piece of legislation and at the moment the use of the Deep Web is partly covered by the Data Protection Act and Computer Misuse ACT. Prior to a major investment in a Deep Web strategy, SMEs should consider how compliance with the law in the country they are based could impact their business activity.

The ethical risks pointed to accidental access and the notoriety the Deep Web has attracted in the media [19]. The PhD student asserted that there is currently no means to censor the TOR-accessible Deep Web part but without a search engine, the chances of stumbling upon disturbing content are very low as the user would need to know the unique TOR address. All business respondents agreed that the media stigma of the Deep Web could, in general, trigger scepticism from traditionalist partners or customers but they trusted their professional network to be open-minded and at least research the concept before dismissing it by default.

Applied Example 2: Companies looking to protect their data online.

Apart from gathering new data and expanding research horizons, knowing how to explore the Deep Web can improve a company's ability to protect their own data. It goes beyond putting sensitive data behind a firewall and reveals how data made publicly available by partners, customers or employees (apparently harmless), can be processed to disclose confidential information.

Company B's representative was the first one to express concerns regarding companies who might want to access the Deep Web not to necessarily gather new intelligence but instead, to find out what kind of information has been made publicly available about their own company. His view was also supported by a brief interest expressed by an SME (Company G) delivering personalised software solutions mostly to publicly-funded organisations on how to use TOR to protect online activity from potential industrial espionage. The protection of SMEs from gigantic data collectors (e.g. corporations which build search engines) is a Deep Web advantage yet to be considered.

While company B has had a chance to evaluate the business use of the Deep Web, company G has not had any experience with it. One of the concerns its representative has expressed was linked to industrial espionage and protecting the data they share online from various data collectors.

On one hand, protection from industrial espionage is the complementary risk associated with what was deemed as a Deep Web advantage by companies interested in business intelligence. Industrial espionage is not necessarily hacking or unlawfully obtaining data from competitors, it might also be using data that has been made publicly available or sold by a third-party but it has been obtained unlawfully. There is also an issue with lawfully accessed data which is in unlawfully analysed or processed (e.g. reverse engineering, which is a typical form of industrial intelligence practice). At the same time, even lawful processing might be problematic for companies for which publicly-available data is manipulated to reveal confidential information. An example is the existence of contact details databases traded on specialised forums.

On the other hand, small companies such as company G feel the need to protect themselves from gigantic data collectors such as companies owning search engines. There have been proved allegations that e-mails, regardless of emails provider, can be fully scanned by smart machines to provide fully personalised features in terms of online search results and malware detection [19]. Giving one of these machines access to a company's digital footprint can reveal a fairly accurate profile and hints about the type of products an SME might develop next or their future marketing strategy.

Awareness of what competitors, partners or customers can see online about a company is of strategic importance. First of all, searching information about the company an individual owns or works for using traditional search engine renders personalised results (based on results' popularity and search history) which are not always comprehensive. Therefore, company representatives will not see everything competitors and customers see. The Deep Web is not currently able to filter information based on personal preferences and profile and therefore offers a better chance to get a more realistic view of what users can actually find out about your company in a matter of seconds.

Secondly, if there is information out there that the company did not know was public or did not want to be public, the company's information security strategy will require amendments. In case of a security breach, the leaked information is more likely to appear on Deep Web forums before being surfaced on the general Web. Monitoring these forums gives the company's IT department a chance to respond and contain the damage, leading to more effective contingency plans.

Although a company needs to be concerned about its online profile, a security strategy that addresses the risks associated with the Deep Web needs to be balanced. While it is challenging to mitigate all the risks derived from what customers or partners share about the company on the Deep Web, the awareness that the Deep Web exists and monitoring of its capabilities and company presence on it can ensure more effective contingency plans. Additionally, understanding and considering the users' individual characteristics and technical skills (employees, customers) can facilitate development of appropriate policies, more effective education and thus support compliance with those policies.

5 Individual Professional Practices

To facilitate the understanding of the context in which the Deep Web can be implemented as a business tool, Systems thinking principles can be employed for a realistic overview. While a SME might not use, or rather not be aware of the use of the Deep Web, some of its employees, customers or partners might benefit or be impacted by it (for example, users of Amazon services use the Deep Web without necessarily deeming the Amazon databases a part of the Deep Web). Systems'

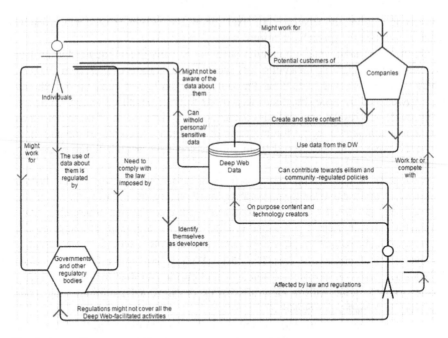

Fig. 4 Actors diagram

thinking facilitates the differentiation between the system as a whole (i.e. the company) and the sum of its parts (employees, customers, market etc.) [20, pp. 18–19]. Additionally, focusing on an SME as an entity may diminish the attention that should be paid to the (socio-technical) human activity system within the organisation [20, p. 28, 21, pp. 3–5]. In the analysis stage of this study, the elements that surfaced as vital were individuals: they asses the Deep Web, they create or exploit the content and ultimately, they dictate the organisation's strategy.

Figure 4 describes the relationships between the Deep Web data and different actors that might impact or benefit from it. It is essential to emphasize that while individuals might be tempted to explore the Deep Web out of curiosity or for personal use, they can also be part of an SME with an interest in technology or a regulatory body. Even if the organisation is not knowingly using the Deep Web, an employee exploring it from a company computer might prompt security concerns or trigger a new business initiative using the Deep Web.

The primary research respondents evaluated the potential of the Deep Web by linking its features to their specific business needs. The recurring codes were customer request and innovation in technology. SMEs' common goal is to be able to meet any customer demand connected to the Deep Web, particularly if later on the Deep Web might become a market norm rather than exception. This is directly linked to technology and innovation as, in their opinion, innovative vision and cutting edge technology are compulsory for long-term business success.

An example provided by company B where they were unable to accept a Bitcoin payment for a web development contract and therefore lost a customer, demonstrates why small and medium enterprises are more prone to use the Deep Web upon customer request. The allure of comprehensive researches is that they would provide more knowledge leading to improved services and innovation. The main potential drawbacks are the reputational costs when dealing with customers who are uncomfortable with the risks associated with the Deep Web such as uncertain data provenance and possible facilitation of illegal activities.

The reduced size of SMEs facilitates more flexibility in implementing new technologies and business strategies compared to larger organisations. SME employees are expected to fulfil various roles at once and have extensive knowledge in the field (being described as generalists) as opposed to large company employees which specialize on specific roles and become proficient at those (specialist) [22]. They tend to have more independence and as a result, explore more innovative technologies and be more proactive in terms of business innovation [23]. While it is easier for them to research the Deep Web and test its business potential, they are also putting their companies at greater risk. At least two of the business representatives interviewed for this project mentioned that they use their personal laptops for business purposes and sometimes work remotely, without having an IS security strategy to comply with.

Their size and limited resources brought into discussion another element of risk. One of the companies interviewed is currently using the Wi-Fi network and sometimes software provided by an academic business supporter. Limited resources make SMEs more vulnerable to using free software or online resources such as e-mail clients or cloud storage space which do not that data is transmitted securely, protected from being accessed by the third party storage provider or if the data is transferred overseas, covered by the same data protection regulation existent in the country where the SME is based [24].

Being smaller organisations means that SMEs are more easily shaped by individuals, employees or customers, compared to giant corporations. While most of the time this leads to flexibility and enables creativity, it also requires additional management and consideration for customer preferences, employees code of practice and position towards controversial areas such as the Deep Web.

6 Conclusion

Each motivation to use the Deep Web as a business tool can be translated into an additional concern or challenge because of its covert nature and lack of incidence under formal regulations. Access to large amounts of data was chosen as an example of how SMEs could both benefit and be threatened by the same Deep Web feature. Accessing countless Deep Web resources could give companies a competitive edge as long as they cautiously take into consideration data quality and provenance. At the same time, having their data (visible on the Deep Web) used and manipulated by other companies represents a major security threat.

A reduced number of employees compared to larger organisations gives SMEs higher flexibility but also makes them more vulnerable to being shaped by individuals. These individuals ultimately decide the inclusion/exclusion of Deep Web resources from the business strategy and their professional practices make the company liable for what and how data is being used or made available on the Deep Web.

The novelty of positioning the Deep Web in a business context represented a challenge throughout the project. The academic literature included materials on querying the Deep Web and more on SME activities but only a reduced number of a correlation of the two. There were no UK or EU pieces of legislation that would specifically target the business use of the Deep Web. This represented the only motive speculated by the primary research respondents to justify why companies who were claiming to use the Deep Web refused to share their experiences.

The main limitations of this project were connected to the companies' reluctance to admit that they are using the Deep Web and share their experience of it. The companies who agreed to comment on the use of the Deep Web for business purpose were either Deep Web technology providers, companies who do not have knowledge of the Deep Web but would be interested in its benefits or companies who have assessed the Deep Web as a business tool but decided that the costs and concerns would outweigh the benefits.

The Deep Web is commonly used for many purposes (e.g. Amazon) and is not only a playground for obscure, surveillance-obsessed technical users. Its existence has been acknowledged and validated by the business world. This means that "*serious information seekers can no longer avoid the importance or quality of Deep Web information*" [25, iii–iv; 26].

The data factor (volume, variety) of the Deep Web has the potential to facilitate faster, more extensive research. The outcome of this research may enable SMEs to accede to the large corporations' league in terms of data collection and give them a competitive edge with many fewer resources. The anonymity provided by the TOR network can represent an additional layer of protection from giant data collectors that own and develop search engines. Researching the Deep Web as opposed to the Surface Web can also free SMEs from the unpredictable search personalisation based on digital footprint of the traditional search engines.

On the other hand, SMEs should be prepared to deal with the scepticism that has been triggered by the media stigma. Another area of concern is the non-existent regulatory framework, especially in the UK and EU. Governments' and regulatory bodies' attention so far has been drawn by the obscure activities facilitated by the Dark Web. However, the speculative association between the Deep Web and Dark Web make any Deep Web regulatory framework virtually unpredictable and therefore, can sensibly impact its business potential.

The future of the Deep Web, as the demand side of the focus group respondents concluded, lies in two variables: motivation and resources. This translates into: If companies are going to want more data than the Surface Web can offer and if they have the resources available, the Deep Web has the potential to become widely used by businesses. From the supplier's point of view, the knowledge gathering market is far from saturated and only starting to learn the benefits of Deep Web technology.

Future research is recommended to observe if the conclusions of this study apply to SMEs who are using the Deep Web in practice. Based on their feedback of the business use of the Deep Web, it would be beneficial to develop a set of legal and ethical recommendations for government and international bodies to consider in their attempt to regulate the business use of the Deep Web.

References

1. Kumar, P.: Visualization of online marketplaces using hidden web services. J. Internet Bus. **6** (2009)
2. UC Berkeley: Invisible or Deep Web: What it is, How to find it, and Its inherent ambiguity. (n. d.) http://www.lib.berkeley.edu/TeachingLib/Guides/Internet/InvisibleWeb.html
3. Deep Web Technologies: Federated Search and My Business. 15 Dec (2014) http://www.deepwebtech.com/company/resource-center/faqs/#bottomline
4. Newton-Small, J.: Why The Deep Web Has Washington Worried. Time.com, 1–1 (2013)
5. Egan, M.: What is the Dark Web? How to access the Dark Web—How to turn out the lights and access the Dark Web (and why you might want to). http://www.pcadvisor.co.uk/how-to/internet/what-is-dark-web-how-access-dark-web-3593569/. (2015)
6. Loecher, U.: Small and medium-sized enterprises-delimitation and the European definition in the area of industrial business. Eur. Bus. Rev. **12**(5), 261–264 (2000)
7. Grossman, L., Newton-Small, J.: The Deep Web. Time: The Secret Web, Where Drugs, Porn and Murder Hide Online. Nov 11 (2013)
8. Bergman, M.K.: White paper: the deep web: surfacing hidden value. J. Electr. Publishing, **7**(1) (2001)
9. He, B., Patel, M., Zhang, Z., Chang, K.C.C.: Accessing the deep web. Commun. ACM **50**(5), 94–101 (2007)
10. Iftikhar, F., Gull, S., Shoaib, M., Shoaib, S., Karim, K.: An Ajax powered forms based approach for crawling the deep web. Pakistan J. Sci. **63**(3) (2011)
11. NYU Politechnic School of Engineering: Decoding the Deep: Juliana Freire and Claudio Silva Join NYU-Poly. http://engineering.nyu.edu/news/2012/02/13/decoding-deep-juliana-freire-and-claudio-silva-join-nyu-poly
12. Devine, J., Egger-Sider, F.: Going Beyond Google Again: Strategies for Using and teaching the invisible web. Facet publishing, London (2014)
13. Hadson, H.: Web of darkness. New Sci. **221**(2961), 44–45 (2014)
14. Langville, A.N., Meyer, C.D.: Google's PageRank and beyond: The science of search engine rankings, Princeton University Press (2011)
15. Dingledine, R., Mathewson, N.: Tor: An anonymous internet communication system. In: Proceedings of Workshop Vanishing Anonymity, the 15th Conference Computers, Freedom, and Privacy (2005)
16. BrightPlanet: Why you should tap into the deep web in 2014. http://www.brightplanet.com/2014/01/why-you-should-tap-into-the-deep-web-in-2014/ (2014)
17. Oboler, A., Welsh, K., Cruz, L.: The danger of big data: social media as computational social science. First Monday **17**(7) (2012)
18. Robb, D.: How search is converging with business intelligence. Bus. Commun. Rev. **37**(8), 28–31 (2007)

19. Poulsen, K.: Visit the wrong website and the FBI could end up in your computer. http://www.wired.com/2014/08/operation_torpedo/ (2014)
20. Checkland, P., Holwell, S.: Information, Systems and Information Systems: Making Sense of the Field. John Wiley, Chichester (1998)
21. Mumford, E.: Designing Human Systems for New Technology: The ETHICS Method. Manchester Business School, Manchester (1983)
22. Turner, R., Ledwith, A., Kelly, J.: Project management in small to medium-sized enterprises. Manag. Decis. **50**(5), 942–957 (2012). doi:10.1108/00251741211227627
23. Gray, D.E., Saunders, M., Goregaokar, H.: Success in Challenging Times: Key Lessons for UK SMEs. Project Report. Kingston Smith LLP, London (2012)
24. Schneider, K.N.: Improving data security in small businesses. J. Technol. Res. **4**(1) (2013)
25. Bindal, S. Muktawat, H.S.: Deep Web. http://www.researchgate.net/profile/Sumit_Bindal/publication/261773660_Deep_Web/links/02e7e5357775467e13000000.pdf (2010)
26. Geller, J., Soon Ae, C., Yoo Jung, A.: Toward the semantic deep web. Computer **41**(9), 95 (2008)
27. Cyber-bullying and Digital Anonymity. http://www.publications.parliament.uk/pa/cm201415/cmhansrd/cm141023/debtext/141023-0004.htm (2014)
28. Gehl, R.W.: Power/freedom on the dark web: a digital ethnography of the Dark Web Social Network. New Media Society (2014). doi:10.1177/1461444814554900

Part II
Specific ICT Enablers in Use for Innovation

New Design Techniques for New Users: An Action Research-Based Approach

Tania Di Mascio and Laura Tarantino

Abstract Novel ICT products based on the idea of phenomenologically situated interaction, along with the demands of their new users, raise the necessity of relying on new design and evaluation methods. Action Research, based on juxtaposition of action and research, is committed to the production of new knowledge through the seeking of solutions and/or improvements to "real-life" practical problem situations, and appears to well cope with these new demands: unlike laboratory experiments, struggling to maintain relevance to the real world, the "laboratory" of Action Research is the real world itself. In this paper we report on our experience within an Action Research project aimed at conceiving a novel children-oriented data gathering technique and using it for the context-of-use analysis of the TERENCE project, which developed a Technology Enhanced Learning system for children. Not only did our experience provide solutions for the problem at hand, but it was also the opportunity for a reflection on Action Research itself in the case in which the objective of the research is the definition of a new method for solving the problem.

Keywords Action research · Data gathering methods · New-users

1 Introduction

ICT products emerged in the last two decades have been characterized by a shift from the idea of interaction as a form of information processing to the idea of interaction as a form of meaning making phenomenologically situated [1]. This new vision—the so called 3rd paradigm of the Human-Computer Interaction (HCI)—requires not only to focus on different topics and questions, but also to rely on

T. Di Mascio (✉) · L. Tarantino
Università degli Studi dell'Aquila, Via Vetoio, 1, Coppito, 67100 L'Aquila, Italy
e-mail: tania.dimascio@univaq.it

L. Tarantino
e-mail: laura.tarantino@univaq.it

© Springer International Publishing Switzerland 2016
L. Caporarello et al. (eds.), *Digitally Supported Innovation*,
Lecture Notes in Information Systems and Organisation 18,
DOI 10.1007/978-3-319-40265-9_6

alternative methods for designing and evaluating interactive products, among which Action Research, as underlined by Harrison et al. in [1].

Action Research (AR) represents a juxtaposition of action (practice) and research (theory) and is committed to the production of new knowledge through the seeking of solutions and/or improvements to "real-life" practical problem situations [2, 3]. Unlike laboratory experiments, which struggle to maintain relevance to the real world, the "laboratory" of AR is the real world, which appears a promising pre-condition for designing and evaluating situated interaction: an AR project is always performed collaboratively by researchers and an organizational "client", under the founding principle that complex social processes can be studied best by introducing changes into these processes and observing the effects of these changes. As observed by Baskerville [2], one area of importance in the ideal domain of AR is new or changed systems development methodologies, since studying new or changed methodologies implicitly involves the introduction of such changes, making AR appropriate for the novel design/research challenges raised by new users brought into the market by new ICT applications. AR has actually recently received attention from HCI researchers, though the focus has been put more on the evaluation of new technology in novel contexts than on conception/evaluation of new design and development methods (see, e.g., [4–8]).

The origins of AR can be traced to the work of Lewin [9, 10] and of researchers at the Tavistock Clinic [11], which inspired a vast stream of work (see [2, 3, 12–14] for discussions and surveys) with the common notion of some kind of cyclical process repeated until a satisfactory outcome is achieved [2, 3]. The seminal paper of Susman and Evered [15] strongly influenced the field: according to their view, after the establishment of a client-system infrastructure (the *researcher-client agreement*) five phases are iterated (Fig. 1a): *diagnosis* corresponds to the identification of the primary problems causing the organization's desire for change and develops a theoretical framework that will guide the process; *action planning* specifies the actions that, guided by the theoretical framework, should solve the organizational problem; *action taking* implements the planned actions; *evaluation* determines

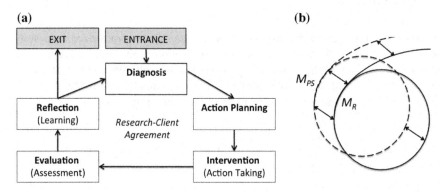

Fig. 1 Two models for the AR process

whether the theoretical effects of the actions were realized and whether they produced desired results; *learning* summarizes and formalizes the knowledge gained throughout the entire process with respect to the immediate problem situation and the scientific community.

Two notable contributions aim at facing criticisms about lack of rigor and ambiguous resemblance with consulting (from which AR anyhow differs, being motivated by scientific prospects and committed to the production of scholarly knowledge [2]): [14] develops a set of interdependent principles and criteria that researchers and reviewers can use both to ensure and to assess the rigor and relevance of Canonical Action Research (CAR), while [3] argues that the issue is related to the way in which AR is conceptualized and proposes a model including two cycles running in tandem (Fig. 1b): one cycle addresses the client's problem solving interest while the other one addresses the researcher's scholarly interest. As outlined in Table 1, this implies that two methods are being used, one (M_R) being action research itself used to investigate on a real world problem situation (A) and the other (M_{PS}) being the one adopted for the problem solving of a real-world example of A (P); rigor requires that a theoretical framework for M_{PS} is selected prior to the intervention.

The TERENCE project (www.terenceproject.eu), aimed at designing a Technology Enhanced Learning system to be integrated into school activities for supporting 7–11 years old poor-text comprehenders, was the occasion for experiencing AR principles and methods within the framework of data gathering activities. Since neither consolidated adult-oriented data gathering techniques nor literature on children-oriented techniques (e.g., [16–18]) turned out to be adequate for the organizational situation (e.g., schools imposed that all children of a class had to be involved at the same time and that the duration of data gathering sessions had to be below 1 h) the need emerged of a dual objective: conceiving an appropriate data gathering approach and applying it to the immediate problem situation.

We adopted an AR view with the multifaceted objective of (i) generating/testing a new children-oriented data gathering technique, (ii) solving the immediate problem (i.e., defining users' classes and personas for the TERENCE project), and (iii) translating the experience into scholarly knowledge related to design and evaluation of children-oriented applications. We based our project on the CAR approach of [14] blended with the tandem view of [3], following the Susman and Evered Cyclical Process Model for individual cycles of the tandem [15].

Table 1 Elements of an AR intervention according to [3]

A	A real world problem situation
P	A real-world example of A allowing the researcher to investigate A
F	A theoretical premise declared by the researcher prior to any intervention in A
M_R	The research method
M_{PS}	The method (M) which is employed to guide the problem solving (PS) intervention

Table 2 Elements of our action research intervention

A	Issues and challenges in effectively gathering dependable children's data on a large-scale basis within school organization
P	Defining the user classification and the personas for the TERENCE project
F	Frameworks from consolidated data gathering techniques can be effectively blended with existing game framework
M_R	Action research
M_{PS}	The new untested evolving technique

Since theoretical and empirical studies show that learners are more motivated to participate in school-class activities if they are shaped like games (e.g., [19, 20]), we decided to base the field study on games. Under this theoretical premise [21], in our case the elements of the AR intervention of Table 1 are instantiated as in Table 2. Differently from [22], where we presented the outcome of the AR project, and from [23], where we discussed the AR process that led to the result, in this paper we discuss some organizational aspects of such a process with focus on the relationships between the two cycles of the tandem, in term of time scheduling (what happens before/while what) and information exchanged. The analysis of such relationships led us to a meta-result related to an original overall structure of a tandem-based AR project in which M_{PS} is itself the object of enquiry.

The remainder of the paper is organized as follows: after sketching in Sect. 2 the situational analysis that motivated the AR project and its foundation in terms of the Research-Client Agreement, Sect. 3 reports an overview of the Cyclical Process. Section 4 then briefly reports reflections on the structure of such process and our proposal for its generalization. Finally, in Sect. 5, conclusions are drawn.

2 The Organizational Situation

TERENCE was a 3 years long European FP7 ICT multidisciplinary project that developed an Adaptive Learning System (ALS), in Italian and in English, for "poor (text) comprehenders", i.e., 7–11 years old children proficient in word decoding and low-level cognitive skills but with problems in deep text comprehension. We converged to the final system in three User Centered Design iterations. In particular, the context-of-use analysis required a preparatory study followed by two rounds of field studies. *The AR project took place during the second rounds of the field studies.*

The Situational Analysis The *preparatory study* was carried on by brainstorming with about 30 domain experts for understanding how children are assessed by psychologists as poor comprehenders [24]. A relevant outcome was the identification of topics to be investigated by field studies to be conducted in schools in UK and Italy according to indications from school deans and teachers: while researchers underlined the need of direct interaction with children, school bodies raised organizational and ethical issues (e.g., they initially requested that data gathering would not interfere with school activities) that forced the project team to structure a *1st round of field studies* as a combination of traditional expert-based and indirect user-based data gathering methods (e.g., diaries), i.e., the approaches followed by the participating schools when involved in research projects. This round, involving about 70 educators and 100 learners, produced main requirements for the learning material and a first cognitive characterization of learners [24] that turned out to be insufficient due to limits of the adopted approach: first of all, since diaries were administered to children as homeworks to be done with educators and family members, results were heavily adult-biased; furthermore, only a small quote (around 30) of the 100 administered diaries were actually returned, mostly poorly filled in. In summary, the indirect approach failed to meet requirements of gen-uineness, dependability, and statistical significance of gathered data. A *2nd round of field studies* was necessary to enrich and refine the results and it was clear that (i) some kind of direct interaction with learners was crucial to gather high quality data, and (ii) a large-scale study was mandatory to ensure pedagogical effectiveness of the system. At this point the TERENCE consortium decided to conduct in parallel two streams of data gathering by two design teams, in UK and Italy. UK activities were conducted according to customary observational methods, while Italy activities followed an AR approach for conducting data gathering while at the same time structuring a new innovative data gathering technique. This reflection phase was the entrance of the cyclical AR process; the considerations about the adequacy of the 1st round results are—de facto—part of the *Diagnosis* stage of the first iteration of the AR project.

The Research Client Agreement In CAR projects the Researcher-Client Agreement (RCA) represents the guiding foundation establishing focus, bound-aries, and objectives of the project, defining roles and responsibilities of the par-ticipants, selecting data collection and analysis methods, and measures to evaluate the results. We here sketch these points by addressing the criteria proposed in [14] to assess the adherence of a CAR project to the *Principle of the RCA* (notice that in practice they are the result of continuous reflections and refinements throughout the project).

The Working Team The team comprised a panel of representatives from the schools involved in TERENCE, including for each school its dean and one teacher per participating class, and a panel of experts from the technical TERENCE team, including two action researchers plus people with background in data gathering, game frameworks, and psychology. Members of the two panels participated to the different CAR activities over different periods of time based on logistics, skills, and expertise issues. The school panel was actually the client of the CAR.

The Focus of the CAR Project We agreed that the boundaries of the CAR project had to coincide with the boundaries of the diagnosed problem, i.e., the context of use analysis phase of the TERENCE project. Teachers stated ethical principles (*Eth*1 and *Eth*2) and organizational constraints (*Org*1 and *Org*2) to be satisfied:

*Eth*1   it would be unfair not to involve all children of a class at the same time (children might perceive unjustified differences in treatment)

*Eth*2   it would be unethical to make children invest time in activities that are not a value for them

*Org*1   activities has to be structured in sessions not longer than 1 h

*Org*2   project activities has to be integrated into regular school activities

Given the constraints and considering related literature (see, e.g., [16, 18, 22, 23, 25]) and teachers' experience, teachers and researchers agreed that a novel technique was to be conceived and decided to have recourse to games as the primary tool for gathering data directly from children. It was decided that the expected duration of the CAR project was of 18 months, coherently with TERENCE project time scheduling.

Client Commitment The client and researchers signed protocol agreements aimed at regulating activities with children, among others: (i) assuring school commitment, (ii) defining rules/roles for in-class activities, (iii) relieving schools from any cost. There was a word-of-mouth agreement related to the participation of teachers into all the stages of the CAR process.

Roles and Responsibilities It was agreed that researchers and the client had to have multiple roles/responsibilities with respect to the design of an innovative game-based data gathering technique and its implementation. As to the design, researchers had to guide the overall process while the clients had to assess design choices; as to the implementation, it was requested by the client that researchers be active parts in game-based activities conducted with children, since, according to the experts' opinion, it would stimulate attention from children. This request was appreciated by us researchers since let us be close to the action while maintaining a clear separation in roles.

Specification of CAR Objectives Objectives of the immediate problem situation and of the CAR project as well as research questions were refined throughout the process. Starting from the general question $Q0$ *"Can data gathering be conducted through games?"* they can be summarized as:

$Q1$ CONSTRAINT COMPLIANCE—Can a game-based technique be designed so to be compatible with given ethical and organizational constraints?

$Q2$ EFFICACY—Can game design be guided by the topics to be investigated and identified in previous phases of a project (preparatory studies)?

$Q3$ EFFICIENCY WRT ACTION—Are data gathering in-class activities playful (i.e., involving children and guaranteeing a correct level of attention during the sessions)?

$Q4$ EFFICIENCY WRT ANALYSIS—Are data gathered through appropriately designed games (see $Q1$ and $Q2$) characterized by quality (genuineness and dependability) and quantity adequate to be statistically significant (the main limitation of diaries)?

In order to investigate on the above research questions, the *problem objective* (PO) and the *research objective* (RO) (corresponding to elements P and A, respectively, in Table 2) for the two cycles of the CPM were defined:

PO TERENCE context of use analysis, with intermediate goals:

*PO*1 population of the TERENCE user data DB

*PO*2 TERENCE user classification

*PO*3 TERENCE persona design

RO definition of a gamed-based children-oriented data gathering technique, with intermediate goals:

*RO*1 identification of the technique stages

*RO*2 design of individual technique stages

*RO*3 definition of implementation instructions

*RO*4 final release of the method according to consolidated frameworks for data gathering techniques (e.g., entries in the method table of usabilitynet.org)

Specification of CAR Evaluation Measures As mentioned, two streams of data gathering were conducted in parallel in UK and Italy. The two design teams were characterized by comparable experience, in User Centered Design in general and in data gathering in particular, and worked under the same TERENCE time constraints. This project organization allowed us to compare the achieved results of the two teams on the basis of data dependability, richness and specificity in users' class description, ease in persona derivation, thus providing a qualitative assessment of CAR results.

Specification of Data Collection and Analysis Methods Notice that, in the context of this issue of the RCA, the term "data collection" refers to the collection of data regarding AR activities and not to the immediate problem situation (we use the term "data gathering" to refer to TERENCE activities). In our case we agreed to involve teachers and deans in intermediate and final brainstorming and semi-structured interviews; data related to such activities have been collected via notes and audiotapes.

3   The Cyclical Process

Overall, our CAR project required three iterations. Figures 2, 3, and 4 show the tandem CAR process schemas of the three iterations, focusing on activities and the relationships between the two cycles in term of time scheduling (vertical arrangements) and information exchanged (dashed arrows) among the various stages of the problem solving cycle (on the left) and the research cycle (on the right).

First Iteration (Fig. 2). It started with the two diagnosis stages that occurred slightly out of phase. Then **Action Planning$_R$** dealt with the CAR project design: we hypothesized that at least two iterations had to involve intervention in schools (for trial and assessment of the technique) and at least one iteration had to be focused on the analysis of gathered data and on personas' definition. Accordingly, schools were aggregated in two groups. Quite in parallel, within **Action Planning$_{PS}$**, the team started working on the activities able to start before the *method design* was released by **Action Taking$_R$** that dealt with the definition of a first version of the data gathering technique structure/characteristics. Then **Action Planning$_{PS}$** could

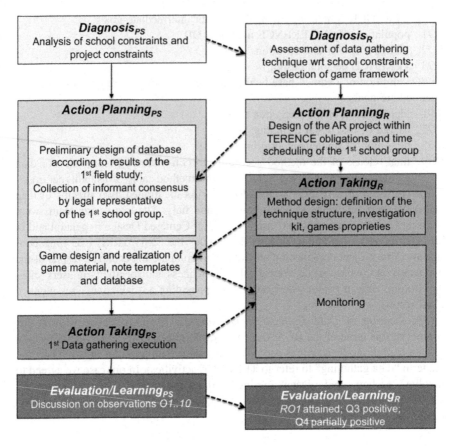

Fig. 2 The first iteration of our tandem CAR process

proceed with design/realization of the games according to the structure of the defined technique; only when all the material was ready, **Action Taking$_{PS}$** started, involving the 1st school group for the data gathering. Meanwhile, the action researchers were *monitoring* problem solving activities. Then **Evaluation/Learning$_{PS}$**, in which observations $O1$–$O10$ were reported (see Table 3), and **Evaluation/Learning$_R$** occurred slightly out of phase.

Second Iteration (Fig. 3). Again, **Diagnosis$_{PS}$** and **Diagnosis$_R$** occurred slightly out of phase. Then, in **Action planning$_R$** time scheduling of activities involving the 2nd school group was assessed and quite in parallel preliminary activities with these schools were performed in **Action planning$_{PS}$**. When the method was re-defined by **Action Taking$_R$** (in particular the method structure was adjusted according to observations $O5$, $O6$, and $O7$ of Table 3), the re-definition of game instances could be performed within **Action Planning$_{PS}$**. Again, as in the first iteration, in this moment **Action Taking$_{PS}$** could start and meanwhile, action researchers were involved also in the *monitoring* task. Finally, **Evaluation/Learning$_{PS}$**, in which

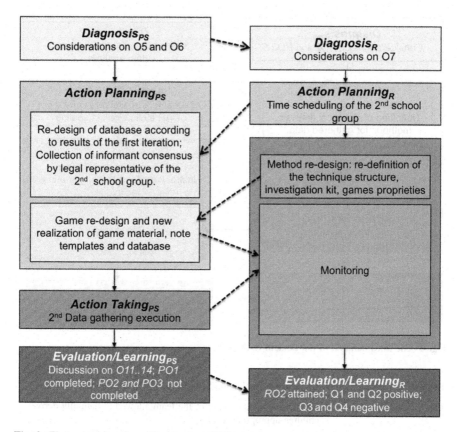

Fig. 3 The second iteration of our tandem CAR process

observations $O11$–$O14$ were reported (see Table 4), and **Evaluation/Learning$_R$** occurred slightly out of phase.

Third Iteration (Fig. 4). **Diagnosis$_{PS}$** and **Diagnosis$_R$** were conducted almost jointly. Notice that, though no real problem was detected during 2nd iteration data gathering activities, the CAR project could not be considered concluded for two inter-related reasons: (i) work for attaining objectives $PO2$ and $PO3$ was not started yet, and (ii) the evaluation of this outcome was crucial for the overall assessment of the method. The main focus of 3rd iteration hence shifted from data gathering to data analysis. **Action planning$_R$**, and **Action planning$_{PS}$** started together with no mutual dependency. On the basis of the experiences gained, in **Action Taking$_R$** the researchers defined the implementation instructions for the new data gathering technique. Meanwhile, they monitored the activities related to objectives $PO2$ e $PO3$ carried on by the two teams in Italy and UK. As in previous iterations, **Evaluation/Learning$_{PS}$** and **Evaluation/Learning$_R$** occurred slightly out of phase. On the basis of the overall experience, action researchers produced a complete formalization of the new game-based children-oriented data gathering technique

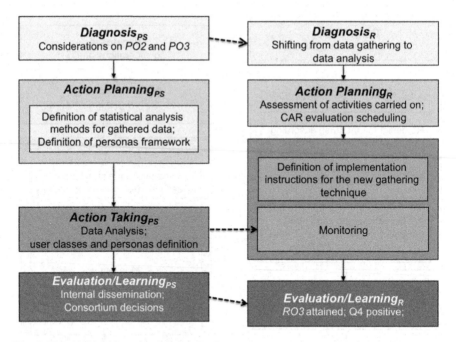

Fig. 4 The third iteration of our tandem CAR process

Table 3 Observations carried out in the Evaluation/Learning$_{PS}$ of the first iteration

Game design	O1: the multidisciplinary of the team allowed to naturally derive children-appropriate games;
Actual experience with the classes	O2: there was a smooth integration between teachers and researchers and between game-based data gathering activities and regular school activities (wrt both contents and modus operandi); O3: deans appreciated the unobtrusiveness of the approach with respect to school resource involvement, cost, and needed time; O4: teachers remarked the value of the activities for children; O5: some children preferred not to participate in the game activities; O6: some children lose interest during the game; O7: in several classes it was not possible to carry on all designed games within one hour;
Gathered data	O8: reliability was supported by evidence from teachers and parents of the involved children (gathered via contextual inquiries); O9: despite withdrawal from some children, the participation was high and consequently we experienced a high rate of returned data; O10: quantity was considered not yet sufficient for statistical significance, as expected.

Table 4 Observations carried out in the Evaluation/Learning$_{PS}$ of the second iteration

Game design	$O11$: no remarkable issue emerged during game redesign;
Actual experience with the classes	$O12$: flexible game administration plan succeeded; $O13$: children were adequately stimulated;
Gathered data	$O14$: their quantity was judged sufficient.

(given in [22]) according to existing frameworks for the description of data gathering techniques, hence completing $RO4$. Furthermore, researchers were able to provide a definitive positive answer to the general question $Q0$ and the decision to exit the CAR project was reached.

4 Reflections on the CAR Project

Post-project reflections on the experience allowed us to derive a general meta-result related to the relationships between the two cycles (and stages) of a tandem-based CAR project in which the outcome of the research cycle is the problem solving method of the immediate problem. One may notice that, while activities performed within our 3rd AR iteration are quite specific for the project at hand, the first two iterations are quite generalizable, as shown in Fig. 5, which highlights an interesting regular structure which constitute an original methodology:

- **Diagnosis$_{PS}$** is the first to start and informs activities in **Diagnosis$_{R}$**, which, among others, has to single out, survey, and assess relevant literature wrt the problem to solve. Objectives and research questions are singled out/refined in these stages.
- **Action planning$_{R}$** refers to planning/designing the research project so to adequately address research questions, validate hypothesis and guide the overall process.
- **Action planning$_{PS}$** refers to planning problem solving activities for the specific problem at hand (in our case: designing/refining games).
- **Action Taking$_{R}$** refers to design/refinement of the problem solving method and must necessarily start before the method is used within **Action planning$_{PS}$** for planning activities that will be carried on during **Action Taking$_{PS}$**: only once the method (or intermediate versions of it) is available, the team (client and researchers) can start to use it, while action researchers involved in **Action Taking$_{R}$** monitor executions of activities.
- For **Evaluation/Learning$_{PS}$** and **Evaluation/Learning$_{R}$**, we have the same kind of relationships observed for the diagnosis stages: the team (1) evaluates effects of actions on the problem and effects of intervention in terms of research questions, so to determine if the results is satisfactory and then exit, or, otherwise, to single out issues to be addressed in the next iteration, where previous results are amended, and (2) reflects on gained knowledge at the immediate

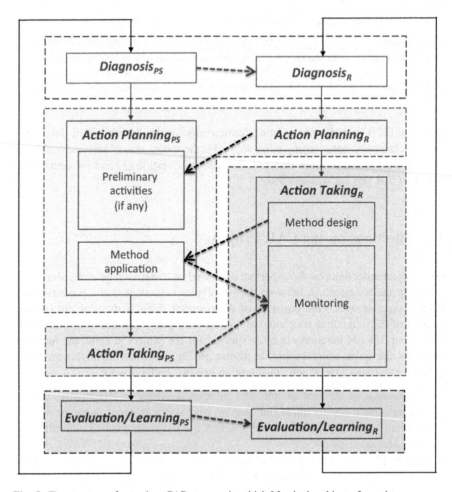

Fig. 5 The structure of a tandem CAR process in which M_{PS} is the object of enquiry

problem level and on the generalization of its solution according to the research questions.

This meta-result extends the discussion in [3] in the case in which M_{PS} is the object of the enquiry.

5   Conclusion

In this paper we discussed the use of Action Research, as part of a UCD process, for conceiving and testing a new data gathering technique. We used AR within the context-of-use analysis of the TERENCE project aimed to realize an ALS for 7–

11 years old poor text comprehenders. The necessity of the AR project derived from the limits that consolidated data gathering approaches showed with respect to the TERENCE context: traditional approaches are not adequate for children, and existing children-oriented techniques were not compliant with organizational and project constraints.

The Italy technical team and its client (the schools involved in the project) agreed to conduct an AR project with the main aim of defining a new game-based children-oriented data gathering technique (research side) and, in tandem, gathering data for the TERENCE project context-of-use analysis (problem side), and defining accordingly user classes and personas. On the other side, the UK team decided to try an observational approach, which allowed to have a benchmark outcome, produced by customary methods, against which to evaluate/assess the outcome of the AR project. The TERENCE consortium discussed the results of the two teams through restricted and plenary meetings. A first appreciation of the work of the Italian team was related to the number of children that the characteristics of the adopted approaches allow to involve: the two rounds of field studies in Italy (1st and 2nd CAR iterations) involved about 50 % more children than the single round of observational studies in UK *within the same period of time*. Furthermore the consortium agreed on the fact that (1) the users' classes produced by the AR process were richer and more specific than the ones produced by the UK observational study, and that (2) personas were more easily derivable. Consequently, the CAR results were taken as a reference for the continuation of the project. Results achieved by the CAR project were also disseminated and assessed outside the consortium via workshops dedicated to HCI researchers and other stakeholders (e.g., teachers), receiving appreciations.

In addition to results on the problem side (users classes and personas) and on the research side (the new data gathering technique [22]), post-project reflections on the experience allowed us to derive a general meta-result related to the relationships between the two cycles (and their stages) of a tandem-based CAR project in which the outcome of the research cycle is the problem solving method of the immediate problem. In particular, we singled out an original regular structure that rules activities to be done, their time scheduling (what happens before/while what) and exchange of information. This novel meta-result contributes to the epistemological discourse of AR by extending the discussion in [3] in the case in which M_{PS} is the object of the enquiry (to the best of our knowledge it is the first contribute in this direction).

References

1. Harrison, S., Sengers, P., Tatar, D.: The three paradigms of HCI. In: International Conference on Human Factors in Computing Systems (CHI2007). ACM Press, New York (2007)
2. Baskerville, R.L.: Investigating information systems with action research. J. Commun. Assoc. Inf. Syst. **3**, Article 4 (1999)

3. McKay, J., Marshall, P.: The dual imperatives of action research. J. Inf. Technol. People **14**, 46–59 (2001)
4. Dix, A.: Action research in HCI. http://alandix.com/blog/2012/12/10/action-research-in-hci/
5. Gulliksen, J., Göransson, B., Boivie, I., Blomkvist, S., Persson, J., Cajander, Å.: Key principles for user-centred system design. J. Behav. Inf. Technol. **22**, 397–409 (2003)
6. Hayes, G.R.: The relationship of action research to human-computer interaction. ACM Trans. Comput. Hum. Interact. **18**, Article 15 (2011)
7. Kock, N.: Action research: its nature and relationship to human-computer interaction. In: Soegaard, M. Dam, R.F. (eds.). The Encyclopedia of Human-Computer Interaction, 2nd edn. Aarhus, Denmark: The Interaction Design Foundation. https://www.interaction-design.org/encyclopedia/action_research.html (2014)
8. Siew S.T., Yeo A.W., Zaman T.: Participatory action research in software development: indigenous knowledge management systems case study. In: International Conference of Human-Computer Interaction (HCI2013). Springer Berlin Heidelberg (2013)
9. Lewin, K.: Frontiers in group dynamics. J. Human Relations **1**, 5–41 (1947)
10. Lewin, K.: Frontiers in group dynamics II. J. Human Relations. **1**, 143–153 (1947)
11. Trist, E., Bamforth, K.: Social and psychological problems of long-wall coal mining. Hum. Relat. **4**, 3–38 (1951)
12. Baskerville, R.L., Heje, J.P.: Grounded action research: a method for understanding IT in practice. J. Account. Manag. Inf. Technol. **9**, 1–23 (1999)
13. Baskerville, R.L., Wood-Harper, A.T.: A critical perspective on action research as a method for information systems research. J. Inf. Technol. **11**, 235–246 (1996)
14. Davison, R.M., Martinsons, M.G., Kock, N.: Principles of canonical action research. J. Inf. Syst. **14**, 65–86 (2004)
15. Susman, G.I., Evered, R.D.: An assessment of the scientific merits of action research. J. Adm. Sci. Q. **23**, 582–603 (1978)
16. Druin, A., Bederson, B., Boltman, A., Miura, A., Knotts-Callahan, D., Platt, M.: Children as our technology design partners. In: Kaufmann M. (Ed.) The design of children's technology, pp. 51–72 (1998)
17. Hourcade, J.P.: Interaction design and children. J. Found. Trends Hum. Comput Interact. **1**, 277–392 (2007)
18. Vaajakallio, K., Lee, J., Mattelmaki, T.: "It has to be a group work!": co-design with children. In: 8th Conference on Interaction Design and Children (IDC'09), pp. 246–249. ACM Press, New York (2009)
19. Jong, M.S., Lee, J., Shang, J.: Educational use of computer games: where we are, and what's next. In: Huang, R., Spector, J.M. (Eds.) Reshaping Learning. New Frontiers of Educational Research, vol. 3, pp. 299–320. Springer, Heidelberg (2013)
20. Prensky, M.: Digital game-based learning. J. Comput. Entertainment **1**, 21–31 (2003)
21. Przybylski, A.K., Rigby, C.S., Ryan, R.M.: A motivational model of video game engagement. Rev. Gen. Psychol. **14**, 154–166 (2010)
22. Di Mascio, T., Gennari, R., Melonio, A., Tarantino, L.: Engaging "New Users" into design activities: the TERENCE experience with children. In: Caporarello, L., et al. (eds.) Smart Organizations and Smart Artifacts. LNISO, vol. 7, pp. 241–250. Springer, International Publishing Switzerland (2014)
23. Di Mascio, T., Tarantino, L.: Designing for children: blending HCI and action research. In: 11th Biannual Conference of the Italian SIGCHI Chapter (2015)
24. Slegers, K., Gennari, R.: State of the art of methods for user analysis and context of use. Technical Report, TERENCE project (2011)
25. Hanna, L., Risden, K., Alexander, K.: Guidelines for usability testing with children. J. Interactions **4**, 9–14 (1997)

Context and Action: A Unitary Vision Within a Logic-Based Multi-agent Environment

Stefania Costantini, Giovanni De Gasperis, Giulio Nazzicone and Laura Tarantino

Abstract Interactive ICT products falling under the umbrella of the 3rd paradigm of the HCI are posing significant challenges to designers. Context—and the way in which it has to be conceptually and epistemologically addressed—is one of the issues central in the general debate around ubiquitous computing and phenomenologically situated interaction: context strays from being yet another non-technological aspect affecting the design to become a central component not separable from activities carried on by means of the interactive application. This paper addresses design issues related to this debate within the case-study of the exploration of a dynamically changing territory upon occurrence of some kind of catastrophic event (e.g. earthquake, fire, flooding), by proposing a logic-based multiagent-oriented framework allowing affordable and flexible planning capabilities, in which dynamic knowledge on environment and activity plans are seamlessly integrated.

Keywords Multi-agent system · Logic programming · Emergency management

S. Costantini · G. De Gasperis · G. Nazzicone · L. Tarantino (✉)
Dipartimento di Ingegneria e Scienze dell'Informazione e Matematica (DISIM),
Universitá degli Studi dell'Aquila, L'Aquila, Italy
e-mail: laura.tarantino@univaq.it

S. Costantini
e-mail: stefania.costantini@univaq.it

G. De Gasperis
e-mail: giovanni.degasperis@univaq.it

G. Nazzicone
e-mail: giulio.nazzicone@graduate.univaq.it

© Springer International Publishing Switzerland 2016
L. Caporarello et al. (eds.), *Digitally Supported Innovation*,
Lecture Notes in Information Systems and Organisation 18,
DOI 10.1007/978-3-319-40265-9_7

1 Introduction

As computation moved beyond the confines of the desk to incorporate itself into the physical and social world, the HCI interest moved away from the specific design of user interfaces to bring into focus the way in which ICT products are incorporated into our environment and our activities. In particular, the notion of context, as loosely specifiable as it can sometimes be, ceases to be yet another non technical information affecting design and becomes central in the discourse of contemporary HCI research. Starting from the visionary view of Weiser [1], the new research lines of ubiquitous computing [2], pervasive computing [3], embodied interaction [4], and context-aware computing [5, 6] all share on the one hand the idea of incorporating the technology into the physical world and, consequently, on the other hand, the primary concern of understanding the relationships between computation and the context in which it is embedded [7]. Dourish [7] in particular underlines the shift from positivist approaches viewing the context as a stable, delineable form of information, separable from the activity (which happens "within" a context), to phenomenological approaches viewing the context as (1) an occasioned relational property that holds between objects or activities, (2) relevant to particular settings and particular instances and/or parties of action, (3) with features characterized by a dynamically defined scope, and (4), above all, not separable from the activity but rather arising from the activity itself [7]. In this view the context is not something that describes a setting but rather something that people do, it is not an observation but rather an achievement; it is an outcome, rather than a premise.

A scenario characterized by such interdependency between action and context is for example the one related to the intervention in a territory upon occurrence of some kind of catastrophic event (earthquake, fire, flooding, etc.) [8]. Organized aid operators may want to explore the area with several purposes, like, e.g., rescuing victims, removing debris and wreckage, fixing holes in the street. Coverage of the territory may be an objective to pursue, unfortunately made difficult by the particular circumstances in which one has to operate in the aftermath of a disaster, among which the impossibility of traversing some locations because of some kind of obstruction and/or the lack of familiarity with or knowledge of the territory by rescuers, often coming from outside the region hit by the catastrophic event. Efficacy and efficiency of organized aids would be greatly improved by a system able to (1) monitor the environment by means of an infrastructure including drones, sensors, robots, and human operators equipped with some kind of system terminals, (2) suggest plans of intervention obeying to physical, ethical and organizational constraints (suggesting, e.g., a sequence of intervention according to priorities), and (3) guide rescuers in the exploration of the territory. Action and context are clearly intertwined and mutually dependent, with actions determined by a context in turn dynamically modified by the actions (e.g., by removal of debris), as well as by external events (like aftershocks in case of an earthquake).

In this paper we propose a solution which seamlessly integrates activity plans and dynamic knowledge on the environment within the framework of a logic-based multiagent-oriented framework. Adaptive autonomous agents are in fact capable of adapting to unknown and potentially changing environment contexts [9], and the MAS (Multi-Agent System) approach not only permits to distribute the computational effort and to increase overall robustness by means of advanced features such as self-monitoring and self-diagnostic, as shown in [10], but can also be based upon a controller agent, which, if necessary, is able to adapt problem-solving criteria to \specific features of the situation at hand and to changing circumstances. In particular, the proposed architecture integrates logical agents, i.e., agents whose syntax and semantics is rooted in Computational Logic [11], with Answer Set Programming (ASP) modules [12], where ASP (cf., among many, [13–16] and the references therein) is a successful logic programming paradigm suitable for planning and reasoning with affordable complexity and many efficient implementation freely available [17].

We implemented this approach in the DALI [18–21] agent-oriented language, and we defined the DALI-ASP [22] interface so to allow an agent to choose among the various solutions (and in particular among the various plans) generated by an ASP module by means of suitable forms of preferences, priorities, and defined strategies.

The remainder of this paper is organized as follows: in Sect. 2 we provide a background on the framework foundations, i.e., the DALI logic-based agent-oriented programming language and Answer Set Programming. Section 3 then presents the general architecture of the multi-agent framework. Finally, in Sect. 4, conclusions are drawn and future work is delineated.

2 Background

2.1 Logical Agents and DALI

Logical agents are agents whose syntax and semantics is rooted in Computational Logic. Traditional logic programming has proved over time to be a good knowledge representation language for rational agents and several approaches to logical agents have been proposed, among which MetateM, 3APL, AgentSpeak, Impact, KGP and DALI [19, 20, 23–29] (for a recent survey the reader may refer to [11]).

In particular, DALI is an Active Logic Programming language, i.e., a logic programming language augmented with reactive and proactive features, designed for executable specification of logical agents; it allows the programmer to define one or more agents, interacting among themselves, with an external environment, or with a user. The integration with ASP modules enhances the planning capability of the framework [22]. While for a comprehensive description of the language we refer, e.g., to [19, 20] (cf. [21] provides a comprehensive list of references), in the following we give a flavor of its features and behavior.

The basic objective of the specification of the language has been the identification and the formalization of the basic patterns for reactivity, proactivity, internal "thinking", and "memory". An important aim has been that of introducing all the essential features in a declarative fashion, keeping the language as close as possible to the syntax and the semantics of the plain Horn-clause language (actually, a Prolog program is a special case of a DALI program). Anyhow, a novel approach to the semantics has been conceived, namely the *evolutionary semantics* [30]: the agent reception of an event is formalized as a program transformation step, and the evolutionary semantics consists of a sequence of logic programs, resulting from this subsequent transformation, together with the sequence of the Least Herbrand Model of these programs. This makes it possible to reason about the "state" of an agent, without introducing explicitly such a notion, and to reason about the conclusions reached and the actions performed at a certain stage.

A DALI agent is a logic program that contains a particular kind of rules, reactive rules, aimed at interacting with an external environment. The environment is perceived in the form of external events, that can be exogenous events, observations, or messages by other agents. In response, a DALI agent can perform actions, send messages, invoke goals. The reactive and proactive behavior of the DALI agent is triggered by several kinds of events: external events, internal, present and past events. It is important to notice that all the events and actions are timestamped, so as to record when they occurred. The new syntactic entities, i.e., predicates related to events and proactivity, are indicated with special postfixes (which are coped with by a pre-processor) so as to be immediately recognized while looking at a program.

External Events The external events are syntactically indicated by the postfix *E*. When an event comes into the agent from its "external world", the agent can perceive it and decide to react. The reaction is defined by a reactive rule which has in its head that external event. The special token : > , used instead of : −, indicates that reactive rules perform forward reasoning. E.g., the body of the reactive rule below specifies the reaction to the external event *bell_ringsE* that is in the head. In this case the agent performs an action, postfix *A*, that consists in opening the door.

$$bell\_ringsE : > open\_the\_doorA.$$

The agent remembers to have reacted by converting the external event into a *past event* (time-stamped).

Operationally, if an incoming external event is recognized, i.e., corresponds to the head of a reactive rule, it is added into a list called EV and consumed according to the arrival order, unless priorities are specified. Priorities are listed in a separate file of directives, where (as we will see) the user can "tune" the agent's behavior under several respect. The advantage introducing a separate initialization file is that for modifying the directives there is no need to modify (or even to understand) the code.

Internal Events The internal events define a kind of "individuality" of a DALI agent, making her proactive independently of the environment, of the user and of the other agents, and allowing her to manipulate and revise her knowledge. An internal event is syntactically indicated by the postfix *I*, and its description is composed of two rules. The first one contains the conditions (knowledge, past events, procedures, etc.) that must be true so that the reaction (in the second rule) may happen.

Internal events are automatically attempted with a default frequency customizable by means of directives in the initialization file. The user's directives can tune several parameters: at which frequency the agent must attempt the internal events; how many times an agent must react to the internal event (forever, once, twice,...) and when (forever, when triggering conditions occur,...); how long the event must be attempted (until some time, until some terminating conditions, forever).

For instance, consider a situation where an agent prepares a soup that must cook on the fire for K minutes. The predicates with postfix *P* are past events, i.e., events or actions that happened before, and have been recorded. Then, the first rule says that the soup is ready if the agent previously turned on the fire, and K minutes have elapsed since when she put the pan on the stove. The goal *soup_ready* will be attempted from time to time, and will finally succeed when the cooking time will have elapsed. At that point, the agent has to react to this (by second rule) thus removing the pan and switching off the fire, which are two actions (postfix *A*).

$$soup\_ready : - turn\_on\_the\_fireP, put\_pan\_on\_the\_stoveP : T,$$
$$cooking\_time(K), time\_elapsed(T, K).$$
$$soup\_readyI : > take\_off\_pan\_from\_stoveA, turn\_off\_the\_fireA.$$

A suitable directive for this internal event can for instance state that it should be attempted every 60 s, starting from when *put_the_pan_on_the_stove* and *turn_on_the_fire* have become past events.

Similarly to external events, internal events which are true by first rule are inserted in a set IV in order to be reacted to (by their second rule). The interpreter, interleaving the different activities, extracts from this set the internal events and triggers the reaction (again according to priorities). A particular kind of internal event is the *goal*, postfix *G*, that stop being attempted as soon as it succeeds for the first time.

Present Events When an agent perceives an event from the "external world", it doesn't necessarily react to it immediately: she has the possibility of reasoning about the event, before (or instead of) triggering a reaction. Reasoning also allows a proactive behavior. In this situation, the event is called present event and is indicated by the suffix *N*.

Actions Actions are the agent's way of affecting her environment, possibly in reaction to an external or internal event. In DALI, actions (indicated with postfix *A*) may have or not preconditions: in the former case, the actions are defined by actions rules, in the latter case they are just action atoms. An action rule is just a plain rule, but in order to emphasize that it is related to an action, we have introduced the new token : <, thus adopting the syntax *action* : <*preconditions*. Similarly to external and internal events, actions are recorded as past actions.

Past events Past events represent the agent's "memory", that makes her capable to perform its future activities while having experience of previous events, and of its own previous conclusions. As we have seen in the examples, past event are indicated by the postfix *P*. For instance, *alarm_clock_ ringsP* is an event to which the agent has reacted and which remains in the agent's memory. Each past event has a timestamp T indicating when the recorded event has happened. Memory of course is not unlimited, neither conceptually nor practically: it is possible to set, for each event, for how long it has to be kept in memory, or until which expiring condition. In the implementation, past events are kept for a certain default amount of time, that can be modified by the user through a suitable directive in the initialization file. Implicitly, if a second version of the same past event arrives, with a more recent time-stamp, the older event is overridden, unless a directive indicates to keep a number of versions.

DALI Communication Architecture The DALI communication architecture consists of four levels. The first level implements the DALI/FIPA communication protocol and a filter on communication, i.e. a set of rules that decide whether or not to receive or send a message. The second level includes a meta-reasoning layer, that tries to understand message contents, possibly based on ontologies and/or on forms of commonsense reasoning. The third level consists of the DALI interpreter. The fourth level implements a filter for the outgoing messages. The DALI/FIPA protocol consists of the main FIPA primitives, plus few new primitives which are particular to DALI. When a message is received, it is examined by a check layer composed of a structure which is adaptable to the context and modifiable by the user. This filter checks the content of the message, and verifies if the conditions for the reception are verified. If the conditions are false, this security level eliminates the supposedly wrong message. Each DALI agent is also provided with a distinguished procedure called *meta*, which is automatically invoked by the interpreter in the attempt to understand message contents. The DALI programming environment at current stage of development [18] offers a multi-platform folder environment, built upon Sicstus Prolog programs, shells scripts, Python scripts to integrate external applications, a JSON/HTML5/jQuery web interface to integrate into DALI applications, with a Python/Twisted/Flask web server capable to interact with A DALI MAS at the backend.

2.2 Answer Set Programming in a Nutshell

"Answer set programming" (ASP) is a well-established logic programming paradigm adopting logic programs with default negation under the *answer set semantics*, which [13, 31] is a view of logic programs as sets of inference rules (more precisely, default inference rules). In fact, one can see an answer set program as a set of *constraints* on the solution of a problem, where each answer set represents a solution compatible with the constraints expressed by the program (for the applications of ASP, the reader can refer for instance to [14, 15, 32]. Several well-developed answer set solvers [17, 33] are able to compute the answer sets of a given program, and can be freely downloaded by potential users.

Syntactically, a program Π is a collection of *rules* of the form

$$H \leftarrow L_1, \ldots, L_m, \, not \, L_{m+1}, \ldots, not \, L_{m+n}$$

where H is an atom, $m \geq 0$ and $n \geq 0$, and each L_i is an atom. Symbol $\leftarrow$ is usually indicated with : − in practical systems. An atom L_i and its negative counterpart $not \, L_i$ are called *literals*. The left-hand side and the right-hand side of the clause are called *head* and *body*, respectively. A rule with empty body is called a *fact*. A rule with empty head is a *constraint*, where a constraint of the form

$$\leftarrow L_1, \ldots, L_n.$$

states that literals $L_1, \ldots, L_n$ cannot be simultaneously true in any answer set.

Unlike other paradigms, a program may have several answer sets, each of which represent a solution to given problem which is consistent w.r.t. the given problem description and constraints, or may have no answer set, which means that no such solution can be found. Whenever a program has no answer sets, it is said to be say that the program is *inconsistent* (w.r.t. *consistent*).

In practical terms a problem encoding, in the form of ASP program, is processed by an ASP solver which computes the answer set(s) of the program, from which the solutions can be easily extracted (by abstracting away from irrelevant details). All solvers provide a number of additional features useful for practical programming, that we will introduce only whenever needed. Solvers are periodically checked and compared over well-established benchmarks, and over challenging sample applications proposed at the yearly ASP competition (cf. [34] for a recent report). The expressive power of ASP and its computational complexity have been deeply investigated [35].

3 The DALI Explorer

In this section we illustrate the DALI MAS solution exploiting ASP modules to fulfill the demands of the application scenario. In particular, the system is in charge of generating plans for inspecting a territory under critical circumstances while accommodating in real time to dynamic updates regarding the territory and exploration strategies and priorities. The exploration can be carried on by humans (e.g., rescuers), by some kind of mobile robot, or by combinations of both, depending on specific conditions.

3.1 The General Exploration Principles

The DALI MAS is intended to fulfill the *bounded rationality principle* [36], by which an exploration plan for the unknown territory/area has to be devised and executed in a timely manner before an ultimate T_{max} deadline. Consequently, there is a second deadline $T_{PlanMax} < T_{Max}$ by which the exploration plan has to be devised, set so that the remaining time should be sufficient for plan execution, i.e., for actual area exploration. Also, for logistic reasons, a requirement and input of the exploration is the *coverage* $C_\%$ parameter, defined by the user, which establishes the percentage of cells of the area which shall be covered by the exploration path.

Exploration paths may have to avoid certain forbidden positions (possibly inaccessible), or mandatorily traverse some others positions (e.g., to check all schools in the region and rescue kids). Forbidden and mandatory positions are possibly dynamically updated over time—by drones, sensors, or operators—as soon as new knowledge is acquired on the territory or events change it. In some case, the system might also determine the number and the nature of "explorers" needed in order to complete the rescuing intervention. For simplicity, we represent the territory (also called "area") as a $N * N$ grid, where some cells are marked as unreachable/forbidden—and therefore considered as "holes" in the grid—and some other cells are marked as mandatory.

Thus, given the input set $T_{PlanMax}, T_{Max}, C_\%, N, F, M$, where $T_{PlanMax}$ and T_{Max} are defined according to the bounded rationality principle, $C_\%$ is the required coverage, N is the size of the grid, F is the set of forbidden cells, and M is the set of mandatory cells, the MAS operates via the following steps.

1. Generate an exploration path within the $T_{PlanMax}$ deadline; in case of failure, return a trivial path of maximum possible length (always possible).
2. Monitor the exploration of the territory at $C_\%$ coverage within the T_{Max} deadline in case of failure (insufficient time), maximize the length of the partially executed plan.

In principle, the exploration can be stopped and a new plan can be devised whenever the list of forbidden/mandatory positions is updated.

3.2 The MAS Architecture

The MAS architecture which implements the desired behavior is illustrated in Fig. 1, where ovals represent DALI agents, the rectangle represents the ASP module, and arrows represent the event-based communication among agents. Most part of the MAS can be deployed over a cloud computing, distributing and balancing the required computational resources. The ASP module is an external solver, configurable depending on the required capabilities. The EXPLORER agent is supposed to work in the field, embedded in a mobile robot or some other facility.

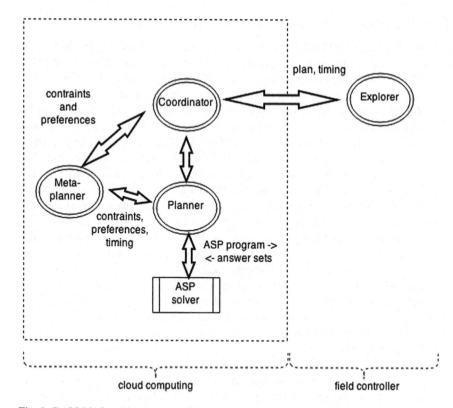

Fig. 1 DALI MAS architecture: coordinator, meta-planner, planner, explorer agents

Generally speaking, the ASP solver is responsible for generating possible solutions and sending them to the PLANNER agent, which has to select a solution depending upon appropriate criteria proposed by the META-PLANNER. Notice that the ASP solver may possibly find more than one answer set (i.e., more than one plan), and it is therefore necessary to define a metric by which a plan could be preferred to another one.

Reasonable metrics could measure a plan in terms of one or more of the following criteria:

- length of the path;
- number of cells that have to be visited when using coverage;
- number of mandatory cells that have to be visited when using coverage;
- predefined priorities about the order in which cells are visited;
- presence of loops;
- plan cost, in case there is a specific cost associated to each cell.

Preference criteria can be be defined by selecting one metric, or by combining different metrics: for instance, a criterium may consist in preferring the shortest path, if it does not exceed a certain cost.

More specifically, the agents behaviors are the following:

- the **COORDINATOR** agent synchronizes all the actions of the MAS and updates the global state of exploration and the number/location of forbidden cells. Its tasks are the following: (a) Ensure the proper activation of the MAS; (b) Communicate with the external world and whenever needed set new objectives for the MAS (its objectives can include: set a new territory to be explored, with its size; set a new preference criterium). Initialize the $T_{PlanMax}$ and T_{Max} deadlines. (c) Activate the **META-PLANNER** agent providing as input the preference criterium for plan selection. (d) Wait to receive from the **META-PLANNER** agent the exploration plan to be executed up to $T_{PlanMax}$; (e) deliver the found plan to the **EXPLORER** agent, which is in charge of executing within maximum time $T_{Max} - T_{PlanMax}$. If time elapses, it cancels the current running exploration. It also logs all events to a log server.
- the **META-PLANNER** agent carries on the following tasks: (a) Receive the triggering event from the **COORDINATOR** to start to search for a new plan. (b) Generate input for the **PLANNER** agent while monitoring its performances. If the **PLANNER** agent does not deliver before $T_{PlanMax}$, cancel the plan request and ask **PLANNER** to generate a trivial plan. It also exploits the given preference criterium in order to select the plan which is closer to present preferences whenever the **PLANNER** returns more than one answer.
- the **PLANNER** agent receives as input the time constraints $T_{PlanMax}$, $T_{Max}, C_\%, N, F, M$ from **META-PLANNER** to generate the best exploration plan using the ASP solver module, if possible within the $T_{PlanMax}$ deadline. If more than a single answer is produced by the ASP solver, it returns all available plans to the **META-PLANNER**. If no solution exists, it generates a trivial maximized path.
- the **EXPLORER** agent is supposed to work in the field, embedded in a mobile robot or some operator-oriented mobile facility; it puts into action the plan provided by the **COORDINATOR**, if possible within the T_{Max} deadline, and notifies the **COORDINATOR** upon completion

3.3 ASP Problem Definition

Though, in general, different strategies can be followed to determine the exploration of the territory (generally depending also on political, logistics, organizational, and ethical constraints), to implement a first prototype and test the effectiveness of the architectural solution, we modeled the problem as a variant of the well-known "knight tour with holes" problem, for which solutions exist, also in ASP.

The Knight Tour problem is known to be practically solvable for small chessboard sizes [37], where the resulting plan is a Hamiltonian path, i.e. a path where each cell is visited exactly once. However, as it is well-known, the problem, as well as its derivatives (including the one with holes that we consider here [38]), is

NP-complete and becomes therefore soon practically intractable with the increasing instance size. Moreover, a Hamiltonian path, restricted to the non forbidden area, in general does not exist, if the area does not present specific geometrical symmetries. Therefore in practice when exploring an area, especially in critical circumstances such as the aftermath of a catastrophic event, one may compromise upon completeness.

Under the bounded rationality principle, the system tries to calculate the Hamiltonian path if exists, possibly under a maximum defined time, otherwise it relies to sub-optimal solutions, calculated with weak constraints or as a trivial greedy deterministic algorithm. Therefore, since we have introduced *coverage* as a problem parameter, in order to make the exploration effective we accept sub-optimal paths that maximize the number of explored cells w.r.t. the coverage parameter. Such solutions can be obtained by introducing weak constraints in the general ASP solution.

The Knight Tour with holes problem has constituted a benchmark in recent ASP competitions, aimed at comparing ASP solvers performances. We performed a number of modifications to the original version [39] concerning: (i) the representation of holes; (ii) the objective of devising a path which, though not Hamiltonian, guarantees the required degree of coverage with the minimum number of multiple-traversals; (iii) simple forms of loop-checking for avoiding at least trivial loops. Our solution is formulated for the DLV ASP solver [40], though it might be easily reformulated for other solvers. We choose DLV because it provides the interesting feature of the so-called *soft constraints*, that are constraints that should possibly, but not mandatorily, satisfied, which come in handy in complex cases like ours. They are denoted by $:\sim$, where, e.g., $:\sim b$ means "satisfy b if possible". The key modifications are the following:

- added the **forbidden(X1, Y1)** facts, meaning that **cell(X1, Y1)** should not be included in the exploration path
- added the **mustReach(X2, Y2)** facts, meaning that **cell(X2, Y2)** must be included in the exploration path

$$: -mustReach(X, Y), notreached(X, Y).$$

- added the new constraint that a **forbidden** cell shall not be **reached**

$$: -forbidden(X, Y), reached(X, Y).$$

- We modified the **reached** constraint, and transformed it into a soft constraint, so as not to be forced to finding a Hamiltonian path.

$$reached(X, Y) : -move(1, 1, X, Y).$$
$$reached(X2, Y2) : -reached(X1, Y1), move(X1, Y1, X2, Y2).$$
$$: \sim cell(X, Y), not(forbidden(X, Y)), not(reached(X, Y)).$$

- We added a new coverage-satisfaction rule, where *coverage* denotes the required degree of coverage of the target area of cells and V is the instance size, i.e., the chessboard edge. The maximum possible coverage is 100 % of the available cells, i.e., $M = V * V$, while the minimum coverage N is computed in terms of *coverage*, considering the holes. Suitable application of the *count* DLV constraint [40] guarantees the desired coverage.

```
coverage(95).
cov(N) :- N <= #count{X,Y : reached(X,Y)} <= M,
   size(V), coverage(Z),
   M = V * V, N2 = M * Z, N = N2 / 100.
```

4 Conclusions and Future Work

Over the years, many ICT-enhanced support tools, categorized as Disaster Management Systems (DMSs), have been developed (e.g., [41–44], aimed at supporting institutions, formal organizations, organized aids, rescuers and citizens in one or more phases of the cyclic emergency management process (prevention, preparedness, response and recovery [45]).

The study reported in this paper refers in particular to the support that a logic-based multi-agent system may provide to the phases of preparedness and response, specifically to organized aids responsible for the exploration of a (possibly unknown) territory in the aftermath of a catastrophic event. The proposed solution seamlessly integrates, in a declarative fashion, activity plans and dynamic knowledge on the environment, mutually dependent: action is determined by the context which is in turn determined by action. Knowledge about the environment is provided by an infrastructure including drones, sensors, robots, and human operators (rescuer and victims); the exploration may be performed by one or more human operators or robots. The system is designed so to be able of generating in real time exploration plans that take into account constraints (e.g., forbidden/mandatory cells) and priorities, while dynamically accommodating changed demands.

The effectiveness of the approach has been tested by a first prototype in which the exploration problem is modeled as a variant of the "knight tour with holes" problem, for which well-known solutions exist, in particular in ASP. However, the knight that can move according to certain rules is to be intended as a metaphor of a rescue vehicle whose movements are constrained by certain external conditions.

Future work will be focused on a generalization of the exploration strategies, aiming at a system able to generate the best combination of explorers (robots, humans, etc.) and exploration plans (response phase) to fulfill the criteria defined by the META-PLANNER (preparedness and response phase) by dynamically tailoring its planning strategies to the changed conditions.

References

1. Weiser, M.: The computer for the 21st century. Sci. Am. **265**(3), 94–104 (1991)
2. Weiser, M.: Some computer science issues in ubiquitous computing. Commun. ACM **36**(7), 75–84 (1993)
3. Ark, W.S., Selker, T.: A look at human interaction with pervasive computers. IBM Syst. J. **38**(4), 504–507 (1999)
4. Dourish, P.: Where the Action Is: The Foundations of Embodied Interaction. MIT Press (2004)
5. Cheverst, K., Davies, N., Mitchell, K., Friday, A., Efstratiou, C.: Developing a context-aware electronic tourist guide: some issues and experiences. In: Proceedings of the SIGCHI Conference on Human Factors in Computing Systems, ACM, pp. 17—24 (2000)
6. Dey, A., Abowd, G., Salber, D.: A conceptual framework and a toolkit for supporting the rapid prototyping of context-aware applications. Human-Comput. Inter. **16**(2), 97–166 (2001)
7. Dourish, P.: What we talk about when we talk about context. Pers. Ubiquit. Comput. **8**(1), 19–30 (2004)
8. Costantini, S., De Gasperis, G., Tarantino, L.: Disaster Response: A Multi-Agent Based Approach. ACM, CHItaly (2015)
9. Costantini, S., De Gasperis, G., Nazzicone, G.: Exploration of unknown territory via dali agents and asp modules. In: Distributed Computing and Artificial Intelligence, 12th International Conference, pp. 285—292. Springer (2015)
10. Bevar, V., Muccini, H., Costantini, S., Gasperis, G.D., Tocchio, A.: A multi-agent system for industrial fault detection and repair. In: Advances on Practical Applications of Agents and Multi-Agent Systems. Advances in Intelligent and Soft Computing, pp. 47–55. Springer, Berlin (2012). Paper and demo
11. Fisher, M., Bordini, R.H., Hirsch, B., Torroni, P.: Computational logics and agents: a road map of current technologies and future trends. Comput. Intell. J. **23**(1), 61–91 (2007)
12. Costantini, S.: Answer set modules for logical agents. In: de Moor, O., Gottlob, G., Furche, T., Sellers, A., (eds.) Datalog Reloaded: First International Workshop, Datalog 2010, vol. 6702 of LNCS. Springer (2011) Revised Selected Papers
13. Gelfond, M., Lifschitz, V.: The stable model semantics for logic programming. In: Kowalski, R., Bowen, K. (eds.) Proceedings of the 5th International Conference and Symposium on Logic Programming (ICLP/SLP'88), pp. 1070—1080. The MIT Press (1988)
14. Baral, C.: Knowledge Representation, Reasoning and Declarative Problem Solving. Cambridge University Press (2003)
15. Truszczyński, M.: Logic programming for knowledge representation. In: Dahl, V., Niemelä, I. (eds.) Logic Programming, 23rd International Conference, ICLP 2007, pp. 76—88 (2007)
16. Gelfond, M.: Answer sets. In: Handbook of Knowledge Representation. Elsevier (2007)
17. Web-references: Some ASP solvers Clasp: potassco.sourceforge.net; Cmodels: www.cs.utexas.edu/users/tag/cmodels; DLV: www.dbai.tuwien.ac.at/proj/dlv; Smodels: www.tcs.hut.fi/Software/smodels
18. De Gasperis, G., Costantini, S., Nazzicone, G.: Dali multi agent systems framework. doi:10.5281/zenodo.11042. DALI GitHub Software Repository (July 2014) DALI: http://github.com/AAAI-DISIM-UnivAQ/DALI
19. Costantini, S., Tocchio, A.: A logic programming language for multi-agent systems. In: Proceedings of the 8th European Conference on Logics in Artificial Intelligence, JELIA 2002. LNAI 2424, Springer-Verlag, Berlin (2002)
20. Costantini, S., Tocchio, A.: The DALI logic programming agent-oriented language. In: Logics in Artificial Intelligence, Proceedings of the 9th European Conference, Jelia 2004. LNAI 3229, Springer-Verlag, Berlin (2004)
21. Costantini, S.: The DALI agent-oriented logic programming language: Summary and references 2015 (2015)

22. Costantini, S., De Gasperis, G., Nazzicone, G.: Exploration of unknown territory via dali agents and asp modules. In: Distributed Computing and Artificial Intelligence, 12th International Conference, pp. 285–292. Springer (2015)

23. Rao, A.S., Georgeff, M.: Modeling rational agents within a BDI-architecture. In: Proceedings of the Second International Conference on Principles of Knowledge Representation and Reasoning (KR'91), pp. 473—484. Morgan Kaufmann (1991)

24. Rao, A.S.: Agentspeak(l): BDI agents speak out in a logical computable language. In: Agents Breaking Away: Proceedings of the Seventh European Workshop on Modelling Autonomous Agents in a Multi-Agent World. Number 1038 in Lecture Notes in Artificial Intelligence, Springer-Verlag (1996)

25. Hindriks, K.V., de Boer, F., van der Hoek, W., Meyer, J.C.: Agent programming in 3APL. Auton. Agents Multi-Agent Syst. **2**(4) (1999)

26. Fisher, M.: Metatem: The story so far. In Bordini, R.H., Dastani, M., Dix, J., Fallah-Seghrouchni, A.E. (eds.) PROMAS. Volume 3862 of Lecture Notes in Computer Science, pp. 3–22. Springer (2005)

27. Subrahmanian, V.S., Bonatti, P., Dix, J., Eiter, T., Kraus, S., Ozcan, F., Ross, R.: Heterogeneous Agent Systems. MIT Press/AAAI Press, Cambridge, MA, USA (2000)

28. Kakas, A.C., Mancarella, P., Sadri, F., Stathis, K., Toni, F.: The KGP model of agency. In: Proceedings ECAI-2004 (2004)

29. Bracciali, A., Demetriou, N., Endriss, U., Kakas, A., Lu, W., Mancarella, P., Sadri, F., Stathis, K., Terreni, G., Toni, F.: The KGP model of agency: computational model and prototype implementation. In: Global Computing: IST/FET International Workshop, Revised Selected Papers. LNAI 3267, pp. 340–367. Springer-Verlag, Berlin (2005)

30. Costantini, S., Tocchio, A.: About declarative semantics of logic-based agent languages. In: Baldoni, M., Torroni, P. (eds.) Declarative Agent Languages and Technologies. LNAI 3229. Springer-Verlag, Berlin (2006)

31. Gelfond, M., Lifschitz, V.: Classical negation in logic programs and disjunctive databases. New Gen. Comput. **9**, 365–385 (1991)

32. Leone, N.: Logic programming and nonmonotonic reasoning: From theory to systems and applications. In Baral, C., Brewka, G., Schlipf, J., (eds.) Logic Programming and Nonmonotonic Reasoning, 9th International Conference, LPNMR 2007 (2007)

33. Calimeri, F., Ianni, G., Ricca, F.: The third open answer set programming competition. TPLP **14**(1), 117–135 (2014)

34. Calimeri, F., Ianni, G., Krennwallner, T., Ricca, F.: The answer set programming competition. AI Mag. **33**(4), 114–118 (2012)

35. Dantsin, E., Eiter, T., Gottlob, G., Voronkov, A.: Complexity and expressive power of logic programming. ACM Comput. Surv. **33**(3), 374–425 (2001)

36. Gigerenzer, G., Selten, R.: Bounded Rationality, The Adaptive Toolbox. The MIT Press (2002)

37. Schwenk, A.J.: Which rectangular chessboards have a knight's tour. Math. Mag. 325–332 (1991)

38. Delei, J.B.S., Wenming, D.: An ant colony optimization algorithm for knight's tour problem on the chessboard with holes. In: IEEE, (ed.) First International Workshop on ETCS'09, vol. 1, pp. 292–296 (2009)

39. Calimeri, F., Zhou, N.F.: Knight tour with holes ASP encoding (2014). See http://www.mat. unical.it/aspcomp2013/files/links/benchmarks/encodings/aspcore-2/22-Knight-Tour-with-holes/encoding.asp

40. Leone, N., Pfeifer, G., Faber, W., Eiter, T., Gottlob, G., Perri, S., Scarcello, F.: The DLV system for knowledge representation and reasoning. ACM Trans. Comput. Logic **7**(3), 499–562 (2006)

41. Barbini, F., D'Atri, A., Tarantino, L., Za, S.: A new generation DMS for supporting social sensemaking. In De Marco, M., Te'eni, D., Albano, V., Za, S. (eds.) Information Systems: Crossroads for Organization, Management, Accounting and Engineering, pp. 105–112. Physica-Verlag HD (2012)

42. Careem, M.: Sahana: Overview of a disaster management system. In: International conference on information and automation (ICIA), Colombo, Sri Lanka, 2006, pp. 361–366 (2007)
43. Turoff, M.: The design of emergency response management information systems. J. Inf. Technol. Theory Appl. **5** 1–35 (2004)
44. Many authors., U.: Ushaidi disaster management system software. http://www.ushahidi.com
45. Alexander, D.: Principles of Emergency Planning and Management. Oxford University Press, New York (2002)

From *Care for Design* to *Becoming Matters*: New Perspectives for the Development of Socio-technical Systems

Federico Cabitza and Angela Locoro

Abstract In this paper, we start by deconstructing the widely-mentioned concept of care in the IS literature, to unveil its inherent shortcomings and ambiguities, and find opportunities to go beyond it while preserving its value for the development of better socio-technical systems. We find an important strand in the feminist studies tradition, and in particular in the contributions related to the so called "new materialism". Notwithstanding their differences, these contrarian and often neglected voices point to the importance of relational thinking and material engagement with our technological objects. For this reason, in continuing the path indicated by Ciborra with his idea of care, we advocate a new shift from this step to the next one, where *becoming matters* more than being, and the caring about matter is more important than design abstractions.

Keywords Care in design · Socio-technical systems · Feminine · New materialism

1 Introduction

The socio-technical discourse has always pervaded the IT literature more or less explicitly, even when scholars preferred to use other terms to indicate the proteiform relation between the social and the technical components of any organizational agency. In many works written in the last 30 years, this relationship has been seen in terms of "strategic alignment". This can be interpreted as the process of adjusting the information technology so that it is not contrasting, nor diverging from, but rather supporting the actors involved at business level, as well as a process of continuous aligning with their values, goals and needs. In short, strategic

F. Cabitza (✉) · A. Locoro
Dipartimento di Informatica, Sistemistica e Comunicazione,
Università degli Studi di Milano Bicocca, Viale Sarca, 336, 20126 Milan, Italy
e-mail: cabitza@disco.unimib.it

A. Locoro
e-mail: angela.locoro@disco.unimib.it

© Springer International Publishing Switzerland 2016
L. Caporarello et al. (eds.), *Digitally Supported Innovation*,
Lecture Notes in Information Systems and Organisation 18,
DOI 10.1007/978-3-319-40265-9_8

alignment seen as designing and deploying a socio-technical system so that its social and technical elements are mutually coordinated and synergic on a strategic and high level, if not locally and in the short term.

We recall this concept not for genealogical purposes, but rather to reconnect our work to the critique moved by Ciborra against the traditional way alignment was (and many would argue, still is) achieved in organizations, that is with a "rational top-down approach [employing] abstract models that are not rooted in the empirically observable everyday practice" [47]. To contrast this perspective, Ciborra proposed the antagonist concept of care and "taking care". In so doing, he advocated that organizations could shift from viewing alignment "as a product of a rational planning process" (which is good "on paper", he used to add) to conceiving it as the continuous development of an in-action (we'd say situated) relation, the "good match between the human organization, the artifact and the context", which requires "a great amount of care taking performed by the various actors involved in the design, implementation and use of IT applications" [10].

So far so good. However, in this paper we move from the realization of the practical failure of the concept of "*care taking*" in making the above-mentioned shift concrete, to focus on its fragilities. Its shortcomings relate to its intrinsic ambiguity and ambivalence: indeed care is also an excessive concern that can result in over-rationalization and control. We will then proceed by focusing on the potential this concept still retains to overcome these limitations: care is a relational concept. Thinking relationally allows to shift focus from objects having "inherent boundaries and properties" to phenomena, which are "ontologically primitive relations—relations without preexisting relata" [1] (p. 814). As such, the related poles are void of real consistency outside of the relation itself. This realization is full of consequences that we will articulate in the following two sections, to then wrap up our proposal in the concluding section.

2 Why We Should Care About Care

The concept of care in the Information Systems discourse has had an odd destiny, between diffusion and neglect. In the last 20 years this term has been mentioned frequently (more or less in 2500 works), but always quite briefly if not scantily (even by Ciborra himself, e.g. in [11], with the exception of [47] from whose analysis we start ours). It is as if the idea of care were as much evocative as obvious, and the readership took it almost for granted, and the metaphor were too powerful for authors to make all the way towards its full implications.

IS researchers like and have pride in the idea of "care", and of "taking care" of a digitization project. This probably happens for the proximity of the term to positive feelings and the so called "human touch". Especially the human touch many feel is missing from the IT discourse, and then sometimes they indulge in it (not without a sort of more or less conscious duplicity). However, the familiarity we feel with this concept must have been an obstacle for concrete applications of the idea to information system design and for deeper investigations in IS research. Not without some responsibilities of Ciborra himself, care has soon lost denotational power to mean a general attitude that can be either exercised or delivered (sic), and that regards both the conception of artifacts (*perception* in Ciborra's jargon), and "practical problem solving and incremental learning" (*circumspection*), as well as even "coping with the main task at hand and the labour of 'being-in-the-world'" (*understanding*) [10]. However, to cut a long academic story short, taking care of socio-technical alignment means to cultivate "familiarity, intimacy and continuous commitment from the initial needs analysis throughout constructing the system, training the users, introducing the system into practice, modifying it as new practices emerge, and so on" [10] (p. 73). However, this is just one side of the coin.

Little wonder that the positive idea of "care" was so convincingly purported by an Italian scholar (Ciborra): in Italian "cura" lost its negative connotation (anxiety, worry and grief) already in the 19th century, and now its common use regards almost exclusively a "thoughtful and attentive (cf. careful) interest for an object (of care)"[1]; notably this interest entails "both our spirit, a practical attitude and active behavior".[2]

English speaking readership could have been less familiar with this positive attitude, as a rapid glance at the most common dictionaries can confirm: care stands primarily for worry, anxiety, sorrow and concern, and only then also solicitude, heed, caution, protection, charge. Moreover, an oft-cited etymology dictionary claims that the word care is in "no way related to Latin 'cura'", but rather it derives from Old English caru, "sorrow, anxiety, grief," also "burdens of mind; serious mental attention," (from the Proto-Germanic *karo "lament; grief, care", from which to cry[3]). The ambivalence of care is found also outside the impersonally defining attitude of dictionary pages: customer care, for instance, is both taking care of the customer and tending to the customer's needs; as well as *caring about* what the customers think of you, about their purchasing behavior, which for many people is but having customers as a continuous source of concern, and often trouble.

However, limiting ourselves to the linguistic aspects of the word would not do justice to Ciborra, who was also deeply concerned with the philosophical roots of our understanding of the "incorporation [of technology] into the daily work life". It is well known that in regard to the concept of care Ciborra took direct inspiration from Heidegger's "Being and Time", where the German philosopher speaks of *sorge*; by this term Heidegger translated (not by common consent, as we saw above) the Latin word Cura.[4] This apparent twine is not cleared up even tracing

---

[1]If Ciborra had spoken of "caring" (usually a loving feeling) rather than of "care", or of "taking care", the positive perspective would have likely been clearer but the overall meaning also less rich, in a way.

[2]"Interessamento solerte e premuroso per un oggetto, che impegna sia il nostro animo sia la nostra attività" Vocabolario On line Treccani—http://www.treccani.it/vocabolario/cura/.

[3]Harper [28].

[4]In so doing, he explicitly drew the term from the semantic well of the Proto-Germanic *surgo "to watch over, worry; be ill, suffer".

back our investigation to the ancient Roman authors: in Latin Cura stands for both physical and mental trouble, anxiety, disquiet, sorrow (cf. sollicitudo, metus), as well as interest and carefulness (cf. diligentia, opera, studium). Since those far times on, many poets and writers have succinctly epitomized this amphiboly in the recurrent quote "to love is to suffer".[5]

However, it is probably less known the fact that Heidegger, in his study of the concept of care, makes an explicit reference to a myth by Hyginus. As this latter one is instrumental in our argumentation, we quote the original myth (with our emphasis) in its entirety below:

> When Cura was crossing a certain river, *she* saw some clayey mud. She took it up *thoughtfully* and began to fashion a man. While she was *pondering* on what she had done, Jove came up; Cura asked him to give the image life, and Jove readily grant this. When Cura wanted to give it her name [cf. the Adam's right in the Genesis], Jove forbade, and said that his name should be given it. But while they were disputing about the name, Tellus arose and said that it should have her name, since she had given her own *body*. They took Saturn for judge; he seems to have decided for them: Jove, since you gave him life [take his soul after death; since Tellus offered her body] let her receive his body; since Cura first fashioned him, let her *posses* him as long as he lives, but since there is controversy about his name, let him be called homo, since he was made from humus.
> (Fabulae, poem 220)

Also Heidegger was aware of the deep allegorical and ambivalent moral of the myth, beyond the mere tale. Just to mention a few points: self-awareness of human beings is ingrained with their sense of existence; things exist for them *in that* they ponder over them; thought shapes our perceptions of the word (as Cura fashions mud); we should be wary of any naming (that is a sort of pinpointing labels to things), as this is only a godly right and option; worrying and caring about things is a constitutive element of all of human beings[6]; and also another point that we present in the words of Froese [21]:

> By giving care such a prominent role, Heidegger challenges the myth of self-sufficiency and individual atomization that has shaped much of modern Western philosophy. In addition, he also tacitly inverts the Christian account of human creation, where woman is made out of the rib of man. However, what Heidegger leaves unquestioned is why cura and earth assume the guise of women. [In] Julia Kristevas semiotic theory, she asserts that Cura is the repressed semiotic that has been driven underground by the symbolic [cf. giving names to things, representing them linguistically]. [...] While the symbolic is Apollonian in its assumption of the essential separateness of things, the semiotic represents a self that is always part of other. (p. 188)

---

[5]Among these authors, it is easy to recall Dostoyevsky (Notes from Underground), Allen (Love and Death), Proust (In Search of Lost Time), but also women writers like Silvina Ocampo and Marguerite-Marie Alacoque.

[6]Heidegger defined sorge as the Being of Dasein, that is the fundamental structure that underlies each and every particular human existence.

This last interpretation acts as a prompt to reconnect the idea of care in information systems, in its original Heideggerian perspective, with the narratives of de-design, which we began outlining in a past contribution [5]. Also for Ciborra the concept of care regards something (in his case "strategic alignment") in-action, as opposed on-paper (see above). This directly relates to an anti-intellectual, anti-abstract, sub-symbolical (but not necessarily anti-representational) activity of engaging in and with the things of concern, in particular with an idea of nurturing, or cultivating [14] a socio-technical system.

To this aim we then recall the distinction that Heidegger makes between authentic care and unauthentic care [30]. The unauthentic care (concern) can "take the other's care away from him and put itself in his place in taking care, it can *leap in* for him. [This kind of care] takes over what is to be taken care of for the other. The other is thus displaced, he steps back so that afterwards [...] he can take things over as something finished and available or disburden himself of it completely. In this [kind of care] the other can become one who is dependent and dominated even if this domination is a tacit one and remains hidden from him". Conversely, there is also an authentic taking care "which does not so much leap in for the other as *leap ahead* of him, not in order to take care away from him, but to first to give it back to him as such. This [taking care] essentially pertains to authentic care; that is, the existence of the other, and not to a *what* which it takes care of, helps the other to become transparent to himself *in* his care and *free for* it. [...] Between the two extremes of [care], the one which does someone's job for him and dominates him, and the one which is in advance of him and frees him, everyday being-with-one-another maintains itself and shows many mixed forms" [30] (p. 114 and ff.).

Thus, in the domain of socio-technical design, there is a care that worries about its object, ponders over it, and ultimately *projects* predetermined futures for the object of care, practically dominating, and shaping it, in the present; and a care that, conversely, enables the full potential of the object of care to let it become itself, by leaving it free to change and evolve in its continuous growth, first of all because no ideal is pro-jected (sic) into its future, but rather a continuous accommodation [29] is allowed to occur on a contingent basis, in closed feedback loops with the world not mediated by abstractions and models. Both attitudes can require a devoted professional role, an expert or what Ciborra suggestively called the "observer-researcher" (to also hint at a detached and judging attitude) that takes care of either the social, or the technical component, or of their mutual alignment, in organizational settings. Moreover, complementing and perhaps extending the notion by Ciborra, we can also take inspiration from another passage by Froese: "one would not care for something else if one were either identical or completely separate from it" (p. 189).

This gives a clue on how to go beyond a dualistic conception of care; that is a conception that requires the observer to be ontologically different from the observed reality and gnosiologically detached from it; and that can be easily deprived of the sentimental (and sometimes rather self-indulgent or, worse yet, patronizing) elements of the care exerted by an external consultant, be it either a designer or a researcher with respect to any socio-technical twine he is not part of. Moreover, to overcome the deadlock between authentic and unauthentic care (because Heidegger is right in pointing that any care encompasses both these aspects to some extent), we should understand the limitations entailed by adopting a relational approach that requires the ontological (that is intrinsic, essential) distinction between subject and object (of care). Instead, we should consider caring as a philosophical alternative to the relational model based on taxonomic thinking and abstract categories [43].

In trying to focus on an alternative perspective where subjects and objects mutually develop and their boundaries blur in the unfolding of the relation itself (that is where the distinction is gnosiological rather than ontological) we are then ready to discuss some perspectives that come from the simple consideration inspired by Hyginus' myth that: cura is a woman.

3   The Feminine and the Differences that Matter

In the vein of the previously outlined perspective, we would like to discuss some marginalized aspects of interaction with technology and attitude toward design that are still in the socio-technical strand as continuously in the making, but tend to represent a contingency route, rather than a mainstream road paved with some consensus [24, 41]. These aspects go along with the feminine nature and way of approaching life (and hence objects of knowledge and technology) that have been discussed by some philosophers, psychologists, sociologists and post-modern thinkers. We would like to summarize these thoughts around the term "feminine", seen as a behavioural, existential and relational stance rather than as a gender-specific attribute. In what follows we will outline some of the main properties that this category brings in regard to technology and technology design.

We introduce this theme by starting from the concepts of "epistemic objectual practice" by Knorr-Cetina [8, 9] and "epistemological pluralism" by Turkle [51]. Their researches deal with a post-modernist paradigm of interaction with objects, which passed from being a performative act with ready-to-hand and black box tools to being a "relationship" act with open-ended objects, filled with care and empathy by their creators and thinkers. Epistemic objects are the knowledge objects of our "knowledge society", to which we project an emotional rather than a detached gaze, i.e., as objects of a scientific inquiry seen as a social endeavor [37]. This kind of intimacy is shaped by our daily interaction with objects of technology,[7] which shapes and is shaped by our "structure of wanting" [9], which is by its very nature doomed to remain unsatisfied. For this reason, and especially in knowledge–and

---

[7]These interactions are sometimes more frequent and durable than the daily interaction with humans, Knorr-Cetina claims. This phenomenon of continuous companionship has assimilated such objects to be part of the so called "lifeworld" [19], a term which can be roughly compared to the Heideggerian "Being-in-the-World", and is defined as "a significant configuration [...] the immediate fundament upon which almost all human experience depends [...] a dynamic horizon in which we live, and which "lives with us" in the sense that nothing can appear in our lifeworld except as *lived*." (our emphasis).

expertise-intensive working activities, this kind of continuous reflection on our epistemic objects and objects of technology has been assigned the property of being capable of continuously changing its boundaries, without fixing the truth or the ends of such objects towards an "ontology". This kind of relational tension with the "other" belongs to the feminine aspect of our human behavior [8].

Studies of personal appropriation of technology discussed in [51] show, for example, how a clear stance may be outlined between soft (feminine) mastery and hard (masculine) mastery of a computer program. In this context, soft is a mastery of objects in terms of "associations and interactions", of a creative, chaotic and flexible approach to the task of programming, an immersion in the white-box details, something that resembles the kind of feminine devotion to "forget the self" and "get lost inside the system" [33]. This kind of appropriation also characterizes the opposition between the soft tinkering of the bricoleur [6] and the hard consultancy of the engineer/planner [50, 51].

Another related dimension of the feminine stance lies in the concept of "multiplicity", or of *becoming instead of being*. This is a point originating from the philosophical work of Nietzsche and, in particular, from his struggle against metaphysics as a device for catching the truth, and the consequent celebration of the authenticity of life through the concept of the *multiplicity of appearances*, which Nietzsche associated to women in highly-disputed passages. For instance the passage where it is claimed that "surface, is woman's soul, a mobile, stormy film on surface water" (Zarathustra, XVIII) was often taken as an evidence of misogyny. However, as clearly argued by Graybeal, in Nietzsche's discourse surface is not a negative or derogatory term as it is simply "what it is, it is appearance, interpretation, mask, relationship, [...] art; it is language in its broadest sense, as the birth of the world, the discernment of meaning and value in otherwise empty experience" [22].[8] The feminine for him represents the *material* creation of life (the only true value, according to Nietzsche) against the nihilistic erudition, a powerful synthesis of the revelation that the continuous and plural *becoming* is "truer" than the static and structured *being*[9] (cf. Sect. 7 in Human, all too Human; Sect. 239 in Beyond Good and Evil).

Becoming has been defined by Grosz as the "the operation of self-differentiation, the elaboration of a difference within a thing, a quality or a *system that emerges or actualizes only in duration*... [our emphasis]" [23]. In the becoming of socio-technical actualizations there is no "the self-identity and [the] stasis necessary for a fixed

---

[8]One should also remember the high esteem attached by Nietzsche to the Greek world, and in particular for their attention to surface: "oh, those Greeks! They knew how to live. What is required for that is to *stop courageously at the surface*, the fold, the skin, to adore appearance, to believe in forms, tones, words, in the whole Olympus of appearance. Those Greeks were superficial—*out of profondity*" (The Gay Science).

[9]Although related to a more existentialist and autobiographic trait of the thought of Nietzsche, this idea is evocatively epitomized by the exhortation "Become, who you are" ("Werde, der du bist"), which he took from Pindar (Genoi hoios essi, Pythians, 2, 72) and that can be found, e.g., in 'Thus Spoke Zarathustra' and 'Ecce Homo'.

identity, [nor] a given boundary and clear-cut states [...] for *objects as they are conceptually understood...* [our emphasis]". In this vision, the dualism of subject and object is overcome; the *relational* term (or "affinity", as Haraway calls it [27]) has become, in its turn, a new a priori instead of identity [31]. This connection is capable of relating other than subject and object, but rather "fields, strata and chaos", (as in [23]), or even "the reality and the not-yet" (as said in [19, 18]).

This dimension gives us the opportunity to leap into an ensemble of (feminist) theories that has been recently grouped under the term of "new materialism" [52]. In the words of the authors:

> "New materialism is then 'new' in the sense that it is an attempt to 'leap into the future without adequate preparation in the present, through becoming, a movement of becoming-more and becoming-other, which involves the orientation to the creation of the new, to an unknown future, what is no longer recognizable in terms of the present.'[...] New materialism wants to do justice to the "material-semiotic," or "material-discursive" character of *all* events".

This may especially open a discussion on what the focus should be when we talk about the design of systems made of artifacts and people, of what should be prioritized beyond "precision, correctness and authority" [19], of what cannot be reduced to a rigid definition (neither the subject-user, nor the object-tool), but instead being studied as the emerging *properties of a system*, considered in its entanglements, its development over time, and in its possibilities of becoming.

The new materialism turn raises the question of how it has being short-sighted (and we may echo the same question for what concerns the design of socio-technical systems) to separate ontology (or the study of what is in the world), epistemology (or the study of what we know about what is in the world) and gnoseology (or the study of how we can know what we know) instead of considering how these are all undifferentiated and influencing one another.

An intriguing story that may clarify this concern is told by Barad when asked to explain her stance on "agential realism", that is her ethico-onto-epistemology of reality as a phenomenon of entanglement (intra-action) between subject and object, in which

> agency is about response-ability, about the possibilities of mutual response, which is not to deny, but to attend to power imbalances. Agency is about possibilities for worldly re-configurings. So agency is not something possessed by humans, or non-humans for that matter. It is an enactment. And it enlists, if you will, 'non-humans' as well as 'humans' [52].

as well as her theory on "diffraction patterns", that is her metaphor to explain the way that this entanglement is indeterminable in its changes and future states, just as the waves when passing through a medium, when even opposite phenomena can be observable (either an amplification or cancellation of the resulting wave intensity). She epitomizes her vision in this description of one physics experiment of measuring atomic properties and behaviors:

> That is, when we make a measurement, what happens is that it is not a matter of disturbing something and our knowledge is uncertain as a result, but rather there are not inherent properties and there are not inherent boundaries of things that we want to call entities before

the measurement intra-action. That is, Bohr is saying that *things are indeterminate; there are no things before the measurement, and that the very act of measurement produces determinate boundaries and properties of things* [our emphasis]. So, his is an ontological principle rather than an epistemological one. In other words, for Bohr particles do not have a position independently of my measuring something called position.

These perspectives are also linked to the "uncertainty of essence" [35, 52] (a powerful perspective we outlined above), and which we would like to reinforce by means of some psychological and social stances, which consider the feminine as a "pre-self" behaviour, the infant world of "desire and imagination", a pre-"socio-symbolic" identity before the imposition of the (male) order over the "indeterminable and plural" being [34].

In our vision, the *response-ability* introduced by Barad in the interview reported in [52] may also characterize socio-technical systems and their design. With this sense of indeterminacy in mind, we should engage in designing *technologies of becoming*, which have nothing to do with identity, entity, and separation of concepts for universal validity, but rather with an unfolding of reality, its singularities (i.e., situated practices) and authenticity (here intended in the Heideggerian sense), together with an impossibility to separate ourselves from them, but instead with a necessity to relate *to* and *through* them [21] to make sense out of them. We would define this kind of design a mirroring, rather than a search for well defined boundaries [35] or for a solution to a problem [46].

We would also define it a "movement beyond dualism" [23] rather than a domination by means of an approach that prioritizes the subject (thinking) over the object (matter). And, finally, we would connect it to a process of unlimited material semiosis [16, 52], seen as a flux of heterogeneous socio-technical negotiations of meaning [49], where the symbolic (the linguistic discourse) does not stifle the semiotic (the material-discursive, à la Barad) [21].

4   Some Implications for (De-)Design

Concretely, one could pose the following question: how can the relational non-dualistic approach we outlined above inform design? This totally sensible question does only partially make sense in the light of our argumentation.

A short answer could be that we have shed light on a design-oriented discourse that actually does not inform design but rather aims to get rid of it, at least of the modernist design. We summarize this point by looking at it from a certain distance, that is on an historical perspective. At the beginning of our contribution we placed our study within the domain of IS research, that is in the strand of speculative research about office automation. This is the automation of the work that is necessary to arrange, organize, articulate and order flows of matter (materials, products) and information (signs, conversations). The technological efficiency required by the capitalist mode of production has been naturally associated with increasing levels of automation just to move and control these flows more and more quickly and increase throughput and hence profit margin [2]. The efficiency rush also required—or was inspired by—(as it is always difficult to detect cause-effect relations in socio-economic entanglements) a modernist stance, which justified two critical decouplings (critical for our aims): the decoupling of production and use (consumers find objects of use "out there" in the market, and acquire them by trading value of exchange, i.e., money, for value of prospective use; these objects are ready-made and come from no-where from the perspective of the consumer); and the decoupling of theory (i.e., planning, modelling, design) and practice ("actual sign action", human work, the working machine).[10]

In short, the design of the office automation, that is the design of the bureaucratic (mega) machine [42] and of its network of sign-manipulating machines [29], realizes the modernist ideals of efficiency, objective detachment, and order. This kind of design, which requires a profession encompassing experts who are proficient in theorizing work from an objective, scientific perspective, speculates and theorizes on static entities, their fixed and immutable relations, and step-like processes where immutable mobiles (cf. Latour) are mobilized.

This idea of design, for its power and ingrainment in the Western culture, can be opposed only by a radical alternative: the bricolage, meant as the tinkering of the non-professional, and the committed and unmediated engagement of the bricoleur/practitioner with the tools of her practice, which is not mediated by any abstraction and any formal (i.e., either diagrammatic or computational) representation of those abstractions. In short, what we call a de-designed activity [5].

We acknowledge that the seminal ideas of bricolage and, especially, care that were proposed by Ciborra are breaches in the modernist, efficientist thinking. However, these are like concessions resulting from a more sympathetic and humanist stance of the professional designer with respect to his object of design: the ideal, efficient, effective, morally upright and wealth-dispensing organization. As such, they are still (more or less) engrained in modernist thinking: what we could denote as a paternalistic mindset, expressed within a patriarchal (managerial) value framework towards organization and work management, which we denoted above as the "inauthentic care", in Heideggerian terms.

From this still immature (not in the sense of callow or shallow bur rather unripe, not yet fully accomplished) idea of care, we argue that we can now move forward, toward its necessary consequences. This move is inspired by feminist studies which challenge the patriarchal attitude and propose a *relational, unobtruding, nondualistic, engaged idea of care* for the others (be these either humans or non-humans), i.e., the care denoted by Heidegger as authentic.

In very short terms, this new kind of care regards *how people (who work) relate to and shape their own tools (of work), shape and are shaped by their objects of*

---

[10]This decoupling can be said to have sealed 25 centuries of gestation of the epistemology of Plato into the philosophy of the *scientific management* of Taylor.

care at the inter-face level,[11] and co-create/negotiate meanings on the surface of the artifacts (the becoming matters).

In this regard, we are not envisioning a future that no one has yet seen, nor we are rehashing discourses already used up in the socio-technical literature. Rather, we are combining still underresearched strands with a particular consideration for the office practices of the pre-automation past. In those practices, meanings were continuously created and recreated in a "radical flux of becoming" [12] rather than being sanctioned in models and enacted in rigid machines. That flow unfolded on the surface of the paper-based records that were (slowly) mobilized in the 18th and 19th century offices. This happened even before the first endeavours of systematic categorization of the words (glossaries, taxonomies), of the material objects (cf. the invention of the filing cabinet), of the people (cf. organigrams) and of their behaviors (the standard operating procedures). These "office technologies" were progressively requested by an orderly ideal that was aimed at imposing *one best way* to have things done (cf. Taylor), and at imposing one order out of possible others (which were more local, temporary, provisional, contingent, and so forth).[12]

We are not advocating the return of the pre-automation age. Rather, we advocate the retreat from automation of the modernist designer. This mainly for these reasons: modernist approach is generally doomed to failure [17]; it is intrinsically unable to cope with complexity (because it is based on necessarily reductionist methodologies); it regards the development of artifacts that enact values and objectives as they have been understood by the designers [16]. Not fully appropriated artifacts could distract the end-users from enjoying the state of "flow", which is the highly productive state in which they can do their best work [15, 45].

Thus, we advocate the shift from the modernist designer to a new-old figure: the empowered and autonomous end-user [18], the active prosumer [3], the office bricoleur [6]. We intend the *bricoleur* (that is an archetype opposed by Levi-Strauss to the *Engineer* one in [39]) as the one who is able to build her own information and automation structures (without necessarily passing through the reification of spurious entities), and to decide for the right amount of automation of her tasks and skills, as they already do in their *shadow tools* [26].[13]

Technologies are becoming more and more capable of supporting this transition from the passive user to the independent worker [18], and to end-user development as a new research strand [40], where new approaches have been recently proposed [4, 6].

This paper contributes (with others) in its own small way, by dispelling the mythologies of the past that would make modernist design irreplaceable [29]. We

---

[11]The interface as situated place where humans and non-humans are mutually constituted [49]. The reader could notice that interface derives from "inter" (between) and "facies" (appearance, form, figure), in its turn from "facere", to make in Latin. Thus the interface can be seen as the place where two entities *make themselves for the other, and each shapes the other in turn.*

[12]Indeed, as Latour points out, "order is extracted not from disorder but from orders" [38] (p. 161).

[13]It is also argued that this would have an effect in minimizing the risk of technology complacency and bias [44].

then advocate the desertion of modernist informatics, for the advent of a post-modern informatics [13], which is grounded on a deeper study of semiology and taps in the power of material configurations[14] [49]. We argue that these configurations must be left as much free as possible to be continuously configured and reconfigured on the surface of artifacts by both human and non-human actants (cf. Latour). These latter actants are not stable themselves, but rather *technologies of becoming*,[15] which are left free to "become" and change all together with the flow of signs that they host, carry, transform and move (sometimes faster than the human hand and eye, sometimes even slower).

5 Conclusions

In this paper, we have affirmed the need to focus on relations, but also on the primacy of relations over the "related", and on the necessity of the entanglement of the observer with the *observed* relation, which actually *absorbes* him and is enacted in its entanglement with him. In short we propose the overcoming of the idea of "caring" *about* and *for* the social and the technical components of a system, in favor of a deeper entanglement in the process of developing, growing and *become the system*.

Our contribution is grounded on a feminine reflection on the role of IT in organizations and human settings more generally. In this process the relationship between the designers, the users and the technology is not of simple design or use.

Both the humans and the non-humans are seen as *agents of becoming*, that is active agents that both produce and are themselves subject to a continuous transformation. In this view, cognition and computation blur and get material, that is are enacted by what Hutchins denotes as "the propagation of representational state" [32] and that in semiotics is generally related to an ever-unfolding *discourse* (sequences of signs) that relates and binds together webs of interpreting agents (actants).

In these webs of actants, *technologies of becoming* are the ones fulfilling the twofold role of being both scaffolding and driver of the full potential of humans in shaping their systems and domesticate their multiple ecologies and socio-technical worlds. As said above, this would also entail the concomitant reallocation of the role of the professional "expert" designer in that of facilitator of this process, as a *further* agent of change. In this view, designers can support the process of continuous adaptation/adoption of the socio-technical system, by seeding and

---

[14]This would probably require a novel "knowledge of the surface", i.e., an epistemology reflecting how we cope with "the multiplicity and confusion on the surface of our existence" (cf. Simmel), which has been tentatively investigated so far by a few authors (e.g., F. Nietzsche, S. Kracauer, G. Simmel, W. Benjamin, E. Bloch, M. Maffesoli, M. Vozza).

[15]To draw an analogy with painting, the most suitable term would be "base support"; in philosophy, this concept has been denoted as "world-sheet", first introduced by Pierce and then speculated by Carlo Sini [48].

facilitating this process, e.g., by providing in-field expertise in the use of scaffolding tools-and-techniques; by cross-fertilizing cooperative settings of either "best practices", effective heuristics or lessons learnt; or by just asking the users the right questions to trigger in them a process of self-empowerment and liberation from the father-designer (cf. the figure of the maieuta-designer proposed in [7]).

The feminine perspectives we discussed above and the mater(ial) creativity that these advocate can be among these valuable lessons learnt: these may challenge the "truth of essence upon the chance of plurality" in regard to the design of technology [51], and conversely emphasize the value of local, temporary, relative *expedients*, notwithstanding their intrinsic shortcomings and weaknesses. To this latter regard, we subscribe the point by Froeze again, when she writes that: "weakness is not the absence of strength but rather signifies a kind of openness that refrains from imposing itself on the world [...] weakness will prevail over strength precisely because of its expansiveness, flexibility and endurance. Strength eventually exhausts itself while the energy of weakness is boundless" [21]. Weakness, multiplicity, materiality, relativity, indeterminacy, superficiality (à la Nietzsche), dynamicity, are all characteristics we attach to the kaleidoscopic concept of *becoming matters*, for the design of socio-technical systems.

Finally, we hope that this contribution will also contribute in favor of the necessity "to decolonize the imaginary" [36] of IS development with terms bound to a (glorious?) past of process re-engineering and automation [25]. To this aim, devoting more research to the feminine element of the creative process of appropriating and socializing people, and their surrounding things, for and about which we can care, can be part of this research path.

References

1. Barad, K.: Posthumanist performativity: toward an understanding of how matter comes to matter. Signs **40**(1), 801–831 (2014)
2. Beniger, J.: The control revolution: technological and economic origins of the information society. Harvard University Press (2009)
3. Bruns, A., Schmidt, J.H.: Produsage: a closer look at continuing developments. New Rev Hypermedia Multimedia **17**(1), 3–7 (2011)
4. Cabitza, F.: "Remain faithful to the earth!"*: reporting experiences of artifact-centered design in healthcare. CSCW **20**(4–5), 231–263 (2011)
5. Cabitza, F.: De-designing the IT artifact. Drafting small narratives for the coming of the socio-technical artifact. In Proceedings of It AIS (2014)
6. Cabitza, F., Simone, C.: Building socially embedded technologies: Implications about design. Designing socially embedded technologies in the real-world, 217 (2015)
7. Cabitza, F., Fogli, D., Piccinno, A.: Fostering participation and co-evolution in sentient multimedia systems. J. Vis. Lang. Comput. **25**(6), 684–694 (2014)
8. Cetina, K.K.: Sociality with objects: social relations in postsocial knowledge societies. Theor. Cult. Soc. **14**(4), 1–30 (1997)
9. Cetina, K.K.: Objectual practice. Knowledge as social order: rethinking the sociology of Barry Barnes. In The Practice Turn in Contemporary Theory, Routledge (2008)

10. Ciborra, C.U.: De profundis? Deconstructing the concept of strategic alignment. Scand. J. Inf. Syst. **9**(1), 2 (1997)
11. Ciborra, C.: Imbrication of representations: risk and digital technologies*. J. Manage. Stud. **43** (6), 1339–1356 (2006)
12. Cox, C.: Nietzsche: naturalism and Interpretation. Univ of California Press (1999)
13. Coyne, R.: Designing Information Technology in the Postmodern Age. MIT Press (1995)
14. Dahlbom, B., Mathiassen, L.: Computers in Context: the Philosophy and Practice of Systems Design. Blackwell Publishers, Inc (1993)
15. Demarco, T., Lister, T.: Peopleware: productive Projects and Teams. Dorset House Publishing Company, Incorporated, New York, NY (1999)
16. De Souza, C. S.: The semiotic engineering of human-computer interaction. MIT press (2005)
17. Dwivedi, Y.K., Wastell, D., Laumer, S., Henriksen, H.Z., Myers, M.D., Bunker, D., Srivastava, S.C.: Research on information systems failures and successes: status update and future directions. Inf. Syst. Front. **17**(1), 143–157 (2015)
18. Fischer, G., Herrmann, T.: Socio-technical systems: a meta-design perspective. IGI Glob. pp. 1–33 (2011)
19. Fors, A.C.: The beauty of the beast: the matter of meaning in digitalization. AI & Soc. **25**(1), 27–33 (2010)
20. Fors, A.C.: Strange familiarity: on the material turn in feminism and HCI. In European Conference on Gender and ICT, Umea University, Sweden (2011)
21. Froese, K.: Nietzsche, Heidegger, and Daoist Thought: Crossing Paths In-between. SUNY Press (2012)
22. Graybeal, J. M.: Language and the Feminine in Nietzsche and Heidegger. Indiana University Press (1990)
23. Grosz, E.: Bergson, Deleuze and the becoming of unbecoming. Parallax **11**(2), 4–13 (2005)
24. Hayles, N.K.: How we became post human: Virtual bodies in cybernetics, literature, and informatics. University of Chicago Press (2008)
25. Hammer, M.: Reengineering work: don't automate, obliterate. Harvard Bus. Rev. **68**(4), 104–112 (1990)
26. Handel, M.J., Poltrock, S.: Working around official applications: experiences from a large engineering project. In CSCW 2011, 309–312, ACM (2011)
27. Haraway, D.J.: Simians, cyborgs, and women: The reinvention of nature. Routledge (2013)
28. Harper, D.: Online Etymology Dictionary. (2015). http://www.etymonline.com/index.php?term=care
29. Harris, J., Henderson, A.: A better mythology for system design. In HCI SIGCHI, pp. 88–95, ACM (1999)
30. Heidegger, M.: Being and Time: A Translation of Sein und Zeit. SUNY Press (1996)
31. Hird, M.J.: Meeting with the microcosmos. Environment and planning. D Soc. Space **28**(1), 36 (2010)
32. Hutchins, E.: Cognition in the Wild. MIT Press (1995)
33. Keller, E.F.: A Feeling for the Organism: The Life and Work of Barbara McClintock. Macmillan (1984)
34. Koshy, A.: The feminine and the question of truth in Nietzschean philosophy. Indian Philos. Q. **26**(1), 89–108 (1999)
35. Kristeva, J.: The subject in process. The Tel Quel Reader, 133–78 (1998)
36. Latouche, S.: Farewell to growth. Polity (2009)
37. Latour, B.: Science in action: how to follow scientists and engineers through society. Harvard University Press (1987)
38. Latour, B.: The pasteurization of France. Harvard University Press (1993)
39. Levi-Strauss, C.: The savage mind. University of Chicago Press (1966)
40. Lieberman, H., Patern, F., Klann, M., Wulf, V.: End-user development: an emerging paradigm, pp. 1–8, Springer (2006)
41. Locoro, A., Cabitza, F.: Should the culture of participation inform a new ethics of design? In CoPDA 2014–2015, Ceur-ws (2015)

42. Mumford, L.: Technics and human development: the myth of the machine, vol. I. Harvest Books (1971)
43. Noddings, N.: Caring: a relational approach to ethics and moral education. Univ of California Press (2013)
44. Parasuraman, R., Manzey, D.H.: Complacency and bias in human use of automation: an attentional integration. Hum. Factors: J. Hum. Factors Ergon. Soc. **52**(3), 381–410 (2010)
45. Pilke, E.: Flow experiences in information technology use. Int. J. Hum. Comput. Stud. **61**(3), 347–357 (2004)
46. Simon, H.A.: The sciences of the artificial, vol. 136. MIT Press (1996)
47. Simonsen, J.: How do we take care of strategic alignment? Scand. J. Inf. Syst. **11**(1), 6 (1999)
48. Sini, C.: On ethical revolution in philosophy. Phainomena (Ljubljana) **21**(82–83), 31–38 (2012)
49. Suchman, L.: Human-Machine Reconfigurations. Cambridge University, Plans and situated actions. New York (1986)
50. Strauss, C.L.: Savage mind. University of Chicago (1962)
51. Turkle, S., Papert, S.: Epistemological pluralism: styles and voices within the computer culture. Signs, pp. 128–157 (1990)
52. Van der Tuin, I., Dolphijn, R.: New materialism: interviews & cartographies. Open Humanities Press (2012)

Redefining the Mutual Positions of the Social and Technical Sides of Socio-Technical Systems

Giorgio De Michelis

Abstract This paper surveys the application of Socio-Technical Design (STD) in the deployment of computer based systems in organizations and tries to explain its successes and difficulties relating it to the evolution of information systems. Moreover, it continues this story recalling the contributions given to the interactions between humans and machines in the work places give by CSCW and related research areas. Finally it shows that a dialogue between STD and CSCW could be beneficial but requires that both of them makes a radical move towards a closer attention to technology, as, today, technological innovation needs to be grounded on what we know about work practices and work organization.

1 Introduction

Socio-Technical Design (STD) has been introduced in the studies about work and organizations to emphasize the, always stricter, interconnection between human beings and machines in the modern factories [31]. Assembly lines, as the main example of this type of ensembles, integrate workers in the production process so that their actions are synchronized with the functioning of the machine. Even if perfect integration of humans and machines has never been achieved, it has remained for almost a century the horizon characterizing most efforts dedicated to increase production automation. Since these efforts were justified by technological innovation offering means to substitute humans with machines, or, at least, to reduce human fatigue, attributing heavy tasks to machines, it has been a natural consequence of them, trying to constrain human to machine behaviors. Doing it was apparently straightforward, since, as indicated by Taylor 's scientific management [28], it could be performed reducing human work to sequences of simple tasks. It did not require much time do discover that work processes had a large number of irregularities (variances, in STD language) making the reduction ineffective. The

G. De Michelis (✉)
Università Degli Studi Di Milano-Bicocca, Viale Sarca 336, 20126 Milan, Italy
e-mail: gdemich@disco.unimib.it

© Springer International Publishing Switzerland 2016
L. Caporarello et al. (eds.), *Digitally Supported Innovation*,
Lecture Notes in Information Systems and Organisation 18,
DOI 10.1007/978-3-319-40265-9_9

researchers of the Tavistock Institute lead by E. Trist, used STD as a means for analyzing the reasons for these variances and for overcoming or managing them. Their inspiring idea was that factory automation needed to take in equal account both machines and humans without subordinating the latter to the regulated machine functioning. 'Joint optimization' was necessary for both respecting human beings and avoiding inefficiencies in production. STD became in this way the approach to innovation accompanying negotiations between trade unions and management to humanize work places in change of higher productivity. Its main principles, having several diverse formulations (e.g., [7, 8]), can be articulated around three pillars: participation of workers in the design process, flexibility and openness of the resulting work organization and, finally, responsible roles for the involved workers.

We can underline here two aspects of STD principles that are very important from our viewpoint: first, STD focuses on work organization and assumes technology as given (this can be easily explained with its focus on manufacturing processes, where technologies require huge investments and embody fully specified production processes); second, human work is characterized in terms of tasks (again, this is easily explained making reference to Taylor's 'scientific analysis of work, and, conversely, it explains the emphasis putted on minimal critical specifications, meaningfulness of tasks, as the means for granting responsible autonomy to workers).

Even if STD had a small number of applications in manufacturing companies, its impact has been quite strong in cultural terms, as it can be seen confronting its principles with those characterizing World Class Manufacturing (WCM; [25]), the work design method that is currently a benchmark in several industrial sectors. It must be underlined that WCM is not a variant of STD: it recalls some of its principles (in particular, those regarding organization flexibility) but, in many respects, it can be considered a reified version of it. A discussion about this controversial issue would be interesting, but we stop here our survey of STD, since this paper does not want to be a summary of STD but it is devoted to its application in the area of Information Systems.

When computers were for the first time introduced within companies, in the late 1960s, the situation reflected, in fact, what was happening in production processes: they were mainframes requiring huge investments, they were used to perform tasks requiring heavy data processing previously needing large amounts of clerical routine work, like payroll, accounting, warehouse management, or management of the operations in services like telephony, electricity distribution, etc. Again we had huge centralized investments, again we had machines reorganizing human work to improve efficiency, and again the attention to workers was low, and the deployment of systems in the workplaces was not having all its expected outcomes. It was natural, therefore, trying to apply, also in this case, STD principles.

This is the beginning of the story that I will summarize in this paper, observing the changes, generated by always new waves of technological and organizational innovation, that have characterized it. It seems to me, in fact, that the major weakness of STD has been to pay little attention to the evolution of technology, being, therefore, unable to renovate itself and to dialogue with the emerging disciplines accompanying it, in particular with Computer Supported Cooperative Work (CSCW). I will show that technological and organizational innovation poses today to both STD and CSCW new challenges requiring to envision new perspectives and paths in the relationships between humans and machines.

I will distinguish, in accordance with a largely agreed periodization [5] of the history of Information Technology (IT), three phases in the evolution of its applications within organizations: the first one where Information Technology was a centralized technology and was used to automate clerical work (mainframes and minis, from the end of the 1960s to the 1980s); a second phase when, with the appearance of the personal computer, work practices have become more autonomous with respect to machines (personal computers, from the 1980s to the end of the 19th century) and, finally, a third phase, that is happening now (pervasive and mobile computing), when technological innovation in the IT sector and new work practices seem to be able to put in crisis the continuous evolution model that has governed up to now the computerization of work-places and to make possible (and, may be, necessary) a newly conceived generation of IT systems. In each phase we will pay attention to how STD has been and is touched by occurring changes.

2 Socio-Technical Design of Information Systems

2.1 Phase 1–Mainframes and Minis

As it is well known, but I need to recall it here to focus the attention of the reader on the changes that have occurred later, computers begin their penetration inside organizations in the late 1960s and continue it during the seventies extending the clerical tasks they are supporting/substituting. Payrolls, accounting, invoicing, warehouse management, are some of the first functions they performed followed by other connected with planning and monitoring in the accounting, logistics, production, and marketing sectors and their expected payoff is increasing efficiency and reducing costs. They are absorbing human work, leaving to some employees only data-entry activities and completely rearranging the work of other employees. For many office workers it is a tsunami, similar to the one that invested textile workers when, at the beginning of 19th century, machines entered in their factories. The impact of computers on office work is still a controversial and debated issue: here we pay attention to its negative aspects, that are, for many observers, mostly temporary and compensated by other more positive effects. These issues are discussed in the literature, e.g.: [16]. Even if they do not loose their job, their working conditions are revolutionized, sometimes, by a radical disqualification of their roles, in other cases, by a big cognitive effort to become capable to use new and 'exoteric' machines, whose interfaces are quite abstract and user-unfriendly and sometimes, impose their unjustified order (from a human viewpoint) in the execution of tasks (even of data entry tasks). The main responsibility remaining to some office workers is, frequently, avoiding errors in copying data. This change process, is also weakening the potential benefits expected by the investments in technology, because frequent and difficult to manage variances affect what is gained by substituting human work. Moreover, rules and procedures in the offices undergo more frequent changes than production processes in the factories, and information systems do not have enough flexibility to absorb them.

It has been natural, therefore, to extend to the deployment of information systems the action research interventions [30] that had been experimented by STD scholars and practitioners in the factories to defend workers from the radical automation of work-processes without affecting work productivity and, on the contrary, trying to increase it. There are, in fact, several similarities between what is done in the offices with IT and manufacturing automation processes; let us recall two of them: progressive automation of routine tasks with expulsion of large number of workers and subordination of workers to the logic and times of technology.

With the aim to overcome these problems, some companies asked to STD practitioners and scholars to assist the introduction of their new computer systems. These projects were participative in that future users at all levels played a major role in design, in particular rethinking jobs and work processes for their own departments before new systems were installed. These user design groups, aided by system analysts who acted as advisors on technical issues, tried to give equal weight to technical and human concerns and introduced teamwork, multiskilling and a degree of self-management [18–20]. Several STD projects were brought to a successful conclusion and implemented, becoming benchmarks for future interventions of the same type.

Their success demonstrated that the principles of STD are well suited for dealing with the problems emerging in the deployment of information systems: minimal critical specifications, adaptability, responsible roles, wholeness and meaningfulness of tasks are all categories capable to qualify changes in socio-technical systems. Moreover, its idea of participation of workers in the design process is important when STD adoption is the outcome of a negotiation between the company and the Trade Unions.

2.2   Phase 2–Personal Computers

In short times, during the 1980s, the personal computer and the ERPs (the reader will forgive me for this over-simplification) change IT, giving raise to systems and tools that are capable to support a larger sets of tasks and can be deployed in a radically new way. They are answering to new requirements emerging within organizations, also as a consequence of the systems that had already been adopted (supporting productivity also at the level of the typical individual office activities, like writing, drawing and computing, and integrating information processing functions around a unique organizational data base). Moreover, they have features qualifying them as commodities that do not require a true design process, needing only to be tailored for each organization adopting them. In 1984, Apple launches Macintosh; in 1992, SAP presents its Sap R/3 system, later named SAP ERP.

Why are these events important? Because Macintosh, at the personal computing level, and Sap R/3, at the organizational computing level, fix, from the user viewpoint, the new standards characterizing, in their specific domains, all the systems proposed to the market up to current days. It is not by chance in fact, that, after the Macintosh, all operating systems for personal computers resemble each other, sharing the desktop metaphor, invented by Allan Kay at Xerox Parc in the late seventies [15], and that the same is true for ERPs, adopted by the majority of medium and large companies all around the world [17].

When they conquer the markets, both are, in essence, in spite of their evident diversity, multi-function devices supporting users in a growing variety of tasks. Their success depends on their capability to solve the problems affecting the diffusion of ICT within work environments. On the one hand, the simple and highly usable interface of Macintosh and imitators allows everyone to use it, making simple its distribution to all office workers, from clerical employees to technicians and managers: typical office work changes dramatically, with the reduction almost to zero, for example, of the clerical work accompanying the activities of intermediate managers and technicians and opening to the latter new possibilities of autonomous information processing. On the other hand, the strong integration of ERP systems gives to enterprises the possibility of planning, managing and controlling their operations in a smooth way, with the certainty that information sharing is granted, almost, without ambiguities and contradictions.

As said above, personal computers (with their suites of productivity tools) and ERPs have several features qualifying them as commodities, so that they do not need, to be designed but only to be tailored when deployed. While this claim captures the essence of the diffusion of personal computers, it is an oversimplification for ERPs, whose introduction in an organization remains a complex and time-consuming project, mainly for the migration of legacy systems it implies. There is no need, with ERPs, of designing information system: STD ceases, therefore, to be an option among those a company may adopt for guiding the introduction of information systems, being slowly marginalized. Enid Mumford [21] attributes this crisis to the reduced interest of companies for work conditions, but I think that ERPs (and personal computers) are systems not needing design, putting therefore out of the game approaches like STD and challenging its scholars and practitioners to renovate their studies of work places in order to understand how they can find new ways to influence technology deployment with the offices.

2.3 Phase 3–Ubiquitous and Mobile Computing

In recent years, in fact, many things happen around IT meriting attention by scholars and practitioners. Let me recall two of them. First, despite the general appreciation that ERPs and personal computers get in the organizations where they are used, always more frequently problems in their use emerge underlining their rigidity: again it is a matter of procedures badly or over specified that workers try to circumvent as they can [2], again it is matter of impossibility of getting information and to process it as needed, to which workers react doing bricolage with what they have (mainly personal computers and their productivity tools; [3, 9]. Second, with the emergence of the new area of research named Computer Supported Cooperative Work (CSCW; in 1986 there is its first international conference) studies on work practices and collaboration get a new radical perspective [24]. The events, to which we make reference here, are too recent to propose them from an historical viewpoint: in the next section we discuss them as indicators of emerging phenomena.

3   CSCW and the Situated Action Perspective

CSCW research has, from its very beginning, opened a new perspective in our understanding of office work practice, showing that what people do is not characterized by the tasks they perform. This has been a radical change of perspective with respect to mainstream thinking, showing that what matters is the knowledge people create and share while trying to fulfill their appointments. Situated action by Lucy Suchman [27], language-action perspective by Terry Winograd and Fernando Flores [32] that have been at the center of CSCW research from its very beginning, but also knowledge creating organizations by Ikujiro Nonaka and Hirotachi Takeuchi [22] propose, in different terms, a similar change in our view of organization behavior. Trying a rough, but not forced, integration of their proposals, we can say that Suchman's studies propose to consider central in human practice its being situated, not only in space and time, but, mainly, in a social context, giving to it sense; Winograd and Flower's language action perspective indicated how a pragmatic viewpoint on human conversations allows to bind what human say and their future actions and interactions; all organizations, in the theory proposed by Nonaka and Takeuchi, are characterized by their capacity of creating unceasingly new knowledge, processing tacit and explicit knowledge already possessed by their members. Despite their different origins, and their different articulation there is a fil rouge connecting these three approaches: people working in knowledge creating organizations are directly engaged in the creation of new knowledge, and knowledge is by necessity situated in the networks of actions and interactions, in which they are immersed.

The issue, here, is understanding how things are correlated with respect to users, what should be ready at their hands while they are acting and interacting. Altogether, the studies recalled above underline that human practice is intrinsically social, that it is situated, and that what people know and say is strictly and bi-directionally linked with what they do. These three hints on human practice recall that the effectiveness of human beings strongly depends on the awareness they have of the context where they are situated. Within the threads of events constituting a social experience, human beings create and circulate also new knowledge. For this reason, being aware of the context in which she is acting and interacting is, for a person, necessary in order to be effective in it. We call these threads 'stories', to underline their sense-making ability [11].

Social contexts are of paramount importance, in particular, for any person who is involved in many different stories, because whichever is the story she is acting and interacting in, what is happening in the others is, both, disturbing (creating noise and confusion) and enriching (opening it to new knowledge) it.

CSCW research has used the hints, deriving from the above recalled new ways of observing and understanding work practice and its relations with knowledge creation and sharing, to investigate collaborative work [24], boundary objects [26], scripts and maps [23], etc., grounding them on a rich and always growing collection of case studies.

Moreover, it has designed a large variety of prototypes of systems capable to support collaboration in the work place, indicating new directions for the development of the technology supporting office workers. Even if almost all of them have remained at the level of research prototypes (this is a question we will raise again in the next section) they indicate new directions for the development of innovative organizational technology that merit to be discussed and known.

In the same years, a community of people, largely overlapping with that doing research in CSCW, met at the Participatory Design Conferences, where the issue of user participation in the design process was discussed. It has been in that framework, for example, that 'meta design' has been discussed [13, 14] as a design after design approach. We have recently surveyed and discussed issues related with design and participation in the book Design Things [29].

It is surprising that all the ideas and findings generated within the CSCW and/or Participatory Design did not raise almost any interest in STD. An occasion has been lost for opening a discussion where the experiences of STD scholars and practitioners could be rejuvenated by the new approaches emerging in CSCW and Participatory Design. But nothing is lost, as we will see in the next section.

4 Towards Situated Computing

We claimed in the previous section that CSCW researchers designed interesting prototypes of collaborative applications, but that most of them remained at the prototype level. So while their work at the analytical and conceptual level became influential in a diversity of disciplines, from anthropology to computer science, the systems they conceived for supporting collaboration, knowledge management, etc. did not reach work places, with few exceptions like Lotus Notes. CSCW has generally avoided to deal with information systems, as well as with organizational processes of technology deployment in the work-places, preferring to dedicate its efforts to the design of systems supporting various forms of collaboration and coordination. This has brought, like I said above, several interesting prototypes but left its outcomes confined, mostly, in research labs.

Moreover, it has to be observed that, also for their being conceived as stand-alone systems, most prototypes designed within CSCW (as also those in which I was involved) have no real chances of leaving the labs where they are created. Despite their innovative aspects, in fact, CSCW systems are generally applications (joint editors, common information spaces, coordination tools, etc.) characterized by new functions and services.

If we go back to situated action and all the issues related with knowledge management in the work places, in fact, we discover that the social context of human actions and interactions is not related, generally, with a particular task or function, but with a story, where human beings execute different tasks and use different functions and services performed by their technological supports. The context traverses applications and several tasks are performed within it: situated action needs for a reconsideration of the systems supporting organizations and their members, and not for new applications delivering new services and executing new functions!

This reconsideration has two complementary consequences, underlining the challenge it poses: on the one hand, it needs to be grounded in what research in CSCW and related areas has brought to our attention about human practice, collaboration and knowledge management; on the other, it needs to invest almost all the technologies populating work-places, from information systems to personal computers, since all of them, together, contribute to make the context of human actions and interactions accessible. But all of them have been designed as multi-function devices supporting specific tasks with limited integration capability, being, therefore, intrinsically unable for supporting situated action. Let me give some hints supporting this claim. ERPs are systems, whose database is accessible only through the pre-defined and optimized access paths they provide: the information they contain is not open to new ways of processing it together with other information coming from different sources; but this openness is exactly what is required by the variable conditions of situatedness. Even the new applications designed for managing knowledge like Business Intelligence [6] require costly data mining [33] activities and have rigid limits. Personal computers are characterized by the interactive and stand-alone tools they offer to their users: from their viewpoint the context of a document is the productivity tool that has created it and allows for its manipulation. Even context-oriented applications like the email, whose conversations take together the interactions characterizing stories, are unable to extend their support to the documents users exchange through it as attachments.

Creating new applications for context management like sophisticated search mechanisms, common information space, etc., risks to increase the complexity of the systems hosting them without solving the problem, because it multiplies the applications a user needs to use while acting and interacting.

There is only one way to overcome this impasse: redesigning both information systems and personal computers as systems supporting situated action, going beyond the task-oriented architecture characterizing them up to now. We have called this new perspective for the design of computer based systems, situated computing [12]. Without repeating, in these pages, what I have written elsewhere, let me illustrate what I mean with this term.

In the presentation of a Workshop organized at CHI 2000 [1] Michel Beaudouin-Lafon and Wendy E. Mackay write: "The term situated computing describes socio-technical systems in which situations of use and context play a central role in the use of computers. Since most computing is arguably situated computing, we need to reflect on our current understanding of context, establish a common language for discussion and define processes for developing systems-in-use." [1]. Continuing this phrase, probably beyond the intentions of its authors, I claim that 'situation of use and context' should play a central role also in the way technology works and in the services it offers. All its functions and services, in fact, should be embedded in the context in which the user aims to use them, increasing her awareness of it as well as her capability of retrieving, almost without any effort, all what she needs to act and interact effectively in it. Situated Computing, for me, is not only characterizing a way of using computers, but indicates also a way of designing them at the scope of supporting situated practice. This is the reason why I think that its innovation should encompass all the most diffused systems human beings use while acting and interacting, as from personal computers and ERPs. Redesigning widely diffused systems, as well as inventing new ones, is difficult and requires, as indicated also by Beaudouin-Lafon and Mackay, all the knowledge we may collect about situated practice and system design and the establishment of a common language. In other terms, situated computing needs for the active contributions of STD, for what it knows about the design processes through which we build socio-technical systems, and of CSCW for what it knows about situatedness of human practice and knowledge related processes and for a common language where their distinct contributions can be discussed.

Moreover, they must do one step further, giving their contribution, in cooperation with technologists, to the definition of the requirements situated computing systems need to satisfy. STD and CSCW have the possibility for playing a major role in this endeavor, since they are multi-disciplinary research fields, where social scientists, technologists and designers have learned to work together.

Situated computing systems are client-server systems. At the server side, systems supporting organizations should be constructible composing modules realizing a strict separation of data and functions, so that data are always directly accessible and systems may evolve substituting and/or adding new modules to the existing ones. This will transform bricolage, from a way of doing what is needed with the available means, into a well-supported form of modular programming (what you do when you buy internet services in a cloud gives some hints on what can be done). At the client side, personal computers should be capable to use meta-data to decorate their files with tags and links and to contextualize access to the data and functions of information systems (see, as an example, the prototype of new Linux front-end for personal computers, itsme, we have built in Milano in these years; [12]) in the stories of the user. Finally, ad here the experience of STD should play the main role, the design of situated computing systems needs to be complemented with a re-visitation of the 'migration of legacy systems', that supported the adoption of ERPs, to make possible and speed up the process of passing from traditional ERPs to situated computing systems.

Even remaining at this generic level, it should be appreciated that the requirements I have outlined are grounded on up tp date technology as cloud computing. But detailing them, we will discover that even open and big data, mash-ups and ontologies are candidate to play a role in situated computing systems [12].

5 Conclusion

The narrative I have proposed in this paper has not the ambition to be a scientifically accurate history of the design of information systems and of the other technologies populating organizations. If the reader expected it, then I am very sorry. I want only to recall to the reader some facts of that history, and to let her reflecting on what those facts can tell us.

STD and CSCW can be considered as two different ways to move social scientists towards multi-disciplinary research: they exhibit two different ways of dealing with technology and technologists, While STD reserves for itself the role of helping to develop technology and technology deployment in such a way that human work is not reduced to an appendix of machines and continues to be necessary in letting machines work appropriately, CSCW opens new perspectives in understanding human practice and in outlining new systems supporting it. In both cases, social scientists, designers and technologists cooperate, moving only partially from their disciplinary fields. But, as I have argued in this paper, disciplinary boundaries, when radical innovation is possible, appear inadequate.

What is required now, is a stronger form of multi-disciplinary work, where each discipline finds ways to influence the other ones on their terrain: I don't think that social scientists should become technologists, nor that designers should become social scientists, etc.: this is unrealistic and may also become dangerous. What I envisions is that technologists design their systems reacting to the requirements proposed by designers and social scientists, and that social scientists test their analysis on the performances of innovative systems, etc.

The social and technical sides of STD, like the computer and work sides of CSCW must become more permeable. This is the only way for giving an impulse to radical innovation in the work places, so that we pass from information to knowledge society.

Acknowledgments My interest for Socio-Technical Systems and Design dates back to the late 1980s and to the beginning of my friendship and collaboration with Federico Butera [10]. It has been Federico who raised my interest on this subject and, for this reason, I am grateful to him. Later, I had several occasions to discuss on the design of ICT with my colleagues Fiorella De Cindio and Carla Simone, with Claudio Ciborra and with several Scandinavian colleagues. In the last years, the interest for the STD experience has revived, while I was elaborating my 'Situated

Computing' manifesto [4]. I discussed it with Federico Cabitza and Carla Simone at the University of Milano–Bicocca, and, within EUSSET, with Liam Bannon, David Randall, Kjeld Schmidt, Ina Wagner and Volker Wulf. To all of them, and to the many others with whom I had occasions to discuss this topic, it goes my gratitude. In any case, the responsibility of what I written in these pages only mine.

References

1. Beaudouin-Lafon, M., Mackay, W.E. (organizers): Workshop on Research Directions in Situated Computing, at the ACM Conference on Human Factors in Computing Systems CHI 2000, Position Papers (2000)
2. Bowers, J., Button, G., Sharrock, W.: Workflow from within and without: technology and cooperative work on the print industry shopfloor. In: Proceedings of ECSCW1995, Dordrecht, Kluwer, pp. 309–324 (1995)
3. Buescher, M., Gill, S., Mogensen, P., Shapiro, D.: Landscapes of practice: Bricolage as a method for situated design. CSCW, Comput. Supported Coop. Work 10(1), 1–28 (2001)
4. Cabitza, F., Simone, C.: Building Socially Embedded Technologies: Implications about Design. In: Wulf, V., Schmidt, K., Randall, D. (eds.) Designing Socially Embedded Technologies in the Real World, pp. 215–268. Springer, London (2015)
5. Ceruzzi, P.E.: A History of Modern Computing, II edn. MIT Press, Cambridge (2003)
6. Chauduri, S., Dayal, U., Narasaaya, V.: An Overview of Business Intelligence Technology. Commun. ACM 34(8), 88–98 (2011)
7. Cherns, A.: The principles of sociotechnical design. Hum. Relat. 29(8), 783–792 (1976)
8. Cherns, A.: The principles of sociotechnical design revisited. Hum. Relat. 40(3), 153–162 (1987)
9. Ciborra, C.: The Labyrinths of Information: Challenging the Wisdom of Systems. Oxford University Press, Oxford (2002)
10. De Michelis, G.: Nuovi Paradigmi per il Disegno Socio-Tecnico (in Italian). Sociologia del Lavoro, 37 (1989)
11. De Michelis, G.: Situated Computing. In: Wulf, V., Schmidt, K., Randall, D. (eds.) Designing Socially Embedded Technologies in the Real World, pp. 63–76. London: Springer (2015a)
12. De Michelis, G.: Interaction Design at itsme. In: Wulf, V., Schmidt, K., Randall, D. (eds.) Designing Socially Embedded Technologies in the Real World, pp. 191–214. Springer, London (2015)
13. Fischer, G.: Social Creativity: Turning Barriers into Opportunities for Collaborative Design. In: Proceedings Pdc'04, Palo Alto CA: CPSR, pp. 152–161 (2004)
14. Fischer, G., Giaccardi, E.: Metadesign: A framework for end-user development. In: Lieberman, H., Paternò, F., Wulf, V. (eds.) End User Development: Empowering People to Flexibly Employ Advanced Information and Communication Technology, pp. 427–457. Kluwer, Dordrecht (2005)
15. Kay, A.: Microelectronics and the personal computer. Sci. Am. 237(3), 230–244 (1977)
16. Kling, R. (ed.): Computerization and Controversy: Value Conflicts and Social Choices. Morgan Kauffman (1996)
17. Kumar, K., Hillergersberg, J.: ERP Experiences and Evolution. Commun. ACM 43(4), 23–26 (2000)
18. Mumford, E.: Effective Systems Design and Requirements Analysis. Wiley, London (1995)
19. Mumford, E.: Ethics Tools for Ethical Change. Macmillan, London (1996)
20. Mumford, E.: Risky ideas in the risk society. J. Inf. Technol. 11, 321–331 (1996)
21. Mumford, E.: The study of socio-technical design: reflections on its successes, failures and potential. Inf. Syst. J. 16, 317–342 (2006)

22. Nonaka, I., Takeuchi, H.: The Knowledge Creating Company. Oxford University Press, Oxford (1995)
23. Schmidt, K.: Of maps and scripts—the status of formal constructs in cooperative work. In: Proceedings of GROUP'97, pp. 138–147, New York: ACM Press (1997)
24. Schmidt, K., Bannon, L.: Taking CSCW seriously: supporting articulation work. CSCW Journal **1**, 7–40 (1992)
25. Schonberger, A.J.: World Class Manufacturing. The Free Press, New York (1986)
26. Star, S.L., Griesemer, J.: Institutional Ecology, 'Translations' and Boundary Objects: Amateurs and Professionals in Berkeley's Museum of Vertebrate Zoology, 1907-39. Soc. Stud. Sci. **19**(3), 387–420 (1989)
27. Suchman, L.: Plans and Situated Actions. Cambridge University Press, New York (1987)
28. Taylor, F.W.: The Principles of Scientific Management. Harper & Brothers, New York (1911)
29. Telier, A., Binder, T., De Michelis, G., Ehn, P., Jacucci, G., Linde, P., Wagner, I.: Design Things. MIT Press, Cambridge (2011)
30. Trist, E.: The evolution of socio-technical systems–a conceptual framework and an action research program. Occasional Paper **2**, 1–67 (1981)
31. Trist, E., Bamforth, K.: Some social and psychological consequences of the longwall method of coal getting. Hum. Relat. **4**, 3–38 (1951)
32. Winograd, T., Flores, C.F.: Understanding Computers and Cognition. A new Foundation for Design. Intellect Books, Wilmington (1986)
33. Wu, X., Zhu, X., Wu, G.-Q., Ding, W.: Data mining with big data. Knowl. Data Eng. IEEE Trans. **26**(1), 97–107 (2014)

Co-production Through ICT in the Public Sector: When Citizens Reframe the Production of Public Services

Andrea Paletti

Abstract Co-production of public services is well known in the public management literature. Many studies show how co-production makes public services not only more efficient but also more effective. It the recent years, the development of several ICT applications and projects have shown that ICT has the potential to make co-production an easy and common practice for all citizens, changing completely how services are delivered on a large scale. The research, after having presented some existing cases of ICTs application that favorite co-production, shows that using ICT for co-production might help the state to deliver public services that generate Public Value. The paper follows with an in depth analysis according to the Actor Network Theory to understand if co-production through ICT might induce structural changes in the public administration allowing in future citizens to be actively involved in the production of public services. The research will conclude by providing a proposal to implement permanently co-production in the public sector.

Keywords Public administration · Co-production · Public value · Actor network theory · Internet of things

1 Introduction and Context

The term co-production was conceptualized to criticize the massive centralization of public management proposed by the dominant theories [1]. Elinor Ostrom, who originally coined the term co-production, won the Nobel Prize in Economy in 2009. She presents co-production as mix of activities that both public service agents and citizens contribute to the provision of public services [2]. However, only in the last

A. Paletti (✉)
London School of Economics, London, UK
e-mail: A.Paletti@lse.ac.uk

© Springer International Publishing Switzerland 2016
L. Caporarello et al. (eds.), *Digitally Supported Innovation*,
Lecture Notes in Information Systems and Organisation 18,
DOI 10.1007/978-3-319-40265-9_10

141

decade, the interest about public sector co-production has found new attention since academics and practitioners have increasingly realised that many public services need the co-participation of citizens to be completely effective.

Although co-production has been largely discussed in the public administration literature, no references or contribution exists to account for the impact of ICTs on the co-production of public services. On the other hand, studies from other fields have seen in ICTs the capability to reshape existing models and frameworks, facilitating new connections within the community, establishing relationships that were not possible before, overcoming problems of geographical dispersion of users and facilitating enormously their participation [3, 4]. These characteristics show how ICTs are strategically important for the success of co-production in the public sector and in proposing new models of participation and of public administration.

However, co-production has to be distinguished from volunteering because citizens act not only to help their community but also to provide services they need for themselves that do not exist, or that are delivered ineffectively [5]. Co-production could be also interpreted as a will of citizens to pursue and propose public values bringing government to concentrate more efforts in collective needs (environment protection, social cohesion, more democratic processes, etc.) [6].

A successful example of co-production and public value is the childcare service in Sweden, where parents voluntarily have created cooperatives to integrate or to offer preschool services to their children, increasing incredibly the quality of the service and making the service available to people that cannot afford private services [7]. In the available researches nearly all the co-production cases show an increase of effectiveness and of cost reduction, proving in small scale experiments or projects the convenience of co-production [6–8]. On the other hand, co-production today is not so diffused or well exploited because there is not an organization or practical channels that make co-production easy and applicable on large scale. ICT has all the properties that can overcome co-production barriers making co-production a common practice for all citizens.

The paper aim to research how co-production is reshaping production of public services and proceeds as follows. First, it provides a wide range presentation of the existing applications developed by citizens that favourite and make easier co-production of public services through the internet of things. Secondly, the co-production through ICT is analysed according to the Public Value paradigm in order to show how the creation of Public Value is intrinsic in co-production practices. There follows an in depth analysis through the Actor Network Theory of how the ICT applications that favourite co-production are gradually changing the existing models of public service production. The final section provides a proposal of a platform to implement co-production in the public administration through the direct involvement of companies and citizens.

2   Co-production Through ICT

ICT is making co-production in the public sector an easier and widely spread practice. There are many apps for smartphones that help citizens to report problems or to be part of the public service. However, looking at Fig. 1 it is possible to see that currently there are three kinds of applications for co-production.

In the first category, we can find applications like Trashout (http://www.trashout. me/) that empowers citizens to report illegal dumps, taking pictures and sending localized information to local authorities. Crimepush (http://crimepush.com/) is another smartphone application that allows citizens to report crime anonymously becoming the eyes and the ears of authorities. The application Liberi di muoversi (http://www.liberidimuoversi.it/map/) allows people with handicaps to report places where there are architectural barriers and places that can be easily accessed through a wheelchair. Another interesting app is Evasori (http://evasori.info/) that allows citizens to report places such as shops or restaurants where they have found fiscal evasion, crowdsourcing all the information on a map and suggesting to the police places that should be controlled.

In the second category, we can find applications to help citizens to crowd source information collected through sensors. An example is AirCasting (http://aircasting. org/) a smartphone application available for Android that empowers users through a portable sensor to analyse the air quality. There is also another sensor Mobosens (http://nanobionics.mntl.illinois.edu/mobosens/) that works according to the same model, analysing the quality of the water through an external device that once connected to the smartphone, processed the data and then send the data on a shared map where everybody can see the quality of the water or polluted areas. Both applications as many other projects, prove that is possible, especially in the future through the internet of things, creating public networks and infrastructures utilizing sensors and devices owned by citizens.

In the third category, it is possible to find applications like Firedepartement (http:// firedepartment.mobi/) and PulsePoint (http://www.pulsepoint.org/) two apps for smartphone that empowers individuals to be part of the rescue operations cooperating actively with paramedics. After registered users have indicated their level of training in cardiopulmonary resuscitation (CPR), they are alerted if someone nearby is affected by hearth attack or needs medical assistance. When the 911 operator receives the call, he is able to see the closest users to the accident. The operator invites trained citizens to reach the area of the accident and to provide CPR to the victim in order to not interrupt the chain of survival until the arrival of the ambulance.

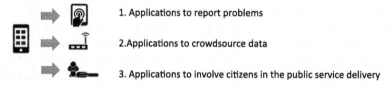

1. Applications to report problems

2. Applications to crowdsource data

3. Applications to involve citizens in the public service delivery

Fig. 1 Type of mobile applications for co-production

These applications able to connect people, sensors and share data with the rest of the community can be also described through the concept of the 'internet of things'. The common definition and vision is that the internet of things links objects such as sensors, tags, smartphones, machine, buildings to the virtual world generating a network of multiple human and non-human agents [9]. Many authors [10] see the internet of things as the enabler for the smart city concept as well as a new way to manage communities based on sharing information and collaboration. In fact, the data collected can improve the ability to forecast problems developing a collective intelligence.

Without ICTs, it would be hardly possible reproducing the connections and the organization that these applications created. Therefore, all these applications, as well as many others, are a clear example of how ICTs could empower citizens to co-produce public services without too many efforts or resources, utilizing common and already available technologies and revolutionizing the existing model of public administration.

3 Co-production Through ICT According to the Public Value Perspective

The existing applications that favourite co-production of public services show that citizens through ICT can also reinvent how public services are delivered according to their own perspective and needs. ICT has empowered citizens to deliver services according to new models. The creation of an application that allows citizens to participate in first aid is not just a new way to deliver a public service together with citizens but it is also a new framework of how public services are delivered. This will to change, the current production of public services can be explained through the paradigm of the Public Value [6] that is intrinsic in the co-production concept. The Public Value paradigm is not the value produced by collective organizations that represent the individual preferences or that pursue the good of the community such as Parliaments, NGOs, government organizations but rather the value that citizens perceived about a specific public good, public service or public policy [11]. Citizens are not just customers of the State and their perception is not only based on the direct benefit they can get from how public services are delivered. Citizens have socio-political values such as aspirations, goals and visions that share with the rest of the community, that make them thinking not as individuals but as part of a community [6, 12].

Therefore citizens evaluate a policy or a public good also according to collective values such as equality, justice, protection of the environment that cannot be evaluated in economic terms and that are more related to the Public Value [11]. This Public Value perspective goes directly against to the New Public Management perspective that thinks that citizens behave just as clients that only want better and more efficient services at a lower price [13]. To understand better the difference between client and citizen perspective we can use an example of a State that decides to not offer anymore the ambulance service to people that do not pay taxes regularly. The ambulance service is a public service and is mainly for emergencies and for people that risk their lives. According to the New Public Management perspective, a citizen behaving just as a customer would be happy of this new law because it would benefit who pays regularly the service making the service more efficient. On the other hand, this new law is not respecting collective values such as equality, justice or the common vision that the emergency service should be free for everyone. This example shows that citizens do no only asses public sector organizations for their ability to deliver efficient services but also for their ability to meet collective expectations [12]. However, Public Value differs according to the culture and is not static because citizens change their collective vision or expectations overtime, making sometimes public services inadequate to meet their perspective [11, 12].

Is the case of how the nuclear disaster of Fukushima led to a radical change in the opinion of Italians and Germans about nuclear energy. In fact, Italians renounced through a referendum to the reintroduction of nuclear power and the Germans accelerated their plans to close their nuclear power reactors [14]. This rapid change of vision among Germans and Italians made inadequate policies and the strategies taken by regularly elected parliaments few years before. However, the mobile applications previously presented, indicate how ICT is enabling today citizens to organize public service delivery according to their current perspective without waiting the political decision of their governments. Therefore, co-production practices naturally generate public value. For example, the application PulsePoints, shows that American citizens, have collectively developed the vision that citizens should be involved in the co-production of first aid services in order to save more people. Consequently they have decided to directly redesign the emergency service through a smartphone application proposing a new model of first aid service that satisfy their current vision of fist aid without passing through policymakers. Other applications such as Trashout or CrimePush and many others similar applications show that citizens are starting perceiving themselves as active actors in the public service production. On the other hand, the current public administration and especially e-government services still perceive citizens as clients and not as active actors [12]. This common will to co-produce public services and the development of these applications show that citizens want to redesign public service delivery to affirm their Public Value perspective. Therefore, ICT is allowing these citizens to change how the public administration delivers services according to their current perspective and ideas forcing public administration to be more flexible and adaptable.

4   ICT for Co-production Is Changing the Public Administration

Extending the co-production of ICT applications for public services to citizens would increase the innovation and the responsiveness of the services [15]. This change of the role of citizens from passive to active actors through ICT is also changing the structure of the public administration. Bovens and Zouridis [16], have already shown how ICT has the power to change the public administration structure and how public services are delivered. However, the difference with the past cases is that this change today is not top-down as in the past but bottom-up and comes from citizens. This means that legislators and public managers are not anymore the only ones that decide how to organize public services. The cases previously shown prove that ICT helps to make political decisions that can change how public sector is shaped and services are produced. According to the Hodgson and Cicmil [17], when standards, infrastructures and categories are implemented in an organization they change how the organization works. In fact, the organization has to adapt to the introduction of a new knowledge, to assimilate the new procedures and to reshape its structure. Behind the introduction of new standards or artefacts there is also a political and ethical meaning [17]. Therefore the assimilation of these ICT applications, has also a political connotation that conflicts with the current structure of the public administration. In fact, these applications show not only that citizens can actively co-produce public services but that they can also create new models of organization to deliver public services. This has clearly a political impact that threats the idea of a public administration just managed by public officers and where there is not space for citizens.

This change in the public administration might find several obstacles. In fact, every time an organization acquires a new technology, infrastructure or standard its actors live a period of stress and alienation [17] that as underlined by Markus [18] can generate resistance. In this case, these applications strongly affect the current organization of the public administration and threat the decisional and political power of many public officers. In addition, co-production increases transparency and then the accountability of public institutions. Furthermore, the Public Sector is usually reluctant to open experiments, to take risks or to implement projects that have been developed by non-public servants [19]. The Actor Network Theory can help to better understand the problems and the process of implementation of co-production to the public sector and how the different actors interact.

Looking at the stage of development of these applications and considering the Actor Network Theory [20] these applications are today in the 'translation phase', trying to modify the structure of the public administration that should be perceived as a network of human and non-human actors. In fact, there are several ICT applications, created by single users and NGOs that are currently involved in changing the existing public administration framework to propose new networks where citizens can start covering an active role. The intermediaries used in this translation process are the smartphone applications previously presented, where are inscribed behaviours and visions that naturally bring citizens to participate and to be involved in the co-production of public services. The translation process that creates or changes a new network has a political nature that in this case consists in making citizens more involved in the production of public services. The first step of the translation process is the "problematization" when actors identifies and explore a problem trying to persuade other actors to accept their favourite solutions and scenarios about how the new network should look like. In this case the problem identified by all the citizens, is the inability of the current public administration model to produce effectively public services and the solution promoted is to use ICT to involve citizens in co-producing public services. In many parts of the world, the translation process is ongoing. In fact, these applications are gradually aligning all the actors to a new network that involves citizens in the co-production and where citizens are not just clients.

However, are still few the cases where the process of translation has been successfully validated through conventions and regulations which have stabilized the network. One of these rare cases, is the IRIS application of Venice Municipality that allows citizens to report damaged streets, illegal dumps and other problems directly to the responsible bureau without calling or writing mails and with the certainty to reach the public officer that might solve their problem [21]. Since the launch of IRIS in Venice in 2008, no other applications for reporting problems in Venice has been created, showing that the network in Venice has been stabilized and the actors have never felt the need to propose new applications to challenge the existing solution. On the other hand, in other parts of Italy many applications such as Decoro Urbano (http://www.decorourbano.org/) or Aid your city (http://www.aidyourcity.com/) have been created and used to report problems but without being fully integrated through conventions with Municipalities. Pisa another Italian city, has its own app to report problems (https://www.androidpit.it) however as it happens in many other cities, the network is still not stabilized because not all the actors are fully aligned and then they continue proposing applications to persuade other actors to choose the application they prefer. Therefore, the Venice case show that when co-production is institutionalized through conventions and norms the rest of the network is temporarily stabilized and the other actors do not try to develop other applications with the same or similar goal. However, beyond the successful IRIS case, there is still not a permanent institutional process of co-production in the public administration that allows citizens to propose new kind of organizations and approaches of public service delivery.

5 Implementing Co-production in the Public Administration

Considering the Actor Network Theory it is therefore necessary to find a way to stabilize the "network" [20] allowing citizens to produce new models of public service that satisfy their changing needs and values. In this new network, the State would become the coordinator and the facilitator of the production in order to generate more Public Value through public services. To reach this goal the final users, in this case the citizens, will be directly involved in the production of ICT applications for the production of public services. This would create an agile, bottom-up and citizen-responsive development process that would improve the innovation reducing costs with the certainty to satisfy citizens' needs [22]. The current proposal is based on the previous research of Fishenden and Thompson [22] where is suggested the importance to build an e-government platform based on open source standards to create an ecosystem of companies in order to reduce the existing oligopoly of few IT companies [23]. However, before creating a platform the government needs to enhance its in-house ICT expertise and skills to successfully adopt and manage an Open Architecture platform [22]. As Google shows, once the platform is created, is necessary to create an ecosystem where the creation of services is completely outsourced to companies, users and other providers [24]. This platform structure is characterized by a centralized power that coordinates and create norms and decentralized structures that develop and deliver services and applications. As already presented in the Digital Era of Governance [25] the creation of a platform would allow new forms of co-creation and co-production not only between government and companies but also between government and citizens.

Social networks, cloud computing, internet of things and emergent digital technologies are opening a new channel of interaction and collaboration between citizens and government [25]. Therefore, the ecosystem of the e-government platform should be opened not only to companies as mentioned by Fishenden and Thompson [22] but also to normal citizens as it happens with Google and Apple. Outsourcing the production to the community would not be something of new. Wikipedia is a successful example of how users can co-produce public goods. However, the structure of Wikipedia allows users to enrich the contents according to predefined rules and frameworks [26]. Considering the experience of Wikipedia [27] and also how Apple manages its market of applications [28, 29], the State should create a platform to collaborate with citizens in order to develop ICT applications for the creation of new services.

Once the trend has been individuated looking at the emergent application features (Fig. 2), the state would open the development of a new module/application on its platform that would work on a national and local scale according to a standardized interface.

The modules could be created by the community and companies. Each module is a project with a specific goal. As the Fig. 3 shows, the module can be used both by local and central government according to their needs and competencies. Once the state has established the rules and a general framework to allow and monitor collaboration, the community (and not the state) starts creating the module according to the "bazar method" [30]. The community would discuss the "to do

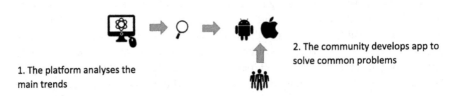

1. The platform analyses the
main trends

2. The community develops app to
solve common problems

Fig. 2 The functioning of the platform

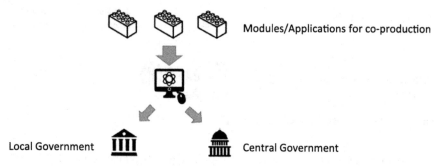

Fig. 3 The modular architecture of the platform

list" as well as the general direction that the development should follow [31]. All members of the community can review and modify the modules. All the users are registered to the platform and their contribution is tracked and awarded by the platform. Considering Fig. 4, once the module is created, a public mix commission composed by public officers and citizens would certify the quality and make the module available on the platform following a similar process already utilized by Apple [28]. The competent authorities responsible in delivering the new public services would be individuated by law in order to avoid misunderstandings or overlapping of duties. Once the application is published, the community could still work on the development of a further and more updated version [24, 27, 31].

The main goal of this platform would be in creating a unique ecosystem of citizens and companies that can freely compete to co-produce the creation of new public services. Basing on the researches about Wikipedia [26, 27, 32] and about Public Value [6, 12] citizens would cooperate because they want to solve common problems (air pollution, criminality, first aid etc.) that the State alone is not able to solve. In addition, they would contribute to the good of the community for a matter of reputation [32] and to affirm their collective aspirations. Shame and honour are probably the most important drivers when all the users registered to the platform could see who is giving more and who is giving less. Utilizing gamification and a dedicated system of incentives would make able citizens to see who contributes to the good of the community. The pressure of the community would incentivize

Fig. 4 Process of certification of a module

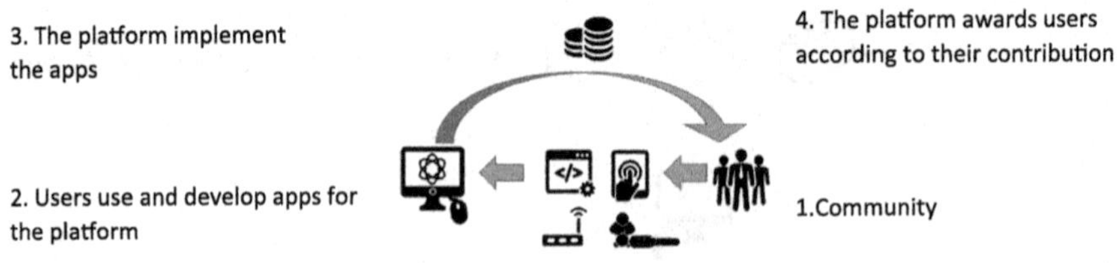

3. The platform implement
the apps

4. The platform awards users
according to their contribution

2. Users use and develop apps for
the platform

1.Community

Fig. 5 Awarding system for users and developers

citizens to behave better and help the co-production of public service [32]. As it possible to see in Fig. 5, co-production can consist both in the development of the applications and in the active participation in co-production of public services (reporting problems, collecting data etc.). In both cases, the platform would award users that contribute more.

6 Conclusions

This research has concentrated on how co-production practices through ICT are changing how public services are delivered and then how the public administration structure is shaped. Although there are many successful cases of co-production of public services through the involvement of citizens, the current public administration model still perceives citizens as costumers. On the other hand, the development of many ICT applications have made co-production an easy practice involving many citizens in collecting data and information about pollution or criminality or in the direct co-production of vital public services such as first aid. According to the Public Value perspective, behind the co-production of public services there is the will of many citizens to create new models of public service production that match their current collective aspirations and ideas and that the current model of public administration is unable to satisfy.

However, these applications are proposing also alternative models of public service delivery that risk to modify the existing public administration structure. Just few cities have started implementing co-production through ICT in their public administration but there is still not a permanent process that can guarantee flexibility and adaptability to the co-production practices. This research tries also to propose an e-government platform that outsources the creation of new modules of public services production to an ecosystem of citizens and companies, nevertheless being a preliminary proposal more research is needed. It would be also interesting to use the framework of Boundary Resources about platforms to understand how to successfully organize the citizen co-production in an ICT context [33]. More research is also needed to better understand the correct implementation of co-production practices through ICT and the possible structural changes that can be generated in the public administration.

References

1. Verschuere, B., Brandsen, T., Pestoff, V.: Co-production: the state of the art in research and the future agenda. Volunt. Int. J. Volunt. Nonprofit Organ. **23**, 1083–1101 (2012). doi:10.1007/s11266-012-9307-8
2. Ostrom: Crossing the great divide: coproduction, synergy, and development. World Dev. **24** (6), 1073–1087 (1996)
3. Bradley, G.: The convergence theory and the good ICT society—trends and visions. Ind. Eng. Ergon. (2009). doi:10.1007/978-3-642-01293-8
4. Hanna, N.K.: Transforming government and building the information society. Innov. Knowl. Manag. 1–25 (2011). doi:10.1007/978-1-4419-1506-1
5. Brandsen, T., Pestoff, V.: Co-production, the third sector and the delivery of public services. Public Manag. Rev. **8**, 493–501 (2006). doi:10.1080/14719030601022874
6. Bovaird, T., Loeffler, E.: From engagement to co-production: the contribution of users and communities to outcomes and public value. Volunt. Int. J. Volunt. Nonprofit Organ. **23**, 1119–1138 (2012). doi:10.1007/s11266-012-9309-6
7. Vamstad, J.: Co-production and service quality: the case of cooperative childcare in Sweden. Volunt. Int. J. Volunt. Nonprofit Organ. **23**, 1173–1188 (2012). doi:10.1007/s11266-012-9312-y
8. Meijer, A.: Co-production in an information age: individual and community engagement supported by new media. Volunt. Int. J. Volunt. Nonprofit Organ. **23**, 1156–1172 (2012). doi:10.1007/s11266-012-9311-z
9. Atzori, L., Iera, A., Morabito, G.: The internet of things: a survey. Comput. Networks **54**(15), 2787–2805 (2010)
10. Schaffers, H., Komninos, N., Pallot, M., Trousse, B., Nilsson, M., Oliveira, A.: Smart cities and the future internet: towards cooperation frameworks for open innova-tion. Futur. Internet Assem. **6656**, 431–446 (2011)
11. Alford, J., Hughes, O.: Public value pragmatism as the next phase of public management. Am. Rev. Public Adm. **38**, 130–148 (2008). doi:10.1177/0275074008314203
12. Cordella, A., Bonina, C.M.: A public value perspective for ICT enabled public sector reforms: a theoretical reflection. Gov. Inf. Q. **29**, 512–520 (2012). doi:10.1016/j.giq.2012.03.004
13. O'Flynn: From new public management to public value: paradigmatic change and managerial implications. Aust. J. Public Adm. **66**(3), 353–366 (2007)
14. Huenteler, J., Schmidt, T.S., Kanie, N.: Japan's post-Fukushima challenge–implications from the German experience on renewable energy policy. Energy Policy **45**, 6–11 (2012)
15. Zouridis, S., Thaens, M., Utrecht, N.: eGovernment: towards a public administration approach. In: 2nd European Conference on e-government, St Catherine's College Oxford, UK, 1–2 Oct 2002, 463 (2002). doi:10.1080/02598272.2003.10800413
16. Bovens, M., Zouridis, S.: From street-level to system-level bureaucracies: how information and communication technology is transforming administrative discretion and constitutional control. Public Adm. Rev. **62**, 174–184 (2002). doi:10.1111/0033-3352.00168
17. Hodgson, D., Cicmil, S.: The politics of standards in modern management: making "the project" a reality. J. Manag. Stud. **44**, 431–450 (2007). doi:10.1111/j.1467-6486.2007.00680.x
18. Markus, M.L.: Power, politics, and MIS implementation. Commun. ACM **26**, 430–444 (1983). doi:10.1145/358141.358148
19. Duivenboden, H.Van, Thaens, M.: ICT-driven innovation and the culture of public administration: A contradiction in terms? Online **13**, 213–232 (2008)
20. Gallon, M.: Actor-network theory—the market test. Sociol. Rev. **47**(S1), 181–195 (1999)
21. Cordella, A., Tempini, N.: E-government and bureaucracy: the role of functional simplification in the case of the Venice municipality. Proc. Transform. Gov. Work tGov'11 **11**, 1–16 (2011)
22. Fishenden, J., Thompson, M.: Digital government, open architecture, and innovation: why public sector it will never be the same again. J. Public Adm. Res. Theory **23**, 977–1004 (2013). doi:10.1093/jopart/mus022

23. Cordella, A., Willcocks, L.: Government policy, public value and IT outsourcing: the strategic case of ASPIRE. J. Strateg. Inf. Syst. **21**, 295–307 (2012). doi:10.1016/j.jsis.2012.10.007
24. Boulos, K., Resch, B., Crowley, D., et al.: Crowdsourcing, citizen sensing and sensor web technologies for public and environmental health surveillance and crisis management: trends, OGC standards and application examples. Int. J. Health Geogr. **10**, 67 (2011). doi:10.1186/1476-072X-10-67
25. Margetts, H., Dunleavy, P., Summers, L.: The second wave of digital-era governance : a quasi-paradigm for government on the Web. R. Soc. (2010)
26. Redondo Olmedilla, J.C.: A review of "Good Faith Collaboration: The Culture of Wikipedia." Inf. Soc. **28**, 53–54 (2012). doi:10.1080/01972243.2011.632286
27. Wielsch, D.: Governance of massive multiauthor collaboration—Linux, Wikipedia, and Other Networks: Governed by Bilateral Contracts, Partnerships, or Something in Between? J. Intellect. Prop. Inf. Technol. E-Commerce Law **1**, 96–108 (2010)
28. Schultz, N., Wulf, J., Zarnekow, R., Nguyen, Q.T.: The new role of developers in the mobile ecosystem: an Apple and Google case study. In: 2011 15th International Conference on Intelligence in Next Generation Networks, ICIN 2011, pp. 103–108 (2011). doi:10.1109/ICIN.2011.6081055
29. Hagiu, A., Yoffie, D.B.: What's Your Google Strategy ? Harv. Bus. Rev. **87**(4), 74–81 (2009)
30. Raymond, E.: The cathedral and the bazaar. Knowl. Technol. Policy **12**(3), 23–49 (1999)
31. Kane, G.C., Ransbotham, S.: Collaborative development in Wikipedia. Collect. Intell. Conf. **2012**, 1–7 (2012)
32. Kuznetsov, S.: Motivations of contributors to Wikipedia. ACM SIGCAS Comput. Soc. **36**, 1–es (2006). doi:10.1145/1215942.1215943
33. Eaton, B., Elaluf-Calderwood, S., Carsten Soresen, Y.Y.: Distributed tuning of boundary resources: the case of Apple's iOS service system. MIS Q. **39**, 217–243 (2015)

3-D Printing in the Spare Parts Supply Chain: An Explorative Study in the Automotive Industry

Marco Savastano, Carlo Amendola, Fabrizio D'Ascenzo and Enrico Massaroni

Abstract Additive manufacturing represents a disruptive technology in comparison to traditional manufacturing. 3-D printing technology discloses companies' inner potential, enabling them to reconsider their strategic positioning, organization, production and distribution processes, offering the potential for new supply chain configurations. Tooling and design processes are greatly simplified, while new materials, shapes, more functional products and applications constantly emerge. More efficient processing methods are able to reduce manufacturing and logistics time and costs in such a way that significant economic and financial benefits can be spread along the entire value chain. The purpose of this research is to shed lights on the state of art of this technique, with a focus on the potential impact on the companies' strategy for the management of spare parts. We considered different scenarios and supply chain configurations related to the Automotive sector, applying the AM to the production of discontinued car parts and evaluating its main benefits.

Keywords Additive manufacturing · 3-D printing · Rapid prototyping · Supply chain management · Spare parts · Automotive industry · On-demand production · Customization · Co-creation · CAD

M. Savastano (✉) · C. Amendola · F. D'Ascenzo · E. Massaroni
Management Department, Sapienza University, Rome, Italy
e-mail: marco.savastano@uniroma1.it

C. Amendola
e-mail: carlo.amendola@uniroma1.it

F. D'Ascenzo
e-mail: fabrizio.dascenzo@uniroma1.it

E. Massaroni
e-mail: enrico.massaroni@uniroma1.it

© Springer International Publishing Switzerland 2016
L. Caporarello et al. (eds.), *Digitally Supported Innovation*,
Lecture Notes in Information Systems and Organisation 18,
DOI 10.1007/978-3-319-40265-9_11

1 Introduction

The possibility to digitalize and produce on a as-needed basis after-sales, in particular spare parts sales, is both a strategic opportunity and a threat for many manufacturers, as the focus of the competition increasingly shifts away from the price and quality of the offerings toward the delivery of value to customers. The accessibility of proper parts and skills whenever a demand occurs, in order to satisfy the needs of customers and reduce downtime and lead time costs, represents the groundwork of maintenance, repair and operations (MRO).

Another important challenge is that companies need to support the previous generation of their products as well as their new products. This obligation amplifies the number of stock keeping units in after-sales inventories and relevant costs [1].

In order to shorten the time of immobilization of a system or a vehicle which has to be repaired, it is essential to have in any place and at any time the availability of the part needed to be replaced. For instance, it is made possible when there is on the shelf an exhaustive and comprehensive stock of spare parts. This solution results in higher inventory levels in different locations obviously connected to high costs, and is not always technically achievable, mostly when the part to be replaced relates to a discontinued model. The alternative strategy is to be able to create, on demand and in situ, the parts required for the manufacturing process or the maintenance intervention. In this context, the use of additive manufacturing (AM) technologies seems to be particularly appropriate [2]. Furthermore, the ability to provide the required parts with high fulfillment rates at low costs is a major challenge to overcome and a goal that digital manufacturing technologies promise to achieve [3]. In fact, the recent emergence of additive manufacturing technologies creates an opportunity to produce parts on demand in order to improve supply chain dynamics [4].

Final products are created by adding different layers of material, starting from a computer aided 3D solid model, without the use of additional fixtures and cutting tools. Consequently, manufacturing lead time can be reduced significantly. In addition, the high material and resource wastage factors are also avoided. In particular, AM technology offers two opportunities: (i) to redesign products with fewer components and (ii) to realize products near the customers (i.e. distributed manufacturing), simplifying the traditional supply chain and reducing the delivery time as well as warehousing, packaging and transportation costs [4].

The idea is that, by adopting 3-D printing technologies, retaining old designs reproducible on demand becomes less costly than excess inventories of spare parts depending on an unpredictable demand [5]. Following this trend, in the present work we argue about the possible integration of the aforementioned technologies into the spare parts supply chain of a specific automotive company.

The purpose of this paper is to explore the impact of 3-D printing application for the production of spare parts in the Automotive industry, with an emphasis on the use of distributed manufacturing strategy to reduce inventory cost and increase the availability of replacement parts for models out of production from 10 years or more, which present an higher degree of complexity.

In particular, our work is structured as follows: the first part provides a review of the literature relevant to our research, in which we present a definition of Additive Manufacturing and 3-D Printing followed by current and possible applications of these technologies in different sectors. Consequently, in the second part we describe the relevant advantages and disadvantages of this new process from several viewpoints and present our hypothesis. Different supply chain configurations for Automotive spare parts industry are further considered. Finally, conclusions and future research avenues are shown.

2 Literature Review

2.1 Additive Manufacturing and 3-D Printing

The American Society for Testing and Materials (ASTM International) defined AM as the "process of joining materials to make objects from 3D model data, usually layer upon layer" [6]. In 1983 design engineer Charles "Chuck" Hull, frustrated by the long wait-time and expense to have new injection molded parts produced, invented the "stereolithography", overcoming these problems and allowing rapid casting of metal parts for industrial manufacturers, such as automotive companies. This process, which forms the basis of actual 3-D printing, differs from traditional production processes in one fundamental way: it is not subtractive [7, 8]. In fact, opposed to a conventional machining process, which takes away superfluous or undesirable material from a block of workpiece, this new technique produces parts by building one layer upon another in an horizontal manner [2]. As a result, it would increase efficiency and help companies to improve the productivity of materials by eliminating waste. Indeed 3-D printing, which employs an additive manufacturing process also known as direct manufacturing, is a digital technology for producing physical objects by fusing a variety of materials with a laser, starting from a three-dimensional computer aided design (CAD) file. This technology, originally introduced as rapid prototyping (RP), was employed by engineers and designers as a method for producing rough physical prototypes of final products. Nowadays, as 3-D printers have become more capable and able to work with a broader variety of materials, including production-grade plastics and metals, additive manufacturing can be used for creating any kind of good, from plastic trinkets and small toys on $300 machines to finished titanium aircraft component parts on industrial printers sold for more than $1 million [7, 8]. Moreover, printer basic models are now available through different channels: they can be purchased not only in specialty stores but also at usual electronics retailers such as Amazon, Ebay, and Wal-Mart. This trend feeds the growth of makers' communities (hobbyists) and FabLab (i.e. *fabrication laboratory*) within universities and business incubators.

According to Terry Wohlers, principal at Wohlers Associates in Fort Collins, which has tracked 3-D printing and additive manufacturing for 20 years, more than 20 % of the output of 3D printers results now in final products rather than prototypes. He also predicted that this datum will rise to 50 % by 2020 [9].

McKinsey recently reported that the capabilities of 3-D printing hardware are evolving rapidly, since now it is possible to build larger components and reach greater precision with finer resolution at higher speeds and lower costs. Together, these advances have brought the technology to appear "ready to emerge from its niche status and become a viable alternative to conventional manufacturing processes in an increasing number of applications" [10].

Based on our review of the existing literature regarding AM technologies and its applications in many industries (i.e. aerospace, healthcare, consumer market, etc.), even in the production of spare parts [1, 2, 4], we found that achievable advantages and critical improvements required to enable distributed production based on AM technologies specifically in Automotive supply chains weren't properly investigated. Since 3-D printing evolves to become a common method of producing final parts, further studies of this computer integrated technology appear necessary. The goal of the present research is to address this gap by estimating the potential impact of additive manufacturing and its future improvements on the configuration of spare parts supply chains in the Automotive industry. In order to reach our purpose, specific hypothesis will be explored.

2.2 Production Process

The additive manufacturing production process can be split into three subsequent steps:

1. Design
2. Printing
3. Post production

The *design phase* (1) begins with generating a three-dimensional CAD model of the object to be produced, including its details and dimensions. Alternatively, users can 3-D scan existing products in different ways, with simple but quite inaccurate scanners made for mobile devices (e.g. iSense 3D scanner), by making 3D models from simple pictures (i.e., 123-D Catch, etc.), or with specific and more powerful 3-D scanners (e.g. MakerBot Digitizer and Rubicon 3D). Once a product is scanned, it can be manipulated using 3-D free design programs such as Blender, 3-DTin, Google SketchUp and TinkerCAD, or more professional and expensive ones like AutoCAD and Pro/Engineer. Recently, a number of online 3D printing services like Shapeways, MakerBot's Thingiverse, or Ponoko have emerged via which users can download, upload or share (either for free or for a fee) the designs for all sorts of products. Once the design stage is completed, the resulting model is exported in the 3-D printer-readable STL (an industry standard stereo-lithography format) file extension.

During the *printing phase* (2), the three-dimensional CAD file will be converted and sliced into very thin two-dimensional (2-D) digital cross sections (layers) by a computer program. Then, the 2D layers are sent one layer at a time to the three-dimensional printing machine [1]. The machine produces the object by building each layer on top of the previous one, utilizing different solidification methods of raw material in its production chamber [11]. Three methods are available for different types of raw materials: Stereolithography (SLA), Fused Deposition Modeling (FDM), also known as Fused Filament Fabrication (FFF), and Selective Laser Sintering (SLS). The process may take from a few minutes to a few days to create an object, depending on its size and required production precision.

To conclude the process, the *post production phase* (3) concerns the surface treatment. Even if today the overall shape and mechanical fit of printed objects seems to be the primary goal of 3-D printing, for many products this phase is essential and consists of deburring, honing, polishing and painting the new objects. Some goods require post-production soldering and friction-welding of separately 3-D printed parts to obtain the final object [5]. For instance, a 3-D printed metal door handle could be polished, painted, or gold-plated to be not just functional, but also aesthetically pleasant. The production process is represented in Fig. 1.

An important benefit of additive manufacturing, which will be stressed later in this work, is that it usually doesn't require any assembly to produce the final object.

2.3 Actual Applications and Leading Industrial Sectors

The first two industrial revolutions, through the mechanisation of the textile industry and the mass production of the 20th century triggered by Henry Ford's moving assembly line, made people richer and more urban. Now we are experiencing a third revolution, whereas manufacturing is going digital. A number of remarkable technologies are converging: clever software, novel materials, more

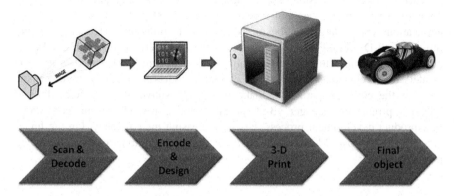

Fig. 1 A representation of 3-D printing production process

dexterous robots, new processes (i.e. 3-D printing) and a complete range of web-based services [12].

3-D printing has been compared to such disruptive technologies as digital books (i.e. e-books) and music downloads (i.e. MP3s) which enable consumers to order their selections online, allow firms to profitably serve small market segments, and permit companies sometimes to operate with no physical stores and with little or no unsold finished goods inventory.

As with previous technologies, 3D printing would mature in those markets where there is an advantage to be gained (either by reducing costs, times and waste or producing highly customized goods). It can be a great complement for the local manufacturing industry, which is today in search of higher levels of customization and competitiveness [13].

Whether or not a specific 3-D application is technically possible or economically feasible largely depends on its production volume, part size, complexity, and material cost. According to some studies [14], 3-D printing is cost effective with plastic injection molding of volumes around 1000 items. In a different research, Sedacca [15] states that this production technology is competitive with plastic injection molding on production runs of 50–5000 units [15]. In the future, some experts believe that efficiency of production will be increased by the wider adoption by firms and consumers of 3-D printing to produce finished goods, which will also reduce raw material costs. Advances in AM have enabled this technology to be employed across a broader range of applications. Earlier versions of 3-D printers could only utilize laser-hardened acrylics, resulting often in the production of fragile parts which required post-manufacturing treatment. Currently, a wider range of materials can be used and more companies will join as the range of printable materials continues to expand. In fact, a key driver of 3-D printers growth is the increasing set of materials available: in addition to basic plastics and photosensitive resins, these already include aluminium; super alloys, such as nickel-based and cobalt chromium; stainless steel; titanium; polymers; ceramics; cement; glass and new thermoplastic composites [5, 16].

Current applications of 3-D printing include: mass-customized products, low production volumes of small-sized parts (e.g. ball bearings) and items having complex design, prototypes and mockups, replacement parts, medical and dental applications [5]. A large number of companies, in different sectors, has already introduced 3-D printing tools. In particular, the Alessi company, a famous Italian designer and manufacturer of high-quality housewares, in 2004 started to use 3-D printers to develop plastic prototypes of new products to obtain a more realistic view of the complex parts that make up its innovative designs. According to Alessi's prototype manager, 3-D printing cut 5–6 weeks from company's new-product development process, largely increasing the efficiency. On the financial side, it also costs Alessi about 70 % less than the traditional method of making prototypes [17].

In the Aerospace industry, the partnership between U.S. Department of Defense, Lockheed Martin, Cincinnati Tool Steel, and Oak Ridge National Laboratory is developing a capability for printing most of the endo and exoskeletons of jet fighters, including the body, wings, internal structural panels, embedded wiring and antennas, and soon the central load-bearing structure. So-called Big Area Additive Manufacturing (BAAM) makes such large-object fabrication possible by using a huge gantry with computerized controls to move the printers into position. At the end of this process, the only assembly required will be the installation of plug-and-play electronics modules for navigation, communications, weaponry, and electronic countermeasure [16]. Avio Aero, a GE Aviation business working on the design, production and maintenance of components and systems for the civil and military aeronautics industry, in 2013 launched in Cameri (Novara, Italy) one of the largest plants in the world (2400 m^2) designed specifically for additive manufacturing. This technology enables any shape of solid object to be produced through a combination of special metal alloys. Therefore, Avio Aero is using 3-D printing to produce mechanical transmissions and low pressure turbines, representing the centre of excellence for the entire General Electric group in this field. The new plant is able to accommodate up to 60 machines for producing components using AM. The plant employs two specific AM technologies: Electron Beam Melting (EBM), which uses an electron beam in the powder melt process, and the Direct Metal Laser Sintering, which consists of using a laser beam to melt metallic powders. Avio Aero's investments in innovation have been constant over the years: regarding AM technology, including the new plant, they reached the area of 20 million euro in the past 4 years. This datum emphasize how Aerospace is one of the most research-intensive sectors using 3-D printing [18].

Regarding the automotive industry, in 2014 Local Motors, Cincinnati Incorporated's BAAM Machine and Oak Ridge National Laboratory, in collaboration with the U.S. Department of Energy's (DOE), presented the world's first 3D-printed car at the annual International Manufacturing Technology Show (IMTS) of Chicago. The vehicle called "Strati" has been 3D printed in one piece using direct digital manufacturing over 44 h, then rapidly assembled by the Local Motors team. Only mechanical components, like battery, electric motor, wiring, and suspension are sourced from a variety of suppliers, including Renault which provided equipments from its electric powered city car "Twizy" [19].

This year, using the BAAM system the Oak Ridge National Laboratory created a new 3-D printed vehicle: a replica of the classic Shelby Cobra, in celebration of the racing car's 50th anniversary. The team took six weeks to design, manufacture and assemble the Shelby, including 24 h of printing time. The car was showcased in January at the 2015 North American International Auto Show in Detroit [20].

The medical and healthcare industry is one of the key industries for new developments of 3-D printing, as this technology can replicate the human shape more accurately than traditional manufacturing techniques. The most common medical applications of the technology are hearing aids, orthopedics and dental implants (more than half a million patients worldwide already, according to IBISWorld, 2013). Further researches and uses in this field include the possibility of bioprinting live cells and tissue (i.e. University of Toronto's Bio Printer project is exploring the use of 3D-printed tissue for the treatment of burned patients), and bone replacements and support structures for growing body parts.

Lastly, consumer market appears to be the field where 3D printing will experience the biggest growth, even outpacing the enterprise market in the short term. In fact, aside from firms, 3-D printers has the potential to bring the factory into consumers' living room, enabling their creativity [7]. Nevertheless, the definitive success of this sector depends mostly on the irruption of a compelling application that would induce consumers to embrace the technology, a "killer app" that, in connection with reduced prices, will finally bring the era of self-production into consumer homes [13].

Currently, 3-D printing accounts for only 28 % of the total manufacturing sector [21], but the market seems destined to grow up fast. Gartner research suggests that this technology has already reached an inflection point, and predicts that the total number of consumer and enterprise 3D printer shipments will grow from 38,002 units in 2012 to 1,083,496 units in 2017, with a compound annual growth rate of 95.4 % [22]. According to Wohlers Report, in terms of turnover the sector may reach \$6 billion in 2017 and exceed \$10 billion in 2021 [23]. Rapid prototyping, small production volumes and customized products will keep driving the commercial usage of 3-D printers in the short term while new niches and wider applications will emerge.

The range of enterprise utilizations of 3-D printing varies depending on the sector and company size [13]. Table 1 shows the sectors expected to see the greater growth in the use of this technology, according to different field studies.

Moreover, a survey conducted by Wohlers [21] indicates which industries are being served by AM technologies and the relevant approximate revenues (as a percentage). Results are shown in Fig. 2.

The chart shows that Consumer products/electronics is the leading industrial sector, followed by Automotive. Medical/dental has established itself as a strong sector for AM and results the third largest over the past years.

Table 1 Estimate of the sectors with highest growth in 3-D printing adoption

Research reference	Industry 1	Industry 2	Industry 3
Wholers	Consumer	Automotive	Medical/dental
Gartner	Consumer	Industrial	Manufacturing
IBISWorld	Aerospace	Medical	Consumer
Frost and Sullivan	Aerospace	Automotive	Medicine
Morgan Stanley	Aerospace	Medical	Consumer

Source MaRS Report 2013

Fig. 2 Industries served and approximate revenues (by percent) for additive manufacturing *Source* Wohlers Report 2013

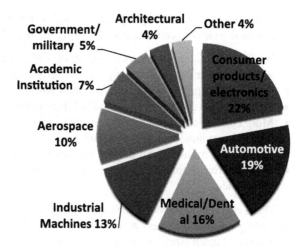

Architectural 4%

Other 4%

Government/ military 5%

Academic Institution 7%

Consumer products/ electronics 22%

Aerospace 10%

Automotive 19%

Industrial Machines 13%

Medical/Dent al 16%

3 Business Impact: Actual and Potential Advantages and Disadvantages of AM Technologies

In this section we will consider advantages and disadvantages of 3-D printing over the conventional manufacturing methods from two different viewpoints: supply-side and demand-side. This analysis will be carried out with reference to the aforementioned sectors. Some important drivers made possible to 3-D printing technology to reach an exciting tipping point, pushing companies to invest in it as a production technology. These drivers can be summarised as follows [24]:

- *Rapid cost reduction:* 3D printers' cost and size decreased, while their accuracy, strength and materials supported improved, becoming a feasible technology for makers and manufacturers;
- *Increase in quality:* higher resolution for industrial printers (i.e. 10 μ) with increased strength and finish quality;
- *Increase in variety of supported materials:* we already discussed how 3D printers have become able to work with a broader variety of materials, including production-grade plastics and metals;
- *Expiration of critical patents:* Chuck Hull's 1984 Additive Manufacturing patent expired in 2009, giving the possibility to the open source community to join the new sector, leading to rapid innovation and improvements. Many other critical patents in the industry will expire in the next years.

From a *supply-side viewpoint*, AM technology with its quick advancements and inherent capabilities, has the potential to fundamentally revolutionize manufacturing operations and supply chain configurations [12]. In fact, its characteristics make this production method a potentially disruptive technology for operations and supply chain management.

Holmstrom et al. [3] highlighted the following benefits of AM methods in comparison with conventional manufacturing methods [3]:

- No need for tooling (since economies of scale does not exist with this technology, customization and design revisions are always possible).
- Feasibility of producing small production batches economically.
- Possibility for quickly change design (customized products).
- More economical custom product manufacturing (batch of one) plus the capability to produce complex geometries (ideally, with 3-D printing the cost of producing a million equal units is the same as one million different pieces).
- Potential for simplifying supply chains, with shorter lead times and lower inventories.

These characteristics may enable the supply chain managers to produce any part (including customized ones) at any time with an enhanced flexibility in terms of locations and batch sizes, significantly reducing the concerns about massive tooling costs. Accordingly, AM will offer original equipment manufacturer companies the opportunity to modify their supply chain configurations by introducing distributed production. This benefit would be turned into location elasticity: (i) supply chains will become more location elastic, bringing manufacturing closer to consumer; (ii) transportation of fewer finished goods will alter global trade flows and logistics settings.

Making low-volume, high-value and customised components is definitely of great interest for companies, but could additive manufacturing really compete with mass-production techniques that have been evolving for over a century? Established techniques are unlikely to be swept away in the short run, especially for mass production of standardized products. However, it is already clear that factories will have 3-D printers working alongside milling machines, presses, foundries and plastic injection-moulding equipment [9]. In fact, AM doesn't offer economies of scale but it avoids the weakness of standard manufacturing concerning the lack of flexibility. That's why it has been widespread for producing one-offs such as prototypes and rare replacement parts. Since each unit is built independently, it can easily be modified to accommodate improvements, changing fashion or to suit unique requests.

At the same time, although the direct costs of producing goods with these new methods and materials are often higher, the greater flexibility afforded could make total costs even substantially lower. And as cost of AM equipments and materials fall, while speed and precision rise, the process increasingly makes sense even at higher scale.

Additive manufacturing also allows to reduce the ecological footprint of actual manufacturing systems and their reliance on physical distribution channels, in order to solve a part of today's intensifying pollution problems. This would benefit both supply-side and demand-side. Printing objects closer to the point of consumption has a positive impact in reducing road and air miles and related delivery times.

Furthermore, in the aerospace and automotive industries, 3-D printing will most often be used in the chase of performance gains. Jet fighters and vehicles fuel efficiency could be improved by reducing their weight, without concerning about this could made them less structurally sturdy. The new technology allows producers to hollow out a part to make it lighter (even 60 %) and more fuel-efficient, since without manufacturing constraints parts can be better optimized for their purpose, and incorporate internal structures that provide greater tensile strength, durability, and resistance to impact. Moreover, new materials with greater heat and chemical resistance can be used in various spots in a product [16]. For instance, the firm EADS started producing planes structures with additive manufacturing, using titanium powder. With this technique, they require only 10 % of the raw material that would be needed otherwise, less energy consumption and time. Lightness is critical in the aircraft sector. A weight reduction of 1 kg in an airliner will save around $3,000-worth of fuel per year as well as cut carbon-dioxide emissions [9].

From a *demand-side viewpoint,* in addition to what we already argued (reduced delivery times, increased sustainability, flexibility, and response speed), a primary advantage of 3-D printing is to allow a great deal of customization. This new process will enhance the concept of customization to an higher level by:

• enabling a real product customization according to personal and demographic needs;
• making possible new retail models to emerge, by involving consumers in the product design process (co-creation) or making them able to create their own products at home.

Table 2 shows schematically advantages and disadvantages of AM technologies from the different perspectives analysed in the text.

Table 2 Advantages and disadvantages of AM/3-D printing technologies

	Advantages	Disadvantages
Supply side	– Enhanced production flexibility in terms of locations (distributed production) and batch sizes ("batches of one")	– No economies of scale
		– Higher direct costs of production
	– On demand production: no unsold products	
	– Reduced costs of logistics. Simplified supply chains: shorter lead times and lower inventories	
	– Higher products' performance	
Demand side	– Reduced delivery times and improved response speed	– Relatively high prices and limited diffusion of 3-D printers
	– Highly customized goods	
	– Co-creation	
	– Consumer self-production	
Ecological footprint	– Reduced pollution, energy consumption and material waste	

So, companies need to understand how their customers could be better served in an era of additive manufacturing and anticipate their future needs. They have to evaluate what designs and features are now possible for their offer that were not in the past, and which aspects can be improved since production restrictions and delivery delays have been eliminated.

3.1 3-D Printing Versus Mass Customization

Based on its characteristics, 3-D Printing has been both compared and contrasted with mass customization [5]. In fact, these two processes present similarities and differences, mainly in terms of manufacturing technology and logistics requirements.

Concerning the differences, while mass customization uses different combinations of pre-assembled modular parts or delayed differentiation strategies such as postponement (i.e. Dell produces personal computers by assembling different hardware parts based on consumers' preferences), 3-D printing uses CAD models and AM technologies to create products by fusing a variety of raw materials with a laser. For this reason, pieces that with traditional manufacturing techniques are used to be molded separately and then assembled, with AM can be produced as one piece in a single run, with no assembly required. According to GE Aviation, which has switched to printing the fuel nozzles of certain jet engines, this represent a significant advantage. Indeed, a nozzle normally assembled from twenty different cast parts can now be printed in one piece, with a cut in cost of manufacturing of 75 % [16]. In addition, mass customization is a team-based process, while 3-D printing is an automated process controlled by a CAD software.

In terms of supply chain settings, on the one hand mass customization relies on multiple suppliers for the component parts needed, requiring a high degree of integration in order to have always the right parts available, in the right quantities at the right moment; on the other one 3-D printing implies readily-available supplies that can be procured from a small number of vendors.

Due to these differences, these two processes are usually applied to the production of different range of goods (but this selection will change over the next years).

Mass customization typical products are: watches, computers, windows, and fast fashion apparel. On the contrary, 3-D printing has been applied to create models, prototypes, replacement parts, dental crowns and artificial limbs.

Regarding similarities, the two processes have in common certain economic characteristics. In fact, they both:

- *Produce custom products at relatively low prices* in comparison to traditional mass-production;
- *minimize inventory risk* since product are made exclusively after an order occurs;

Table 3 Differences and similarities of mass customization and 3-D printing

	Characteristic	Mass customization	3-D printing
Differences	Manufacturing technology	– Different combinations of pre-assembled modular parts or delayed differentiation strategies	– Digital manufacturing based on CAD models and AM technologies
		– Assembly required	– No assembly required
	Supply chain configuration	– Highly-integrated supply chain management with Just-in-time (JIT) inventory replenishment	– Readily available supplies from multiple vendors
Similarities	Economic advantages	– Produce custom products at relatively low prices	
		– Minimize inventory risk	
		– No unsold products inventory	
		– Improved working capital management	

- have no unsold products inventory;
- improve working capital management since goods are paid before being produced.

Table 3 summarizes similarities and differences of the two processes.

4 Research Design

The research goal is to explore possible positive correlations between the adoption of AM technologies in the Automotive industry and improved efficiency of the supply chain. In particular, two specific research questions directed the design and execution of our research:

(1) What are the potential impacts of 3-D printing technologies on the company's spare parts management strategy?
(2) Is this transition convenient for the company, in terms of improved efficiency, cost effectiveness and increased service level provided?

According to evidence presented so far, we decided to build up our study focusing on the application of additive manufacturing in a specific sector (Automotive), in the production of spare parts for a discontinued vehicle. This category of vehicles involves particularly unpredictable demand (which presents an extremely random component) for its parts, making requirements planning complex and uncertain. Moreover, relevant spare parts presents a long warehousing time which effects inventory management costs, and involves the immobilization of capital.

Our starting point was the regulatory standard that obliges auto manufacturers to ensure the availability of spare parts on the market for 10 years after the end production of any model [25]. Some companies offer a temporal limit even longer.

For our study we needed a model with the following features:

- city car (A-segment; e.g. first generation Smart ForTwo by Mercedes);
- widespread on the market;
- out of production;
- characterized by an high percentage of plastic parts (internal/external).

After evaluating different possibilities, we finally chose these characteristics in order to benefit the most from the AM advantages shown in previous paragraphs. According to them, in fact, an old car usually requires a low volume of demanded spare parts which can be satisfied by small production batches. In addition, we focused on a basket of plastic parts since 3-D printing is a mature technology within these material productions, offering relatively lower costs and a wide number of data from market applications, which allows the possibility to make reliable prediction models.

Our hypothesis is that decentralizing the production of specific spare parts categories by adopting the additive manufacturing technologies, companies would achieve better performances in terms of costs and times reduction, and an increase value provided to the customer.

Following a deductive approach, we considered the following alternative spare parts provision scenarios:

(1) The *actual scenario*, with a supply chain configuration characterized by a traditional centralized production. It is based on the spare parts supplier's current practice which requires high logistics costs of handling/transporting genuine parts from the headquarters' warehouse to the local logistics centres of different countries. In addition, we have to consider costs of:

- Inventory management
- Immobilization of capital
- Inventory obsolescence
- Warehouse rent
- Maintenance
- Personnel
- 3PLs (third-party logistics providers)

(2) The *distributed production scenario*. We assumed that the possible future decentralization of production and expected improvements in AM technologies [1] will allow companies to produce spare parts "on demand", closer to the consumption points. Shorter traveling distance for products or parts not only saves money, it also saves time (e.g. down-time, delivery time, waiting time, etc.). In this configuration, transportation for inventory replenishment and relevant costs are estimated to be not relevant. In fact, past studies showed how 3-D printing technologies can benefit both firms and consumers. From an inventory management perspective, firms can save space and costs by on-demand reproduction of stock items with a 3-D printer rather than keeping them stockpiled in anticipation of a future demand. Indeed, for many industries, additive manufacturing can become the new *kanban* by providing a true

just-in-time inventory management solution [8]. According to this perspective, companies could no longer keep the physical items/parts, but printable files containing their original designs.

As we have previously discussed, 3-D printers offer the possibility of realizing any type of shape without particular limitations or additional machining. So, in this second configuration we wouldn't have to consider transportation/inventory costs but the necessary investments in AM machines and their depreciation costs.

However, an alternative solution to such high investments is possible: some big players (e.g. eBay, IBM, Autodesk, Materialise, Stratasys, 3D Systems, etc.) already in the business of additive manufacturing, are developing the platforms on which other companies will build and connect to. In particular, some companies are already setting up contract "printer farms" that will effectively commoditize the making of products on demand [16].

Following this business model (3), the manufacturing of original spare parts could be outsourced from automobile manufacturers to these printer farms, granting the use of items' original designs in exchange for payment of royalties on units sold.

Radicalizing this process, in the future if firms enabled the downloading of repair instructions as well as the 3-D printing pars needed, they would not only capture the market of parts suppliers, but also speed up the abovementioned repair or replacement process for their customers. Strongly depending on the future development and diffusion of 3-D printers over end users, they would be able also to print small-sized parts on their own, after purchasing the model file from the manufacturer.

The matrix in Fig. 3 represent the different possible scenarios above outlined.

Fig. 3 Different scenarios and supply chain configurations

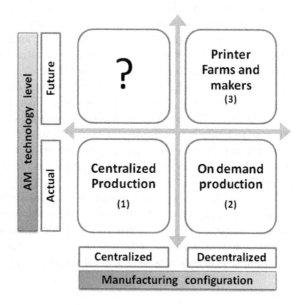

5 Conclusions and Future Research Directions

This study examined the state of art of additive manufacturing and 3-D printing technologies among different sectors. It also provides a framework of *pros and cons* characterizing this disruptive revolution, that would help companies to reconsider their management strategies and business models.

According to our research questions, we analyzed some practical evidences and estimated the benefits from both supply and demand sides in specific fields (automotive, aerospace, biomedical and consumer market).

Based on the possible evolution and adoption of additive techniques and 3-D printers, different scenarios could be possible (see Fig. 3).

In a hybrid world of traditional and new manufacturing methods, producers would have many more options. They could decide which components or items to move to additive manufacturing, and in what order according to their strategic plans. Indeed, not every component will be the right candidate for this new process and reap its benefits (cost reductions, performance improvements, or both). Companies should understand the favorable characteristics in order to determine the right ones. As already mentioned, they include components with a high labor-cost element (i.e. time-consuming assembly and secondary machining processes), complex tooling requirements, relatively low production volumes (which involve high tooling costs), high obsolescence or waste rates [10]. If we compare 3-D printing with another disruptive technology, the Internet, we can find similarities according to the impact on the companies' strategy. On this topic Porter [26] argued that the best way of integrating the Internet into company's overall strategy and operations is in the perspective of complementing, rather than cannibalizing, established competitive approaches and creating systemic advantages that competitors cannot copy. Therefore, the right question is not whether to use the new process/technology or traditional methods to compete, but how to use both coordinated in order to obtain the greatest strategic advantage [26]. Naturally, it will be necessary to rethink business models and align internal/core resources to the new technology in order to fully exploit its potential.

Forward-looking manufacturers have to lay out a road map to determine the best strategy in adopting additive manufacturing. There will be much competition among incumbents and upstarts in order to capture shares of the enormous value this new technology will create and reach the first-mover advantage (FMA) on the market. Entrepreneurs and managers would need to determine whether it's wise to wait for this fast-evolving technology to mature before making certain investments or whether the risk of waiting becomes too great. Their answers will differ, nevertheless for all of them it's clear that the time for strategic thinking is right now.

For instance, BMW and Honda, among other automakers, are moving toward the additive manufacturing of many industrial tools and end-use car parts in their factories and dealerships. This is due to new metal, composite plastic, and carbon-fiber materials now available for use in 3-D printers [16].

Another benefit from the application of this new process regards the environmental aspect: it allows producers to reduce material waste; energy consumption; pollution due to product transportation and fuel consumption due to the lower weight of printed parts and materials in comparison to machined ones.

The main barriers to the effective implementation of this model are today consisting in lack of adequate standards regarding the certification of raw materials, machines and manufacturing processes, and final products. Furthermore, in order to expand its application to a large scale production, it would certainly need further development and innovation. This represents the big challenge now.

Since the present work is an explorative research, further studies would be necessary to confirm and quantify the real convenience of this new process. In order to have reliable data and integrate this research with richer insights, in-depth interviews with managers and quantitative analysis based on big data-sets are needed.

References

1. Khajavi, S.H., Partanen, J., Holmström, J.: Additive manufacturing in the spare parts supply chain. Comput. Indus. **65**, 50–63 (2014)
2. Pérès, F., Noyes, D.: Envisioning e-logistics developments: making spare parts in situ and on demand. state of the art and guidelines for future developments. Comput. Indus. **57**, 490–503 (2006)
3. Holmström, J., Partanen, J., Tuomi, J., Walter., M.: Rapid manufacturing in the spare parts supply chain: alternative approaches to capacity deployment. J. Manuf. Technol. Manag. **21** (6), 687–697 (2010)
4. Liu, P., Huang, S.H., Mokasdar, A., Zhou, H., Hou, L.: The impact of additive manufacturing in the aircraft spare parts supply chain: supply chain operation reference (Scor) model based analysis. Prod. Plann. Control: The Manag. Oper. **25**(13–14), 1169–1181 (2013)
5. Berman, B.: 3-D printing: the new industrial revolution. Bus. Horizons **55**, 155–162 (2012)
6. ASTM 2010: Standard terminology for additive manufacturing technologies. http://www.astm.org/
7. Hessman, T.: Take 5: Q&A with Chuck Hull, Co-Founder. 3D Systems. Industry Week (2013)
8. Kietzmann, J., Leyland, P., Berthon, P.: Disruptions, decisions, and destinations: enter the age of 3-d printing and additive manufacturing. Bus. Horizons **58**, 209–215 (2015)
9. The Economist: 3D Printing: The Printed World. http://www.economist.com/node/18114221 (2011)
10. Cohen, D., Sargeant, M., Somers, K.: 3-D printing takes shape. McKinsey Q. http://www.mckinsey.com/insights/manufacturing/3-d_printing_takes_shape (2014)
11. Gibson, I., Rosen, D.W., Stucker, B.: Additive Manufacturing Technologies: Rapid Prototyping to Direct Digital Manufacturing. Springer, New York, USA (2009)
12. The Economist: The Third Industrial Revolution. http://www.economist.com/node/21553017 (2012)
13. MaRS Market Insights: Layer-by-Layer: Opportunities in 3D printing technology. Trends, growth drivers and the emergence of innovative applications in 3D printing (2013)
14. The Economist: Print Me a Stradivarius. http://www.economist.com/node/18114327 (2011)
15. Sedacca, B.: Hand built by lasers. Eng. Technol. **6**(1), 58–60 (2011)
16. D'Aveni, R.: The big idea. The 3-D Printing Revolution. Harvard Bus. Rev. 40–48 (2015)

17. D Systems: 3D Printer Case Study. http://www.3dsystems.com/sites/www.3dsystems.com/files/3DS_CS_Alessi.pdf (2010)
18. Avio Aero, https://www.avioaero.com/Press-releases/AVIO-AERO-Piedmont-witnesses-the-birth-of-3D-printing-for-the-aeronautics-industry-of-the-futuress
19. IMTS, http://www.imts.com/media/imts_releases/20140908.html
20. Oak Ridge National Laboratory, http://www.ornl.gov/ornl/news/news-releases/2015/3-d-printed-shelby-cobra-highlights-ornl-rd-at-detroit-auto-show
21. Wohlers Associates: State of Additive Manufacturing (2013)
22. Gartner, Inc.: Forecast: 3D Printers, Worldwide (2013)
23. Il Sole 24 ORE: Fabbrica 4.0: La Rivoluzione della Manifattura Digitale (2015)
24. IBM Institute for Business Value: The New Software-Defined Supply Chain (2013)
25. Cavalieri, S., Pinto, R.: Orientare al Successo la Supply Chain. Isedi (2007)
26. Porter, M.E.: Strategy and the internet. Harvard Bus. Rev. **79**(3), 62–78 (2001)

4D Printing: An Emerging Technology in Manufacturing?

Alessandra Ghi and Francesca Rossetti

Abstract The paper highlights the possible technological evolution in the Lean manufacturing that concerns 4D Printing. To date there are not case studies of 4D printing application able to demonstrate the effective use of 4D Printing, and its results on the production cycles. The purpose of this article is to review the state of the art of the developments in four dimensional (4D) Printing, through a literature review, in order to define the 4D Printing characteristics, to examine its perspectives for the future application in manufacturing and to identify the potential benefits and manufacturing advantages.

Keywords 4D printing · Lean manufacturing · Additive manufacturing · Self-assembly · Internet of things

1 Introduction

There have been many improvements in manufacturing in the last few years because of the solid imaging process known as stereolithography, or 3D Printing, a process for viewing and testing designs before investing in full production. The rapid prototyping and the Additive Manufacturing (AM) have gained wide approval since its invention in 1980s (Fig. 1).

The Additive Manufacturing is a process in which material is added to generate products. Instead of subtracted, as in traditional manufacturing processes, the switch from traditional subtractive manufacturing has enabled the rapid production of complex components and systems at a reasonable cost. It's a viable alternative to traditional manufacturing methods at lower production quantities [1]. The additive

A. Ghi (✉) · F. Rossetti
Department of Management, Università Di Roma, Sapienza, Italy
e-mail: alessandra.ghi@uniroma1.it

F. Rossetti
e-mail: francesca.rossetti@uniroma1.it

© Springer International Publishing Switzerland 2016   171
L. Caporarello et al. (eds.), *Digitally Supported Innovation*,
Lecture Notes in Information Systems and Organisation 18,
DOI 10.1007/978-3-319-40265-9_12

Characteristics	Problematization
Materials	How do we create materials with multifunctional properties?
Energy	How can we generate, store, and use passive and abundant energy sources?
Environment	How do we program and design environmentally?
Design	How do we program future CAD software with dynamic components?
Programming	How do we program variable state-changes?
Electronic	How do we insert controllable electronics at the sub-millimeter scale?
Assembly	What external forces would be needed to self-assembly?
Recycling	How can we ensure the reconfiguration for reuse or error-correcting for self-repair?
Standardization	Can standards be created?
Manufacturing Techniques	Can manufacturing be made economically viable for small- and large-scale manufacturers?
Certifications	Can programmable matter systems be certified technically?

Fig. 1 Technical challenges (*Source* adapted from [15])

manufacturing can easily be modified to suit unique needs or, more broadly, to accommodate improvements [2].

The number and variety of additive manufacturing systems is set to grow, in line with the increased demand. According to [3], the market for additive manufacturing, consisting of all AM products and services worldwide, grew at a compound annual growth rate (CAGR) of 35.2 % to $4.1 billion in 2014; the industry expanded by more than $1 billion in 2014, with 49 manufacturers producing and selling industrial-grade AM machines. The CAGR over the past 3 years (2012–2014) was 33.8 %. The use of industrial metal AM systems for demanding production applications in the aerospace and medical markets also grew strongly.

Actually, one of the radical advantages of additive manufacturing is the capacity to mass-produce customized components without the increase in wastes expressed in terms of material, inefficiency and time. Today several applications for Printing include proof-of-concept prototypes, but according to Hayes [4], the main hurdles for additive manufacturing are:

- Multi-functional and smart/responsive materials.
- Increased scale for printing applications.
- Structural materials that can be used in high performance settings.

"Each of these hurdles will need to be addressed and likely combined in order to truly demonstrate the scalability of additive manufacturing to rival existing manufacturing efficiencies" [5].

We are participating in a development termed 4D Printing, where the fourth dimension, the "time" is an extension of conventional 3D Printing technologies. It is not about how long it takes for a part to be printed, but rather the fact that the 3D printed object still continues to "shape shift" and evolve over a period of time [6–11].

The Self-Assembly Lab at the Massachusetts Institute of Technology (MIT) is focused on the development of programmable materials, adaptive technology and self-assembly for industrial applications. These operations are the most important processes in synthetic and natural systems, offering an opportunity for making better construction techniques. Programmable material prototypes and self-assembling have been developed, highlighting principles through materials and methodology of fabrication.

"4D Printing is a first glimpse into the world of evolvable materials that can respond to user needs or environmental changes" [5].

Our attention for this technology, comes from the interest on the consequences that the technological evolution of 4D Printing can have on recent production paradigms. Nowadays, the production process techniques must be "lean", focused on waste reduction, production speed, decreasing lead time, saving and reducing the purchase and maintenance costs. Within the features of 4D Printing, it is possible to better achieve the goals of lean manufacturing, but some questions arise, including the following: how much it will be the total cost of production by 4D Printing? What will be the 4D printing production environmental impact? The purpose of this paper is to review the state of the art of the developments of 4D Printing, in order to investigate on the interest among the researchers about this technology and if 4D print will be able to meet certain requirements of production or if the technology in testing will have no future.

2 Methodology

In order to review the state of the art of 4D Printing technology, the methodology used is only exploratory. At the moment, there are no case-studies that demonstrate the effective use of 4D print, because the technology still needs to be tested.

The databases we used to generate the literature review were the following: Google Scholar, Proquest, Science Direct, Ebsco, Scopus.

We inserted the 4D Printing keyword and selected the period 2010–2015 per database. We used descriptive statistic models to calculate the absolute frequency on the results for each database and for all the considered databases.

We calculated the relative frequency using descriptive statistic methods, expressing the results in percentage. The results from 2010 to 2015 were the following: Google Scholar (72.3 %), Proquest (10.8 %), Science Direct (10.4 %), Ebsco (6.4 %), Scopus (0.1 %).

We calculated the absolute frequency of the papers for every database, for every year, from 2010 to 2015.

Then, to compare the results, we decided to split the period from 2010 to 2015 in two periods: from 2010 to 2012 and from 2013 to 2015.

In order to verify if the literature output increased or decreased from 2013 to 2015, at first we calculated the relative frequency in percentage from 2010 to 2012, obtaining the following results: Google Scholar (75.1 %), Proquest (8.1 %), Science Direct (8.9 %), Ebsco (7.9 %), Scopus (0.1 %). Then, we calculated the relative frequency expressed in percentage, from 2013 to 2015, obtaining the following results: Google Scholar (69.8 %), Proquest (13.3 %), Science Direct (11.6 %), Ebsco (5.1 %), Scopus (0.2 %).

Finally, in order to analyze the increment or decrement rate, we compared the number of papers of the two periods 2010–2012 and 2013–2015. We observed that there was an incredible growth of literature output for about 80 % in the considered databases. In particular, the number of the papers increased with the following rates per: Scopus (275 %), Proquest (84.8 %), Science Direct (46.9 %), Google Scholar (4.2 %) and only negative Ebsco (−27.6 %).

As Qi [12] said "The momentum's there, this field is developing really fast".

3   The Fourth Dimension

The concept begins with additive manufacturing in which a technology builds a 3D object by depositing successive layers of material in any shape it is possible to imagine [13]. Despite several benefits, a disadvantage of additive manufactured parts is that they generally incline to be inanimate and static [9, 10].

The researchers are going to the next step by adding a fourth dimension, the time. 4D Printing is a new process that demonstrates a fundamental shift in the manufacturing sector. With its capability to change from one shape to another configuration, it entails to transform over time multi-material prints or a customized material system.

As mentioned above, the fourth dimension is the transformation over time, printed structures are programmable active and they are able to transform independently. The materials are activated in a controlled manner to change the solid physical form in response to an external stimuli [12, 14].

According to [9, 10], three aspects must be discovered from the 4D printing use.

1. The use of stimuli-responsive composite materials that are incorporate multi-materials with several properties, layer on layer.
2. The stimuli that will act on the material. An example of stimulus regards cooling, ultraviolet light, water, humidity, heating, magnetic energy and wind.

3. The amount of time for the simulation and the final effect is the change of configuration of the object.

The operation of the object transformation is termed self-assembly, the concept has been used inter-changeable with 4D Print, in this way the entire system becomes "smarter" [5–8]. The 4D technology definition is "a process of building a physical object using appropriate additive manufacturing technology, laying down successive layers of stimuli-responsive composite or multi-materials with varying properties. After being built, the object reacts to stimuli from the natural environment or through human intervention, resulting in a physical or chemical change of state through time. This means that the result of 4D printing is not limited to self-assemblies but also other states of change" [10].

To date, the only company in the world that builds 4D prints is Stratasys Ltd., the multi-material technology allows specific material properties to be programmed into controlled zones of the designed geometry [15]. The printers are able to mix three dissimilar resins in ratios within a single print operation. The system uses synthetic blends based on acrylic-based photopolymer resins. These materials are plunged in a liquid and once a material is deposited, there is a UV light to form a solid.

The researcher group of MIT Self-Assembly Lab claims that the next step is to build structures which use energy from hydraulics, wind resistance, heating, fluids and capillary action, contraction of materials and pre/post tensional forces [9, 10].

What will determine the success of 4D Printing? According to [16], there are several advantages over traditional manufacturing.

The ability to shape-shift physical objects, the adaptability from any shape to another, the capability to design of dynamic objects, the facility to adapt their geometry and structure, on-demand, as forces and requirements change, increasing material efficiency, they can raise product design freedom. Once that the processes are streamlined, 4DP would require no additional cost for complexity or time to embed actuation, logic and sensing into printable parts. The products could be customizable in batches of one or more since 4DP won't add complexity or cost to the printing process itself. 4D Printing allows to customize the product, the concept changes from mass production to mass customization (user-responsive products, environmentally adaptive structures). The manufacturing process would become even simpler, the structures can be printed and then activated by external stimulus to change into complex functional systems, the printed part can now be produced, shipped, and unmonitored while it senses and responds physically to its surrounding environment. The digitization permits to take a collection of voxels[1] anywhere in the world to form a multifunctional object offering an instant

---

[1]"A voxel is a volumetric pixel, often used to define the fundamental unit of digital space and Programmable Matter. Voxels can be both digital and physical. Digital voxel are computational representation in 3D models. Physical voxel may be comprised of materials as diverse as basic raw materials (e.g., titanium), nanomaterials, integrated circuits, biological materials, and micro-robotics, among others" [16].

production on a global scale, a game changing design-to-production cycle and the decoupling of the need to manufacture traditional on site. The supply chains and assembly lines could dramatically change or become obsolete with widespread adoption of 4DP.

4D Printing would inherently boost innovation because the design and fabrication of voxels would become a new industry as new materials and functionality are enabled beyond what exists today with traditional manufacturing processes [16].

The economic sectors probably involved in 4D Printing are Construction, Infrastructure and Manufacturing. The multiple applications regard conceptual modeling, functional prototypes, manufacturing tools, finished parts, advanced applications. In particular, conceptual modeling allows businesses that deal with design and engineering to expand its reach with the ability to test more ideas and develop only the appropriate products [9, 10, 16].

The functional prototypes permit to correct the mistakes and make improvements in the early stages of the design process when these operations are less expensive [10].

The areas mainly involved in 4D print innovation could be buildings or structures, airplane wings that change shape in response of environmental conditions, tyres that change traction depending on the road conditions, clothes that adapt to the user's performance, bridges that adapt to varying load weather and smart sensors for infrastructure lines that can respond to control flow-rates [16].

What are 4D Printing technical challenges? And will, the 4D Print technology, be able to answer all the challenges in charge? According to [16], we show in the following table, main 4D Printing characteristics and problematizations in the coming years.

4   Conclusions

4D Printing allows to create self-modifying outputs, to product materials that can adapt independently to changing environments, toward a kind of interaction between physical and the human world [17]. However, 4D Print could be the next evolution of lean manufacturing: the error-correcting for self-repair or self-assembly materials could impact directly and positively on the reduction of wastes, errors and loss of products.

We need to know more about this issue, but in a first moment 4D Printing could be used in lean manufacturing since materials should be programmed to adapt in response to environmental conditions. We can't apply any lean principles without a proper design (for assembly, manufacture and product). Thus 4D Printing could be used in lean production as well as a robot is used in some assembly lines.

What will determine the success of one or another tool? May be the design process and the configuration mode.

Furthermore, 4D Printing can be faced as a Kaikaku[2] [18], regarding lean principles for improvements, what justify researches and economic feasibility. All the future programmable products will self-repair, self-disassemble for recyclability and error-correct to meet the new market needs. Thus, programmable active materials and 4D printing offer special opportunities for the manufacturing sectors and the future of the products. The additive manufacturing will likely increase to become a set of materials with boundless response to exogenous force [5–8].

Although not commercially available yet, the self-assembly is just a beginning of innovative world of manufacturing with minimum energy spending. As variables continue to fluctuate, like environmental, economic and human factors, there is a need of dynamic systems that could respond with ease and agility. 4D Printing is the first to offer this exciting capability. This is truly an essential shift in understanding such structures which remain static and rigid (aerospace, automotive, building industries) and will soon be dynamic, adaptable and tunable for on-demand performance.

To date, no one can prove how the 4D Printing technology impacts on production processes, which are the effective costs of manufacturing and which is the energy impact required for the production of materials in 4D. Our investigation shows that the interest among researchers for this technology has strongly increased in the last 2 years. Given the 4D Printing characteristics, benefits and potential new manufacturing advantages above explained, future researches could solve the questions regarding the satisfaction of the production requirements through the 4D Printing application and highlight the challenges of technological innovation in the lean manufacturing processes. Specifically, the application of 4D Printing to lean manufacturing could produce an improvement in the lean production three-areas: realization of activities that do not produce value (e.g.: waste characterized by an excessive amount of input into the printer of composite material formed by the polymer fiber) reduction of defects, scrap and rework, over-production.

In conclusion, lean manufacturing processes are characterized by the search of continuous improvement of the process/product, expressed in terms of increasing flexibility and reduction of defects and waste. In this context, the application of 4D printing technology based on the main concepts of programmable materials, adaptive technology and self–assembly in manufacturing lean process, could be able to reduce to the maximum the complexity of the production by focusing on the material/product flexibility, designing production and enhancement.

At the materials level there is an influx of research around smart materials and self-assembly processes to efficiently manufacture new material properties [19]. Gazing into the future, the range and availability of some materials derived mostly from existing substances [20], probably increase in terms of strength, durability, quality of surface finish and added functionality. Other materials probably won't be

---

[2]Kaikaku is characterized by two terms: "Kai", meaning to change and "Kaku", meaning to transform. The method is a radical change and it aims to reform entire system. Kaikaku creates a breakthrough using new model in the lean production [18].

able to be used again, due to health concerns [21]. As print volumes increase and as associated costs fall, the developments in 4D printing will be very exciting [10].

As [9, 10] says: "Perhaps, for now, time as the fourth dimension in 4D printing could refer to both paradigms—strategies that can be used to reduce the print process and the use of smart materials where parts adapt themselves in response to the surrounding environment, supporting the notion of self-assemblies. So 4D printing, whether fad or truly revolutionary, you decide, time will tell!".

References

1. Kurfess, T., Cass, W.J.: Rethinking additive manufacturing and intellectual property protection. Res. Technol. Manag. **57**(5), 35–42 (2014)
2. D'Aveni, R.: The 3D printing revolution. Harvard Business Review, pp. 41–48 (2015)
3. Wholer's Report: http://www.wohlersassociates.com/2015report.htm (2015)
4. Hayes, M.: Developing and deploying new technologies – industry perspectives. Boeing presentation at the US Manufacturing Competitiveness Initiative Dialogue on Additive Manufacturing, Oak Ridge National Laboratory, Oak Ridge, Tennessee (2013)
5. Tibbits, S., Linor, S., Dikovsky, D., Hirsch, S.: High Definition: Zero Tolerance in Design and Production. John Wiley & Sons, London (2014)
6. Tibbits, S.: Logic matter: digital logic as heuristics for physical self-guided assembly. MIT, Department of Architecture & Department of Electrical Engineering and Computer Science, Master Thesis (2010)
7. Tibbits, S.: A model for intelligence of large-scale self-assembly. In: Proceedings of the Association for Computer Aided Design in Architecture, pp. 342–349. Banff, Alberta, pp. 13–16 (2011)
8. Tibbits, S.: Logic Matter. Proceedings of Fabricate. London, England (2011)
9. Pei, E.: 4D printing—revolution or fad? Assembly Autom. **34**(2), 123–127 (2014)
10. Pei, E.: 4D Printing: dawn of an emerging technology cycle. Assembly Autom. **34**(4), 310–314 (2014)
12. Tibbits, S.: 4D Printing: Multi-Material Shape Change. In: Sheil, B. (ed.) 2 High Definition, Jan/Feb (n.1), pp. 116–21 (2014)
11. Ge, Q., Jerry, H.Q., Dunn, M.L.: Active materials by four-dimension printing. Appl. Phys. Lett. **103**(131901), 1–5 (2013)
13. Savage, N.: Time Change Tech. **57**(6), 16–18 (2014)
14. Ge, Q., Dunn, C.K., Jerry, H.Q., Dunn, M.L.: Active origami by 4D printing. Smart Mater. Struct. **23**(9), 1–15 (2014)
15. Stratays Ltd.: http://www.stratasys.com/industries/education/4d-printing-project (2013)
16. Campbell, T.A., Tibbits, K., Garrett, B.: The next wave: 4D Printing programming the material world, vol 202, pp. 778–4952, pp. 1–15 www.AtlanticCouncil.org (2014)
17. Headrick, D.: 4D printing transforms product design. Res. Technol. Manage. **58**(2), 7/8 (2015)
18. Munro, A.: Kaikaku: Manufacturing Re-Imagined. Manufacturing Engineering, pp. 99–104 (2012)
19. Tibbits, S., Young, A., Kara'in, L., Gomez-Marquez, J., Schaeffer, J., de Puig, H.: DNA DISPLAY—Programmable Bioactive Materials Using CNC Patterning,, pp 104–111. MIT, John Wiley & Sons Ltd. (2014)
20. Al Rhodan, N.: Programmable Matter: 4D Printing's Promises and Risks. Georgetown Journal of International Affairs (2014)
21. Hoskins, S.: 3D Printing for Artists. Designers and Makers. Bloomsbury Publishing, London (2013)

Part III
Implementing Innovative
ICT Enablers

How to Manage the Application Portfolio Over Time: A Qualitative Analysis

Roberto Candiotto, Silvia Gandini and Giulia Palmarini

Abstract The ability to understand, or even to anticipate, business needs is the necessary input to create value for the whole organization and so to transform IT into «business technology». In this context, it is important to capture expectations and to rationalize the application portfolio, in order to avoid obsolescence, manage related costs, and support the convergence with companies' business goals. The purpose of this paper is to understand if it is possible to define a useful model to manage the application portfolio over time. To answer this question, the case of Edison S.p.A. has been analyzed. Against a critical situation, the IT Management of the company investigated a way of increasing the control over the application portfolio and defined a strategy for its migration to an integrated platform, in order to increase the level of alignment between IT and business processes and to prepare for changing requirements in the future.

Keywords Application portfolio · IT management · IT governance · Business strategy · Change management

---

Although this work is the result of a common will, every paragraph has been written by a single author; particularly.

- 1st section by Giulia Palmarini.
- 2nd section by Roberto Candiotto.
- 3rd and 4th sections by Silvia Gandini.

R. Candiotto (✉) · S. Gandini
Dipartimento Di Studi Per L'Economia E L'Impresa,
Università Del Piemonte Orientale, Vercelli, Italy
e-mail: roberto.candiotto@uniupo.it

S. Gandini
e-mail: silvia.gandini@uniupo.it

G. Palmarini
Edison S.p.A., Milan, Italy
e-mail: Giulia.Palmarini@edison.it

© Springer International Publishing Switzerland 2016
L. Caporarello et al. (eds.), *Digitally Supported Innovation*,
Lecture Notes in Information Systems and Organisation 18,
DOI 10.1007/978-3-319-40265-9_13

1   Introduction

Today, most organizations in all sectors of industry, commerce and government are fundamentally dependent on their information systems [18]; moreover, IT invest-ments represent a great deal of many organizations annual budget [9]. From their invention to the present, an increasing number of computer-based information systems have been supporting an increasing number of functions and processes within and between businesses. Enormous numbers of applications gives rise to a high level of complexity for IT Management, responsible for implementing, inte-grating, operating, and further developing them. With the increasing focus on corporate globalization, Chief Information Officers (CIO) face even more complex challenges to rationalize their IT portfolio, since they have to optimize IT systems deployment within the organization.

As the scale and complexity of the data and information companies produce and consume within their business continues to grow so too has the requirement to share it across and beyond organizational units [1]. How then is it possible to continu-ously maintain a clear understanding of which applications are relevant and sup-porting today business objectives? It is possible, but requires a shift in the IT governance and strategic planning processes with a greater understanding of business capabilities and organizational characteristics [13].

Scientific literature about the management of application portfolio is mainly focused on matrices, which are useful for obtaining an overview but not sufficient for reaching informed decisions about how to deal with an application and for interpreting the management of application portfolio as an organizational challenge.

According to Magoulas and Pessi [10], «application architecture» and «system architecture» are synonymous and they define the main applications needed to handle data and support the organizational functions. The authors also states that the focus of IT management is, among other things, to give guidance for which systems are needed, how they are going to interoperate and how to migrate from the current situation, in order to: (a) get control over this great number of systems; (b) terminate systems that do not provide sufficient business value anymore; (c) find several ways to get more out of the legacy systems compared to actual organization.

According to Ward [19], the most common way of visualizing a portfolio is using different matrices; the approach has been widely adopted because it reduces a large set of alternatives into a comprehensible number of options. One of the first and most well-known matrices for the classification of information system envi-ronments is the *Strategic Grid*, which was developed for the purpose of assessing the whole application portfolio and determining the management approach required from the business [11].

Since then, the Strategic Grid has been complemented and enhanced by other various models. Weill and Vitale [21] introduced the *Health Grid*, based on the concept that, considering «technical quality» and «management value» as dimen-sions of analysis, it is possible to distinguish the following options: *Upgrade, Nurture, Question* or *Consolidate/Eliminate*. The Health Grid is not very different from the *Legacy Matrix* proposed by Sommerville [15], which is focused on the dimension «business value» instead of «management value».

Nhampossa [12] investigated strategies to deal with legacy information systems using Sommerville's Legacy Matrix, taking as the primary concern of the study the processes involved when dealing with legacy information systems. Instead, Hirvonen [5] investigated how the maturity of an enterprise can affect the organizational benefits using application portfolio models for plan, evaluate and manage information systems. And he concluded that, in order to use the matrices, a certain level of maturity is necessary.

Fabriek et al. [3] defined a rationalization approach for the application portfolio, dealing with reducing the complexity of existing applications. By using the *rationalization approach*, companies can analyze their applications basing on technical quality and uncommon programming language, and thereby make a decision about the whole category, to *discard* (parts of) them, *replace* them, *redevelop* them or *invest* in new applications.

Kwan and West [8] proposed a model for the analysis of all systems in an organization considering the relative importance of the applications and the respective alignment to strategic goals. The resulting framework contains four stages of IT importance: *support, mission critical, strategic* and *laboratory*. These showed that the importance of an application changes over time.

At last, Swanson and Dans [16] made their study in the area of systems retirement and replacement. They investigated the relation between maintenance effort and system life expectancy and found, among other things, that larger systems are associated with a greater life expectancy, and not only with a greater maintenance effort. They also found that older systems have shorter remaining life expectancy, as should be expected, but also that there is no direct association between older systems and greater maintenance effort.

Hence, the scientific literature relates to several different application portfolio methods, which generally aim to «assess the health of an IT application portfolio» [21], «rationalize the application portfolio» [3], «propose strategies to deal with legacy information systems» [12] and «enterprise IT portfolio management» [8].

The management of application portfolio however represents a business challenge, since technologies can deeply affect information, products, and services flows of a value chain, becoming a way to coordinate activities and resources in the organization and between organizations [2]. IT can assume a determinant role both for the reengineering of internal processes, and for the redesign and integration of business processes [17].

The linkage between IT and business, often referred to as «alignment» [4], is an important objective for CIO [6]. Obtaining a fit between IT and business is not going to happen by itself, and will not bring any benefits unless it is continuously exploited and shaped to the business needs [4].

The way of managing IT assets is more important for companies' performance than the level of spending [7] but, actually, the business impact of application portfolio has been explored only by advisory companies, and mainly by Gartner.[1] The gap has been confirmed by the analysis of academic contributions of the last five years,[2] denoting a substantial lack of case studies that could be useful to improve existing models.

In the light of previous considerations, we decided to analyze the case of Edison S.p.A. In March 2013 the company started a process for the application portfolio assessment, in order to obtain detailed information about existing applications and to enforce the organizational know-how about them. The main problem areas were low rate of application flexibility, difficulties related to legacy applications and lacking control of the application portfolio.

Basing on the assumption that the management of the application portfolio is a long-term process of phasing out an IT asset, that needs to be integrated into the global IT governance framework [14], we asked if it is possible to define a standardized model to: (a) realize a comprehensive inventory of existing applications, (b) make an evaluation of applications in terms of business value, maintenance and support costs, and risk acceptance, and (c) define a roadmap for all transformation initiatives.

2 Research Project Description

In the last 30 years, application portfolios of complex organizations have been characterized by great and continuous expansion. This trend is supported by growing business requirements, new technologies diffusion over the market, and major focus on globalization. In this context, CIO must face more and more complicated challenges: that of optimizing the IT application portfolio of their companies.

The model actually used by Edison to manage applications has been realized through a more than a year project, characterized by continuous reflections and reviews as to the starting concept, not only to assure the quality of deliverables but also to create a wide and flexible database for organizational needs.

---

[1]http://www.gartner.com/.

[2]Literature analysis has been realized on the abstract of contributions, in the years from 2010 to 2014, of these publications: *European Journal of Information Systems, Information Systems Journal, Information Systems Research, Journal of AIS, Journal of MIS, MIS Quarterly* (first 6 excellence journal and review according to the ranking of Association for Information Systems (AIS)), *Information and Management, Management Science, Sviluppo e Organizzazione* and *Economia and Management.* The same results has been produced by the analysis of the first 20 pages of Jstor Archive Collection and Google Scholar, related to the keywords «Application Portfolio Management» and «Management of Application Portfolio».

Research methodology qualitative analysis through direct interviews
Interviewed people IT Manager and Project Consultant
Period December 2014–February 2015
Goals

- how an application portfolio can be successfully managed by organizations?
- how decisions about the destiny of an application are related to business processes?
- is it possible to manage different applications through the same approach?

Considering the complexity of the project, we structured interviews basing on the following sections:

(1) **Application strategy**

The idea that organizations need to develop a strategy for their applications is a matter of supreme importance. An application strategy must be responsive to all of the decisions that have gone before and provide a degree of comprehension about the business and technology changes that are occurring in the organization.

In this section, questions were focused on:

- the main aspects the company considered in order to improve knowledge about existing applications;
- how the company found a relation between the characteristics of existing applications and involved organizational functions.

(2) **Application inventory**

The creation of a register of all applications in use, the projects in-flight, and the proposals for new applications considered by the organization allows to improve the quality of actual and future decision making. The inventory should start one process at a time, and must be capable of being analyzed from many different perspectives and used for many different purposes.

In this section, questions were focused on:

- the main characteristics and the granularity degree of captured information;
- how the consolidation of collected information allowed the company to better understand the alignment between applications, organizational activities, and business strategy.

(3) **Application assessment**

Independent business unit decisions often can overlap with existing capabilities in the organization, and perhaps even with initiatives being conducted in other business units at the same time. The assessment is fundamental to understand if the applications in use or being proposed may not meet the current and the future needs of the organization, and to avoid applications become unwieldy to manage, because of duplications and aging technology.

In this section, questions were focused on:

- the relation between the assessment degree of complexity and the company degree of maturity;
- the main approaches used to realized the assessment activities;
- the evaluated performance aspects that allowed company to understand the organizational and business impact of applications.

3   Main Findings and Contributions

Interviews has allowed to understand the approach Edison used to improve the management of application portfolio and how this kind of projects can be suitable also for future technological evolutions.

The evaluation activities are based both on applications' value and risk profile, and can have different complexity degree in coherence with the organization's maturity stage. In Edison, the starting concept of the analysis was specifically focused on enterprise architecture and so characterized by a purely technical nature. The following data collection has pointed out all limits of the above said concept and lead to a wider focus, including further differentiated values and involving a plurality of different actors (organization, infrastructures, and security).

The analysis of application portfolio requires not only to consider the link between applications and supporting infrastructures, but also to comprehend how applications can sustain different functions, in order to identify the company's capability maps and cross-functional relations, under a process perspective [20]. The standardization and the consolidation of data about the application portfolio must be based on a rational analysis of the goals and the informative depth a company wants to obtain. It is fundamental the file tuning on various data cluster, to be defined in relation with the purport of inventory activities and the informative needs of specific process owners.

In Edison, all information about existing applications have been included in a single database and organized in complementary sections, to reduce data fragmentation and simplify their consultation. In order to understand the relation between its application portfolio and business peculiarities, for each application the company decided to collect information about: (a) used technologies and main functionalities; (b) actual conditions and criticalities; (c) internal and external referents; (d) supported functions, business lines, and processes; (e) the impact on business risks, for the ability to support utilities production, and on image risks, for the capacity to improve relations with final customers.

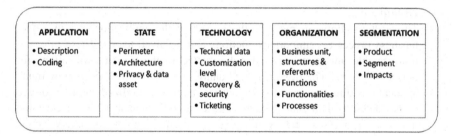

APPLICATION	STATE	TECHNOLOGY	ORGANIZATION	SEGMENTATION

• Description
• Coding
	• Perimeter
	• Architecture
	• Privacy & data
	  asset
		• Technical data
		• Customization
		  level
		• Recovery &
		  security
		• Ticketing
			• Business unit,
			  structures &
			  referents
			• Functions
			• Functionalities
			• Processes
				• Product
				• Segment
				• Impacts

Fig. 1 Application inventory in Edison

Hence, the so created application master can be represented as follows Fig. 1:

(1) **Application**

This section allows to identify the general characteristics of applications, to create coordination between different company's systems (data asset, trouble ticketing, etc.). Each application is described under a business oriented perspective, in order to understand what it really is able to do. The attribution of a special code lets to standardize every application for each company's system, overcoming the problem of different views.

(2) **State**

This section describes how applications can change during their lifecycle. These information are important to understand the positioning, the obsolescence and the strategic impact of each application the company decided to implement. The analysis of application's perimeter allows to understand if it is used by a little number of people or instead by different organizations. The architecture evaluation leads to some considerations about planning activities, according to the state of applications (still to be developed, operative, etc.) and so to their importance for the company strategy. Finally, it is important to identify all characteristics related to privacy and security, in order to respect what rules and norms say about the management of application portfolio.

(3) **Technology**

This section allows to describe each application under a technical and technological point of view. These information are important not only to measure the strategic value of the application portfolio but also to make some considerations about the applications' obsolescence and lifecycle. Moreover, it is indispensable to know the customization level of each application, in order to evaluate the potential dependence on provider and to determine the application portfolio complexity. The analysis of security systems, business continuity, and disaster recovery, is related to the applications' capacity to support critical business and to satisfy specific legal obligations. Finally, the check about the presence of ticketing systems supporting an application leads to make some considerations about the service management approach and the related capacity to realize customer satisfaction.

(4) **Organization**

This section allows to measure the impact of the application portfolio over business processes, supported functions and involved teams. These information are relevant to understand risks related to the use of applications for business matters. The organizational analysis is useful to evaluate how much applications' functions and functionalities can be standardized, in order to save costs related to their management, but also to distinguish between core and non core processes and so to give a specific weight for every single application.

(5) **Segmentation**

This section is aimed to analyze the capacity of applications to support specific product lines or market segments. Segmentation is fundamental to understand what kinds of final customers each application can serve and so to measure its ability to increase, or decrease, the company's competitive advantage.

The application master is steadily updated, after new information have been checked both by Demand Manager, for technical aspects, and Project Manager, for business process aspects. Finally, the application assessment involves reflections about the capacity of IT to be an enabler and requires to do leverage on core applications (about 10 % of the total portfolio). In order to identify its most strategic applications and to obtain a complete evaluation, Edison decided to structure the assessment activities basing on the following qualitative and quantitative aspects: (1) the support to business processes and to strategies that have a direct impact over the mission; (2) the contribution to organizational operations; (3) the technical match with to-be architecture.

4   Conclusions

Although the research project is still *in itinere*, because the analysis of one case is not sufficient to test the above said assumption, this introductory work has shown how companies' ability to structure a repeatable process to assess what they have, and if an application is not performing or does not meet their architectural requirements, eliminating it and freeing up money to invest in new and better performing applications can be effectively supported through the definition of a standardized model.

The analysis has allowed to consider how is possible for classical methods to evolve to more strategic approaches, in order to respect the relation between IT and business processes. But as organization grows and change so the application database do. Constant updating activities allow to increase values reliability, to develop useful know-how, and to favor the cultural change. Edison is actually analyzing how the introduction of digital technologies can have an impact on the realized model and lead to eventually rethink used variables.

The above said considerations should be substantially revised in the light of the profound changes that are affecting the business application portfolios. The first challenge is closely related to the applications' ownership: moving from legacy and on premise systems to digital technologies it is necessary to completely revise: (a) the logic by which the ability of applications to contribute to the achievement of business goals is analyzed, and (b) the drivers through which the applications themselves are weighed, organized and analyzed.

The profound change that involves a review of the application portfolio management itself can have an impact on the use and exploitation of the variables that allow to capture the contribution of each application, expressed in terms of business. So different is the value proposition expressed by the application itself. This consideration becomes even more important considering not only the type of application and its ownership, but also the trends that are emerging in today context.

With the advent of the digital business it is emerging more and more the substantial presence of two different speeds in IT, better known as «bimodal». Hence, is it possible to speak about application portfolio management facing applications characterized by a completely different approach in terms of value, time to market, cost of ownership, governance, lifecycle? Under this point of view, it could make sense to talk about two different approaches, as an expression of that part of the above said bimodal IT.

The realized analysis has shown how each application must have a set of defined formal requirements, and these requirements must be able to capture what the business expects and often must be able to anticipate the business needs or be flexible enough if markets change. The real challenge, however, lies in the management skills needed to capture the requirements of internal and external business customers, that are more and more able to handle applications user friendly and apparently free and available 24/7.

The ability to quickly apply the strategy through a rapid change of the business operations is increasingly important in the digital era. Even the management of application portfolio must therefore be able to meet the challenges of business transformation that is under way: in a world characterized by an extremely fast evolving value system traditional drivers are unlikely to capture the full meaning of an application (considering, for example, the value expressed by a digital application that is born and dies in a cycle life of 2 years, and comparing it with that of a legacy system whose life cycle is estimated about 10–12 years).

The change, however, does not impact only on the system of values to be determined but also on the risks to be accounted for and incorporate in the weighting systems. It will be therefore indispensable to set up a robust system for the change management, through the adoption ex-ante evaluation activities to identify what may be the new frontier for integration of sophisticated technologies in the processes and business functions.

Hence, although the contribution of application portfolio management is today still relevant, it is possible to say that companies potentially will need a revision of data and variables to consider. And information could be managed through the same identified model or instead require a change in the model itself.

The next step of the research will consist in:

- a deeper analysis of Edison case, in order to better understand opportunities and threats of the implemented model;
- the study of some cases of companies that already implemented similar projects, in order to enlarge the sample of analysis.

References

1. Champy, J.: Reengineering Management. Harper Collins, New York (1995)
2. Champy, J.: X-engineering. Ripensare l'azienda nell'era digitale, Sperling & Kupfer, Milano (2003)
3. Fabriek, M., Brinkkemper, S., Van Dullemen, J.: A Method for Application Portfolio Rationalization. Institute of Information and Computer Science, Utrecht University (2007)
4. Henderson, J.C., Venkatraman, N.: Strategic alignment: Leveraging information technology for transforming organizations. IBM Syst. J. **38** (1999)
5. Hirvonen, A.P.: Application Portfolio Models in Practise—Tools for ICT Planning, Management and Business Value Evaluation. Jyväskylä, Finland (2004)
6. Horner Reich, B., Benbasat, I.: Measuring the Linkage between Business and Information Technology Objectives, MIS Quarterly. Management Information Systems Research Center, University of Minnesota, vol. 20 (1996)
7. Irani, Z., Information Systems Evaluation: Navigating Through the Problem Domain. Information and management, Elsevier Science, vol. 40 (2002)
8. Kwan, S.K., West, J: Heterogeneity of IT Importance: Implications for Enterprise IT Portfolio Management, San José State University (2004)
9. Lin, C., Pervan, G.: A Review of IS/IT Investment Evaluation and Benefits Management Issues, Problems, and Processes, Idea Group Publishing (2001)
10. Magoulas, T., Pessi, K.: Strategic IT-management, University of Göteborg, Department of Informatics (1998)
11. McFarlan, F.W., McKenney, J.L., Pyburn, P.: The Information Archipelago—Plotting a Course, Harvard Business Review (1983)
12. Nhampossa, J.L.: Strategies to Deal With Legacy Information Systems: A Case Study from the Mozambican Health Sector, Department of Informatics, University of Oslo (2004)
13. Parsons G.: Strategic Information Technology, Harvard Business School Case, No. 183–121 (1984)
14. Ross J.: Maturity Matters: How Firms Generate Value from Enterprise Architecture, CISR WP 359 (2006)
15. Sommerville, I.: Software Engineering, 6th Edn. (2001)
16. Swanson, B.E., Dans, E.: System life expectancy and the maintenance effort: exploring their equilibration, MIS Q. **24**(2), (2000)
17. Venkatraman, N.: IT-enabled Business Transformation: From Automation to Business Scope Redefinition, Sloan Management Review, Winter (1994)
18. Ward, J., Peppard, J.: Strategic Planning for Information Systems, 3rd edn. John Wiley & Sons, Ltd (2002)

19. Ward, J.: Information Systems and Technology Application Portfolio Management—An Assessment of Matrix Based Analyses. Cranfield School of Management, Cranfield University (1987)
20. Weill, P., Ross, J.W.: IT Governance—How Top Performers Manage IT Decision Rights for Superior Results. Harvard Business School Press (2004)
21. Weill, P., Vitale, M.: Assessing the Health of an Information Systems Application Portfolio: An Example from Process Manufacturing. MIS Q. **23**(4), (1999)

Marks & Spencer's RFID Initiative: Laying the Foundation for Omnichannel Retailing

Rebecca Angeles

Abstract This case study features the experiences of Marks & Spencer, a leading U.K. retailer, in deploying the latest round of its radio frequency identification (RFID) initiative as a way of laying the foundation for attaining omnichannel retailing capabilities. The prize to be obtained is inventory accuracy and reliability; this study focuses on attempts to reach inventory management improvements in the retail stores first. The exploration of M&S is successful and in the future, M&S would like to extend its RFID enablement to its entire supply chain which would include its manufacturers and distribution centers. This case study also uses the qualitative research method of content analysis of conference transcripts of talks given by key M&S executives who deployed their RFID initiatives.

Keywords Radio frequency identification (RFID) · Supply chain management (SCM) for retailing · Omnichannel retailing · Inventory management

1 Introduction

Interesting changes are happening in the retail marketplace that are clearly being dictated by customers' needs in the light of the multiple touch points by which they could reach the retailer. Customers have the longest experience walking into a brick-and-mortar stores. But with the onset of the Internet, online electronic, virtual stores and marketplaces became commonplace. Currently, use of smartphones and global positioning systems, along with the influences of social media marketing, has powered location based mobile commerce, following the tracks of customers who are now demanding retailers to provide the ability to purchase anything, anytime, anywhere. Thus, the concept of "omnichannel retailing" emerged dissolving the boundaries separating the physical, virtual, and mobile storefronts. "...The omnichannel concept is perceived as an evolution of the multichannel. While the

R. Angeles (✉)
University of New Brunswick Fredericton, Fredericton, NB, Canada
e-mail: rangeles@unb.ca

© Springer International Publishing Switzerland 2016   193
L. Caporarello et al. (eds.), *Digitally Supported Innovation*,
Lecture Notes in Information Systems and Organisation 18,
DOI 10.1007/978-3-319-40265-9_14

multichannel implies a division between the physical and online store, in the omnichannel world, customers move freely between the online (PC), mobile devices, and physical store, all within a single transaction process….the journey should be smooth and should provide a seamless, unified customer experience, regardless of the channels used…." [1] This case study features the radio frequency identification (RFID) initiatives of Marks & Spencer (M&S), a well-known U.K. retailer, in its bid to become one of the top omnichannel retailers in the marketplace. Omnichannel retailing is a broad and timely concept but, at this time, what M&S is laying the foundation for full omnichannel retailing capability by establishing a tight inventory management system that will produce inventory count accuracy and reliability.

2 Literature Review

2.1 RFID and Retailing and Omni-Channel Retailing

M&S has repeatedly expressed its desire to be a leading omnichannel retailer and considers the role of RFID item-level tagging as critical in this endeavor [2, 3]. The concept of "omnichannel retailing" has been defined by a number of scholars. To Vanheems, omnichannel retailing refers to "…a strategy of assembling various channels into a single distribution system promoting interchangeability and the transfer of customers between channels…." [4]. The Aberdeen Group, an IT consulting firm in the U.S., on the other hand, considers omnichannel retailing "…as a set of integrated processes and decisions that support a unified view of a brand from the perspective of product purchase, return, and exchange, irrespective of the channel (in-store, online, mobile, call center, or social)…." [5]. The critical role of item-level RFID tagging has also been articulated by Bill Hardgrave, founder and former director of the RFID Research Center of the University of Arkansas [6, 7]: "'Anywhere, anytime, any product' is the mantra of omnichannel retailing and retailers of all types are clamoring to make it happen….Customers should have a consistent and seamless experience whether they're shopping in a store, on a mobile device, on a home computer or via a catalog….But omnichannel retailing starts with operations—in particular, those that deliver real-time, accurate inventory data efficiently and cost-effectively. If you don't know what you have, where you have it and when you have it, the great mobile or online app you created for your customers is worthless." [7].

2.2 Marks & Spencer RFID Initiative: Background

Marks & Spencer, a leading U.K. retailer, has physical 800 stores in Britain and 420 international retail outlets, and trade out of 55 territories [2]. About 49 % of the retail business is in general merchandise and 51 %, in food. As of late, M&S has about 2,000 suppliers and an estimated 34 million customers who visit their U.K. retail stores. Currently, M&S is in the midst of transforming itself from a traditional brick-and-mortal retailer to an international multi-channel retailer, cultivating the capabilities of omnichannel retailing as well. The firm is relying heavily in RFID technology to enable this transformation. M&S has recently participated in the e-commerce marketplace as well and currently has a virtual presence in 12 different countries [8]. A series of RFID pilot projects were undertaken by M&S since 2000, each with specific incremental goals, all of which are intended to progressively increase the firm's capabilities towards omnichannel retailing.

2.3   Structurational Model of Technology

This study applies Orlikowski's "Structurational Model of Technology," [9, 10] to understand how information technology (IT) interacts with organizations. This model draws on Giddens' [11–13] theory of structuration, which proposed the concept of the "duality of structure," "...which refers to the notion that the structure or institutional properties of social systems are created by human action, and then serve to shape future human action...." [10, p. 147]. "...In Giddens' theory, structure is understood to be an abstract property of social systems. Structure is not something concrete, situated in time and space, and it lacks material characteristics. Structure cannot exist apart from the human actors who enact and interpret its dimensions. Structure has only virtual existence. Interestingly, people readily allow their actions to be constrained by these shared abstractions as social structure....The ability of organizational structures to elicit compliance and conformity in the absence of material constraints attests to the power of those socially constructed abstractions....Social structure conditions these social practices by providing the contextual rules and resources that allow human actors to make sense of their own acts and those of other people." [10, p. 147]. Furthermore, Giddens specifies that human interactions are an amalgamation of structures of meaning, power, and moral frameworks enacted in what he calls the "modalities" of these interactions: interpretive schemes, resources, and norms.

"Interpretive schemes...form the core of mutual knowledge whereby an accountable universe of meaning is sustained through and in processes of interaction [12, p. 83]. Orlikowski and Robey [10] translate Giddens' concept of "interpretive scheme" within the realm of IT and explain that IT represents reality through a set of concepts of symbols embedded in it by which end users understand their world. Thus, IT is not only a medium for the construction of social reality, but also a means of institutionalizing certain "interpretive schemes" or stocks of knowledge within the organization by standardizing, sharing, and taking them for granted.

Resources are the media through which power is exercised by human actors because it is through these resources that humans can accomplish their objectives and thus, gain "domination" [10]. Therefore, the deployment of IT institutes a certain order of authority, dictating the way work will be performed, and also, resulting in the differential distribution of power in the organization.

Norms are understood as organizational rules that shape "legitimate" behavior. IT is a medium for installing such norms in order to control human behavior in an organization [10].

Orlikowski incorporates the following components in her framework: first, the human agents, consisting of technology designers, end users, and decision makers; second, the material artifacts that constitute IT itself, and third, the institutional properties of organizations—structural arrangements, business strategies, ideology, culture, control mechanisms, standard operating procedures, division of labor, expertise, communication patterns, and environmental pressures [9, 10].

The structurational model of technology discusses four critical issues [10]. First, IT is the product of human action, which is responsible for the creation, use, and maintenance of different forms of IT. It is only through the human appropriation of IT that it is able to influence human activity. Second, technology is the medium of human action. Since different forms of IT are used by organizational workers, they mediate organizational work either by facilitating it and in some ways, also constraining it. Third, organizational contexts shape human action within organizations. Human agents are influenced by the institutional properties of their setting which provide the resources, norms, and knowledge they need to work. Furthermore, IT is created and used within certain social and historical circumstances which influence the form and features of this technology. Fourth, human agents either reinforce or transform the institutional properties of an organization when using IT. Weick [14] characterized technology as "enacted environment" whose construction is determined by an organization's structures of signification, domination, and legitimation. Any change in these three structures indicate the "appropriation" and use of technology.

"Structure of signification" refers to the way the concepts and procedures intrinsic to the knowledge embedded in IT directs the manner in which problems are interpreted and work is conducted in the organization [9]. "Structure of domination" refers to IT's ability to control the work of organizational members once it is deployed. "Structure of legitimation" refers to the ability of IT to sanction a particular mode of conducting the work and thus, propagate a set of norms about what is considered legitimate business practice. Orlikowski also incorporates the three modalities of structuration—interpretive schemes, resources, and norms—in her application of the structures of signification, domination, and legitimation in the deployment of IT in an organization.

3   Research Method

This study uses the case study approach in aligning the concepts prescribed by Orlikowski's framework [9, 10] to M&S' RFID system. The case study is an appropriate methodology in testing the application of a conceptual framework to a real firm. Primary data based on the transcription of the conference presentations of a number of M&S executives during the RFID Journal Live! 2015, 2014, 2013, and 2006 Conferences was used [15–18]. In addition, secondary data sources from academic and trade articles were content analyzed using key concepts in the model. The following are accepted definitions of the content analysis method:

> "Content analysis is any research technique for making inferences by systematically and objectively identifying specified characteristics within text." [19, p. 5]."Content analysis is a research technique for making replicable and valid inferences from data to their context." [20, p. 21]."Content analysis is a research method that uses a set of procedures to make valid inferences from text." [21, p. 9].

In this study, the concepts used for content analysis were derived from the structurational model of technology. This framework forms the "context" of the content analysis method as applied to M&S' RFID system. The secondary data was analyzed within the context provided by the Orlikowski framework, which is considered the "prior theory." "Analytical constructs operationalize what the content analyst knows about the context, specifically the network of correlations that are assumed to explain how available text are connected to the possible answers to the analyst's questions and the conditions under which these correlations could change....analytical constructs ensure that an analysis of given texts models the texts' context of use..." [22, p. 34].

The following key conceptual elements of the content analysis method as stipulated by Krippendorf [22] were used in this study: (1) body of text selected for the analysis; (2) research question that needed to be addressed; (3) a context of analysis within which interpretations will be made; (4) analytical constructs that operationalize what the analyst knows about the context; and (5) inferences that will be arrived at to address the research question.

4 Research Findings

4.1 Structure of Signification

"The structure of signification" will show how the RFID initiative at M&S embedded the way the technology works in the form of concepts and procedures has directed in the manner in which inventory management and tracking issues have been interpreted at M&S and how business processes have been redesigned to make full use of RFID.

M&S Business Process Steps Involved in RFID Inventory Tracking

The following are the brief steps that represent take place in the journey of the merchandise at M&S from the suppliers to the retail stores:

(1) Avery Dennison, the RFID tag vendor, prepares the RFID tags for the M&S's use. The RFID tag has a microchip in the label that holds a unique number.

(2) An RFID printer is used to add a UPC bar code and reads the chip number.

(3) The resulting intelligent RFID labels are sent to the 200 or so suppliers of M&S in over 20 countries so that they could be attached to the M&S merchandise. These suppliers produce merchandise strictly for M&S's own brand and so, it is fairly easy to manage these suppliers [8, 23].

(4) RFID tagged garments are shipped to the appropriate M&S distribution center where they are temporarily stored.

(5) RFID tagged garments arrive the M&S retail stores where they are scanned on either a 2-week or 4-week cycle.

(6) Store personnel use GEN 2 handheld RFID readers could be used to scan the GEN 2 RFID tag IDs.

(7) The scanned RFID data goes to a central database and is processed by RFID software, both developed and managed by M&S independently [23]. Data on product code (UPC) or stock keeping unit (SKU) [24] is captured.

(8) The merchandise count was validated and sent through to the stock management report; the stock file is corrected based on the latest scans.

(9) Stock files could get critically inaccurate within about 6 weeks (typical in the industry); at this point, a manual count is made.

(10) Replenishment requests from stores are also based on the data and the distribution center sends the requested merchandise to the stores.

RFID Infrastructure Used By M&S

Today, M&S uses Gen 2 HHT handheld RFID readers to read the relatively new GEN 2 RFID tags. M&S approved the transition to Gen 2 RFID technology in 2012 for all general merchandise. Thus, far, M&S has used well over 400 million RFID tags as of 2014 [2]. Avery Dennison has supplied M&S with nearly one billion RFID tags as of May 2013 and continues to be the tag supplier for the firm [25]. M&S uses different types of GEN 2 RFID tags for various types of store merchandise, resulting in a total of 70 RFID tag variations [26]. Previously in 2005, M&S used "intelligent labels" operating at 868 megahertz (MHz). It also used 5-in long paper labels developed by Paxar, a printing and retail technology vendor [27]. The French firm IER based in Suresnes, France used microchips from the Swiss firm EM Microelectronic to make RFID inlays, which were then inserted by Paxar in the intelligent labels. The RFID inlays hold a single unique serial number which EM Microelectronic encoded onto the microchip. As a result of this, M&S reported that the mobile RFID readers and inlays have provided 100 % successful read rates at a range of 0.7 m [27].

In prior years, M&S used fixed RFID readers built into shopping trolleys powered by lead-acid batteries. Motorola and other vendors supplied these older readers. M&S also used fix portals with RFID readers at the distribution centers. Then, in 2006 and 2007, two-piece RFID readers consisting of a mobile base station and a handheld RFID scanner communicated with the reader via Bluetooth. These two-piece RFID readers also communicated with M&S' network. U.K.'s BT Group developed and deployed a hosted database to manage the RFID system and integrated this database with M&S' enterprise IT systems [27].

The RFID readers are usually fielded out to the sales floor for tag readings early in the mornings or in the evenings. The Gen 2 HHT handheld RFID readers connect with the store server using a radio frequency network or a docking station. The handheld RFID readers allow sales assistants on the floor to select a store department using a drop-down menu on the handheld reader. The RFID readers can read up to 15,000 items hourly and remove duplicate reads. Upon completion of the scans, the reader uploads the RFID data to the RFID database through the store's wireless network. The RFID system is programmed to filter out stray reads from other departments and following verification of the final RFID data, the latest RFID scan data overwrites the database's stock data automatically [26]. The RFID software also updates the daily delivery list to facilitate the replenishment of missing items [26].

M&S developed its own proprietary software to manage the RFID system and uses its own database to store RFID data [25]. The software generates weekly reports showing product data at the merchandise and store levels.

M&S' top 380 stores that account for about 97 % of the firm's sales revenue count their stock using the mobile RFID reader to correct their inventory data [2]. About 59 merchandise categories are tagged and counted in the stores, accounting for about 93 % of sales revenue [2]. M&S had planned to extend item-level tagging to the remaining merchandise categories and deploy in all stores by 2016 [2].

Impact of RFID System on the Inventory Systems of M&S

The following are the significant observed impacts of RFID item-level tagging on the inventory system of M&S.

- Item-level RFID tagging is appropriate specifically for inventory that has the following attributes: (1) relative high retail price of the item and (2) size complexity for the item as in the case of men's trousers, for instance. Men's trousers could have five different leg lengths and ten different waist sizes—ten multiplied by five is fifty. One product, men's trousers, has fifty different sizes— it could be very costly to have, say, ten for each of these fifty different sizes. A store is more likely to have one or two of each size. Thus, it is critical to have accurate information on the location of men's trousers of other sizes in other stores in order to meet customer orders and needs.

- The typical expectation is that the inventory count would be about 8 % inaccurate. "….At that stage we are looking for it to be within what we call a "tolerance," so within the ballpark of acceptability in terms of what we were expecting to have found. Typically, that's 8 %. You would not expect that after 2 weeks or even after four weeks that your inventory would be 50 % inaccurate or 40 % inaccurate. But 4, 5, 6 %…yeah you would. That is fairly typical and I think most retailers would probably be able to corroborate that for us. So if it is within that margin of error, within that acceptability bracket, as it were, then we use that count to overwrite our stock management system. So we've a lot of confidence in RFID…." expressed Kim Phillips, M&S Head of General Merchandise Packaging [23]. If the inventory inaccuracy exceeds 8 %, M&S could request another recount, though, not necessarily a full recount to satisfy the need the ensure some measure of due diligence is done:

"…Quite often, is the answer to that. 8 % is a number that we've judged whereby it's a fine line between, you know, you want the store to be conscientious. Have they counted everything that's in the back rooms? Have they counted the windows and all of the mannequin displays? Have they made sure that they really have captured everything that's within the building? If they have, then you need to accept that count, whatever it is, you know it is the ugly truth, but you have to accept it, because otherwise there's no value in the exercise…." [24]

"….We wouldn't need to do a full recount, actually, we'd ask the store team to take the handheld to recall the count that's already been done and if they find there's anything that they've missed, which is very easily done, you know maybe you've missed what's behind the refund desk or in the fitting rooms, you can just add that one bit, you don't need to count everything all over again…." [24].

- RFID has helped to identify items that were flagged as being "out-of-stock" in specific stores and to use RFID system reported figures to correct the supposed "out-of-stock" status for the item [24].
- RFID has helped identify where misplaced inventory might be: "….So we're now using 40 stores and we're checking our delivery discrepancies and we've made great strides in terms of identifying where the flow of merchandise into stores is not what it should be in terms of the level of accuracy and changes have been made as a result of new information, brand new information, which RFID has provided us with for the first time…." [24].
- The RFID system provided information on the items that remained in the stores at the end of the day [28]. This information was forwarded to the central inventory database to enable the delivery of the right inventory items the following day. Prior to the pilots involved, this type of data was previously collected using point-of-sale terminals with bar code scanners. There were significant differences between the inventory figures reported by the RFID system against these those coming from point-of-sale terminals, with the former delivering much better results. Without RFID, most retail stores simply estimated inventory in the store by subtracting inventory sold from the inventory sent to the store—but this resulted in errors.
- RFID has helped deal with misplaced inventory involving logistics activities: "….we were even able to pinpoint how some of these things had occurred, how some of these errors had happened and some of it, I mean a very large part of it, was around timing issues, for example, where distribution centers from a systems point of view have done one thing but the reality of what they have loaded or not loaded is different. In a non-RFID world, that doesn't matter too much, but when you're counting every day, something every day in every store, you are writing off and writing on vast quantities of stock and you are sending product that is not required to stores that don't need it which of course, by default, means that if you're purchasing the correct amount of product in the first place, you're sending things to places that don't need it such that other stores that do need it cannot then have it and you will inevitably be selling that product at a loss eventually, or certainly a mark down. And we were able to identify how some of this was happening and to work with them to tighten some of our standard operating

procedures in order to make sure that that was much improved in the future. And what we've actually found is that we've been able to more than halve the level of delivery inaccuracy within our business...." according to Richard Jenkins, Head of RFID Strategic Development, M&S [8, pp. 9–10].

- RFID will be used to update M&S' stock management system automatically upon receipt of RFID-tagged items during deliveries and this will enable the store staff to detect discrepancies immediately as opposed to waiting for up to 3 weeks before discrepancies are detected.

- The RFID software system also allows the store personnel to confirm the accuracy of any count and check for missing items, if any discrepancy is detected [26]. The software also supports an in-store store personnel feedback system that facilitates ongoing evaluation, refinement, and upgrading of the RFID system.

- Doing the cycle count every two weeks for items with product size complexity will eliminate the need to do manual inventory barcode checking done twice a year, but could lead to more frequent electronic counting using RFID readers:

"....So the business case objectives for RFID in clothing. So it's about getting accurate information on stock position in each store and keeping it accurate. Yeah. Improving the true availability of all sizes, colors for the customer. Known for 'the store that can always find your size.' Increase customer satisfaction and reduce manual stock checking by staff. We do a twice annually barcode manual checking. By actually reading everything on a two week cycle, then we don't need to do this. Deliver increased sales and rapid return on our investment is the idea for that. But absolutely, absolutely right to get the accurate stock file for all the multi-channel things that we need to do...." explained Kim Phillips. [23].

"....I think that manual counting will cease, yeah. And I think we'll count more often because the speed of the counting device is now actually fantastic and before it used to take use a night shift to scan T33. T33 are our bras, boxed bras, which are very size and color complex and that now took an hour and a half with the new Gen 2 reader. So, changing, and that's fast. You know, why should you not count all the time? You know, if you've got enough hours and the store staff to do it, but then the quicker, the more accurate the equipment, the better it is...." explained Kim Phillips. [23].

4.2 Structure of Domination

M&S signified its intention to explore and discover RFID's potential role in improving its retail inventory systems by mandating a series of RFID pilot initiatives starting with the first one in the year 2000. That year, M&S used high frequency (HF) RFID tags to track 10 million food totes (i.e., plastic trays carrying food items) between its suppliers and distribution centers. Then, in 2003, M&S stepped up by using ultra-high frequency (UHF) RFID tags to track selected clothing items—men's suits, shirts, and ties first in one of the firm's 400 stores [27]. This initial trial for clothing items was partially financially supported by U.K.'s Department of Trade and Industry as part of its New Wave Technology Program [28].

In 2004, M&S expanded its men's suit tagging to nine other stores but stopped tagging shirts and ties. Then, in 2006, M&S decided to attach RFID tags to all items in its men's suit, jacket, and formal trousers set and all items in its ladies' lingerie, suit-and-jacket, and formal-trousers-and-skirt departments [27]. The firm started tagging only ladies' bras in the lingerie department, since each bra style comes in 48 different sizes. Ladies' bras are one example of a clothing item that exhibits "product size complexity," a requisite attribute of merchandise that require item-level tagging for accurate inventory stock reads.

The success of these prior RFID pilots convinced M&S of the business value of RFID and thus, in 2012, its Board of Directors mandated a global rollout of item-level tagging for all its apparel and general merchandise including bedding, home goods, kitchenware, beauty products, etc., at all its 760 stores, involving about 69 key departments [29, 23]. In the same year, M&S stepped up its use of RFID technology by adopting the Gen 2 RFID tags and readers.

The ability of the RFID-enabled system to prevail over M&S subsequent inventory and tracking systems and thus, manifest its "structure of domination" is due to the numerous benefits realized since the inception of RFID pilots. The commitment to this initiative was manifested with the commitment of ten million pounds to the project to cover 100 million RFID tags and involving 14 M&S departments [30].

M&S maintained that RFID readers installed in the portals of its distribution centers had a 95–98 % read rate, whereas the mobile readers used in the sales floor turned in as high as 100 % read rates [28]. When it comes to the technical accuracy of the RFID tag technology used, Kim Phillips confirmed no data loss or duplication reported. Richard Jenkins also indicated that the series of RFID projects have enabled them to isolate improvements in sales revenues due specifically to item-level RFID tagging on the merchandise.

Another evidence of RFID's importance in terms of the "structure of domination" is the element of importance accorded to this technology for six key areas in M&S' RFID strategic development plan: (1) general merchandise supply chain; (2) food supply chain; (3) retail stores; (4) property and assets; (5) international supply chain/international business; and (6) e-commerce customer channels [8]. All RFID pilots to date have led to the current status of M&S tagging all general merchandise at the item level, which should have direct impacts on its supply chain. Thus, far, the discussions on the RFID system in place have focused on the inventory management system for M&S's various general merchandise categories. Within M&S's food category, the firm is eyeing item-level tagging wine and expensive meats as both are high-value items [8]. With respect to enhancing the customer experience in the brick-and-mortar store, M&S is already piloting RFID-enabled features in its trials in three stores in Blue Water, Lennon Coney, and the Pantheon in Oxford Street London. In these sites, item-level RFID tagged shoes are put on shelves which read the tags and activate interactive screens that bring up images of handbags, scarves, and other apparel that could go nicely with the pair of shoes in a complete ensemble design package [23]. Using in-store touch screens, customers should also be able to browse products, obtain product information, review interactive product guides, and order products that are not physically in the store [26]. M&S should also be able to push product information to the customers' iPads or smartphones. Regarding asset management, Jenkins expressed concern that M&S is spending too much money buying assets used to transport merchandise at different touch points in its supply chain simply because they could not be located after they are used [8]. M&S has expanded its forays into retail merchandising and is aspiring to be an omnichannel retailer [31]. In 2007, M&S used Amazon.com as the outsourcing service provider to support its online website. By venturing into the online world, M&S expanded its supply chain globally and in 2008, it started international delivery services to France, Germany, Spain, the U.S., Canada, Australia, and New Zealand. Then, in 2011, M&S appointed former Tesco employee Laura Wade-Gery to manage the firm's multichannel division. Under Wade-Gery's oversight, M&S launched its own new website in 2014, which is promoted to its customers through the retailer's email and social media channels.

4.3 Structure of Legitimation

The RFID initiative at M&S has attained a "structure of legitimation" due to a number of developments recently in the retailing industry. Having "structure of legitimation," RFID item-level tagging has been the technological means by which retailers have sanctioned a specific way of developing information systems to address certain business operations needs and propagate a set of norms about what is and what is not "professional" social practice.

What is happening now is that by item-level tagging with RFID for all categories of general merchandise, M&S is laying the foundation for omnichannel retailing. This concept is complex, bridges the linkages among the multiple channels of selling to customers, and will require the integration of the IT infrastructure pieces used for capturing, storing, and processing order transactions and creating integrated customer profiles via these different channels. This case study focuses solely on M&S's efforts to achieve a robust inventory management system as its groundwork for taking on the challenge of linking transaction data from the various channels that would have to sit on top of an inventory system serving all these channels.

The other pillar supporting the "structure of legitimation" underlining RFID item-level tagging are the initiatives of the organization called GS1, a nonprofit international organization that develops and maintains standards for supply and demand chains across industries. Firms in the retailing industry use GS 1 electronic product code or EPC global standards that govern the workings of RFID technology. For instance, RFID Gen 2 was released by GS 1 as a worldwide standard for ultra-high frequency (UHF) RFID to simplify visibility, boost read rates, and improve RFID tag performance [32].

4.4 Social Consequences of RFID System at Marks & Spencer

4.4.1 Social structure and social consequences of IT

In looking at the "social structure and social consequences of IT," the structurational model of technology investigates how the IT, in this case, the RFID system for inventory control, is implemented, assimilated, and adopted by the end users, and the consequences of usage [10]. IT, once again, acts as a medium of human action, and human action is also shaped by the use of IT. The end users' behavior at M&S in the process of using the RFID system is mediated by interpretive schemes, resources, and norms perceived to be embedded in the technology. Since the RFID system is a medium of human action at M&S, it will shape the end users' behavior in the firm, resulting in facilitating certain outcomes and constraining others.

In M&S's earnest attempt to improve its inventory control and management systems through the years, RFID served as a focal point of a number of pilot projects prior to the 2012 mandated directed to deploy item-level tagging on all categories of general merchandise, presumably because of the positive outcomes from these pilots. M&S was so pleased with the results that project proponents were able to successfully obtain near 100 % store compliance in deploying item-level tagging. Internally structurally, therefore, the RFID system is tightly knitting M&S stores together so that they are in near or full compliance with the technology requirements for reaching higher levels of inventory management accuracy and reliability. It is critical that all M&S retail outlets use RFID-tagging so that all these brick-and-mortar outlets can function as fulfillment centers not just for in-store customer orders, but also for orders placed online such as those placed through smartphones and iPads. In other words, omnichannel retailing has now redefined the functions of the brick-and-mortar outlets, which should now be poised to serve the interests of a unified marketing strategy aimed to reach the customer anytime, anywhere.

Also, with the mandate to tag all general merchandise at the item level, M&S has to address the technical RFID issues involving handling liquids and metals. The ability to do so requires M&S to collaborate closely with different types of RFID vendors—thus extending its interorganizational linkages to achieve the ultimate goals of omnichannel retailing.

4.4.2 Action and social consequences of IT

The "action and social consequences of IT" discussion refers to the current and future changes needed in terms of "action initiatives" to more clearly delineate the path towards omnichannel retailing. More future changes are still needed in affected business processes and actions in order to fully meet the requirements of omnichannel retailing. The following is M&S's future vision for its RFID deployment at three key points of its supply chains: manufacturing plants, logistics/distribution centers, and M&S retail stores [2]. In the manufacturing plants, M&S plans automated RFID shipping and automated advance ship notice generation. In the logistics/distribution centers, the desired RFID enabled tasks are: automated RFID receiving of merchandise from the manufacturing plants; RFID inventory counts; RFID-verified pick-and-pack cartons; and automated RFID advanced ship notices to the appropriate retail stores. In the M&S retail stores, the future RFID-enabled tasks include: automated RFID receiving from the distribution centers; RFID integrated systemic inventory counts; rapid RFID inventory scanning; RFID point-of-sale transaction support; RFID tag scanning for loss prevention; generation of exception reports for immediate replenishment; and RFID-enabled enhanced customer in-store experience [2]. Once the entire M&S supply chain is RFID enabled at the preferred points, the manner in which cross-channel inventory management will be conducted still has to be determined. The higher demands of omnichannel retailing involve decisions covering in-store order fulfillment; store-to-store transfers; store fulfillment of on-line orders; online site to store transfers; ecommerce fulfillment; and processing returns and exchanges [33].

5 Conclusions and Future Research Direction

In the near future, it would be interesting to track the progress of M&S after it has successfully item-level tagged all merchandise in all its stores and measure key performance indicators. Then, further into the future, it is suggested that the narrative be extended to include the experience of M&S after RFID tagging important selected business processes in its entire supply chain. Still another thread—and perhaps, this is the more topical one—is to investigate how well M&S's RFID systems uphold the firm's goals with respect to ecommerce and omnichannel retailing. The case study approach would still be the qualitative research method of choice to address these research questions in the future.

References

1. Pioytrowicz, W., Cuthbertson, R.: Introduction to the special issue information technology in retail: toward omnichannel retailing. MISQ **18**(4), Summer, 5–15 (2014)
2. RFID Journal: RFID Journal Live! Europe: M&S' Journey—Past, Present, and Future. Slides, Part 1. London, England (2014)
3. RFID Journal: RFID Journal Live! Europe: Moving to 100 % RFID Tagging of General Merchandise. Slides, Part 1. London, England (2013)
4. Vanheems, R.: Multichannel retailing: Why do multichannel customers deserve special attention. Dec. Mktg. **55**, 41–52 (2009)
5. The Aberdeen Group: The 2012 Omni-Channel Retail Experience. Boston (2012). www.stores.org/assets/whitepapers/EpicorThe2012OmniChannelRetailExperience.pdf

6. Hardgrave, B.: Get Hip TO BOPIS. RFID J. 5 April 2015. http://www.rfidjournal.com/articles/view?12911
7. Hardgrave, B.: Omnichannel Retailing: You Can't Do it Without RFID. RFID J. 18 Dec 2012. http://www.rfidjournal.com/articles/view?10247
8. Jenkins, R.: M&S' RFID Journey—Past, Present, and Future. Transcription of Talk. London, England (2014)
9. Orlikowski, W.J.: The duality of technology: rethinking the concept of technology in organizations. Org. Sci. 3(3), 398–427 (1992)
10. Orlikowski, W.J., Robey, D.: Information technology and the structuring of organizations. Info. Sys. Res. 2(2), 143–169 (1991)
11. Giddens, A.: The Constitution of Society: Outline of the Theory of Structure. University of California Press, Berkeley (1984)
12. Giddens, A.: Central Problems in Social Theory: Action, Structure and Contradiction in Social Analysis. University of California Press, Berkeley (1979)
13. Giddens, A.: New Rules of Sociological Method. Basic Books, New York (1976)
14. Weick, K.: The Social Psychology of Organizing. Addison-Wesley, Reading, MA (1979)
15. RFID Journal: RFID Journal Live! Marks & Spencer Broadens and Deepens Its RFID Use. Slides. San Diego, California (2015)
16. RFID Journal: RFID Journal Live! Europe: M&S' Journey—Past, Present, and Future. Slides, Part 2. London, England (2014)
17. RFID Journal: RFID Journal Live! Europe: Moving to 100 % RFID Tagging of General Merchandise. Slides, Part 2. London, England (2013)
18. RFID Journal: RFID Journal Live! Using RFID to Improve Customer Service and Retail Productivity. Slides, (2006)
19. Stone, P.J., Dunphy, D.C., Smith, M.S., Ogilvie, D.M.: The General Inquirer: A Computer Approach to Content Analysis. MIT Press, Cambridge (1966)
20. Krippendorff, K.: Content Analysis: An Introduction to Its Methodology. Sage Publications, Beverly Hills, CA (1980)
21. Weber, R.P.: Basic Content Analysis, 2nd edn. Sage Publications, Newbury Park, CA (1990)
22. Krippendorff, K.: Content Analysis: An Introduction to Its Methodology. Sage Publications, Thousand Oaks, CA (2004)
23. Phillips, K.: Marks & Spencer Expands RFID to All Its Stores. Transcription of Talk: Part 3. Orange County, Florida (2014)
24. Phillips, K., Jenkins, R.: Marks & Spencer Expands RFID to All Its Stores. Transcription of Talk: Part 2. Orange County, Florida (2014)
25. Violino, B.: Marks & Spencer Rolls out RFID to All its Stores. RFIDJ J. 25 May 2013. http://www.rfidjournal.com/articles/view?10536
26. Greengard, S.: Marks & Spencer Embraces Change. RFID J. 6 July 2014. http://www.rfidjournal.com/articles/view?11952
27. Collins, M.: Marks & Spencer to Extend Trial to 53 Stores. RFID J. 18 Feb 2005. http://www.rfidjournal.com/articles/view?1412
28. Collins, M.: Marks & Spencer Expands RFID Trial. RFID J. 10 Feb 2004. http://www.rfidjournal.com/articles/view?791
29. Roberti, M.: Marks & Spencer Leads the Way. RFID J. 21 Oct 2013. http://www.rfidjournal.com/articles/view?11106/2
30. Phillips, K., Jenkins, R.: Marks & Spencer Expands RFID to All Its Stores. Transcription of Talk: Part 1. Orange County, Florida (2014)
31. Sharma, N.: Marks & Spencer's Standalone E-Commerce Foray to Spruce Up Retail. Case Number 515-030-1, Amity Research Centers Headquarter, Bangalore (2015)
32. Swedberg, C.: GS1 Ratifies EPC Gen2v2, Adds Security Features, More Memory. RFID J. 8 Nov 2013. http://www.rfidjournal.com/articles/view?11168
33. Lodwig, D.: Omni-Channel Fulfillment in a Changing Retail World. Technical Report, WHS Systems (2014)

M-Health and Self Care Management in Chronic Diseases—Territorial Intelligence Can Make the Difference

Monica Sebillo, Maurizio Tucci, Genny Tortora, Giuliana Vitiello and Athula Ginige

Abstract The healthcare domain represents a field where the territorial intelligence and ICT can be profitably combined to strengthen the skills of a territory, to understand its phenomena, to interpret local dynamics concerning the ordinary arrangement as well as extraordinary phenomena involving patients, institutions and organizations. The results presented in this paper are addressed to face the challenges of territory sustainable development, encouraging mutualisation and cooperative exploitation of information between individuals and communities. In particular, the main goal of the research carried out within the healthcare domain is to provide patients with personalized services based on a technology with a limited invasive effect, through the experimentation of new solutions meant to share information and integrate software components. The process model discussed in this paper and the derived application, MyDDiary, represent a concrete modality of interrelationships among territorial actors devoted to the patients' empowerment.

M. Sebillo (✉) · M. Tucci · G. Tortora · G. Vitiello
Department of Computer Science, Università di Salerno, Fisciano, Italy
e-mail: msebillo@unisa.it

M. Tucci
e-mail: mtucci@unisa.it

G. Tortora
e-mail: tortora@unisa.it

G. Vitiello
e-mail: gvitiello@unisa.it

A. Ginige
School of Computing, Engineering and Math,
University of Western Sydney, Sydney, Australia
e-mail: A.Ginige@westernsydney.edu.au

© Springer International Publishing Switzerland 2016
L. Caporarello et al. (eds.), *Digitally Supported Innovation*,
Lecture Notes in Information Systems and Organisation 18,
DOI 10.1007/978-3-319-40265-9_15

1 Introduction

Territorial Intelligence (TI) is a system of models, methods, processes, people and tools that allows for a regular and organized collection of data heritage generated by a territory. In particular, it consists in the availability and exchange of know-how among local actors of different cultures [1]. Through data processing, analyses and aggregations, TI allows data transformation into information, its preservation and availability, and its presentation into a simple, flexible and effective form so that to constitute a support for strategic, tactical and operating decisions.

Currently, TI is gaining an important role for organizations and companies belonging to the same geographic area because it works as a collector of diverse knowledge and contributes to improve the exchange of strategic information at the local level [2, 3]. As an example, the goal of a territory homogeneous in terms of population, environmental resources and economic activities requires an analytical design approach that takes into account several aspects, ranging from communication lines to public work, from social policies to services for citizens. In this context, the interrelationship among territorial actors is strongly beneficial because it can play a significant role within the participatory city planning with the involvement of local stakeholders and citizens who can express their needs and share their knowledge.

A relevant contribution to these new forms of governance could be guaranteed by exploiting ICT as fundamental support to the collaborative work and to the transformation of information into knowledge. In particular, making the collective knowledge accessible and deployable by decision makers represents the first step towards the automation of a transparent federation process addressed to build networks and clusters to which specific actions can be linked.

The goal of the research we are carrying out is to define methods and techniques for handling the multidisciplinary complexity of data coming from a spatially enabled territory. In particular, we investigate new ways to exchange strategic information at the different levels, through processes that encourage local dynamics and improve the relationships between ultimate users and the territory.

The healthcare domain represents a field where TI and ICT can be profitably combined to strengthen the skills of a territory, to understand its phenomena, to interpret local dynamics concerning the ordinary arrangement as well as extraordinary phenomena involving patients, institutions and organizations.

The results presented here fall in the healthcare domain, and are meant to provide patients with personalized services based on a technology with a limited invasive effect, through the experimentation of new process models meant to share information and integrate software components. We also aim to extend the impact of those results in order to address the challenges of territory sustainable development, encouraging mutualisation and cooperative exploitation of information between individuals and communities.

The experimentation we are conducting concerns an environment neighboring a local community of diabetic patients. We are developing new types of connections among patients and among patients, physicians and medical facilities, in order to improve the healthcare coordination. A spatio-temporal database has been designed to collect, aggregate and manage both the metadata generated by user-performed activities and those captured through the sensors available on a smartphone device. On the basis of this infrastructure diabetic patients are provided with innovative functionalities and may also automate several recurring operations. Moreover, metadata collected from individual patients can be aggregated and managed to support public healthcare services, allowing for, e.g., planning, management and research activities. The final goal is to enrich collective knowledge and produce territorial intelligence addressed to improve the decision making by healthcare experts and organizations.

Mobile applications are gaining increasing consensus as a valuable means to improve healthcare services. A detailed review of 42 controlled trials that investigate the use and limitations of mobile-based systems in the context of healthcare services can be found in [4]. A detailed analysis about the present support level of existing mobile applications designed to help patients with the self-management of their diabetes can be found in [2]. The majority of reviewed applications support the basic tasks needed by a diabetic patient such as diet, physical exercise, insulin dosage or blood glucose level and, according to the authors, can represent a suitable solution for diabetes self-management. However, the study shows also how, although mobile applications are usually preferred to traditional computer or Web-based solutions, several usability issues and limitations still exist, related, e.g., to data entry difficulty, lack of personalized feedback and missing integration with existing health records.

The paper is organized as follows. Section 2 describes the role that ICT could play in establishing and supporting interrelationships among territory actors meant to improve the collective knowledge and territorial intelligence. In Sect. 3, the mobile Health solution, MyDDiary, is described both in terms of architecture and functionality. It has been realized on the basis of the analysis of users requirements collected from a preliminary study. Each function is properly described and the corresponding interface is detailed also discussing the resulting improvement of the user's experience. Finally, in order to investigate the technical feasibility of the proposed healthcare self-management model, the prototype has been tested simulating realistic interaction scenarios, as described in Sect. 4, where some future activities also are planned.

2 Discovering New Process Models to Support Patients' Empowerment

In the healthcare domain, one of the present challenges is to provide patients with personalized ICT-based services which may leverage all relevant information coming from the surrounding environment, with a low invasive impact. In the present research, we have investigated and experimented an innovative process model conceived to share information and integrate software components. In order to address the challenges of territory sustainable development, the model supports cooperation and information sharing between individuals and communities. This goal can be achieved by a profitable combination of territorial knowledge with personal data and events, able to support the development of special-purpose applications meant to improve users' experience while creating public value for services. In order to design and develop such an information system infrastructure, the factors of primary importance that should be taken into account are the need of a shared communication protocol among all the involved entities, extensibility (i.e., the ability to add new features without affecting the existing components), and the opportunity to hide the format differences of data coming from heterogeneous data sources.

Raw data generated by users through devices and sensors, can be properly processed, aggregated and shared. In order to perform those tasks, datasets from patients have to be associated with appropriate metadata thus guaranteeing their interoperability. Moreover, once shared and enriched by personal sense making, they can contribute to the collective meaning making. On this basis, the territory can finally take advantage of collective knowledge, produce innovation in the healthcare management, and create cross-fertilization in terms of added value for different domains.

An example of such a progressing is illustrated in Fig. 1, where the expected interrelationships among territory actors are depicted and supported by the under-lying technology. Each diabetic patient is able to use specific (mobile) applications

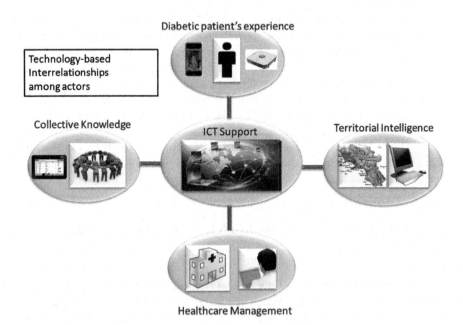

Fig. 1 ICT support for collective knowledge and territorial intelligence

that collect data (and metadata) about some of his relevant parameters, such as blood, physical condition, food, and physical exercise. The goal for this collection is wide. Those parameters can be collected and shared with the physician in charge of monitoring his health condition, with the local healthcare institutions to take part to campaigns for monitoring global trends and tuning existing protocols, with other patients to build a collective awareness as well as social artifacts (social constructivism). As for the ICT support, it is paramount for both improving patients' life and contributing to a sustainable development by extending the impact of TI processes to a broader context. In the example depicted in the figure, if a patient has a positive experience with a restaurant where a gluten-free cooking for diabetics is available, the value of this information is multifaceted.[1] It can be shared with the diabetes community (collective knowledge), it can be properly managed by caregivers and healthcare institutions (healthcare management), and it can eventually represent a peculiarity of that territory to be promoted by institutional web sites for tourism (territorial intelligence).

3 A Mobile Health Solution in a Spatially Enabled Territory

Our recent research activities have been focused on the design of personal healthcare applications that may benefit from complex data coming from a given spatially enabled territory. In this section we describe a special-purpose application, named *MyDDiary*, developed to improve care experience of diabetic patients while creating public value for territorial services. Diabetic patients are provided with an application for the self-management, which includes the monitoring of several parameters, such as the blood glucose level and the amount of carbohydrate ingested. Moreover, metadata collected from individual patients can be aggregated and managed to support public healthcare services.

From a high level point of view, the system is characterized by a traditional client-server architecture. The backend is designed around the principles of Service Oriented Computing (SOC) [5–7], while the client side is entirely deployed as a mobile solution. A detailed description of the backend module is out of the scope for the present paper. In the following, we rather focus on patients' perspective and describe the metadata collection framework and the mobile interaction experience built upon that framework.

---

[1]There exists a strong relationship between diabetes and celiac disease. They are both autoimmune diseases and it is rather frequent that people suffering from an autoimmune disease have a particular predisposition to develop other ones.

3.1 The Metadata Collection Framework

The first module of the client side is the Metadata Collection Framework that is responsible to aggregate and manage metadata either directly generated by user-performed activities or coming from the various sensors usually available on an Android device. In addition, it offers a high level API that simplifies the development of mobile applications addressed to exploit such metadata. As shown in Fig. 2, the framework main components are the Metadata Collection and Aggregation Background modules and the High Level Library that lets developers make use of such metadata.

The first task performed is metadata retrieval. It is carried out by the Background Module, namely an Android service that scans (at regular or user-defined intervals) all metadata sources available on a mobile device. A list of the most important traceable metadata sources freely accessible on the Android platform can be found in Table 1. Every single metadata is subsequently stored in the internal database of the framework. It is worth noting that every time the service is launched it performs the operations and then stops until the next iteration. In that way the impact on other user's activities and on the device battery life is reduced. The only significant exception happens when tracking user's fitness activity (walking, running, driving or still), by means of the built-in functions provided by the recent versions of the

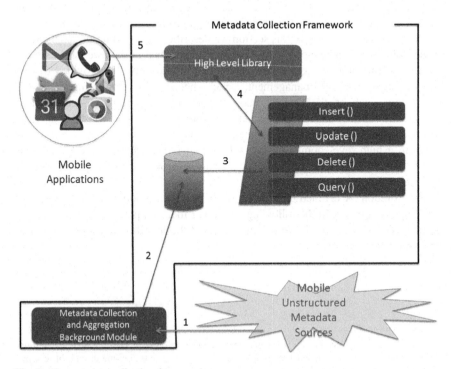

Fig. 2 The metadata collection framework

Table 1 Traceable metadata sources accessible through android

Metadata sources		
Basics	Android telephony framework	Android media store framework
Alarm clock Browser history Browser Bookmarks Calendar Contacts	Calls log and details Service state Signal strength SMS details	Images Videos Audio files
Android location framework	Android hardware framework	
GPS status	Camera details Geomagnetic field Accelerometer Gyroscope Light sensor Pressure sensor Proximity	

Android platform. To enhance the query performance and avoid privacy and security violation issues, we chose to store only metadata, while the real referred content, such as pictures and documents, is retrieved by the High Level Library according to parameters chosen by the developer. In particular, the stored metadata are grouped into several classes of objects, such as images, videos, phone calls, and browser history, and for each class, we have designed a table which stores all relevant metadata. Moreover, in order to facilitate spatio-temporal queries we decided to add information about time and space for each type of metadata collected. In fact, some of them are not automatically acquired by the Android platform. As an example, when the users receive a phone call only the temporal information, namely the date, time and duration, is automatically inserted.

In order to use the database content, we have created a supporting library to allow filter and display of information on the basis of specific combinations of space and time. Such a library is in charge of translating complex queries which involve, as parameters, non-trivial time series and/or spatial information, into appropriate invocations to the standard component of the Android platform, namely the Content Provider, which allows to share information by means of simple methods to retrieve and store data.

3.2 Interface Design to Enhance User's Experience

MyDDiary has been designed to be a comprehensive solution for the self-management of several aspects of diabetes care. Moreover, it embeds empowerment and context functionalities within a more general environment where their interrelationships can be exploited in a transparent manner. Figure 3a shows *MyDDiary* home screen displaying three sets of functionalities, related to selfcare, empowerment and context, respectively. In Appendix I the complete list of *MyDDiary* functionalities is given.

3.2.1 Diabetes' Selfcare

The first set covers the basic self-care treatments, namely the glycemic index, the insulin dosage and ingestion, and the calorie count. Due to the extensive amount of information that a diabetic user may need to input every day, a desirable

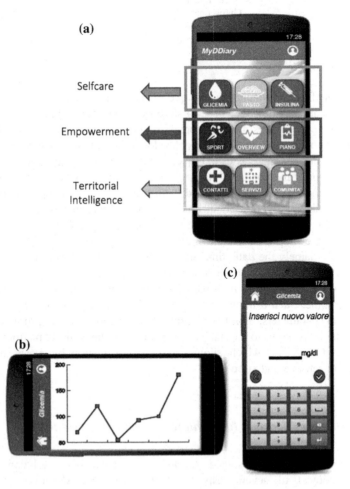

Fig. 3 **a** MyDDiary home **b** the trend of the glycemic index and **c** the insertion of a new georeferenced value

requirement is the automation of repetitive tasks. To this aim, for each functionality *MyDDiary* offers an immediate overview of the last week trend through a graphic, then it allows the user to add new values and update his/her diary. Figure 3b displays the graphic of the glycemic index over the last week and Fig. 3c shows the interface for the insertion of a new glycaemia value, automatically associated with its geolocalization. This last feature can be relevant for medical studies, considering that for instance a scientific relationship has been discovered between the blood glucose level and the elevation of the place where a patient lives.

3.2.2　Empowerment

As for the Empowerment set of functionalities, the goal of our research has been to extend the set of automated tasks by embedding also those that currently require a more invasive technology and repetitive actions, such as the survey of fitness activity. By properly exploiting the functionality offered by the Metadata Collection Framework, we are testing some feasible solutions to automate, as much as possible and without the use of CPU-intensive methods, most of those daily activities.

Let us consider the following scenario. A diabetic user has set on the calendar of his/her mobile device a recurring fitness plan: Gym from 19.00 to 20.00 from Monday to Wednesday and running on Thursday and Friday. Let us also suppose that on the corresponding calendar entry such activities are marked as "Gym" and "Run". The user decides to use *MyDDiary* to monitor his fitness activity and compute the number of times he missed the scheduled training during the last 2 months. Moreover, he/she needs to obtain an immediate overview that compares the fitness activity, calorie counts and glycemic values of the last week.

The application checks that the gym activity has been actually performed by verifying whether user's position and the gym location were inside a reasonable convex hull for a certain temporal range. The run activity is instead checked by calculating the speed value within a time range of a calendar entry taken from the personal planning, on the basis of user's position stored as metadata.

As for the Overview function, we have defined a visual metaphor capable to integrate three different parameters within a unique view, namely the glycemic index (a raw data), the calorie count (an aggregated value) and the percentage of fitness activity (a calculated value) done in a given temporal range. Figure 4a shows the list of such parameters where each entry can be selected for a subsequent detailed access. In Fig. 4b the summarizing metaphor is illustrated that represents respectively the glycemic index as the length of a slice, the calorie count as the slice color based on the semaphore metaphor, and the percentage of fitness activity done. Besides the hint that the patient himself can obtain from such a view, this function allows different stakeholders to gain an immediate overview of the current health state of a diabetic user. As an example, the physician could profitably receive the image and make decisions about the trend of a specific treatment or detect alert situations.

(a)   (b)

Fig. 4 a The textual synthesis of user's activities and **b** the corresponding visual representation. The *red ring* corresponds to the warning customized threshold for the glycemic index

3.2.3 Territorial Intelligence

The last set of functionalities concern some relevant context information. The T (erritorial) I(ntelligence) functionalities are useful to establish some relationships among patients, territorial communities and services. Indeed, the local database stores information about patient's customized parameters as well as events and activities planned within the personal diary. A portion of that information can be properly exchanged by the patient on a dedicated social network where new patterns can be discovered and additional facts built. The derived collective knowledge could be in turn convenient for the patient himself/herself when it is offered through location based services.

Besides personal and health data accessible from the profile, the user can manage the POI geolocalization which can be useful also in a wider domain, such as the acquisition of location-based services. As an example, when reaching a new area, it can be classified and described in terms of relevance for the diabetic patient. This classification is also stored within the local database, thus every subsequent access to that area will invoke and filter the POIs advisory on the basis of the user's needs.

When designing the application we also took into account the privacy issue, especially important when dealing with highly sensitive information. In fact, not all the information caught by patient's smartphone (e.g., personal calls) should be transmitted to the backend module. Therefore, *MyDDiary* has been designed to

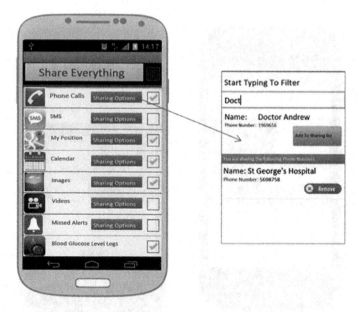

Fig. 5 Handling privacy issues with MyDDiary

provide users with a fine-grained control over the data that can be actually sent and shared. For example, the user may choose to send his/her current location only when he/she is at the hospital or he/she may decide to share only the phone calls metadata that match some fixed keywords such as "Doctor's phone number" or to share only the multimedia files directly taken through the *MyDDiary* application. Figure 5 shows the screen for information sharing settings.

4 Experimental Usability Evaluation and Future Work

The prototype has been tested simulating realistic interaction scenarios, also relying on territorial knowledge, on events exposed through Web services and on a set of anonymized data, provided by a company which performs periodic statistics to analyze the care trend of the diabetes at a national level.

Diverse scenarios customized on the patient's needs have been experimented during prototype testing, as follows. Once a diabetic patient reaches a new place, he automatically receives (1) some relevant information, such as the location of the closest center for therapy of diabetes, where emergency medications and insulin can be prescribed and obtained, (2) recommendations about restaurants offering breakfast and meals customized for diabetic patients' diet (with the calorie count), and finally (3) information on the presence of fruit and vegetables biological markets. Moreover, based on the fitness activity planned for that day, (4) he/she can

(a) (b)

Fig. 6 **a** The information about the closest pharmacy and **b** the information about a restaurant with the calorie count facility

be informed about the sport facility available in that area with the corresponding opening times.

Figures 6a, b show the information the diabetic patient receives when visiting a new city. In particular, Fig. 6a illustrates the notification of a pharmacy satisfying his treatment needs, it is displayed through Google Maps. Analogously, Fig. 6b shows the information that the user receives at dinner time about a restaurant nearby, where food intolerances are properly handled.

The experiments were carried out in three different sites and involved two groups of diabetes patients, 10 used to mobile technology (*Experts*) and 10 who only use smartphones for voice communication and sms exchange (*Novices*). We followed a Think Aloud approach to annotate any comments/criticisms coming from participants. Each participant was asked to perform a set of 10 representative tasks, while an observer was encouraging comments on the perceived interaction experience. Usability-related measures, such as medium time to complete a task, number of errors and number of clicks per task, were computed during the experiments, whereas a reaction questionnaire was submitted to each participant soon after each experimental session. The achieved results indicated the technical feasibility of the proposed healthcare self-management model and at the same time encouraged us to further refine the interface design also based on users' feedback. As soon as the new version of the prototype is available, we plan to set up a longitudinal field user study to properly estimate the achieved patient's empowerment, in terms of appropriate metrics.

References

1. Bertacchini, Y., Rodriguez-Salvador, M., Souari, W.: From territorial intelligence to compositive and sustainable system. In: Procs of International Conference of Territorial Intelligence, pp. 106–124. Case studies in Mexico & in Gafsa University, Huelva Spain, Oct 2007
2. El-Gayar, O., Timsina, P., Nawar, N., Eid, W.: Mobile applications for diabetes self-management: status and potential. J. Diab. Sci. Technol. 7(1), 247–262 (2013)
3. European Network of Territorial Intelligence (ENTI). http://www.territorial-intelligence.eu. Accessed June 2015
4. Free, C., Phillips, G., Watson, L., Galli, L., Felix, L., Edwards, P., Patel, V., Haines, A.: The effectiveness of mobile-health technologies to improve health care service selivery processes: a systematic review and meta-analysis. PLOS Med. 10(1), (2013)
5. Bertolotto, M., Di Giovanni, P., Sebillo, M., Vitiello, G.: Standard-based integration of W3C and geospatial services: quality challenges. In: Casteleyn, S., Rossi, G., Winckler, M. (Eds.) Procs of the 14th International Conference on Web Engineering ICWE 2014, Toulouse, France, pp. 460–469, 2014. © Springer International Publishing Switzerland, 1–4 July 2014
6. Di Giovanni, P., Bertolotto, M., Vitiello, G., Sebillo, M.: Web Services Composition and Geographic Information. In: Elaheh Pourabbas (ed.) Geographical Information Systems— Trends and Technologies, pp. 104–141. Taylor and Francis Group. 978-1-46-659693-1 (2014)
7. Papazoglou, M.P.: Service oriented computing: concepts characteristics and directions. In: Proceedings of the Fourth International Conference Web Information Systems Engineering, pp. 3–12 (2003)

Enforcing Software Developers' Productivity by Using Knowledge and Experience

Pasquale Ardimento, Maria Teresa Baldassarre, Nicola Boffoli,
Danilo Caivano, Michele Scalera and Giuseppe Visaggio

Abstract *Objective*—Explore the relation between developers, a Knowledge Experience Base (KEB) called PROMETHEUS and their presentation in the development of enterprise applications used to propose a theory that expresses relations based on empirical evidences. *Methods*—Case study carried out in a real context with 5 development teams each of 6 staff members, who have in turn carried out evolutive maintenance tasks on 5 Software Packages commercialized by the enterprise with 5 different process models. *Results*—In the 5 experimental teams that used KEB productivity is almost double compared to previous data without the KEB. *Conclusions*—We can assume that the theory is extendible to the development process according to which using KEB in maintenance processes improves developer productivity as it mitigates the errors made due to the amount of decisions taken during project execution. Experience collected in PROMETHEUS becomes part of the organizational culture, being it formalized.

Keywords Knowledge packaging · Knowledge base · Software production

P. Ardimento (✉) · M.T. Baldassarre · N. Boffoli · D. Caivano · M. Scalera · G. Visaggio
Department of Informatics, University of Bari, Bari, Italy
e-mail: pasquale.ardimento@uniba.it

M.T. Baldassarre
e-mail: mariateresa.baldassarre@uniba.it

N. Boffoli
e-mail: nicola.boffoli@uniba.it

D. Caivano
e-mail: danilo.caivano@uniba.it

M. Scalera
e-mail: michele.scalera@uniba.it

G. Visaggio
e-mail: giuseppe.visaggio@uniba.it

M.T. Baldassarre · D. Caivano · G. Visaggio
SER&Practices Spinoff of University of Bari, Bari, Italy

© Springer International Publishing Switzerland 2016   221
L. Caporarello et al. (eds.), *Digitally Supported Innovation*,
Lecture Notes in Information Systems and Organisation 18,
DOI 10.1007/978-3-319-40265-9_16

1 Introduction

Software development (production and maintenance) is a knowledge-intensive business involving many people working in different phases and activities. The available resources are not increasing at the same pace as the needs; therefore, software organizations expect an increment in productivity.

However, currently development teams do not benefit from existing experience and they repeat mistakes even though some individuals in the organization know how to avoid them. Project team members acquire valuable individual experience with each project; the organization and individuals could gain much more if they were able to share this knowledge. Knowledge, therefore, is a critical factor and affects many different aspects of software development such as:

- Accessing domain knowledge. Software development requires access to knowledge not only about its domain and new technologies but also about the domain for which the software is being developed. An organization must acquire new domain knowledge either by training or by hiring knowledgeable employees and spreading it throughout the team.
- Acquiring knowledge about new technologies. It is difficult for developers to become proficient with a new technology and managers to understand its impact and estimate a project's cost when using it. When developers or project managers use a technology that project team members are unfamiliar with, engineers often resort to the "learning by doing" approach, which can result in serious delays. So, organizations must quickly acquire knowledge about new technologies and master them. Research produces knowledge that should be transferred to production processes as innovation in order to be valuable. Consequently, domain knowledge must be enriched by technical and economical knowledge that allows identifying the best approach for introducing new knowledge in processes together with the resources, risks and mitigation actions [1].
- Sharing knowledge about local policies and practices. Every organization has its own policies, practices, and culture, which are not only technical but also managerial and administrative. New developers in an organization need knowledge about the existing software assets and local programming conventions. Experienced developers often disseminate it to inexperienced developers through ad hoc informal meetings; consequently, not everyone has access to the knowledge they need. Passing knowledge informally is an important aspect of a knowledge-sharing culture that should be encouraged. Nonetheless, formal knowledge capturing and sharing ensures that all employees can access it. So, organizations must formalize knowledge sharing while continuing informal knowledge sharing.
- Capturing knowledge and knowing who knows what. Software organizations depend heavily on knowledgeable employees because they are key to the project's success [2, 3]. However, access to these people can be difficult. Software developers apply just as much effort and attention determining whom to contact in an organization as they do getting the job done. These knowledgeable people

are also very mobile. When a person with critical knowledge suddenly leaves an organization, it creates severe knowledge gaps. Knowing what employees know is necessary for organizations to create a strategy for preventing valuable knowledge from disappearing. Knowing "who has what knowledge" is also a requirement for efficiently staffing projects, identifying training needs, and matching employees with training offers. So, until knowledge is transferable or reusable, it cannot be considered as part of an organization's assets [2].

All these needs require both formalizing knowledge so that it is comprehensible and reusable by others that are not the author of the knowledge and experience packaging able to guide the user in applying the knowledge in a context.

Given these premises, this paper describes an approach for Knowledge Packaging and Representation and reports preliminary results of a first experimentation of the approach in an industrial context.

In our proposed approach, we have formalized a Knowledge Experience Package (KEP) and we have defined some packages that are stored in a Knowledge Experience Base (KEB) [4–7], [8]. The KEPs are obtained by using paper and other resources available on the Web and by giving them a predefined structure in order to facilitate stakeholders in the comprehension and the acquisition of the knowledge that they contain.

We have conducted a validation through a controlled experiment with the aim of answering the following Research Question (RQ): does the proposed knowledge description approach increase the productivity of software development?

The rest of the paper is organized as follows: related works are described in Sect. 2; Sect. 3 illustrates, briefly, the proposed approach for knowledge representation, Sect. 4 illustrates the investigation planning, Sect. 5 empirical execution and measurement model used; results of the study and lessons learned are presented in Sect. 6; finally, in Sect. 7 conclusions are drawn.

2 Related Works

The problem of knowledge packaging for better usage is being studied by research centers [5, 9–11], some of these are enterprises [4, 11], showing interest of the industrial community to the same problem. Knowledge bases sometimes have a semantically limited scope. This is the case of the Daimler-Benz base [5, 11], that collects lessons learned or mathematical prediction models or results of controlled experiments in the automobile domain only. In other cases, the scope is wider but the knowledge is too general and therefore not very usable. This applies to the MIT knowledge base [10] that describes business processes but only at one or two levels of abstraction. There are probably other knowledge bases that cover wider fields with greater operative details [11] but we do not know much about them because they are private knowledge bases. Our approach focuses on a knowledge base whose contents make it easier to achieve knowledge transfer among different stakeholders involved during software development. The knowledge base must be hybrid, public, as we wish, or private, depending on KEP authors preferences. The public KEB allows one or more interested communities to develop around it and exchange knowledge. In particular, it must be possible for Small and Medium sized Enterprise (SME) to become members of these communities.

3 Proposed Approach

Our approach focuses on a knowledge base, named PROMETHEUS [12–16], whose stored knowledge is formalized as KEP. A KEP is any cluster of knowledge, sufficiently familiar that it can be remembered rather than derived.

3.1 Knowledge Experience Package Structure

Authors use the term KEP to refer to an organized set of: knowledge content, teaching units on the use of the demonstration prototypes or tools and all other information that may strengthen the package's ability to achieve the proposed goal. The knowledge package must be usable independently of its author or authors and for this purpose the content must have a particular structure: distance education and training must be available through an e-learning system. In short, the proposed knowledge package contains knowledge content integrated with an e-learning function. In the proposed approach, the KEP can be made up of all the elements shown in Fig. 1. Evidence component is the only one KEP component that requires, for being defined, to be related to the Art and Practices component. A user can access one of the package components and then navigate along all the components of the same package according to her/his needs. Search inside the package starting from any of its components is facilitated by the component's Attributes.

To support the different needs that may arise during software development different kind of packages were defined as shown in Table 1.

3.2 Attributes

As shown in Fig. 1, each component in the KEP has its own attributes structure. For all the components, these allow rapid selection of the relative elements in the knowledge base. To facilitate the research a set of selection classifiers and a set of descriptors summarizing the contents are used.

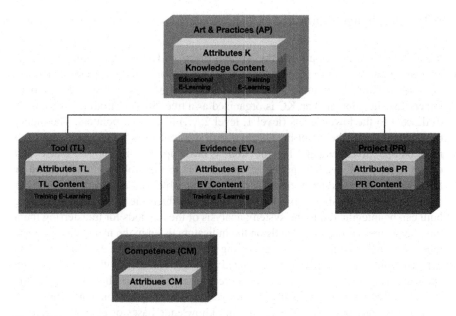

Fig. 1 Diagram of a knowledge/experience package

Table 1 Different kind of packages

Name	Description
Experience package	Contains experiences about processes, methods, and techniques used to develop software. Are expressed as theories
Product package	contains artifacts expressed in the form of source code, documents, analysis of architecture, test cases, etc.; template-guide for all the documentation

The classifiers include the keywords and the problems the package is intended to solve. The summary descriptors include a brief description of the content and a history of the essential events occurring during the life cycle of the package, giving the reader an idea of how it has been applied, improved, and how mature it is. Brief description may also include information telling the reader that the content of all or some parts of the package are currently undergoing improvements.

The package also provides the following indicators: necessary competence to acquire it, prerequisite conditions for a correct execution of the package, adoption plan describing how to acquire the package and estimating the resources required for each activity. To assess the benefits of acquisition, they contain a list of: the economic impact generated by application of the package; the value for the stakeholders in the company that might be interested in acquiring the innovation. There are also indicators estimating the costs and risks. It is important to note that each kind of package has other specific attributes.

3.3   Knowledge Contents

It can be seen in the figure that the Art and Practices Knowledge Content (KC) is the central one. It contains the knowledge package expressed in a hypermedia form in order to include figures, graphs, formulas and whatever else may help to understand the content. The KC is organized as a tree. Starting from the root (level 0) descent to the lower levels (level 1, level 2, ...) is through pointers. The higher the level of a node the lower the abstraction of the content, which focuses more and more on operative elements. The root node is made up of a "Thoughtful Index" and one or more problems. The nodes are the answers to the problems: the solution or the solutions proposed for each of the announced problems. Each answer consists of the following: analysis of how far the results on which the innovation should be built can be integrated into the system; analysis of the methods for transferring them into the business processes; details on the indicators listed in the metadata of the KC inherent to the specific package, analyzing and generalizing the experimental data evinced from the evidence and associated projects; analysis of the results of any applications of the package in one or more projects; details on how to acquire the package. The research results integrated by a package may be contained within the same knowledge base or derive from other knowledge bases or other laboratories. PROMETHEUS also allows to capture, share and retain content to ensure that one or more software processes are automated and managed. To achieve these results PROMETHEUS was interfaced with a well known Content Management System (CMS), Alfresco [17]. More details can be found in [18]. In the remaining part of the paper reference to KEB is intended structured according to PROMETHEUS.

4   Investigation Planning

4.1   Research Goal

The Research Goal (RG) has been defined as: analyze software development process with the aim of evaluating the efficacy of PROMETHEUS with respect to productivity from the view point of the software developer in the context of a company.

The investigation was carried out in a large enterprise (over 2000 developers) geographically distributed with several sites in Italy. For privacy reasons we cannot cite the company, referred to as "company" in the rest of the paper.

4.2   Variables

The independent variables. The development process with four levels, the most used by the company: WaterFall (WF), POD (Process Oriented Development);

LWRUP (Light Weight-Rational Unified Process), LASAP (Light AcceleratedSAP; a methodology for speeding up the implementation of a SAP R/3 system).

The dependent variable of the study is Productivity, defined by the company in terms of Function Points/person-day.

4.3 Investigation Design

The investigation design adopted is a typical case study, i.e. carried out in the company context and appropriately adapted to the environment and resources made available. The experimental units are five evolutive maintenance processes of Software Packages (SP) {SP1, SP2, SP3, SP4, SP5} marketed by the company needing frequent maintenance interventions. Table 2 describes the application domain and the development process uses for each experimental SP.

A maintenance session begins when the number of maintenance requests for a SP is accountable to 50 new Function Points [19]. An average of 20 solar days are necessary to collect the number of maintenance requests summing up to an average of 50 new FP. Each maintenance session is an experimental RUN. Given the budget of the investigation 4 RUNS were scheduled for each SP: {RUN1, RUN2, RUN3, RUN4}. Each RUN generated a new version for each SP: SP_{ij} indicates the ith SP following the jth RUN.

Five teams {T1, T2, T3, T4, T5} were defined, each of 6 developers. Each team included competences on analysis (1 person), design (1 person) and coding (4 people). The team members were not involved full time, their involvement depended on the development process adopted.

The experimental design is shown in Table 3. Each SP has four maintenance sessions and each team changes the SP used in every RUN. Furthermore, in each RUN all the teams use a KEP and designer and programmer change SP according to Table 3, while the analyst always collaborates on the same SP, being the application domain expert.

Table 2 SP representing the experimental material

Id. project	Brief description	Software methodology
SP_1	management of utilities energetic	WF
SP_2	Management of Curriculum Vitae of a company	POD
SP_3	sharing of tacit and non structured knowledge present in an industrial context	XP
SP_4	support the migration to a new SAP version or maintenance of a SAP installation	LWRUP
SP_5	upgrading of a SAP preconfigured system	LASAP

Table 3 Experimental design

Id. team	RUN$_1$	RUN$_2$	RUN$_3$	RUN$_4$
T$_1$	SP$_{11}$	SP$_{52}$	SP$_{43}$	SP$_{34}$
T$_2$	SP$_{21}$	SP$_{12}$	SP$_{53}$	SP$_{44}$
T$_3$	SP$_{31}$	SP$_{22}$	SP$_{13}$	SP$_{54}$
T$_4$	SP$_{41}$	SP$_{32}$	SP$_{23}$	SP$_{14}$
T$_5$	SP$_{51}$	SP$_{42}$	SP$_{33}$	SP$_{24}$

4.4 Selection of Experimental Subjects

The experimental subjects involved in the experimentation are developers belonging to the same company. The company has provided experimental subjects represented by analysts, designers and developers with long working experience in the company. None of the subjects were knowledgeable with PROMETHEUS. A stratified random sample was carried out to identify 5 analysts, 5 designers and 20 developers. From this sample the developers were selected to make up 5 teams.

5 Executing the Investigation

When preparing the investigation as first step we initialized the KEP to make it available at the first RUN. To this end we considered empirical evidence from the literature related to general development processes used in the experimentation as well as specific ones adopted. We selected the experiences supported by empirical evidence that could be relevant for the developers of the company. These experiences were enriched with other ones following from a survey carried out on data collected by the company. The survey allowed to select useful information to calculate FP produced by the company. Once data was collected, the KEP was initialized and the KEB was populated. Training was carried out for 8 h where the structure of the KEP and its use was illustrated. A seminar was also organized to validate the relevance of the experience collected in PROMETHEUS. It was helpful for both experimental subjects involved in the experimentation as well as a manner for collecting their comments and remarks for improving the KEP. The SP selected by the company as experimental objects were validated in terms of quality, documentation and source code by the authors of this study, and, if the case, improved. It is the case to point out that the activities of a RUN did not necessarily begin on the same day for each team as it was necessary that maintenance requests summed to about 50 new FP for the SP. Once the RUN was completed each development team met with two authors of this paper to identify new experiences to add or modify in the KEP included in the KEB. The authors also analyzed possible contradictions between collected experience and that registered in the KEB. When this occurred, the authors together with the experimental subjects modified the contents of the KEB and eliminated the contradiction.

5.1 Material and Instrumentation

The experimental material for each SP included:

- analysis specifications, design specifications, source code, integration and system test cases updated to the last version, all according to the company standards. The SP in input to RUN1 were verified by the experimenters during the preparation phase of the investigation, while the ones in input to RUNi are the ones verified during the previous RUNi-1
- maintenance requests expressed according to the company standards.

The instruments used for the investigation were the same as the ones adopted regularly by the company during their production processes.

5.2 Measurement Model

The indirect measurement used was Productivity, as intended by the company:

$$\text{Productivity} = \text{Size} / \text{Effort}$$

where

$$\text{Effort} = \sum_{i=1}^{6} T_i$$

where T_i = time implied by the ith person

$$\text{Size} = \text{FP\_New} - \text{FP\_Old}$$

FP_New is the total number of Function Points of SP after the developing run. In case of new development FP_Old = 0. In the RUNs of the investigation we refer to maintenance, as so, FP_New correspond to the FP of the SP produced by the maintenance process. On the other hand, FP_Old are the ones related to the FP undergoing maintenance. Some of the FP calculated in Size refer to the reused components either during development or maintenance and made available from PROMETHEUS. Effort is the person-time, expressed in person days (1 person-day = 8 h) spent for production or maintenance of the SP.

Two types of effort are not considered in Productivity:

- effort for eliminating data and functions of the SP that are no longer necessary;
- effort for correcting failures identified and included in the corrective maintenance requests. The maintenance requests in input to each RUN are the ones actually collected by the project manager during the following two RUNs.

Ignoring these two types of effort is a way for inducing developers to maintain a high software quality level. In fact, only a high level of quality can lead to an insignificant effort for correcting and eliminating failures. In case of low quality, the effort needed for both types of intervention would not be negligible nor could it be calculated in the developer's performances.

6 Experimental Results

The productivity baseline used was calculated as average performance that the enterprise had before introducing PROMETHEUS. This was calculated by using data collected in the survey previously mentioned. Figure 2 reports the performance box plots without baseline and with the KEB. It is evident that performances improve considerably going from an average of 0,94/day and 1,38 in RUN1, 1,9 in RUN2, 2,66 in RUN3 and 2,46 in RUN4. The historical series shows the continuous improvement of the performance until it stabilized at 2,5 FP/Day. Adopting the KEB increased productivity in time thanks to the following factors:

- increased experience in the KEB usable by the developers;
- increased reuse of reusable components included in the KEB;
- improved use of PROMETHEUS by developers. This occurs timely if we consider that in RUN2 the average performances are already close to 2FP/Day.

After each cycle the data collected was analyzed to produce new knowledge and generalize it in explicable experience formalized in the KEB. From the description of the empirical investigation we can see that this activity requires an extra 20 % of

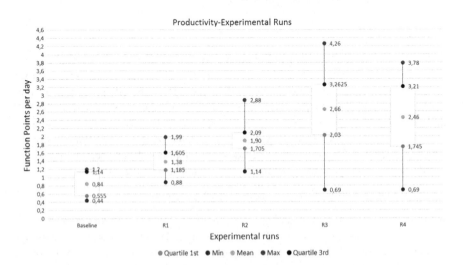

Fig. 2 Productivity: baseline (without PROMETHEUS) and RUN₁₋₄ (with PROMETHEUS)

time with respect to the time spent for development only. This means that the performances in each RUN should be adjusted with a corrective factor of 0,8. As so, the corrected performances come out to: $RUN_1 = 1,10$; $RUN_2 = 1,52$; $RUN_3 = 2,13$; $RUN_4 = 1,97$. Summarizing, KEB tends to double the company's developer performances. Improvement of the performances derives from reusing experience as well as products. Reusing experience is systematic while reusing products occurs only if one or more products contained in the KEB are part of the capabilities or functionalities that must be developed in the SP. In summary, reusing experience is certainly the most significant component of performance improvement. In RUN_4 reuse was less intensive than in the previous RUN, as so the performance value is slightly lower.

Figure 3 shows the average productivity values in the four RUNs where PROMETHEUS was adopted. It can be seen how developer performance improves whatever the process model used.

Figure 4 shows the performance trends for each team in every experimental RUN. See how all teams improve their performances with a similar trend to the one shown in Fig. 2. This means that:

- all the developers are equally enhanced by using the KEB;
- exchanging experience between teams from one SP to another through the KEB is effective, so that a developer's performance continuously improves even though he moves from one SP to another, i.e. even though the project a developer is assigned to changes in time. In other words, the KEB is able to turn experience into a cultural and organizational asset rather than being restricted to the individual developer.

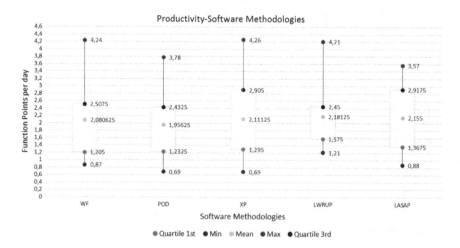

Fig. 3 Productivity: software development methodologies

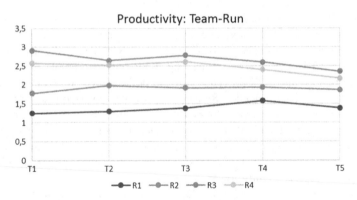

Fig. 4 Productivity: development team

7 Conclusions and Future Works

The empirical study carried out proves that adopting a KEB in software maintenance activities, based on 5 different process models and applied to 4 different SP enhances developers' productivity. Results are significant and encouraging: developer performances double with PROMETHEUS, independently from the development process model used and from the application domain; all the developers that use PROMETHEUS improve their performances with a similar trend; PROMETHEUS enhances formalizing experience collected and transferring it to developers.

Given the above findings, we can hypothesize the following theory, extendible to the entire development process: using KEB in maintenance enhances developers' productivity because it mitigates the errors that they tend to make given the large amount of decisions made during project execution. Furthermore, the experience collected in PROMETHEUS is capitalized in the by the company, i.e. transferable because formalized and organized. This theory is based on empirical observations collected throughout our investigation. It however requires to be confirmed through replications. As so, future replication studies must extend the field of application and validity of our theory so it can be applied to production processes other than maintenance ones. Finally, new knowledge and experience must be collected from other replications, in other disciplines, in order to increase the level of abstraction of our theory.

References

1. Reifer, D.J.: Is the software engineering state of the practice getting closer to the state of the art? IEEE Softw. **20**(6), 78–83 (2003)
2. Foray, D.: L'economia della conoscenza. Il Mulino (2006)

3. Myers, P.: Knowledge Management and Organizational Design: An Introduction, Knowledge Management and Organizational Design. Butterworth-Heinemann, MA (1996)
4. Schneider, K., Schwinn, T.: Maturing experience base concepts at DaimlerChrysler. Softw. Process Improv. Pract. **6**, 85–96 (2001)
5. Malone, T.W., Crowston, K., Herman, G.A.: Organizing Business Knowledge-The MIT Process Handbook. MIT Press Cambridge (2003)
6. Basili, V.R., Caldiera, G., McGarry, F., Pajerski, R., Page, G., Waligora, S.: The software engineering laboratory—an operational software experience factory. In: Proceedings of the 14th International Conference on Software Engineering, pp. 370–381. ACM (1992)
7. Schneider, K., Hunnius, J.V.: Effective experience repositories for software engineering. In: 25th International Conference on Software Engineering, pp. 534–39. IEEE (2003)
8. Ardimento, P., Cimitile, M., Visaggio, G.: Distributed software development with knowledge experience packages. In: Demey, Y.T., Panetto, H. (eds.) OTM 2013. LNCS, vol. 8186, pp. 263–273. Springer, Berlin Heidelberg (2013)
9. Jedlitschka, A., Pfahl, D.: Experience-based model-driven improvement management with combined data sources from industry and academia. In: International Symposium on Empirical Software Engineering, pp. 154–161. IEEE (2003)
10. Klein, M.: Combining and relating ontologies: an analysis of problems and solutions. In: Workshop on ontologies and information sharing, pp. 53–62. Seattle, USA (2001)
11. Schneider, K., Schwinn, T.: Maturing experience base concepts at DaimlerChrysler. Softw. Process Improv. Pract. **6**(2), 85–96 (2001)
12. Ardimento, P., Caivano, D., Visaggio, G.: Experience formalized as a service for geographical and temporal remote collaboration. In: 3rd International Conference on Advanced Applied Informatics, pp. 48–53. IEEE (2014)
13. Ardimento, P., Baldassarre, M.T., Cimitile, M., Visaggio, G.: Empirical experimentation for validating the usability of knowledge packages in the innovation transfer. In: Filipe, J., Shishkov, B., Helfert, M., Maciaszek, L.A. (eds.) ICSOFT/ENASE 2007. CCIS, vol. 22, pp. 357–370. Springer, Berlin Heidelberg (2008)
14. Ardimento, P., Cimitile, M.: An empirical study on software engineering knowledge/experience packages. In: Jedlitschka, A., Salo, O. (eds.) PROFES 2008. LNCS, vol. 5089, pp. 298–303. Springer, Berlin Heidelberg (2008)
15. Ardimento, P., Baldassarre, M.T., Cimitile, M., Visaggio, G.: Empirical validation on knowledge packaging supporting knowledge transfer. In: 2nd International Conference on Software and Data Technologies (ICSOFT), pp. 212–219. INSTICC (2007)
16. Ardimento, P., Cimitile, M., Visaggio, G.: Knowledge management integrated with e-learning in open innovation. J. e-Learn. Knowl. Soc. **2**(3), 343–354 (2006)
17. Open platform for business software. http://www.alfresco.com/
18. Ardimento, P., Convertini, V.N., Visaggio, G.: Building a knowledge experience base for facilitating innovation. Int. J. E-Services Mob. Appl. **5**(4), 40–49 (2013)
19. International Function Point Users Group. http://www.ifpug.org/

Digital Services for New Model of Sustainable Mobility

Giuliana Vinci and Martina Musarra

Abstract The use of technology is increasing in our society, leading to an evolution in the consumers' behaviours and opening new frontiers in the communication modalities. Transportation sector is pervaded by this progress: new models of mobility are rising, mainly connected to the preeminent role of technology. Sharing economy is the new aspect of future society, focusing the attention on the goods' distribution and allocation. This study looks at the economic, environmental and social benefit of this new approach, considering the lack of policies to regulate this phenomenon.

Keyword Technology · Transportation · Mobility · Environment · Sharing economy

1 Introduction

In the 1990s the phenomenon of car sharing rose up, becoming a new economic model, having sound basis on the relationship between individuals in the society and on the respect of the environment and the promotion of biodiversity. This new business has influenced many countries around the world, especially United States of America (US) and Europe. Car sharing is an integration service for the public transport, which aim is reducing the use of private cars, especially in congested cities [1]. The service is managed by public and private organizations that allow users who pay a membership fee to use at individual level a number of vehicles in various points of the city, by reservation. Today car sharing is an international phenomenon, big companies are facing the potentiality to integrate it in new business models.

G. Vinci (✉) · M. Musarra
Department of Management, Sapienza University of Rome,
Via Del Castro Laurenziano 9, 00161 Rome, Italy
e-mail: giuliana.vinci@uniroma1.it

M. Musarra
e-mail: martina.musarra@uniroma1.it

© Springer International Publishing Switzerland 2016
L. Caporarello et al. (eds.), *Digitally Supported Innovation*,
Lecture Notes in Information Systems and Organisation 18,
DOI 10.1007/978-3-319-40265-9_17

At the meantime, thanks to technology, the barriers between people are slightly fall down, and new modalities of transfer are changing mobility. By considering the society' evolution, the study is focused on the importance of technology applied in the automotive industry, according to the new economy of sharing. The network created by technologies leads to a collaborative consumption that change the way of thinking to the market, by moving away from the old industrial economy and invite consumers to exchange all types of their assets [2]. A confront between the Car Sharing (CS) and the Uber (U) model of business is done, in order to underline the costs and the benefits in terms of environment, economy and society implications.

2 Changing the Modality to Live Mobility

Sharing is a fundamental consumer behaviour that is overlook or confuse with commodity exchange and gift giving. The act of sharing dissolves interpersonal boundaries posed by materialism and possession attachment trough expanding the aggregate extended self [3]. According to the study of Price in 1975 [4] the act of share has been the most basic form of economic distribution in the ancient society, by considering it the basic form of human economic behaviour. Thus, the first car sharing model was organised in small sharing vehicles cooperatives, where time and kilometres travelled were appointed on a report [5]. With the development of technologies and infrastructures, as well as economies of scale, new companies started to generate added value from this business, by increasing their penetration index into the market and the car sharing model has evolved. The new model is characterised by the interaction between people with same needs, high level of technology and no information asymmetries. The European car sharing market faces a growth especially during the years 2008–2011, by registering an increase of about 60 % in the subscription rate, from 500,000 to more than 800,000 members, with future perspective to reach 750,000 users in 2020 [6]. The market rate is growing constantly, presenting a 40 % compound annual growth rate for traditional and a 20 % for peer-to-peer (P2P) car sharing. Differently from the traditional car sharing, P2P car sharing allows car owners to convert their personal vehicles into shared cars that can be rented to other drivers on a short-term basis [7]. The phenomenon of car sharing is enhancing its rate for several reason:

- The economic crisis started in 2008 coerced people to rethink about expenditures, promoting new approaches in the perception of value. The new business model focuses the attention on a collaborative dimension, based on P2P business and a win-win situation. The P2P activities redefine traditional forms of ownership, lending and renting, establishing strong affinity to shared access to goods and knowledge, even between strangers.

- Increasing the population density at global level, and considering the number of people in 2050 will reach the 9.6 billion of inhabitants [8] also the spatial geography has to be redefine. In fact, in the biggest cities the construction industry must face distributional problems, in order to implement a functional usage of space, infrastructures and technology. To support this hypothesis, we consider the study that demonstrates that an owned car is used only for the 10 % during the day, while it is unused for the rest of the time [9], we can consider this asset as a waste also in term of money, representing a cost.
- The car sharing phenomenon is strictly connected to the environment. In fact, the impact of cars in terms of depletion of resources and pollution released into the atmosphere is linked to the importance of logistic and transportation optimization in urban areas.
- Interconnection between people is the most important variable of the system: car sharing platform is composed by users that towards social networks and technological tools are able to enter in contact each other to fulfil their needs, improve their satisfaction, and reduce total costs [10]. The opportunity to be connected with other users that have the same needs is useful for sharing success and costs.
- Undoubtedly, the investments in infrastructures and technology are fundamental to pull the demand and to achieve tangible results in terms of users' access and implementation of the new business model.

2.1 Car Sharing

Car sharing service in Italy is available in ten cities: Bologna, Brescia, Florence, Genoa, Milan, Padua, Palermo, Parma, Rome, Scandicci, Turin, Savona and Venice (Table 1). To support local cities in the establishment of a car sharing system, the *Iniziativa Car Sharing* (ICS) has been created by the Italian Ministry of Environment, Protection of the Territory and the Sea. This framework supports the identification of local companies (public or private), for the implementation of mobility operations according to required standards. Car sharing is a complementary public transport service, and cities' governments allow free parks for cars, generally in dedicated parking slots, to enter in no-traffic zone, without any traffic limitations, and to use taxi and buses reserved lanes. These mobility advantages for customers contribute to the creation of added value for the operating companies. Actually, the Italian market is rather fragmented: the national service is available in 16 cities with 12 small operative companies, with approximately 20.000 users with 600 cars and 400 parking slots. Investments for about € 20 billion in infrastructures and € 20 billion in smart mobility and new car park slots are required, in order to get to a flawless model of sharing mobility.

Table 1 Car sharing availability in Italy, by cities (*data processed by the authors on* www. icscarsharing.it, *2015*)

Cities	Started date	No. of cars	No. of users	No. of parks
Milan	Sept. 2001	141	6,274	85
Bologna	Aug. 2002	41	1,261	31
Venice	Aug. 2002	43	3,574	16
Turin	Nov. 2002	122	2,795	78
Genoa	Jul. 2004	52	2,542	15
Rome	Mar. 2005	124	3,430	86
Florence	Apr. 2005	15	420	15
Parma	Feb. 2007	11	328	11
Palermo	Mar. 2009	100	1,625	63
Savona	Jun. 2009	52	2,524	44
Brescia	Feb. 2010	11	328	11
Padua	Sept. 2011	11	163	13
Total		**666**	**22,500**	**447**

Modalities. Italian users must proceed with the registration on an online platform, which can work also as an app on a smartphone or on a tablet. Users can reserve and choose a car model accordingly to their needs and to their geographical position, in the closest parking area, at each hours, during the day and/or the night. The most relevant strength of the car sharing system is the availability of the service 24 h, besides the autonomy of the user to choose the nearest car, by using the technology support.

The total cost the users have to face for the service' exercise can be divided into:

- *Fixed cost* it includes an amount of money (monthly or yearly) to be part of the association and a reimbursable deposit.
- *Variable cost* it depends on the kilometres driven, the rent time, the type of vehicle used, the time slot and extra services.

Tools. To access to the car sharing service, users must register their personal data and proceed with the payment of a money amount defined by the company, which can be private or public, depending on the city's policies. After the registration and the payment, a smartcard with a personal identification number (PIN) is provided to the users. The smartcard is an individual instrument which is composed by a microchip and a PIN code, necessary to rent and return the car (open and close the vehicle) and to settle the service. The invoice is delivered to the user monthly or bimonthly (according to the company's rules), by using an electronical device installed on the car, which records the travel detail for each consumer (thanks to the PIN). To reserve cars, consumer can use internet or can phone to a call centre service (24 h): those tools provide information on the type of car to rent, its availability and distance position from the user. The rent period can be one-hour minimum.

2.2 Uber App

In 2009 in the US was founded a company with the aim to simplify the citizens' mobility in the urban areas. The service offered by Uber (U) is based on the creation of a network in order to connect drivers and passengers towards a mobile software application. Thus, U is an intermediate between user and driver, combining the supply and the demand. For that reason a percentage of the total cost the user pays, only using a credit card, is direct to U company. To be part of the drivers' community, there are some requirements as well as benefits.

Modalities. Users have to find a driver on the online app, accordingly with the geographical position and with the final destination they would reach. The total cost users have to pay to the driver is divided into two different percentage:

- *80 % of the total cost* is directed to the driver, in order to support the fixed and variable car costs (fuel, insurance, maintenance and refund);
- *20 % of the total cost* is directed to U company, which define the policies to regulate the tariffs and hold the operating system for the app.

U system tariffs are cheaper than a normal taxi service. The expenses are calculated according to the distance travelled, (if the speed is higher than 17 km/h), or based on the elapsed time (if the speed is less than the threshold just cited). U offers different cars options, according to the quality the customer wants:

1. UberPop: the low cost option of Uber, running is done on a small car.
2. UberTAXI: the classic version Uber taxi.
3. UberBLACK: the race takes place on a sedan.
4. UberSUV: the driver will be aboard an SUV.
5. UberXL: the driver will be in a car with six or more seats.
6. UberLUX: the race takes place through a very stylish and expensive.

Furthermore, because the service works mainly between people that do not knows each other's, U company established some general requirements to accede to the platform: be 21 years of age; owning a car 4-door covered by insurance and no older than 8 years; have a clean criminal record; have at least 10 points remaining on the license; not having a license suspended for at least 10 years. Moreover, the company provides to the driver: a smartphone with the U app installed, to be detectable by users; the revision of the car to check the conditions; the insurance against damage to third parties.

Tools. To access to the service, users have to register their personal data on the app available for smartphone and tablet. During the registration process, it is necessary to insert the credit card coordinate, because the payment for using the service is allowed only with this modality. To use the service, users must enter on the online platform in order to activate the GPS coordinate, which are sent to the switchboard to calculate the travel' costs and the time needed to reach the final destination. If a user decides to benefit the service, the payment will occur with a charge on the credit card. The customers will keep track in real time the position of the car booked. The service of UberPop is actually suspended in some European countries, mainly for a problem of responsibility connected to the taxis category.

3   Role of Technology

A pivotal element for the access to the new paradigm of social mobility is technology [11], in particular internet availability. The tool necessary to enter into this market as user or driver, both in terms of renting a car with the car sharing or a driver with U company, is a smartphone with an internet access. The World Bank indicators [12] estimate some key data about the access to technology instruments: in the Fig. 1 and in the Fig. 2 are represented the development of technology usage

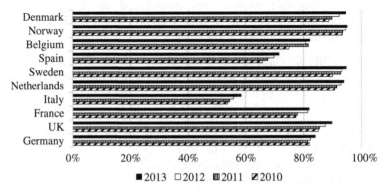

Fig. 1 Internet users (percentage per 100 people). Internet users are people with access to the worldwide network (*data processed by the authors on International Communication union, world Telecommunication/ICT Development report and database, and World Bank estimates, 2015*)

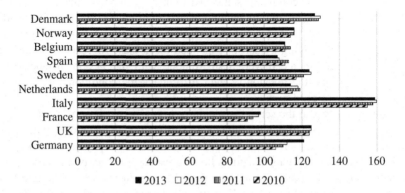

Fig. 2 Mobile cellular subscription. Mobile cellular telephone subscriptions includes the number of post-paid subscriptions, and the number of active prepaid accounts (*data processed by the authors on World Bank report, 2015*)

in different countries, across time series. In Fig. 1 is represented the internet access: in Europe it is advanced in the North-Europe countries, Denmark, Norway, Sweden, with an important role played by Netherlands, Germany and United Kingdom, while Italy reports an internet access capacity nearly to the 60 %. In Italy, the impossibility to access the network is a big challenge related to low investments in the broadband, which delay the connection' speed. Even though Italy has not a high rate of internet access compared to the total population, the Country has the first place in Europe for the possession of mobile phone. In fact, in the Fig. 2 is shown the total number of mobile phones per 100 persons (the indicator excludes: via data cards or USB modems, subscriptions to public mobile data services, private trunked mobile radio, telepoint, radio paging and telemetry services), and Italy represents the highest value, with 160 mobile phone on 100 persons. This aspect will be relevant dealing with the transportation sector if the investments on internet availability will be made in the near future [13]. Technology is playing an important role in the modern society [14], simplifying the capacity to connect people, with the growing usage of social networks and apps for smartphones and tablets [15]. Technology is also important in relation to the growing share on social mobility in the urban areas [16]: increasing the interconnection between people, the access rate to the share mobility will increase, by leading to some benefits in not only economics terms, but also growing the interconnection and the sense of citizens between members of the same society.

4 Environmental and Economic Aspects

In the recent years the automotive industry has registered a positive growth, especially in the US market ($ 13 million in 2008) and, even though with less profitability, in Europe. Annual sales have reached prerecession levels, but the uncertainty about future remains. Furthermore, this particular industry is strictly connected to the environment, especially considering the transformation process of commodities, for the substances released during the production process and during the usage of the final products. In the decade 2000–2010 the total hectares disappeared each years has been $ 5.2 million. The total cost of the environment degradation in terms of GDP loss at world level is equal to 8 %: in this scenario transportation sector plays an important role in terms of changing the environment equilibria, being an important source of pollutant emissions. This sector accounts for approximately 16 % of the global annual mean anthropogenic radiative forcing of black carbon, the vast majority of which is from diesel-fueled vehicles [17]. About 19 % of all carbon emissions were attributable to transportation in the year 2000 [18]. Approximately 9 % of global carbon emissions were attributable to the on-road sector alone, of which 99 % were from diesel engines [19]. Black carbon emissions were the most potent contributor to temperature change per unit mass emitted of any pollutant from the transportation sector from 1990–1999 [20]. The impact of the emissions generated by the gasoline and diesel-fueled transportation (equivalent to Euro 6/VI) are related to the geographical distribution. Modeling experiments have demonstrated that the climate impacts of black carbon and other non-CO_2 emissions will peak between 2000–2050, contributing to a global temperature increase of 0.1°K under projected emissions growth scenarios [21]. Cars, light trucks, heavy-duty trucks, buses, and coaches are the vehicle types that will contribute the most to the near-term climate forcing of transportation-related black carbon [22]. The implementation of international policies focused on the reduction in sulphates, besides the Kyoto protocol and the Horizon 2020, is required, in order to contrast the global warming effects. By considering those factors, the benefits of diesel controls may be more complicated once regional factors and magnitude of baseline sulphate emissions are considered [23]. Assuming the adoption of international standards for the emissions' reduction, new transportation model should be implemented with the aim to redefine the sector [24]. Actually, there is no jurisdiction regulating diesel lack carbon directly, but the practices implemented in OECD countries are the basis to regulate diesel emissions in developing countries [25]. In the specific case of sharing vision, a problem in the OECD countries is the government regulation for some categories, as taxis. The main constrain for U in OECD countries is strictly connected to the imputation of unfair competition: the app has been suspended in five European countries, Germany, Spain, France, Netherlands, and Italy with the objective to preserve the rights of taxis. Changes is both fuels and policies are required in order to promote a sustainable impact for the environment [26]. Undoubtedly, technology, feasibility of implementation, institutional capacity to support the market, and specific policies' definitions are fundamental to lead the transportation topic to new frontiers as the promotion of sharing cars' vision. Successful strategies tend to take a holistic approach that integrates all maximum feasible and cost-effective emissions reduction strategies [27]. As well as environmental aspects, the economic benefits should be underlined. In the automotive, with a particular focus on the Italian market, in 2014 cars sales increased, after some years of null growth and recession. In the Fig. 3 is represented the cars sell trend in Italy from 2007 to 2014. The trend decreased for the economic crisis started in 2008, but in 2014 the sector weakly

Fig. 3 Italy car market share, 2007–2014 (*data processed by the authors on* www.fiat. net, *2015*)

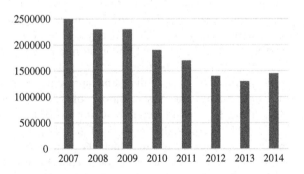

increased the total cars sold. During the period 2007–2014 the concept of economy and mobility has changed, especially for the delicate financial situation in the world. In fact, new models of transportation have entered in the society with the aim to substitute the ancient vision of property. The phenomenon of car sharing is nowadays increasing its popularity in the modern societies: the OECD countries are more developed in terms of accessibility, penetration index and management of the services provided to the consumers.

The new concept of the economy of sharing is following the transformation and the evolution of the society [28], supported by social networks, nowadays always more present in the citizens' lives. The increase of the sharing economy concept, especially in the transportation sector, has to be researched in its strengths: reduction of costs, increase of profits, positive environmental and social impacts. In particular, the phenomenon of car sharing is in rapid expansion in terms of investments: the most important operator is Zipcar (850,000 members globally in 2013), followed by Car2Go (600,000 members globally in 2013). In 2015 the market will reach five million members, mainly for the combinations of growing established car sharing markets and a rapid growth in a new wave of car sharing locations. The car sharing phenomenon is largely penetrated in the US market and only recently is growing in importance in Europe. The leader companies on the

Table 2 International car sharing leader companies (*data processed by the authors on reviewers.com-industrial experts, 2015*)

	Zipcar	Car2Go	Getaround	Hertz	City car share
Age requirement	18	18	19	18	21
Availability	170 cities in US, Canada, England, France, Spain	Select North America and European cities	San Francisco, Portland, Chicago, Austin, San Diego	Select North American, European, and Australian cities	San Francisco Bay area
Free daily mileage limit	180	150	200	180	200
Annual fee ($)	72	None	None	None	None
Daily rate ($)	69–77	84.99	Varies by owner	None	48-62 (+0.10/mile)
Hourly rate	8-10	14.99	Varies by owner	starts at 8.50 (varies by vehicle)	5.75–7.50 (+0.35/mile)
Late fee ($)	50/h (150 max)	None	50/h (up to 500)	10 per 15 min	15–50
Low fuel fee ($)	20	None	8/gallon + 30	25	25

international scene are six, and only two are serving the European market, as reported in Table 2.

In the specific case of Italy, the penetration of users grew from 30,000 to over 130,000 members from 2012–2013, led by Car2Go and Enjoy (ENI/Fiat) in particular, both of whom doubled their fleet size within a few months of launching owing to impressive member adoption. In the next future, the scenario will be positive: the rate of new users is constantly growing, leading to new investments in the car sharing sector. New investments are fundamental to enlarge the stock of cars available for the users. In fact, as shown in Table 1, in Italy the access to the potentiality of car sharing methodology is limited to the furniture of cars. For UberPop the future scenario will be more complicated for the legislation and the regulation for the competition in the sector to allow the maximization of the consumers' satisfaction at the lowest cost is necessary.

5 Conclusions

The depletion of natural resources is an important challenge for the society. In particular, the transportation sector involves energy, human and ecological habitats, atmospheric carbon loading capacity, and individuals' available time. To invert this negative trend it is necessary the combination of different variables that can change the paradigm of mobility [29]. The most important aspect for the implementation of decisions in the transportation sector deals with the economy [30]: economic growth and job creation, the character and intensity of land use, and socioeconomic and geographic transfers of wealth. The policies goals have to became sustainable in a holistic optimization, by defining standards for renewable resources usage, fuel substitutes and health standards for nitrogen oxides, ozone, particulates, and noise. The implementation of car sharing systems can represent a practical solution in terms of natural resources employment, environmental standards, economic benefits and social integration [31]. In order to develop this new model the following criteria must be met: international objectives for transportation sector emissions of carbon dioxide; and ecosystem protection objectives relating to land protection in urban areas. Research demonstrates that for each usage of a car in a shared system, there is a reduction between 12 and 15 cars [32]. Nowadays the global car sharing market is growing, with particular attention to the Italian situation, where a 70 % increasing is registered. The technological situation in our country is uncertain, especially for the delay in the infrastructure and smart mobility, which can be annulled with an investment of about € 40 billion. Furthermore, is necessary to establish a regulation for UberPop to understand the possible market evolution, both for the category of consumers and taxis. By concluding, it is possible to affirm that the society is changing thanks to the technology and the new paradigm of mobility: our century is facing the capability of individuals to share resources, with the aim to be in a win-win situation in terms of costs, revenues and environmental benefits.

References

1. Hamilton-Baillie, B.: Urban design: why don't we do it in the road? Modifying traffic behaviour through legible urban design. J. Urb. Technol. **11**, 43–62 (2004)
2. Yeager, K.: Electricity for the 21st century: digital electricity for a digital economy. J. Technol. Soc. **26**, 209–221 (2004)
3. Belk, R.: Shar. J. Cons. Res. **36**, 715–734 (2009)
4. Price, J.: Sharing: the integration of intimate economics. J. Anthrop. **17**, 3–27 (1975)
5. Nair, R., Miller-Hooks, E.: Fleet management for vehicle sharing operations. J. Trans. Sci. **45**, 524 (2010)
6. Le Vine, S., Zolfaghari, A., Polak, J.: Carsharing: evolution, challenges and opportunities. Scientific advisory group report, 22 ACEA, **7** (2014)
7. Hampshire, R.C., Gaites, C.: Peer-to-peer carsharing market analysis and potential growth. J. Trans. Res. Rec. **2217**, 119–126 (2011)
8. United Nations Department of Social and Economic Affairs: World Population Prospects: the 2012 revision. Report. http://esa.un.org/wpp/
9. Hampshire, R.C., Sinha, S.: A simulation study of Peer-to-Peer car sharing. J. Int. Sust. Trans. Sys. (FISTS) 59–163 (2011)
10. Xu, Y., Yan, J.: A cloud based information integration platform for smart cars. In: Second International Conference, SUComS 2011on Security-Enriched Urban Computing and Smart Grid Communications in Computer and Information Science, pp 241–250, Taiwan (2011)
11. Kulash, D.: Working together to address induced demand. Eno Transportation Foundation Report, Washington Forum (2002)
12. World Bank indicators, 2015. http://data.worldbank.org/indicator
13. Bromley, A.: Tech. Policy. J. Technol. Soc. **26**, 455–468 (2004)
14. Bijker, W., Hughes, T., Pinch, T.: The Social Construction of Technological Systems: New Directions in the Sociology and History of Technology. MIT Press, (1987)
15. Magsamen-Conrad, K., Billotte-Verhoff, C., Greene, K.: Technology addiction's contribution to mental wellbeing: the positive effect of online social capital. J. Comput. Hum. Behav. **40**, 23–30 (2014)
16. Fan, P., Watanabe, C.: Promoting industrial development through technology policy: lessons from Japan and China. J. Technol. Soc. **28**, 303–320 (2006)
17. Koch, D., Bond, T.C., Streets, D., Unger, N., Van Der Werf, G.R.: Global Impacts of Aerosols from Particular Source Regions and Sectors. J. Geop. Res. Atm. **112** (2007)
18. Lamarque, J.-F., Bond, T.C., Eyring, V., Granier, C., Heil, A., Klimont, Z., Lee, D., et al.: Historical (1850–2000) gridded anthropogenic and biomass burning emissions of reactive gases and aerosols: methodology and application. J. Atm. Chem. Phys. **10**, 7017–7039 (2010)
19. Uherek, E., Halenka, T., Borken-Kleefeld, J., Balkanski, Y., Berntsen, T., Borrego, C., Gauss, M., Hoor, P., JudaRezler, K., Lelieveld, J., Melas, D., Rypdal, K., Schmid, S.: Transport impacts on atmosphere and climate: land transport. J. Atm. Environ. **44**, 4772–4816 (2010)
20. Fuglestvedt, J.S., Shine, K.P., Berntsen, T., Cook, J., Lee, D.S., Stenke, A., Skeie, R.B., Velders, G.J.M., Waitz, I.A.: Transport impacts on atmosphere and climate: metrics. J. Atm. Environ. **44**, 4648–4677 (2010)
21. Olivié, D.J.L., Cariolle, D., Teyssèdre, H., Salas, D., Voldoire, A., Clark, H., Saint-Martin, D., Michou, M., Karcher, F., Balkanski, Y., Gauss, M., Dessens, O., Koffi, B., Sausen, R.: Modeling the climate impact of road transport, maritime shipping and aviation over the period 1860–2100 with an AOGCM. J. Atm. Chem. Phys. **12**, 1449–1480 (2012)
22. Borken-Kleefeld, J., Berntsen, T., Fuglestvedt, J.: Specific climate impact of passenger and freight transport. J. Environ. Sci. Technol. **44**, 5700–5706 (2010)
23. Shinnar, R., Citro, F.: Decarbonization: Achieving near-total energy independence and near-total elimination of greenhouse emissions with available technologies. J. Technol. Soc. **30**, 1–16 (2008)

24. Organization for Economic Cooperation and Development: Environmental criteria for sustainable transport: report on phase 1 of the project on environmentally sustainable transport. OECD, Paris (1996)
25. European conference of ministers of transport: Urban travel and sustainable development: overview of the project. http://www.cemt.org/UrbTrav/overview.htm
26. Antonis, A., Vassilis, J.: Automotive industry challenges in meeting EU 2015 environmental standard. J. Technol. Soc. **34**, 55–83 (2012)
27. Hesse, M.: Urban space and logistics: on the road to sustainability? J. Wor. Transp. Policy Pract. **1**, 39–45 (1995)
28. Turner, B., Rojek, C.: Society and culture: Principles of scarcity and solidarity,. London sage. (2001)
29. Tengström, E.: An analytic framework with which to consider society's response to new technologies: the automobile as a case in point. J. Technol. Soc. **17**, 215–229 (1995)
30. Fan, P., Watanabe, C.: Promoting industrial development through technology policy: lessons from Japan and China. J. Technol. Soc. **28**, 303–320 (2006)
31. Rodriguez, D., Busco, C., Flores, R.: Information technology within society's evolution. J. Technol. Soc. **40**, 64–72 (2015)
32. Markets and Markets Smart Transportation Market by Solutions- Global Forecast to 2020. Report (2015)

Part IV
Innovating Novel ICT Solutions

Towards a Design Pattern Language to Assist the Design of Alarm Visualizations for Operating Control Systems

Rosa Romero-Gómez and Paloma Díaz

Abstract With the growing emphasis on visualization as a mechanism for analyzing and exploring large and complex data sets, visualization research has recognized the need of reusing prior design knowledge instead of starting from scratch. This fact is especially relevant in designing control systems in which alarm visualizations are key artifacts for human operators to maintain an awareness of the state of the process under control. In this context, there is a plethora of design material in the form of design rules that collect design knowledge about known ways to design alarm visualizations. However, these design rules can be too abstract, not comprehensive enough, and loosely coupled, being difficult to be interpreted and applied by non-experienced designers. Aiming at overcoming this situation, this paper proposes a design pattern language as a fitting approach to disseminate reusable alarm visualization design knowledge. The final aim is to provide designers with an easy access to the existing body of knowledge of recognized alarm visualization design solutions for operating control systems.

Keywords Alarm visualization · Design knowledge reuse · Design pattern languages · Design patterns · Control systems

1 Introduction

A control system is defined as '*a device, or set of devices, that manages, commands, directs or regulates the behavior of other device(s) or system(s)*' [27]. Control systems have been used over time to solve problems of practical importance with enormous impact on society. They can be found within a range of

R. Romero-Gómez (✉) · P. Díaz
Interactive Systems Group (DEI LAB), Computer Science Department,
Universidad Carlos III de Madrid, Madrid, Spain
e-mail: rmromero@inf.uc3m.es

P. Díaz
e-mail: pdp@inf.uc3m.es

© Springer International Publishing Switzerland 2016
L. Caporarello et al. (eds.), *Digitally Supported Innovation*,
Lecture Notes in Information Systems and Organisation 18,
DOI 10.1007/978-3-319-40265-9_18

industrial domains, including *electric power grids, transportation networks*, or *water management systems*. Lately, the intensive use of information technologies has resulted in a proliferation of these control systems in other domains such as *emergency response* [22, 23]; in particular, in case of natural disasters including earthquakes or floods. In current control systems, equipment is separated in functional areas and is installed in different work areas of a controlled process. The human operator monitors and manipulates the set points of the process parameter from a central control room. In particular, he/she visualizes the information transmitted from the process area and displayed on the computer terminal through information displays. With the help of these computer-based information displays, human operators decide on the actions required for controlling the process. Owing to the high complexity of controlled processes, where many parameters on many different locations need to be monitored, operating control systems through information displays can be characterized under the notion of *alarm-initiated activities* [30]. This notion describes the human operators' behaviors as triggered into action by an upcoming alarm. Aiming at supporting human operators to maintain an awareness of the state of the controlled process, alarm visualizations have become key artifacts for operating control systems. Alarm visualizations refer to as '*the visual method(s) by which alarm coding and messages are presented to control room operators*' [2].

Designing effective alarm visualizations has a number of implications that go beyond the visual display of alarms. It requires designers to take into consideration the role of the human operator in response to alarms. It also requires designers to recognize the human operator's capabilities, goals and needs. However, no single designer can be an expert in every relevant field, and becoming proficient may require years of experience [18]. One relevant approach is to reuse design knowledge instead of starting from scratch. A variety of *design principles, guidelines, standards*, and *visual languages* have been used to disseminate reusable alarm visualization design knowledge. In the remaining of this paper we will refer to them design rules that are defined as '*a rule that a designer can follow to provide direction for the design process*' [14]. These design rules may be useful for ensuring a degree of consistency across alarm visualization designs. Nevertheless, they are too abstract, loosely coupled, and not comprehensive enough, being difficult to be applied effectively by non-experienced designers. As previous research on visualization has stated [8], providing a collection of visualization designs that show the same data in different ways will often provide new insights to designers into important properties that exist in the dataset. Lead by this idea, the purpose of this paper is to provide designers with an easy access to the existing body of knowledge of recognized alarm visualization design options for operating control systems. The key intention is to provide an intermediate perspective, a level between high-level design rules and highly specific details. To achieve this, a design pattern language is a convenient way to help designers place abstract design rules in the context of concrete projects they are working on. In particular, this design pattern language is composed by the following elements: (i) a *catalogue of 29 design patterns* that captures design practice and embodies knowledge about successful alarm visualization design solutions; (ii) a *classification scheme* that organizes the existing design knowledge according to two different criteria; and (iii) a *design pattern language* that defines 5 types of relations between design patterns in order to provide a more holistic view of alarm visualization design.

The remaining of this paper is structured as follows. Next section reviews diverse factors that determine the design of alarm visualizations and discusses the limitations of current design knowledge reuse approaches in alarm visualization design. Third section describes the proposed design pattern language in further detail. Fourth section presents an evaluation of this design pattern language by designers. Finally, some conclusions are drawn.

2 Background

ANSI/ISA 8.2-2009 [2], one of the de facto standards for alarm management established by the International Society of Automation (ISA), defines an alarm as '*an announcement to the operator initiated by a process variable passing a defined limit as it approaches an undesirable or unsafe value*'. An alarm can be characterized by relevant attributes such as *the alarm state, the alarm priority,* and *the alarm typology* [2]. According to its definition, alarms are regarded as significant attractors of attention for human operators. In this way, the role of the human operator in response to alarms may be firstly examined to determine how to design alarm visualizations.

There exist different descriptive models of human operators in response to alarms that may split into two types: those models that don't distinguish operators' activities among operation situations and those that do. Under the first distinction, most authors [21, 24] have agreed about characterizing alarm-initiated activities as a process comprising three-level activity stages. For example, Lees' model [21] comprises: (i) *detection* (detecting the fault); (ii) *diagnosis* (identifying the cause of the fault); and (iii) *correction* (dealing with the fault). These models thus emphasize the role of the human operator as a problem solver when faults arise. However, they describe such role as static across different operation situations, without considering the diverse range of controlled process states or different information requirements. In real work settings, human operators are dependent on the information provided by the alarm visualization, which can vary according to the status of the controlled process. Under the second distinction, Stanton [24] has proposed the most complete and well-known descriptive model of alarm-initiated activities. In contrast to the previous models, this model distinguishes human operator's activities between two operating situations: *routine events* involving alarms and *critical events* involving alarms. For routine events, this model is composed by a sequence of six generic activity stages: (i) *observe* (initial detection of abnormal conditions); (ii) *accept* (the acceptance of an alarm or receipt); (iii) *analyze* (the assessment of the alarm within the context of the task that is to be performed and the dynamics of the system); (iv) *correct* (to adjust so as to meet the required conditions of the system);

(v) *monitor* (the assessment of the outcome of one's actions); and (vi) reset (to restore to normal operating conditions). For critical events, this model adds one activity stage to this sequence; *investigate*, which is depicted as '*seeking to discover the underlying cause of the alarm with the intention of dealing with the fault*'. This model therefore not only establishes the distinction of human operator's activities among operating situations but also emphasizes the need of an investigation process to diagnose the fault during critical events. During these types of events, the cause of the failure can be not so clear. For this reason, it can be necessary to explore through different types and volumes of information in order to diagnose its cause.

The human factors and ergonomics field also recognizes the need of designing alarm visualizations with all the human operator's capabilities, goals and needs in mind. In handling alarm information, Situation Awareness (SA) can be characterized as the most relevant goal for human operators [17]. In particular, SA can be defined informally as '*being aware of what is happening around you and understanding what that information means to you now and in the future*' [17]. However, building and maintaining this SA can be a difficult process when people supervise complex and dynamic processes. As an example, in real-time operations, the analyses of recent operating problems have shown that the ability of human operators for acquiring SA is one of the major factors that affects the propagation of failures [19]. Moreover, there is a large body of literature in SA, and this continues to be an active area of research. In particular, reviews of definitions and theories from varied sources provide a clear indication of the variety of approaches about SA. For example, Micah Endsley describes SA as '*the perception of the elements in the environment within a volume of time and space, the comprehension of their meaning and the projection of their status in the near future*'. Endsley uses the term to define a state of knowledge and she describes the associated process as situation assessment. However, several other authors have agreed about considering SA as a label for a range of cognitive processes or processing activities. For example, Dekker and Lutzhoft [10] describe the concept of SA as '*an intrinsic feature of the functional relationship between the environment and the person*'. This empiricist view of SA breaks down the process into perception of information elements and is highly consistent with current ideas about *sense making* as an active strategy when the available information is uncertain or conflicting, and maintained or recovered after surprising events, which are typical situations that a human operator has to deal with.

Trying to address and considering these complicated issues, in the context of alarm visualization design, a variety of *design principles, guidelines, standards*, and *visual languages* have been used, which document what are considered the expectations and best practices for designing effective alarm visualizations. The set of existing design rules for alarm visualization design and their limitations are displayed using a colored *Venn* diagram, which is shown in Fig. 1. This diagram encodes the different fields of expertise involved in alarm visualization design as colored circles (Alarm Management, Visualization and Human Factors); the variety of models and perspectives within these fields as lined circles; and existing design rules as rhombuses located according to the perspectives adopted within these fields.

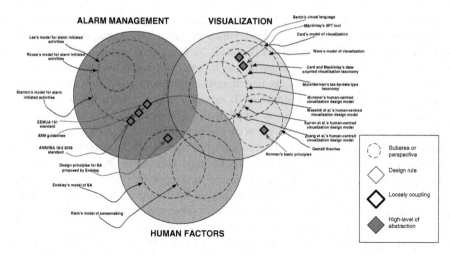

Fig. 1 Venn diagram showing the state-of-the-art of knowledge reuse approaches for alarm visualization design

As Fig. 1 shows, there are not design rules that consider all required factors for alarm visualization design, which correspond to the area where the three circles overlap. In particular, the design principles for SA proposed by Endsley [17] can be characterized as the most comprehensive rules, considering a more extensive range of key design factors than other existing artifacts for alarm visualization design. However, these design rules are still limited in two other main aspects. They are too abstract (shown as a grey rhombus in Fig. 1). For an abstraction of a reusable design component to be effective, it must express all of the information that is needed by the designer who uses it. This may include space and time character-istics, precision statistics, or scalability limits. Finally, they are loosely coupled (shown as a rhombus with a black border in Fig. 1). To combine a variety of reusable components, the designer must clearly understand the components' interfaces; it means those properties of the component that interact with other components. These limitations of existing design rules for alarm visualization design may lead not only to an expensive and time-consuming design process but also to create alarm visualizations without sound reasoning and therefore ineffective for supporting human operator's tasks.

3 A Design Pattern Language for Alarm Visualization Design

Incorporating design patterns into the design process can facilitate the construction of new visualization design solutions [14]. Compared to other efforts to reuse design knowledge, design patterns capture design practice, facilitate multiple levels of abstraction, include the statement of a problem that they address, and deliberately scope their context of application [26]. However, taken in isolation, design patterns are, as Dearden and Finlay [9] firstly stated, '*at best, unrelated good ideas*'. They need to be organized in a meaningful way in order to provide coherent support for design generation. A key concept in distinguishing pattern collections from pattern languages is the idea of generativity. It means a design pattern language allows designers to generate designs by implicit sequencing of decisions, derived by traversing the network of links between the individual patterns [9]. It provides a more cohesive structure, with higher-level patterns yielding contexts, which are resolved by more detailed patterns. In keeping with these features, this paper proposes a design pattern language as a fitting approach for representing and articulating previous alarm visualization design knowledge. Previous work related to the definition of design pattern languages for other purposes such as the design of visualization-based computational tools for complex cognitive activities [27], object-oriented software [18], user interfaces, interaction design, security systems [19], web systems [24], and web information systems for emergency management [11] has been considered.

3.1 The Design Patterns Catalogue

Cataloguing is a key step of growing a pattern language in a specific domain. It consists of the selection and classification of a set of suitable design patterns for the purpose at hand. Nevertheless, there is no objective metric indicating the abstraction level of the problem addressed by patterns. According to Seeman [26], design patterns that are abstract are usually ideal for reuse purposes. The more specialized a design pattern gets the more difficult to reuse it. In this work, adapting the widely used definition of a design pattern proposed by Gamma et al. [18] in software engineering, design patterns are referred to as '*descriptions of features, visual structures, and view transformations to define computer-based interactive visual representations of alarm information*'.

   This catalogue of design patterns results from an extensive literature review from different areas such as Alarm Management, Human Factors, and Visualization. In particular, the literature reviewed includes two main standards for alarm management [2, 15], two collections of guidelines for human-system interface design [3, 13], a collection of design principles for human factors [17], twenty-six reports on control systems from companies such as Siemens [28] or ABB [1], a variety of books on human factors [17] and visualization design [4, 6, 7, 29], and different papers on visualization and interaction techniques such as the proposed by Eick and Karr [16] to assist visual scalability. As a result of this review, the catalogue contains 29 design patterns that describe the design space for alarm visualizations. The main criteria of including a design pattern in the catalogue are both the maturity of its description, and its application in more than one design situation. Patterns can be found at http://dei.inf.uc3m.es/AlarmVisualizationPatternLanguage/. Figure 2 shows the structure of these design patterns.

As an example of the selection of a design pattern to be included in this catalogue, *Details hierarchy* pattern results from a variety of sources such as standards for alarm management [3, 13], control system reports [28], and guidelines for

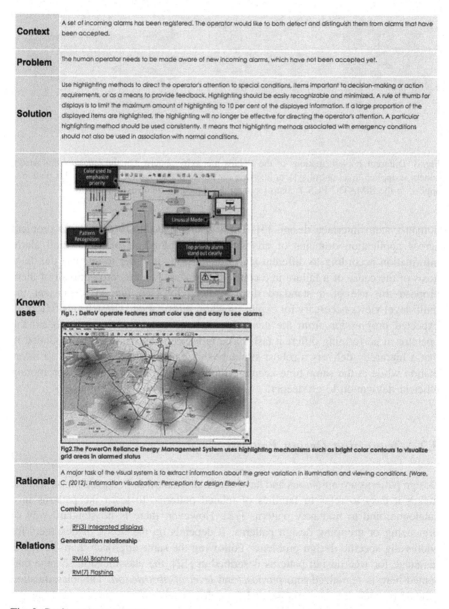

Context — A set of incoming alarms has been registered. The operator would like to both detect and distinguish them from alarms that have been accepted.

Problem — The human operator needs to be made aware of new incoming alarms, which have not been accepted yet.

Solution — Use highlighting methods to direct the operator's attention to special conditions, items important to decision-making or action requirements, or as a means to provide feedback. Highlighting should be easily recognizable and minimized. A rule of thumb for displays is to limit the maximum amount of highlighting to 10 per cent of the displayed information. If a large proportion of the displayed items are highlighted, the highlighting will no longer be effective for directing the operator's attention. A particular highlighting method should be used consistently. It means that highlighting methods associated with emergency conditions should not also be used in association with normal conditions.

Known uses — Fig1. : DeltaV operate features smart color use and easy to see alarms

Fig2.The PowerOn Reliance Energy Management System uses highlighting mechanisms such as bright color contours to visualize grid areas in alarmed status

Rationale — A major task of the visual system is to extract information about the great variation in illumination and viewing conditions. (Ware, C. (2012). Information visualization: Perception for design Elsevier.)

Relations —
Combination relationship
- RF(3) Integrated displays

Generalization relationship
- RM(6) Brightness
- RM(7) Flashing

Fig. 2 Design pattern structure

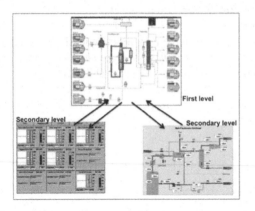
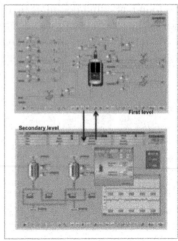

Fig. 3 Different implementations of the Details hierarchy pattern. On the *left side*, this design pattern is applied to a control system interface for power plants. On the *right side*, this pattern is applied to the SIMATIC PCS 7 control system developed by Siemens [28]

human-system interface design [3]. These sources recognize the design problem across application domains of addressing the exploration of the overall alarm information according to different alarm dimensions in order to support the diagnosis of the cause of a failure in a controlled process. To this problem, all of them propose the use of a standard display hierarchy (see Fig. 3) to present the multi-level views necessary for exploring alarm information. These levels follow an expected progression from the general to the more detailed in order to aid the operator in performing different tasks. The rationale of this solution is grounded in that a hierarchy delivers a robust structure that encourages ready access to information while at the same time keeping important situation context and promoting efficient navigation to go deeper.

3.2 Organizing Design Patterns

Design patterns are numerous and have common properties. A classification scheme makes it easy to refer to families of related patterns, to learn the patterns in a catalogue, and to find new patterns [18]. However, there is no standard way of organizing or grouping design patterns. It depends on the needs of designers for addressing specific design problems. Following the same approach than the visual language for web design patterns described at [12], the classification scheme presented here is organized into *purpose* and *level of abstraction*. This classification scheme provides two criteria general enough to enable non-experienced designers the search of design patterns. Design patterns provide more detailed instructions of

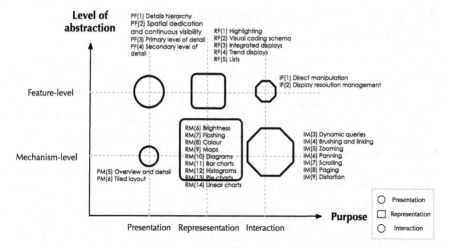

Fig. 4 Alarm visualization design patterns classified according to the classification scheme

how certain recurring problems can be solved according to high-level design principles. Figure 4 shows all twenty-nine design-patterns using this classification scheme. It uses three different shapes of different sizes to encode the number of design patterns classified according to both purpose and level of abstraction. Note, as it shown in Fig. 4, that the two criteria of this classification scheme are orthogonal. This classification scheme forms the basis for growing the pattern language.

The first criterion, called purpose, reflects what a design pattern does. Design patterns can have *presentation*, *representation*, or *interaction* purposes [6]. In particular, *presentation patterns* are related to how to organize the alarm information on the interface; *representation patterns* refer to the assignment of specific marks and graphic properties to alarm information attributes; and, *interaction patterns* are associated with those graphical parameters that allow the human operator producing a change in a view of a corpus of alarm information, easing the acquisition of insight. There are interdependences between presentation, representation and interaction patterns. Even if represented alarm information is chosen to be displayed, there remains the question as to whether its display should be under interactive control. The second criterion, called level of abstraction, specifies whether the design pattern reflects visual features that an alarm visualization should support, thus, the design pattern is very general, or depicts how these features should be supported. Alarm visualization design literature includes different levels of abstraction. *Feature-level patterns* are the more general patterns. They describe visual features that the alarm visualization should support. A feature in this work is a grouping of visual capabilities that provides value to the user. *Mechanism-level patterns* are of a detailed nature depicting how the visual features of an alarm visualization should be addressed. In particular, they describe different visual mechanisms such as visual structures and view transformations that should be applied to support such visual features.

3.3   From the Patterns Catalogue to a Design Pattern Language

The previous collection of design patterns captures the essence of the design problems and solutions when designing alarm visualizations. It provides design patterns classified by purpose in combination with level of abstraction, easing the selection of an appropriate solution for the problem at hand. However, as afore-mentioned, design patterns by themselves are not enough for communicating a holistic view of the design; they need to be combined in a pattern language in order to support a more general design purpose. The construction of this design pattern language follows the strategy applied by Hafiz et al. [20] to grow a pattern language for security systems. This strategy is based on the study of the connections among design patterns in the small scale. In particular, following the connective rules for pattern languages proposed by Salingaros [25], this design pattern language displays five types of connections between design patterns:

- ─────────▶ *Composition relationship.* This relationship indicates that a pattern is composed of one or more other patterns.
- ◀─ ─ ── ─ ─▶ *Combination relationship.* This relationship indicates an alliance of patterns to be applied together in order to address a specific human operator task.
- ◀·················▶ *Alternative relationship.* This relationship indicates several design patterns that lead more or less, to the same design result.
- ─·──·──·──·▷ Specialization *relationship.* This relationship indicates when a pattern shares the same functionality than other but possesses more specialized characteristics. The logical consequence of the specialization pattern is its inversion: the *generalization.* This relationship indicates that a pattern has rather generic features to serve a more universal purpose.

According to these connections, three small pattern languages have been created, one for each cluster of patterns corresponding to the purpose categories, including a pattern language of presentation patterns, a pattern language of representation patterns, and a pattern language of interaction patterns. These small design pattern languages are relatively self-contained, because they describe solutions for different classes of alarm visualization design problems. In each small pattern language, the design patterns were ordered in the typical order they would be applied in practice and considering the references on the literature. Then, these small pattern languages were combined into one large pattern language diagram showed on the Appendix, adding some inter-group relationships. These small pattern languages are distinguished by using colored frames. In particular, the pattern language of presentation patterns is colored in orange, the pattern language of representation patterns colored in light blue, and the pattern language of interaction patterns is colored in purple.

For example, aiming at providing a first level of detail of alarm information combines the *PF(3) Primary level* design pattern with *RF(3) Integrated displays*, *RF(4) Trend displays* and *RF(5) Lists* design patterns. Similarly, interacting with alarm information that does not fit the display space involves combining *IM(5) Zooming*, *IM(6) Panning*, and *ID(9) Distortion* with the *RF(3) Integrated displays* pattern. Figure 4 also shows how the design patterns in the higher-level fragments of each small pattern language use the patterns in the lower-level fragments. For instance, the *PF(2) Spatial dedication and continuous visibility* pattern can be implemented by using the *PM(6) Tiled layout* pattern. The *PM(6) Tiled layout* pattern recommends using a tiled structure to present a summary of the most relevant alarms visible at all times.

4   Evaluation

This evaluation used the knowledge of designers to identify misunderstandings, or ambiguous terminologies in order to both refine the design pattern language and validate their quality. To these purposes, *card-sorting exercises* and a *mix-questionnaire* were used. Card sorting is a method used to understand users' expectations and understanding of a specific topic [6]. A mix-questionnaire combines both open-ended questions and closed-ended questions. Open-ended questions enabled the respondents to highlight the issues that they find most relevant. Closed-ended questions made it possible to validate some quality attributes of the design patterns by using a four-level summated rating scale ranging from *strongly disagree* to *strongly agree*.

4.1   Procedure

Seven designers (three women and four men) performed this evaluation. They had experience in visualization design, interaction design, software design, and web design. In particular, four of them had also experience in designing tools and visualizations for the emergency context. The range of experience went from two to more than six years. All of the participants were familiar with the use of design rules. Each participant's session was conducted individually and consisted of two main steps. On average, these sessions lasted about 40 min. One researcher directed all these sessions and assisted participants throughout.

The first step focused on asking the participant to physically sort 29 textual cards of pattern descriptions according to pre-defined categories. Each textual card contained a pattern name, pattern problem description and pattern solution description. An overview of the meaning of the pre-defined categories was provided. Once the cards were sorted into groups, the participant was asked to look at each card and mark its quality of fit in the category he/she selected for it: *poor, fair* or *perfect*. The participant could also propose new categories labels that make more sense to them if required. Therefore, a combined card sorting method was used. This combination helped to see both how well the pre-defined categories labels worked and how designers grouped the design patterns. This step typically took around 35 min. In the second step, a mix-questionnaire including three open-ended questions (*Q1. Does the categories labels and terminology used to refer design patterns make sense to you? Q2. Do you consider that some of the categories labels do not reflect their purpose? Q3. Do you consider pattern names are not expressive enough according to the pattern description?*) and two closed-ended questions (*Q4. Do you consider patterns descriptions teach how to build alarm visualization designs? Q5. Do you consider patterns descriptions are descriptive enough?*) was given to the participants. These questions were related to both the terminology used to refer and categorize design patterns and the quality of design patterns descriptions throughout the language. A four-value Likert scale was used to collect the opinion of designers in closed-ended questions: *strongly agree* (4), *agree* (3), *disagree* (2), and *strongly disagree* (1). This scale was chosen to avoid neutral responses.

4.2 Results

The results obtained from the card sorting exercises were analyzed using Syncaps v3 [32], a card-sorting analysis package. In card sorting, cluster analysis is used to decide which items are most frequently grouped together by participants. This package allows automatizing it. In particular, an item dendogram and a pairs matrix were generated to display the results of this cluster analysis.

The item dendogram (see Fig. 5a) shows the distances between patterns using a similarity matrix. The more times a pattern is sorted together with another pattern, the more similar they are. They then appear closer in proximity in the dendogram. The clear result from the item dendogram is that a group of seven design patterns classified under different categories within the catalogue (within the cyan band in Fig. 5a) tended to be sorted together by the seven participants. These design patterns describe design decisions mostly related to both limited display space and navigation issues. This grouping could possibility be because most of design patterns related to display space issues involve interaction capabilities such as *zooming* or *panning*. This interactive nature seems to be more relevant for designers to identify these design patterns than the need of handling limited display spaces.

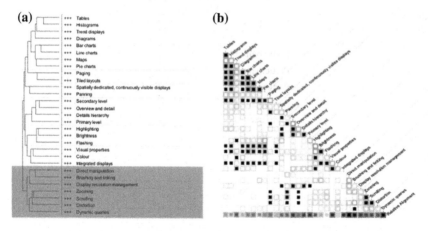

Fig. 5 Item dendogram card sorting results **a** and pairs matrix card sorting results **b**

The pairs matrix (shown in Fig. 5b) also supported this result. This matrix shows the frequency with which every possible pair of items appeared together in the same groups. The matrix uses colour saturation to display this so that a white cell shows a pairing that did not occur while a dark cell shows a pairing that was made by most participants. For instance, the Trend displays pattern and the Diagrams pattern tended to be sorted together by most participants. As expert data is used in this analysis, the central portion of each cell indicates the expert pairings and alignment. An example of that is the pair of patterns Primary level and Secondary level. The bottom row shows relative alignment. In this row, darker cells represent items that were consistently grouped while lighter cells indicate less agreement between participants. Considering the results supported by these two diagrams, a refinement of the preliminary version of the catalogue of design patterns was carried out. This refinement consisted of the movement of Direct manipulation, Zooming, Scrolling, Paging, Panning, and Distortion patterns from the Presentation category to the Interaction category. Finally, the participants' responses to the mix-questionnaire were analysed. The set of participants' responses to the open-ended questions suggested that some dimensions of the classification scheme were ambiguous or misleading. For instance, *Principles* and *Techniques* categories were considered difficult to distinguish. Therefore, some changes and additions in the preliminary version of the classification scheme were conducted, such as the replacement of *Principles* and *Techniques* categories for *Feature-level* and *Mechanism-level* categories. Similarly, the set of participants' responses to the closed-ended questions were also analysed. Since summated rating scales do not provide concrete values but categories, this study used the median to identify the agreement of designers (see Table 1): the design patterns will be considered as valid if the median of designers' opinion is equal or higher than three (agreement level).

Table 1 Results and final score of each designer to the closed-ended questions

Participants	Score	
	Q4	Q5
Participant 1	3	4
Participant 2	4	4
Participant 3	3	3
Participant 4	3	3
Participant 5	4	4
Participant 6	3	4
Participant 7	3	4

5 Conclusions

Reusing previous design knowledge provides useful starting points for existing or new design problems. It can not only avoid repeated design effort but also help the designer adapt the original design to new situation for design innovation. In keeping with that, this paper has presented a design pattern language to provide designers with an easy access to the existing body of knowledge of alarm visualization design. The aim of creating a design pattern language is not to provide something that a designer must use. Pattern languages are intended as a tool that designers can use as they see and change if they feel they have a better solution.

By describing a particular way of design, a design pattern language opens that way to scrutiny and improvement. In this regard, the plan is to have this design pattern language reviewed by more designers to help becoming more standardized. Similarly, using a design pattern language to design a system shows both missing patterns and when descriptions of individual patterns are incomplete. The intention is to use this pattern language to design alarm visualizations for operating control systems in different application domains. Like reusable components, design patterns develop in an iterative and evolving process through repeated reuse. These uses may provide new insights and interesting future research opportunities. Finally, this design pattern language also opens to debate the relevance of knowledge reuse for visualization design, which still remains relatively unexplored.

Acknowledgments This work is supported by the project emerCien grant funded by the Spanish Ministry of Economy and Competitivity (TIN2012-09687).

Appendix: Design Pattern Language for Designing Alarm Visualizations for Operating Control Systems

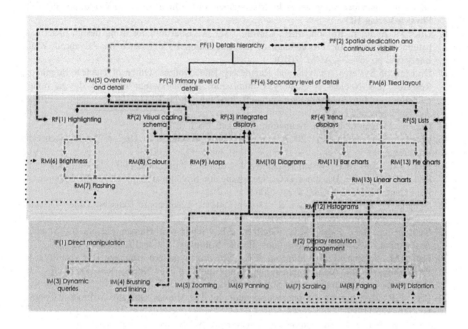

References

1. ABB control systems. http://www.directindustry.es/prod/abb-control-systems/interfaces-hombre-maquina-30259-149900.html
2. ANSI/ISA-18.2:2009 Management of Alarm Systems for the Process Industries (2009)
3. ASM consortium guidelines. Effective operator display design. Abnormal Situation Management. https://www.asmconsortium.net/Documents/2009%20ASM%20Displays%20GL%20Webinar%20v014.pdf. Accessed March 12 2015
4. Bertin, J.: Semiology of Graphics: Diagrams, Networks, Maps. The University of Wisconsin Press, Ltd., Madison, WI (1983)
5. Card Sorting. http://www.usability.gov/how-to-and-tools/methods/card-sorting.html
6. Card, S.K., Mackinlay, J.D., Shneiderman, B.: Readings in information visualization: using vision to think. Morgan Kaufmann Pub. (1999)
7. Chen, C.: Information Visualization: Beyond the Horizon, 2nd edn. Springer Science & Business (2006)
8. Chen, C.: Information visualization. Wiley Interdisciplinary Rev.: Comput. Statis. 2(4), 387–403 (2010)
9. Dearden, A., Finlay, J.: Pattern languages in HCI: A critical review. Human–Comput. Inter. 21 (1), 49–102 (2006)

10. Dekker, S., Lutzhoft, M.: Correspondence, cognition and sensemaking: A radical empiricist view of situation awareness. In: A Cognitive Approach to Situation Awareness: Theory and Application, pp. 22–41. Ashgate Publishing Company, Burlington, VT (2004)
11. Diaz, P., Acuña, P., Aedo, I., Malizia, A. (2010). A design patterns catalog for web-based emergency management systems. In: Management of the Interconnected World, pp. 387–394. Physica-Verlag HD
12. Díaz, P., Aedo, I., Rosson, M.B., Carroll, J.M.: A visual tool for using design patterns as pattern languages. In: Proceedings of the International Conference on Advanced Visual Interfaces, pp. 67–74. ACM (2010)
13. Division of Systems Analysis and Regulatory Effectiveness, Office of Nuclear Regulatory Research, US Nuclear Regulatory Commission: Human-system interface design review guidelines. http://www.bnl.gov/humanfactors/files/pdf/NUREG-0700_Rev2.pdf (2002). Accessed March 12 2015
14. Dix, A.: Human-Computer Interaction. Springer, US (2009)
15. EEMUA Publication 191: 2007 Alarm Systems: A Guide to Design, Management and Procurement
16. Eick, S.G., Karr, A.F.: Visual scalability. J. Comput. Graph. Stat. **11**(1), 22–43 (2002)
17. Endsley, M., Bolté, B., Jones D.G.: Designing for Situational Awareness: An Approach to User-Centered Design. CRC Press (2003)
18. Gamma, E., Helm, R., Johnson, R.: Design Patterns: Elements of Reusable Object-Oriented Software. Pearson Education (1994)
19. Guttromson, R.T., Paget, M.L., Greitzer, F.L., Schur, A.: Human Factors for Situation Assessment in Power Grid Operations. Pacific Northwest National Laboratory (2008)
20. Hafiz, M., Adamczyk, P., Johnson, R.E.: Growing a pattern language (for security). In: Proceedings of the ACM International Symposium on New Ideas, New Paradigms, and Reflections on Programming and Software (2012)
21. Lees, F.P.: Research on the process operator. In: The Human Operator in Process Control, pp. 386–425 (1974)
22. Lohs, S., Karnapke, R., Nolte, J., Lagemann, A.: Self-stabilizing sensor networks for emergency management. In: Pervasive Computing and Communications Workshops (PERCOM Workshops), pp. 715–720 (2012)
23. Lorincz, K., Malan, D.J., Fulford-Jones, T.R., Nawoj, A., Clavel, A., Shnayder, V., Mainland, G., Welsh, M.: Sensor networks for emergency response: challenges and opportunities. Pervasive Comput. IEEE **3**(4), 16–23 (2004)
24. Rouse, W.: Models of human problem solving: detection, diagnosis, and compensation for system failures. Automatica **19**(6), 613–625 (1983)
25. Salingaros, N.A.: The structure of pattern languages. Architect. Res. Q. **4**(02), 149–162 (2000)
26. Seemann, N.A.: design pattern oriented programming environment. PhD Thesis, University of Rokstok, Germany (1999)
27. Sheridan, T.B.: Telerobotics, Automation, and Human Supervisory Control. MIT press (1992)
28. Siemens AG. The SIMATIC PCS 7 Process Control System. Technical report (2009)
29. Spence, R.: Information Visualization: Design for Interaction, 2nd edn. Pearson-Prentice Hall (2006)
30. Stanton, N.A.: Alarm initiated activities. In: Taylor & Francis (eds.) Human Factors in Alarm Design, pp. 93–117 (1999)
31. Stolte, C., Tang, D., Hanrahan, P.: Multiscale visualization using data cubes. IEEE Trans. Vis. Comput. Graph. **9**(2), 176–187 (2003)
32. Syncaps Card Sorting Software, http://www.syntagm.co.uk/design/cardsortdl.shtml#syncapsv3
33. Thomas, J.J., Cook, K.A.: Illuminating the Path: The Research and Development Agenda for Visual Analytics. IEEE Computer Society Press (2005)
34. Zhang, J., Johnson, K.A., Malin, J.T., Smith, J.W.: Human-centered information visualization. In: International Workshop on Dynamic Visualizations and Learning, Germany (2002)

A Generic, Multimodal Framework for Sensorial Feedback on Android Systems

Rosario Sensale, Francesco Cutugno and Antonio Origlia

Abstract The success of software applications, in a worldwide setup offering simple development and distribution models, is often determined by the quality and ease of use of provided interfaces. In this paper, we present a framework for multimodal signal analysis operating in conjunction with any other Android application to estimate the cognitive load imposed by its interface. The framework integrates seamlessly with such applications, even existing ones, by acting as middleware between the sensors layer and the application logic. The interaction between interface elements is mainly targeted in this work: a game presenting an increasingly complex interface was designed and tracking modules for touch events and eye movements were implemented. We show that the framework is able to capture and present raw data together with underlying models estimated by least squares approximation. We then discuss the implications of such a framework for the evaluation of efficient application interfaces.

1 Introduction

Human-Computer interfaces have been constantly evolving since the first computing machines were constructed. There are multiple motivations for this. Making interaction easier allows wider groups of people to take advantage of the technology and also improves the experience itself if new sensors aimed at multimodal interaction are involved. Command line interfaces, oriented towards expert users, have first been substituted by Graphical User Interfaces built around the concepts of Windows, Icons, Mouse and Pointer (WIMP), favoring the diffusion of computer

R. Sensale · F. Cutugno · A. Origlia (✉)
University of Naples Federico II, Naples, Italy
e-mail: antori@gmail.com

R. Sensale
e-mail: rosario.sensale@gmail.com

F. Cutugno
e-mail: cutugno@unina.it

© Springer International Publishing Switzerland 2016
L. Caporarello et al. (eds.), *Digitally Supported Innovation*,
Lecture Notes in Information Systems and Organisation 18,
DOI 10.1007/978-3-319-40265-9_19

265

systems. Nowadays, these interfaces are being subsided by new interface protocols that aim at being *natural*, by giving the machines limited capabilities to adapt to the users. This opposes the traditional concept assuming that humans need to adapt to the machine in order to access its services. On the other hand, this approach increases the risk of producing interfaces that are not clear enough and, therefore, the chance of users becoming unsatisfied is also higher. An unclear interface that is perceived as confusing by the users produces sums itself to the intrinsic difficulty of a given task, resulting in increased *cognitive load* for the user.

In this paper, we present a framework to evaluate the cognitive load imposed to the users by multimodal applications. The framework can be combined with any existing software to introduce a logging layer aimed at detecting indicators of stress in eye movements and interface touch behavior. Obtained data can be examined to identify correlations between interface design and users reactions in order to spot problems during the design phase. This framework builds on previous work presented in [1] by explicitly linking the signal analysis framework to software interfaces evaluation.

1.1 Cognitive Load Theory

The term *working memory* indicates the system dedicated to the storage of data that are useful to accomplish complex activities like comprehension, learning and reasoning. This system allows the integration between data coming from sensory systems and long term memory data [2]. Working memory has a fundamental role in complex cognition: processes involved in cognitive tasks often produce intermediate results that must be used together in order to pursue a goal [3].

This section will mainly refer to Cognitive Load Theories (hereafter CLT) developed by Sweller [4–6]. Sweller defines three types of cognitive load which are expected to concur in the process of learning. The first, intrinsic cognitive load, is related to the intrinsic complexity of information per se. In more recent developments of his theory, Sweller states that it depends on the number of elements to be learned and on the degree of their mutual interactivity: i.e. learning words of a foreign language is an example of low element interactivity, as each word can be, at least in first approximation, learned independently. At the same time learning syntax, i.e. learning ho to define the correct word order to build sentences, is an example of high element interactivity. The second type of cognitive load is called "extraneous" and it is connected to how instructions are given to learners: Sweller states than non optimal instructions tend to impose extraneous cognitive load. A learning process can be seen as non optimal when it requires different mental processes involving different abilities at the same time. Even in this case Sweller states the importance of process interactivity and propose strategies to reduce extraneous cognitive load (CL) due to it.

The final type of cognitive load, Germane CL is related to learner characteristics. It appears when learner activates her working memory resources to afford the complexity of the challenging the intrinsic CL associated with the learning task. Germane cognitive load is independent of the information presented.

2 System Architecture

The architecture of the system presented here has been thought to favor the integration with existing applications in order to provide feedback about the cognitive load it imposes on users. To accomplish this goal, the framework presents the following characteristics:

- it is able to accept different input modalities;
- it is transparent with respect to the application it is connected to;
- it extracts and analyzes the input signals independently.

The framework can be represented by two main logical blocks:

- a Core Component (CC) block implementing the main functions of the framework;
- a set of Input Hot Spots (IHS) blocks implementing the interfaces used by programmers to link their code to the framework.

The CC calls the tested software procedures by means of the IHS so the software designer should not necessarily be aware of how the framework analyzes the input signals. In detail, the CC is composed of the following submodules:

- Input recognizer: this component captures user interactions with the device. Details about how the device interacts with the framework are specified here.
- Input Manager: this component manages the interaction of the input sources with the analysis modules of the framework.
- Log Manager: this component collects and stores data about incoming input data.

The IHS layer contains an Input Forward module collecting and sending incoming multiple inputs to the underlying application after the logging phase. The full architectural design is presented in Fig. 1.

3 Cognitive Loading Game

In order to test the framework, we developed an Android application designed to propose a simple task with an increasingly complex interface. The experimental setup was based on the Wizard of Oz paradigm, in which a user believes it is interacting with a machine while another human, hidden in another room, controls the application reactions. The setup is summarized in Fig. 2.

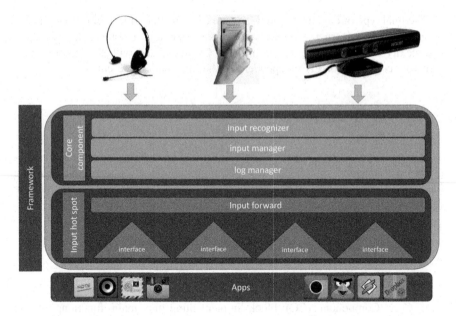

Fig. 1 System architecture

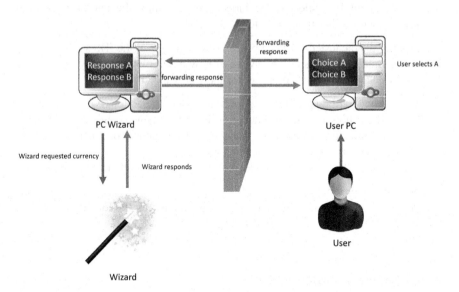

Fig. 2 The wizard of Oz setup

The game itself consists in selecting the appropriate objects to complete a given task. The chosen objects should be selected by dragging and dropping the corresponding icons inside a specific *target* area. A screenshot of the application is presented in Fig. 3.

Fig. 3 A mockup of the cognitive loading game interface

A time limit of three minutes was introduced to complete the tasks to introduce a first element of stress. To gradually increase the stressful experience imposed by the application, the Wizard of Oz was controlling the success/failure responses of the application after each user interaction. The hidden operator initially simulated a *honest* system providing the correct reactions to the users' stimuli. As time was running out, however, the Wizard was instructed to intentionally disrupt the interaction by providing wrong reactions, thus provoking the users' and increasing their stress level.

4 Results

In this work, we present an example of the measures it is possible to extract from the framework and how they are interpreted. First of all, we compute the different degree of difficulty of the game level as the product between the number of icons presented on screen and the number of combinations provided in the level. This is motivated by the fact that icon combinations generate new icons, thus modifying the interface in a way that is unpredictable to the user and representing a substantial factor of cognitive stress. We normalize the difficulty score by the maximum value obtained so that level 4 is assigned a value of 1 while level 1, which does not include icon combinations, is assigned a value of 0. In Fig. 4 we report the difficulty curve as computed with this method.

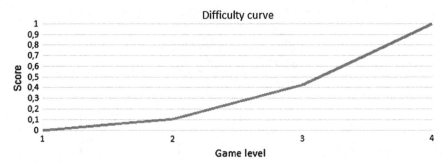

Fig. 4 The difficulty curve of the game levels

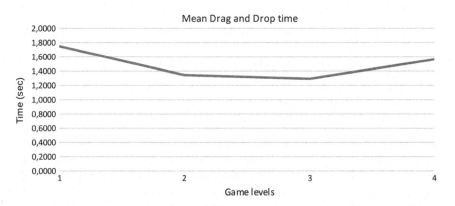

Fig. 5 Mean drag and drop time over increasing difficulty levels

In order to illustrate the intended use of this framework, we first consider the mean time used by the participants to complete a drag and drop operation. Figure 5 shows how this measure varies depending on the level.

We observe a decrease in the amount of time needed when moving from level 1 to level 2, moving to level 3 shows little difference with level 2 while moving to level 4 shows an increase in the computed measure. We can interpret the first movement as a manifestation of the training effect: as we did not let the participants try the application before starting the experiment, the increase in difficulty, shown in the first movement of the curve in Fig. 4, is not strong enough to compensate the effect of the experience gained while playing level 1. The second movement in Fig. 5 corresponds to a stronger increase in difficulty, shown in Fig. 4. In this case, the experience gained by the users in performing the motor task is not enough to compensate the difficulty increase, which is more significant than the first movement in Fig. 4. The last movement in Fig. 5 highlights an increase in the mean drag and drop time together with the last movement in Fig. 4. Being this last movement of the difficulty curve the strongest one, we interpret the last increase of the drag

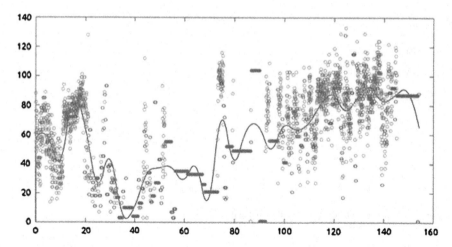

Fig. 6 ENDs for a subject's *left* pupil. The *blue line* indicates the approximating least squares spline (color online)

and drop time curve as an indication of the impossibility of experience to compensate the significant difficulty increase when moving from level 3 to level 4.

More complex analyses can be conducted with the proposed framework. As an example, in Fig. 6, the trace of the x component of a subject's left eye's pupil is shown. Both the raw data and the underlying model obtained with cubic spline approximation are presented. The data were obtained by linking an eye tracking module to the framework. When the tracking is momentarily lost, the module holds the last position.

As an example of the analysis it is possible to conduct with this kind of data, we consider the full stream collected over the four levels of the game for each participant and we analyse the data streams tracking the eyes on X and Y coordinates. Each time the absolute difference between the observed value and the value of the approximating splice is higher than the mean difference, indicating a strong change in the eyes position, we count an *event*. By plotting the total number of events in each level, we obtain the curve shown in Fig. 7.

This Figure is intended to describe the effort put by a user in analysing the interface. We can observe a strong increase in this effort when moving from level 1 to level 2: this is caused by the fact that, while in level 0 the icons disposition does not change, in level 1 the interface changes during the game as soon as the combination of two icons produces a new icon. The training effect reduces this effort when moving from level 1 to level 2, while the strong increase in the task difficulty in level 4 causes another increase of the effort the user must provide to keep track of the changing interface.

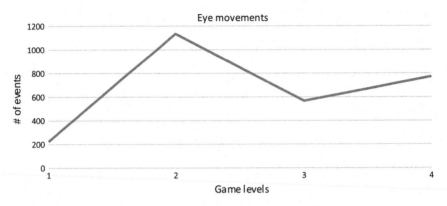

Fig. 7 Eye movement events over the four game levels

5 Conclusions

We have presented a framework for cognitive load evaluation studies on software interfaces. The framework allows to analyze the connection between interface structure changes and cognitive load estimation on the basis of the theories presented in [5]. This goes beyond the framework presented in [1], where only the software architecture was presented without considering explicit theoretical links with interfaces organization. Future work will focus on obtaining a formal model of the connection between observed signals and interface complexity.

Acknowledgments Antonio Origlia's work is supported by the Italian PAC project *Cultural Heritage Emotional Experience See-Through Eyewear* (CHEESE).

References

1. Calandra, D., Caso, A., Cutugno, F., Origlia, A., Rossi, S.: Cowme: a general framework to evaluate cognitive workload during multimodal interaction. In: Proceedings of International Conference on Multimodal Interfaces. pp. 111–118 (2013)
2. Baddeley, A.D.: Working Memory. Oxford University Press (1986)
3. Miyake, A., Shah, P.: Toward unified theories of working memory: Emerging general consensus, unresolved theoretical issues, and future research directions. In: Models of Working Memory: Mechanisms of Active Maintenance and Executive Control. pp. 442–481. Cambridge University Press (1999)
4. Sweller, J.: Cognitive load as a factor in the structuring of technical material. J. Exp. Psychol. **119**, 176–192 (1990)
5. Sweller, J.: Cognitive load during problem solving—effect on learning. Cogn. Sci. **12**, 257–285 (1998)
6. Sweller, J.: Element interactivity and intrinsic, extraneous, and germane cognitive load. Educ. Psychol. Rev. **22**(2), 123–138 (2010). doi:10.1007/s10648-010-9128-5

Modeling Replication and Erasure Coding in Large Scale Distributed Storage Systems Based on CEPH

Daniele Manini, Marco Gribaudo and Mauro Iacono

Abstract The efficiency of storage systems is a key factor to ensure sustainability in data centers devoted to provide cloud services. A proper management of storage infrastructures can ensure the best trade off between costs, reliability and quality of service, enabling the provider to be competitive in the market. Heterogeneity of nodes, and the need for frequent expansion and reconfiguration of the subsystems fostered the development of efficient approaches that replace traditional data replication, by exploiting more advanced techniques, such the ones that leverage erasure codes. In this paper we use an *ad-hoc* discrete event simulation approach to study the performances of replication and erasure coding with different parametric configurations, aiming at the minimization of overheads while obtaining the desired reliability. The approach is demonstrated with a practical application to the erasure coding plugins of the increasingly popular CEPH distributed file system.

Keywords Performance modeling · Cloud computing and big data infrastructures · Storage systems · Erasure codes · CEPH

D. Manini
Dip. Di Informatica, Università Di Torino, Corso Svizzera, 185,
10129 Torino, Italy
e-mail: manini@di.unito.it

M. Gribaudo
Dip. Di Elettronica, Informazione E Bioingegneria, Politecnico Di Milano,
Via Ponzio 34/5, 20133 Milan, Italy
e-mail: marco.gribaudo@polimi.it

M. Iacono (✉)
Dip. Di Scienze Politiche, Seconda Università Degli Studi Di Napoli,
Viale Ellittico 31, 81100 Caserta, Italy
e-mail: mauro.iacono@unina2.it

© Springer International Publishing Switzerland 2016
L. Caporarello et al. (eds.), *Digitally Supported Innovation*,
Lecture Notes in Information Systems and Organisation 18,
DOI 10.1007/978-3-319-40265-9_20

273

1   Introduction

The management of huge computing infrastructures, typical of the cloud computing oriented market, is a challenge that a provider has to face in order to keep the pace with competitors. Besides the technical factors, costs are the main leverage on which providers have to found their strategies. Efficiency in using expensive resources, such as energy, computation and storage, is an effective way to balance costs and revenues while providing affordable services with sufficient quality. The complexity of such infrastructures requires a higher management effort, but paves the way to more sophisticated solutions to pursue efficiency.

The authors already investigated the main aspects of massively distributed architectures for data centers in [2–8, 12]. In this paper, that extends the results that can be found in [12] and apply them to an emerging technology for storage in datacenters, we present a simulative approach for the evaluation of erasure coding based approaches for space and performance efficient data resilience solutions. Our approach uses user defined storage entity grouping blocks across different nodes to improve system reliability, by exploiting erasure codes to define and implement data redundancy while using a low space and computing overhead. With respect to [12], this paper extends the number of parameters that can be evaluated by the proposed *ad-hoc* simulator and applies the approach to the use of the erasure coding plugins of the CEPH distributed file system.

The paper is organized as follows: after the discussion of the related work in Sect. 2, an overview about the CEPH architecture is provided in Sect. 3. The modeling approach is discussed in Sect. 4 and results presented in Sect. 5. Final remarks and future works are discussed in Sect. 6.

2   Related Works

A general introduction to storage problems can be found in [26, 27]. The problem of replica placement in distributed storage systems is studied in [15], that presents some interesting results. A solution with a massively distributed approach that aims at cost reduction is presented in [20], in which an analytical model is used to analyze the characterization of lost chunks reconstruction processes. Erasure coding has been extensively studied, with its applications, specially in peer to peer systems: [1] provides a good application, [22] presents a quantitative evaluation of the benefits deriving from the adoption of erasure coding and replication strategies in resilient storage subsystems, while [13] presents a low overhead erasure codes family applied to peer systems and [9] presents an empirical simulation based statistical analysis of reconstruction of data blocks in peer to peer architectures. Applications to distributed hash tables can be found in [24, 17]. Applications in Big Data oriented systems can be found in [18] or [25], that analyzes the causes and management of latency. In [11] a two-phase solution to combine efficiency of coding devoted space and reconstruction traffic amount is presented and analyzed by means of analytical models, focusing on chunk and files, with similar aims to this paper, that is rather oriented to the analysis of the effects of node failures, and to provide a simulation study that also encompasses the transient behaviors. For a wider perspective of the topic, the problem of storage resources selection is dealt in [10], an introduction to resource scheduling in these architectures can be found in [19, 21] and some new results about energy efficiency in management are pointed by [14] and related papers.

3 CEPH Overview

CEPH, as defined by it authors, is a distributed object store and file system designed to provide performance, reliability and scalability. It is a very complex systems that, among all its other features, can protect against node failures using both replication and erasure coding. In the following we provide an overview of this system, in particular, we will focus on the components that are explicitly described in our simulator.

3.1 CEPH Architecture

CEPH stores its data at two levels: a physical one that is represented by a set of interconnected machines called CEPH nodes, and a logical one composed of a set of Object Storage Devices (OSD). Each physical node can contain one or more OSDs where data are spread using an algorithm called CRUSH.

The system, which provides a large scalable storage cluster based upon RADOS [23], is composed of two types of daemons: CEPH Monitor and CEPH OSD Daemon. The former maintains a master copy of the cluster map, the latter checks its own state and the state of other OSDs and reports back to monitors. The combination of these two logic components ensures a reliable updating of the network and the self managing of the data. CEPH OSD Daemons use a flat namespace with no hierarchy of directory, characterizing each object with an identifier. Even if these entities are not explicitly represented in the simulator, we rely on their correct behavior to abstract our model and focus only on the reliability aspects of the system.

OSDs are constructed from commodity components. They include a CPU, a network interface, a local cache and several disks or RAIDs. OSDs replace the conventional fixed size blocks with named variable-length objects. The CEPH monitors manages the CEPH clusters through a cluster map that compactly specifies how data is distributed across the devices of the system. Each object stored by the system is as first mapped into a *placement group* (PG), a logical collection of objects that are replicated by the same set of devices. Replication is performed by the OSDs themselves: clients submit a single write operation to the first primary OSD, who is then responsible for consistently and safely updating all replicas. Each object stored in the system uses the concept of PG to simplify the distribution among the nodes. In particular, as replication and erasure coding can be used to increase the reliability of the system, each object is spread among several OSDs. Placement groups represent logical collections of objects that use the same set of OSDs.

Clients submit a single write operation to one specific OSD, which is then responsible for updating all replicas. At the highest possible abstraction level, data is divided in *pools*, which are logical partitions for storing objects. Each pool determines the way CRUSH maps the data to the OSDs. Moreover, pools can be characterized by either *replication* or *erasure* coding to improve the availability. In the following we will focus on the analysis of these two mechanisms. Each pool has a number of placement groups which CRUSH maps dynamically to OSDs. When a CEPH Client stores objects, CRUSH will map each object to a placement group.

3.2 Pools: Replication and Erasure Coding

Replication pools store several different copies of the same object, as shown in Fig. 1. For sake of simplicity, let us assume that there are 8 objects (A to G) and that each node hosts a single OSD. In this example there are 4 PGs: n_1 and n_2, n_2 and n_3, n_3 and n_4, and n_4 and n_1, and the replication factor $s = 2$. The CRUSH algorithm defines where to store an object, for instance it maps objects A and E to first PG and thus on node n_1 and n_2, B and F to the second PG and so on. Moreover, the algorithm identifies a *primary node* among the OSDs of a PG: the CEPH clients will communicate only with the selected node. The primary OSD will then contact the other nodes in the group in order to perform replication. In Fig. 1 copies on primary OSDs are represented with continuous lines whereas dashed boxes represents objects stored on secondary nodes.

With the ability to perform data replication, CEPH OSD daemons ensure high data availability and data safety, relieving the application from this duty. For instance, if node n_1 fails, objects A and E are still available on the secondary

Fig. 1 Example of replication pool

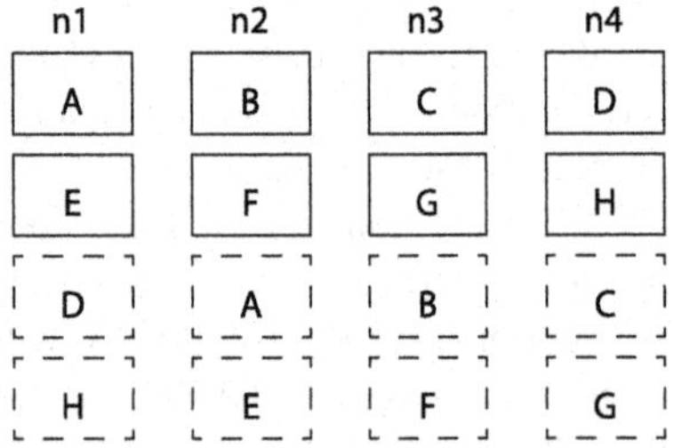

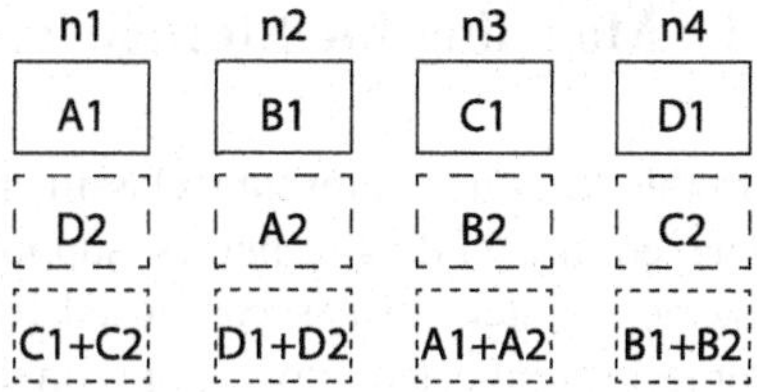

Fig. 2 Example of erasure coded pool

n1	n2	n3	n4
A1	B1	C1	D1
D2	A2	B2	C2
C1+C2	D1+D2	A1+A2	B1+B2

node n_2. On the other hand, using this schema, the amount of required resources increases proportionally with the replication factor.

Erasure coded pools aim to guarantee reliability while reducing the storage required. In particular, they store each object as $k + m$ chunks where k are data chunks and m are coding chunks. The $k + m$ chunks are stored in different OSDs according to the PG associated to the original object. The objects can then be reconstructed from any subset of k out of $k + m$ chunks (either data or coding). The techniques that can be used to compute coding chunks exploit *Forward Error Correcting* codes, and in particular the *Maximum Distance Separable Codes*. A well known example of Maximum Distance Separable codes are the *Solomon-Reed* codes, used to protect RAID 6 [16] disk arrays from multiple disks failures. For example, Fig. 2 shows a case with $k = 2$ and $m = 1$. There are 4 objects belonging to 4 different PGs ($n_1 n_2 n_3$, $n_2 n_3 n_4$, and so on). The primary OSDs are responsible for encoding the objects into $k + m$ chunks and send them to the other OSDs. In this case, object A is divided into chunks $A1$, $A2$, and $A1 + A2$ (the first two are data chunks, the third is the coding chunk). The primary node is n_1, holding chunk $A1$, while $A2$ and $A1 + A2$ are hosted in the other OSDs of the PG. If node n_1 fails, object A can be reconstructed from data chunk A_2 on node n_2 and coding chunk $A1 + A2$ on node n_3. The amount of storage required by the erasure coded pool presented in Fig. 2 is 25 %} smaller if compared with the amount used by the replication approach shown in Fig. 1. This is due to the fact that erasure coded schema is based on chunks that are just a fraction of an object.

CEPH allows the user to configure a specific error correcting code profile for each erasure coded pool: each profile is characterized by different performances in terms of reliability, storage overhead and efficiency during reconstruction. The ones supported by the current version of CEPH are: Jerasure, ISA, Locally Repairable, SHEC (and its extended version mSHEC). Jerasure is the default plugin for CEPH coded pools, and it is the most flexible and generic one. ISA runs only on INTEL processors, it comes in two Solomon-Reed forms: Vandermonde and Cauchy. The Locally Repairable erasure code plugin allows to recover the loss of one OSD by using a minor number of other OSDs, for instance with Jerasure when a OSD is loss then all the other OSDs are required to recover. SHEC and mSHEC allow CEPH to recover data more efficiently than Solomon-Reed codes. A more detailed description of the coding profile will be given in the following section.

4   Modeling the Storage System

In this section we present a classification framework that can be used to characterize the erasure coding schemes supported by CEPH. In particular, we consider a storage system that is composed by n OSDs that store q *objects* ($q \gg n$). Each object is replicated into s copies on different nodes. Let us recall that a PG is a set of chunks in which an object that is stored in an erasure coded pool is divided and that each object in the CEPH architecture, depending on whether it is stored in a replicated pool or erasure coded pool with a given profile, belongs to p parity groups. Every parity group i, with $1 \leq i \leq p$, is composed by k_i *data chunks*, and m_i *coding chunks*. Note that the number of data chunks and coding chunks might be different in each parity group.

Let us call b_j the size in bytes of object j, with $1 \leq j \leq q$. The total storage capacity used by the system to store the q objects can then be computed as:

$$B = \sum_{j=1}^{q} \left[b_j \cdot \left(s + \sum_{i=1}^{p} \frac{m_i}{k_i} \right) \right] \tag{1}$$

since each byte of each file is repeated s times for the replicas in replication pools, and m_i coding bytes are added every k_i data bytes for every parity group i that form the p levels used by the coding profile. Thus the overhead θ of the coding can be defined as:

$$\theta = \frac{B}{\sum_{j=1}^{q} b_j} - 1 = s - 1 + \sum_{i=1}^{p} \frac{m_i}{k_i} \tag{2}$$

The -1 term in the previous expression excludes the storage space that is needed to hold the entire copy of the object, focusing measure θ on the additional space requirements used to improve the reliability of the data.

The different types of pools used in the CEPH can then be identified by a proper assignment of s, p, m_i and k_i: let us analyze how this can be accomplished in more detail.

Replicated pools

In replicated pools, data is repeated several times in different nodes of the system. In our characterization, it can be obtained by setting s to the total number of copies of the data ($s > 1$), and by setting $p = 0$ since no coding chunks are used.

Erasure coded pools: *Jerasure* or *ISA*

The ISA and Jerasure coding profiles, although characterized by different software and hardware implementations and by different types of Solomon-Reed encoding, all share the same redundancy structure. In particular they are all characterized by having only one single complete set of data chunks that is reflected in our modeling framework by setting $s = 1$. There is only one single parity group

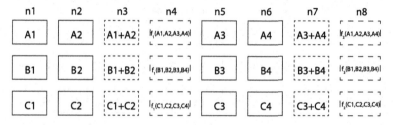

Fig. 3 Local Repairable codes

$p = 1$, and parameters k_1 and m_1 respectively represent the number of data chunks K and of coding chunks M configured by the user.

Erasure coded pools: *Locally Repairable*

Locally repairable codes encode k data with m coding chunks as standard Solomon-Reed codes. In addition, they place an extra coding chunk every l blocks. In particular, they create $g = (k+m)/l$ groups, that are protected by an extra coding chunks: in this way, if a single chunk in a local group is missing, it can be reconstructed by accessing only the local data and the corresponding coding chunk. If up to m chunks are missing from a group, but all the chunks in the other groups are available, they can be reconstructed using the global parity at the higher level. Even if it is not a strict requirement, thanks to the special algorithms that are used, normally g is an integer number and both m and k are integer multiples of g. In this work we will focus only on this case. Figure 3 shows an example of Locally repairable codes: in particular, data chunks A1, A2, A3 and A4 on nodes n_1, n_2, n_5 and n_6 are protected by the two coding chunks on nodes n_4 and n_8, allowing to repair up to two broken chunks. In addition, a coding chunk for A1 and A2 is placed in node n_3 and one for A3 and A4 is placed on n_7. If node n_1 fails, its data can be reconstructed using only n_2 and n_3. If also n_5 fails, then A1 and A3 can be reconstructed using the information on nodes n_2, n_4, n_6 and n_8. Locally repairable codes can be included in our framework by setting $p = 2$ to model the two different levels of the coding scheme. The first group represents the local codes and it can be defined with $k_1 = k/g$ and $m_1 = 1$. The second level represents the global coding and can be described with $k_2 = k$ and $m_2 = m$.

Erasure coded pools: *SHEC* and *mSHEC*

Shingled Erasure Codes (SHEC) protect each block by means of several parity groups, each one shifted and partially overlapped with the others. In particular, it is defined by three parameters: k and m, that are respectively the number of data and coding chunks, and c, that defines the number of failures in the system that must occur to have a data loss (called *durability* parameter). From k, m and c, the number l of chunks that must be used for each coding chunk can be determined. In particular, it can be shown that $l = k \cdot c/m$. Figure 4 shows an example of SHEC coding with $k = 6$, $m = 3$ and $c = 2$ and $l = 4$. In this case, if node n_1 fails, it can be reconstructed using nodes n_2 to n_5. If also node n_2 fails, both nodes can be reconstructed using n_3 to n_5 and n_7 to n_9. In our framework, SHEC can be

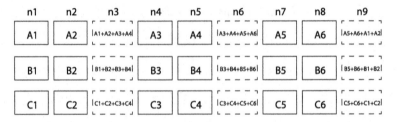

Fig. 4 Shingled Erasure Codes (SHEC)

introduced by setting the number of parity groups $p = c$, and by setting the number of chunks in each group $k_i = l$, and the number of parity blocks per group $m_i = 1$. mSHEC extends the code by repeating the SHEC schema two times, dividing the number of parity information $m = m_1 + m_2$ and the durability factor $c = c_1 + c_2$ such to maximize the recovery efficiency. In our schema, it can be introduced by setting $l_1 = k \cdot c_1/m_1$, $l_2 = k \cdot c_2/m_2$, $p = c$, $m_i = 1$ and $k_i = l_1$ for $i \le c_1$, and $k_i = l_2$ for $i > c_1$.

In order to evaluate the performances of the considered CEPH configuration, we must study its dynamic behavior. Users access objects with rate c. Node failures happen with rate d, duplications in replicated pools happen with rate r, redundancy computation in erasure coded pools happens with rate η and data reconstruction happens at rate σ. A summary of the parameters in Table 1. Performance indices have been computed using an *ad-hoc* simulator: interested readers can find a more thorough discussion in [12]. The simulator starts from a plain configuration of the system, with no object replication, and, according to the parameters of the considered CEPH configuration, builds the desired replication and redundancy configuration. For this work, the simulator has been extended to consider also more parity groups (i.e. $p > 1$).

Table 1 Parameters of the model

Parm.	Description
n	Number of nodes
q	Number of objects
s	Number of full copies per object
v_{max}	Max. # of blocks on a node
p	Number of parity groups
k	Data chunks per object
m	Coding chunks per object
d	Node failure rate
r	Duplication rate
η	Redundancy computation rate
σ	Reconstruction from redundancy rate
c	Block request rate

5 Experiments

We consider a scenario composed by $n = 40$ OSDs and $q = 200$ objects. Simulations have been computed on a standard Macbook Air laptop, based on an Intel i5 processor, with 4 GB of RAM and required few minutes to reach the desired confidence level. Even if confidence intervals were always evaluated, we present only the mean results to simplify the plots. We have chosen a very slow and faulty environment to test the system in extreme conditions. Node failure rate was set to $d = 0.01$ (one failure every 100 h), duplication rate was $r = 0.1$ (10 h to complete a copy), redundancy computation was $\eta = 0.1$ (redundancy is computed every 10 h) and reconstruction rate was $\sigma = 0.2$ (in average, 5 h are required to identify a missing chunk and reconstruct it).

5.1 Reliability of Replicated Pools

Figure 5 shows the evolution of the number of objects in the system as a function of time. The number of objects starts with q, since at time $t = 0$ all the objects are available, and gradually reduces, with a rate that becomes smaller as the replication factor increases. Figure 6 considers instead the evolution of the total number of copies for each object. As it can be seen, since initially (left side of the figure) there is only one copy per object, the plot starts with q for all the considered values of s. However, since the copy mechanism starts copying the objects, the number of copies increases to $q \cdot s$ during the initial evolution of the system. This limit however is not reached due to the OSDs that fail before the first copy has been completed. The right hand side of Fig. 6 focuses on larger time scales: in this case the evolution of the average number of copies tends to the average number of objects, multiplied by s.

Fig. 5 Evolution of the number of objects in time for replicated pools

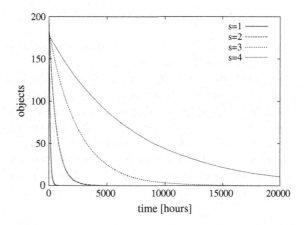

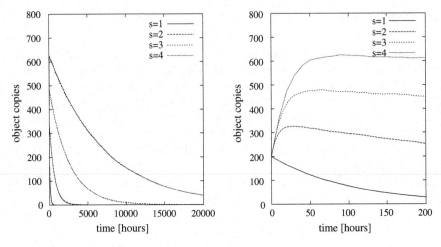

Fig. 6 Evolution of the total number of copies of the objects for replicated pools: small time scale (*left*) and larger time scale (*right*)

Fig. 7 Evolution of the number of objects in time for erasure code pools using Jerasure or ISA profiles

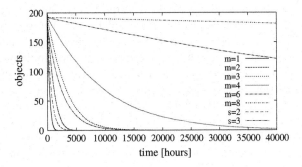

5.2 Reliability in Erasure Coded Poools

We next consider the coding mechanisms used in the erasure coded pools based on either the ISA or Jerasure profiles.

Figure 7 shows the effect of changing the number of coding chunks m used for objects split into $k = 4$ data chunks. As expected, increasing the number of coding information improves the lifetime of the objects. It is interesting to compare the curve of $m = 4$ with the one with $s = 2$, that represents a replicated pool with two copies per object. Both configurations have the same overhead (i.e. twice the size of the objects); however, the parity mechanism provides a higher reliability, at the expense of a performance reduction due to the complexity of the reconstruction procedure.

6 Conclusions and Future Works

In this paper we have presented a modeling approach to support management and design of large scale distributed storage systems, aiming at the analysis of the effects on reliability of replication or erasure coding. The approach has been applied to a specific case study, the increasingly popular CEPH distributed file system, by examining the pool configuration and its the erasure coding plugins. Future work includes the analysis of CEPH erasure coding profiles based on Locally Repairable codes or SHEC, and the extension of the approach to include a more detailed physical subsystem characterization, the effect of limited bandwidth and power absorption related aspects.

References

1. Aguilera, M., Janakiraman, R., Xu, L.: Using erasure codes efficiently for storage in a distributed system. In: Proceedings. International Conference on Dependable Systems and Networks, 2005. DSN 2005, pp. 336–345 (2005)
2. Barbierato, E., Gribaudo, M., Iacono, M.: Modeling apache hive based applications in big data architectures. In: Proceedings of the 7th International Conference on Performance Evaluation Methodologies and Tools, pp. 30–38. ValueTools'13, ICST (Institute for Computer Sciences, Social-Informatics and Telecommunications Engineering), ICST, Brussels, Belgium (2013)
3. Barbierato, E., Gribaudo, M., Iacono, M.: A performance modeling language for big data architectures. In: Rekdalsbakken, W., Bye, R.T., Zhang, H. (eds.) ECMS, pp. 511–517. European Council for Modeling and Simulation (2013)
4. Barbierato, E., Gribaudo, M., Iacono, M.: Performance evaluation of NoSQL big-data applications using multi-formalism models. Future Gen. Comput. Syst. 37, 345–353 (2014)
5. Barbierato, E., Gribaudo, M., Iacono, M.: Modeling and evaluating the effects of big data storage resource allocation in global scale cloud architectures. Int. J. Data Warehousing Min. (2015)
6. Castiglione, A., Gribaudo, M., Iacono, M., Palmieri, F.: Exploiting mean field analysis to model performances of big data architectures. Future Gen. Comput. Syst. 37, 203–211 (2014)
7. Castiglione, A., Gribaudo, M., Iacono, M., Palmieri, F.: Modeling performances of concurrent big data applications. Software: Practice and Experience (2014)
8. Cerotti, D., Gribaudo, M., Iacono, M., Piazzolla, P.: Modeling and analysis of performances for concurrent multithread applications on multicore and graphics processing unit systems. Concurrency and Computation: Practice and Experience (2015)
9. Dandoush, A., Alouf, S., Nain, P.: Simulation analysis of download and recovery processes in p2p storage systems. In: 21st International Teletraffic Congress, 2009. ITC 21 2009, pp. 1–8 (2009)
10. Esposito, C., Ficco, M., Palmieri, F., Castiglione, A.: Smart cloud storage service selection based on fuzzy logic, theory of evidence and game theory. IEEE Transac. Comput. PP(99), 1–1 (2015)
11. Friedman, R., Kantor, Y., Kantor, A.: Replicated erasure codes for storage and repair-traffic efficiency. In: 14th IEEE International Conference on Peer-to-Peer Computing, P2P 2014, London, United Kingdom, September 9–11, 2014, Proceedings, pp. 1–10 (2014)
12. Gribaudo, M., Iacono, M., Manini, D.: Improving reliability and performances in large scale distributed applications with erasure codes and replication. Future Generation Computer Systems (2015)

13. Kameyama, H., Sato, Y.: Erasure codes with small overhead factor and their distributed storage applications. In: 41st Annual Conference on Information Sciences and Systems, 2007. CISS'07, pp. 80–85 (2007)
14. Kolodziej, J., Burczynski, T., Zomaya, A.Y.: A note on energy efficient data, services and memory management in big data information systems. Inform. Sci. **319**, 69–70 (2015), energy Efficient Data, Services and Memory Management in Big Data Information Systems
15. Lian, Q., Chen, W., Zhang, Z.: On the impact of replica placement to the reliability of distributed brick storage systems. In: Proceedings of the 25th IEEE International Conference on Distributed Computing Systems, 2005, ICDCS 2005, pp. 187–196 (2005)
16. Plank, J.S.: A tutorial on reed-solomon coding for fault-tolerance in raid-like systems. Softw. Pract. Exper. **27**(9), 995–1012 (1997)
17. Rodrigues, R., Liskov, B.: High availability in dhts: Erasure coding vs. replication. In: 4th International Workshop on Peer-to-Peer Systems IV, IPTPS 2005. Ithaca, New York (Feb 2005)
18. Sathiamoorthy, M., Asteris, M., Papailiopoulos, D., Dimakis, A.G., Vadali, R., Chen, S., Borthakur, D.: Xoring elephants: novel erasure codes for big data. In: Proceedings of the 39th International Conference on Very Large Data Bases. pp. 325–336. PVLDB'13, VLDB Endowment (2013)
19. Sfrent, A., Pop, F.: Asymptotic scheduling for many task computing in big data platforms. Inform. Sci. *319*, 71–91 (2015), energy Efficient Data, Services and Memory Management in Big Data Information Systems
20. Simon, V., Monnet, S., Feuillet, M., Robert, P., Sens, P.: SPLAD: scattering and placing data replicas to enhance long-term durability. Rapport de recherche RR-8533, INRIA (2014), http:// hal.inria.fr/hal-00988374
21. Vasile, M.A., Pop, F., Tutueanu, R.I., Cristea, V., KoÅ,odziej, J.: Resource-aware hybrid scheduling algorithm in heterogeneous distributed computing. Future Gen. Comput. Syst. **51**, 61–71 (2015), special Section: A Note on New Trends in Data-Aware Scheduling and Resource Provisioning in Modern {HPC} Systems
22. Weatherspoon, H., Kubiatowicz, J.: Erasure coding versus replication: a quantitative comparison. In: Revised Papers from the First International Workshop on Peer-to-Peer Systems, pp. 328–338. IPTPS'01, Springer, London (2002)
23. Weil, S.A., Leung, A.W., Brandt, S.A., Maltzahn, C.: RADOS: a Scalable, Reliable Storage Service for Petabyte-scale Storage Clusters, http://ceph.com/papers/weil-rados-pdsw07.pdf
24. Wu, F., Qiu, T., Chen, Y., Chen, G.: Redundancy schemes for high availability in dhts. In: Pan, Y., Chen, D., Guo, M., Cao, J., Dongarra, J. (eds.) ISPA. Lecture Notes in Computer Science, vol. 3758, pp. 990–1000. Springer (2005)
25. Xiang, Y., Lan, T., Aggarwal, V., Chen, Y.F.R.: Joint latency and cost optimization for erasurecoded data center storage. SIGMETRICS Perform. Eval. Rev. **42**(2), 3–14 (2014)
26. Xu, L., Cipar, J., Krevat, E., Tumanov, A., Gupta, N., Kozuch, M.A., Ganger, G.R.: Agility and performance in elastic distributed storage. Trans. Storage **10**(4), 16:1–16:27 (2014)
27. Yan, F., Riska, A., Smirni, E.: Fast eventual consistency with performance guarantees for distributed storage. In: 32nd International Conference on Distributed Computing Systems Workshops (ICDCSW), 2012. pp. 23–28 (June 2012)

Power Consumption Analysis of Replicated Virtual Applications in Heterogeneous Architectures

Gianfranco Ciardo, Marco Gribaudo, Mauro Iacono, Andrew Miner and Pietro Piazzolla

Abstract Nowadays, power consumption in IT infrastructures is a major area of concern for both academia and industry. In data centers where computational power is provided by means of virtualized resources, like virtual machines, the policy to allocate them on physical servers can strongly impact the power consumption of the entire system. This affects data center management, and proper estimation means can offer an important guidance to administrators. We propose a lumped Petri net model to investigate the contribution to energy efficiency due to different allocation and deallocation policies on heterogeneous machines with different power demands, to support estimation and planning of datacenter needs.

Keywords Energy efficiency · Generalized stochastic petrinets · Virtualized datacenters Allocation policies Performance evaluation

G. Ciardo · A. Miner
Department of Computer Science, Iowa State University, 226 Atanasoff Hall,
50011 Ames, USA
e-mail: ciardo@iastate.edu

A. Miner
e-mail: asminer@iastate.edu

M. Gribaudo (✉) · P. Piazzolla
Dipartimento Di Elettronica, Informazione E Bioingegneria, Politecnico Di Milano,
Via Ponzio 34/5, 20133 Milano, Italy
e-mail: marco.gribaudo@polimi.it

P. Piazzolla
e-mail: pietro.piazzolla@polimi.it

M. Iacono
Dipartimento Di Scienze Politiche, Seconda Università Degli Studi Di Napoli,
Viale Ellittico 31, 81100 Caserta, Italy

© Springer International Publishing Switzerland 2016
L. Caporarello et al. (eds.), *Digitally Supported Innovation*,
Lecture Notes in Information Systems and Organisation 18,
DOI 10.1007/978-3-319-40265-9_21

285

1 Introduction

The commercial scenario of IT in the current decade is dominated by a constant demand for intelligent services and the availability of increasingly massive volumes of data. These two forces drive the market towards a consolidation of complex software systems into large data centers that host evolving, heterogeneous, high–performance computing architectures.

The aspects related to computing, networking, and storage are very complex, as a consequence of the scale, the interrelation, the volume of data, the reliability requirements, and the diversity in workload. The authors already investigated these aspects in [1–4, 7, 8, 16]. However, there are other reasons for which the management of such infrastructures is a challenging problem: besides issues strictly connected to computing and networking, energy problems arise for both powering the infrastructure and cooling down its components. Energy requirements represent a significant part of costs and affect the ability of providers to stay in the market (at the point that energy related attacks have been designed to damage providers (see [14, 20])). Virtualization is a key software technology on which proper resource scheduling solutions can be designed: the literature offers many proposals (e.g. see [24, 26]), but the research field is just opening. Recent results on energy issues in these systems are pointed by [18] and related papers.

Because large–scale empirical experiments are expensive, as they need to be performed on large, complex architectures and require non–negligible time shares on the system, a model–based approach is a more viable way to approach the problem of designing optimal power–oriented management strategies, at least in a first stage of the process, and in support of operations on existing systems. This paper presents a model to evaluate the power requirements of different allocation strategies for virtual machines (VMs) on the nodes of a datacenter. The modeling approach exploits the modular organization of commercial datacenters, so that energy–related problems can be similarly addressed with a modular logic dependent on the organization of the power subsystem. The model accounts for allocation and deallocation of VMs on heterogeneous nodes and exploits lumping to scale up to significant datacenter sizes. A case study is presented to show the effectiveness of the approach, evaluated with the software tool SMART [12].

The paper is organized as follows: Sect. 2 describes related works. Section 3 discusses the modeling approach, while Sect. 4 presents the model analyzed in Sect. 5. Section 6 concludes the paper with final considerations and future research directions.

2 Background and Related Works

A basic support technology to power management is provided in hardware by two essential mechanisms [5]: Dynamic Performance Scaling enables components to operate at different performance levels, depending on the workload; Dynamic

Component Deactivation allows to shut off unnecessary components (or parts of them) when they are not required by the workload. The literature [9] shows that in general there is a linear relation between instantaneous power consumption and CPU utilization, with a significant baseline power consumption level even when the utilization is zero, to keep the system on and ready. Hardware mechanisms are not enough to provide sufficient savings when the architecture scales up to systems that involve different nodes: in this case, major savings can be achieved by a proper allocation of tasks to the nodes, e.g., to keep as many components in a lower consumption state or to allow some nodes to shut off, or at least to switch to the lowest consumption state. The problem is not straightforward, as state switching is not instantaneous and affects the overall performances of the system, and system workload is not constant. Some results about node scheduling can be found in [22].

Virtualization allows a flexible management of scheduling between and within computing nodes, e.g., enabling server consolidation or migration of VMs. Consolidation allows to increase the number of idle nodes in a system, but there may be other resource allocation schemata that enable a lower overall average power absorption at the system level. The literature offers some solutions for optimal allocation of resources in virtualized computing environments, mainly based on probabilistic approaches [6, 19, 27], but different metrics and goals have been proposed: a survey of the main issues and solutions suitable for large data centers can be found in [5]. Workload– and application–dependent solutions have been presented: [15] deals with the problems related to multitier web applications; [23] presents different policies for the management of average data center power consumption; [25] targets the improvement of resource utilization as a means to lower power consumption; and [10, 17] study power consumption and replication of services.

3 Modeling Approach

We consider a datacenter dedicated to provisioning of on–demand computing resources. The datacenter has heterogeneous computing nodes, or Physical Machines (PMs), meaning that there are different classes of architectures, each capable of providing a different amount of resources to the system. We assume network bandwidth is sufficient to support application requests and administrative needs. Resources are provisioned as Virtual Machines (VMs), allocated on demand by an application so that it can scale accordingly to users' requests. All VMs are assumed to be identical, thus able to replicate the same services. When the resources of a single VM are no longer able to satisfy all incoming requests, a new VM is allocated. When the workload lowers and VMs are not needed anymore, under the hypothesis that requests are routed according to the chosen management strategy, VMs are chosen to be deallocated.

Resource management is based on the allocation and deallocation of VMs, which have an operational life spanning in time intervals that are significantly wider than allocation and deallocation times. Since VM migration (and, consequently, consolidation) are expensive processes, management is instead oriented to identify the best allocation and deallocation strategy, avoiding migrations. Depending on incoming user requests, which vary over time, the system reacts by allocating or releasing VMs to ensure that all requests are served. Every VM can support a certain volume of requests, according to the nature of the hosted applications, whose specifics are outside the scope of this paper. No particular assumption is made about the nature of the application or any special usage patterns. The goal of the datacenter's provider is to optimize the usage of the system, guaranteeing the users a given service level while keeping energy consumption low. The allocation and deallocation strategies are crucial for power consumption, because they allow to put one or more nodes in lower consumption states: studying such strategies and their effects on consumption, according to a proper power estimation criterion, provides insights on datacenter power needs. The aim of this modeling approach is to support provider management decisions on the basis of performance and power consumption estimations.

We focus on different allocation and deallocation policies that place or remove VMs from PMs, focusing on some common approaches [28] that take into consideration the partial homogeneity of the architectures we consider. In particular, we focus on datacenters where resources have been acquired in different times, leading to a heterogenous architecture were PMs with different characteristics coexist. The heterogeneity is manifested by using policies that give priority, when selecting a physical server, to those belonging to a class supplying fewer cores to the system's resources as *Smallest-first(SF)*. With *Biggest-First(BF)*, instead, we refer to those policies that give priority to nodes belonging to a class supplying a higher number of cores per machine. For the allocation we analyze the following policies:

- *Random*: a randomly–determined computing node is selected to host the new VM.
- *Least-loaded(All)*: among all the different computing nodes, the new VM is placed on the one with the smallest number of allocated resources.
- *Most-loaded(SF)*: among all the different computing nodes, the new VM is placed on the one with the highest number of resources used. This policy gives priority to PMs belonging to the classes that have the smallest number of resources.
- *Most-loaded(BF)*: among all the different computing nodes, the new VM is placed on the one with the fewest available resources. This policy gives priority to nodes capable of hosting the largest number of resources.

When a VM is not serving requests anymore because of a lower workload, it can be immediately removed. Dealloccation policies we analyze are:

- *Random*: a randomly–determined PM is selected to deallocate the VM.
- *Least-loaded(SF)*: among all the different computing nodes, the VM is deallocated from the one with the fewest used resources. This policy gives priority to nodes belonging to the class that contributes the smallest number of resources.

- *Least-loaded(BF)*: among all the different computing nodes, the VM is deallocated from the one with the fewest used resources. This policy gives priority to nodes belonging to the class that contributes the largest number of resources.
- *Most-loaded(All)*: among all the different computing nodes, the new VM is released from the one with the most used resources.

The approach presented in this paper extends that of [21]. With respect to [21], the contributions are the extension to heterogeneous nodes and a new model that provides higher scalability in the dimensions of target systems while requiring the same computational resources for its evaluation.

4 The Model

Consider a system composed of K classes of physical machines or nodes, each class defined by a different architecture in terms of resources that can be provided for the allocation of VMs. Each class k, $1 \leq k \leq K$, is characterized by PM_k physical machines in the system. Let C_k be the maximum number of VMs that can be allocated on a machine of class k. Up to N VMs can be allocated on the $\sum_{k=1}^{K} PM_k$ machines that compose the hardware of the system. We assume that the system always has enough resources for the allocation of all N VMs, that is:

$$\sum_{k=1}^{K} PM_k \cdot C_K \geq N \qquad (1)$$

Two events change the state of the system: α^+, which requests the provision of a new VM, and α^-, which requests to deallocate a VM from one of the physical machines. α^+ events follow a Poisson process with an interarrival rate λ. α^- events follow a Poisson process with service rate μ. The policies listed in Sect. 3 define how the state of the system changes after the occurrence of an event α^+ or α^-.

For our study, the most significant quantity to minimize is P_{idle}, the amount of power that a node consumes for being powered on, ready to handle incoming requests, required by a running PM. To reduce their P_{idle} contribution, unutilised servers must be put in a state where their power consumption is negligible or null, using one or more Dynamic Component Deactivation techniques. We assume that a server is turned off when it hosts no VMs, and is turned on when no resources are available in the pool of currently active servers to allocate a new VM.

We study how the policies that determine the allocation and deallocation of VMs among PMs can influence the power consumption of a datacenter. In particular, allocating and deallocating resources for VM instances according to a specific strategy can determine different levels of utilization among the servers, placing a higher or lower number of them in idle state. Since idle PMs can be deactivated to save power, policies can be seen as a tool to increase power efficiency by reducing the P_{idle} contribution. We define the energy consumption function or *efficiency* $E(t)$ as the number of PMs powered off at time t. Since we assume that no time is required to start or stop a PM, the new PMs are instantaneously available while PMs without VMs on it are automatically turned off. Let $n_k(n, t)$ be the number of PMs of class k with n VM allocated on them at time t. We can then define $E(t)$ as:

$$E(t) = \sum_{k=1}^{K} n_k(0, t) \tag{2}$$

To compute the power consumption of the running PMs, instead, a more accurate approach is required. It has been shown [13] that a good approximation of the power consumption of a server can be described by a linear function of the utilization:

$$P(U) = P_{idle} + U \cdot (P_{max} - P_{idle}) \tag{3}$$

where P_{max} is the maximum power consumption of the considered resource. We can approximate the utilization of a PM of class k as $U_k(n) = n/C_k$, where n is the number of VMs running on the considered PM. Moreover, we consider that each class of PM is characterized by different values for $P_{idle(k)}$ and $P_{max(k)}$. To measure the energy consumption of the system we define an *estimated power consumption function* $P(t)$ that considers the number of PMs powered on at time t and the number of VMs running on them. We can then define $P(t)$ as:

$$P(t) = \sum_{k=1}^{K} \sum_{n=1}^{C_k} n_k(n, t) \cdot \left(P_{idle(k)} + \frac{n}{C_k} \cdot \left(P_{max(k)} - P_{idle(k)} \right) \right) \tag{4}$$

4.1 The Petri Net Model

Figure 1 shows a lumped GSPN model for a specific configuration of the system. Place p represents VMs not yet requested for allocation by the application and may contain tokens up to the maximum number N of VMs that the application can start. The PM_k tokens are the number of physical machines available for each class k. Places $VM_{k,c}$ hold the number of servers PM_k that are hosting exactly c VMs. Each class of servers can have up to $VM_{k,C+1}$ such places, with $VM_{k,0}$ holding the number of servers that are powered off, thus do not contribute to the P_{idle} power consumption.

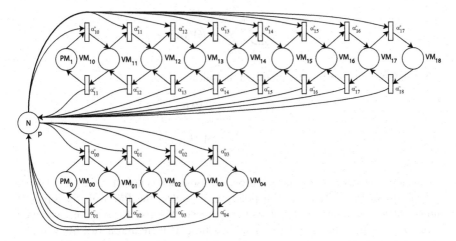

Fig. 1 The lumped GSPN model

When the request for allocating a new VM is issued, one transition among the $\alpha_{k,c}^+$ fires according to a given policy (see Sect. 4.2), and places a VM on an available PM (it changes the place of one PM_k token, meaning that it now hosts one more VM). The firing of transition $\alpha_{k,c}^-$ issues a request to stop one of the running VMs.

4.2 Implementing the Policies

We implement our policies as guards to transitions $\alpha_{k,c}^+$ and $\alpha_{k,c}^-$, denoted respectively as $g(\alpha_{k,c}^+)$ and $g(\alpha_{k,c}^-)$. The rates are proportional to the number of active transitions of the same type (i.e., all active $\alpha_{k,c}^+$ or all active $\alpha_{k,c}^-$) and will be denoted as $r(\alpha_{k,c}^+)$ and $r(\alpha_{k,c}^-)$. In the following we will present into details only the main policies.

Random server. No guards are required for this policy, whether for allocation or deallocation. The rates are instead modified as follows:

$$r(\alpha_{k,c}^+) = \frac{n_k(c) \cdot \alpha^+}{\sum_{k=1}^{K}(PM_k - n_k(C_k))} \qquad r(\alpha_{k,c}^-) = \frac{n_k(c) \cdot \alpha^-}{\sum_{k=1}^{K}(PM_k - n_k(0))}.$$

Least-loaded(All). Among all available classes of physical machines, the least loaded is the one selected to host the next VM. We consider this policy for allocation only. Guards are provided to the $\alpha_{k,c}^+$ transitions. In particular

$$g(\alpha_{k,c}^+) \equiv \sum_{k=1}^{K} \sum_{i=1}^{\min(c,C_k)} \#VM_{k,i} = 0.$$

Transition rates are instead modified as follows:

$$r(\alpha_{k,c}^+) = \frac{\lambda_{\alpha_k^+} \cdot \#VM_{k,c}}{\displaystyle\sum_{k=1}^{K} \#VM_{k,0}}.$$

This rate change only affects transitions whose index is not shared by all classes.

Least-loaded(SF). Deallocation policy only. Select the PM with the smallest number of VMs running on it. Favors the smallest PMs first. Rates are not changed since only one transition can be enabled at a time. If there are more PMs with the same load level, the choice is taken randomly among them.

Least-loaded(LF). Deallocation policy only. As the previous policy but favors the largest PMs first. Rates are not changed since only one transition can be enabled at a time. If there are more PMs with the same load level, the choice is taken randomly among them.

Most-loaded(All). This policy is implemented for deallocation only. Guards provided to $\alpha_{k,c}^-$ transitions are defined differently for places that share the c index with another transition, and those that do not. In particular:

$$g(\alpha_{k,c}^-) \equiv \sum_{k=1,C_k \geq c}^{K} \left(\sum_{i=c+1}^{C_k} \#VM_{k,i} \right) = 0.$$

Rates are changed as follows:

$$r(\alpha_{k,c}^-) = \begin{cases} 0 & C_k < c \\[2ex] \dfrac{\lambda_{\alpha_k^+} \cdot \#VM_{k,c}}{\sum_{k=1,C_k \geq c}^{K} \#VM_{k,c}} & C_k \geq c \end{cases}$$

Most-loaded(SF). Allocation policy only. Select the PM with the highest number of VMs running on it, favoring the smallest PMs first. Rates are not changed since only one transition can be enabled at a time. If there are more PMs with the same load level, the choice is taken randomly among them.

Most-loaded(LF). Allocation policy only. As above but it favors the smallest PMs first. Rates are not changed since only one transition can be enabled at a time. If there are more PMs with the same load level, the choice is taken randomly among them.

5 Experimental Results

This section presents results obtained solving the models of the previous section using the SMART [11] tool (Stochastic Model checking Analyzer for Reliability and Timing). SMART takes as input a GSPN, then generates and analyzes the underlying continuous-time Markov chain (CTMC). To compute the steady-state distribution of the CTMC for models in Fig. 1, we use the Gauss-Seidel option (#Solver GAUSS_SEIDEL) with an exact symbolic representation of the transition rate matrix (#SolutionType EXACT_EVMDD). The study was performed an i 7 ASUS machine, running Ubuntu 14.04 OS.

For all the tests, we consider a system made of $K = 2$ classes of physical machines, with $C_1 = 4$ and $C_2 = 8$. We set the number of VMs to $N = 64$, and determined various mixes of PM_1 and PM_2 satisfying Eq. 1. The goal is to compare different policies in terms of their contribution to the system energy efficiency. The two type of machines have different energy consumption, as shown in Table 1.

5.1 Allocation Policies

Figure 2 presents the results obtained from applying the different allocation policies of Sect. 4.2 and the *Random* deallocation policy. As expected, the best policies assign new VMs to the most loaded resources. It is interesting to note that giving priority to smaller machines can further reduce the power consumption.

Table 1 Power consumption parameters

	Large (C_2) (Watts)	Small (C_1) (Watts)
P_{Idle}	70	30
P_{Busy}	140	70

Fig. 2 Allocation policies

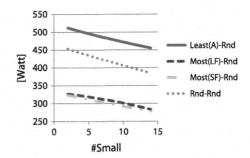

5.2   Deallocation Policies

Figure 3 presents the results obtained from applying the different deallocation policies of Sect. 4.2 and the *Random* allocation policy. In this case, the best results are obtained when releasing the VMs from the least loaded resources, giving priority to larger machines.

5.3   Best Performing Policies

We now focus on those pairs of allocation-deallocation policies that from previous works and experiments performed well in terms of efficiency. In particular we consider the combination of *Most-loaded* allocation with *Least-loaded* deallocation, using different priorities of assignment on different types of PMs (i.e., *Biggest-first* Vs. *Smallest-first*). Figure 4 shows the results: almost all combinations have good energy performance. However, giving priority to smaller machines in allocation, and to larger machine in deallocation, we can obtain a significant reduction in the overall power consumption.

Fig. 3 Deallocation policies

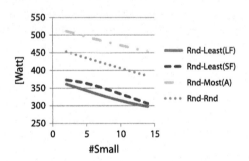

Fig. 4 Changing machine type order for best policies

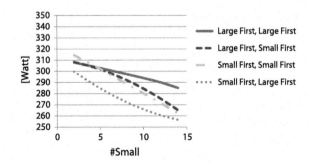

6 Conclusions and Future Work

We presented a lumped model to support the management of power consumption in datacenters. The model allows a provider to gain insights about the best use of resources, in the form of different allocation and deallocation strategies for VMs, can be easily adapted to different configurations, and is useful to evaluate large sections of a datacenter consisting of heterogeneous nodes. Results on a case study show the effectiveness of the approach.

Future work includes extending the analysis to include the effects of VM migration and power consumption of the network infrastructure in larger configurations.

References

1. Barbierato, E., Gribaudo, M., Iacono, M.: Modeling apache hive based applications in big data architectures. In: Proceedings of the 7th International Conference on Performance Evaluation Methodologies and Tools. pp. 30–38. ValueTools'13, ICST (Institute for Computer Sciences, Social-Informatics and Telecommunications Engineering), ICST, Brussels, Belgium (2013), http://dx.doi.org/10.4108/icst.valuetools.2013.254398
2. Barbierato, E., Gribaudo, M., Iacono, M.: A performance modeling language for big data architectures. In: Rekdalsbakken, W., Bye, R.T., Zhang, H. (eds.) ECMS. pp. 511–517. European Council for Modeling and Simulation (2013), http://dblp.uni-trier.de/db/conf/ecms/ecms2013.html
3. Barbierato, E., Gribaudo, M., Iacono, M.: Performance evaluation of NoSQL big-data applications using multi-formalism models. Future Generation Computer Systems 37(0), 345–353 (2014), special Section: Innovative Methods and Algorithms for Advanced Data-Intensive Computing Special Section: Semantics, Intelligent processing and services for big data Special Section: Advances in Data-Intensive Modelling and Simulation Special Section: Hybrid Intelligence for Growing Internet and its Applications
4. Barbierato, E., Gribaudo, M., Iacono, M.: Modeling and evaluating the effects of big data storage resource allocation in global scale cloud architectures. International Journal of Data Warehousing and Mining (2015 (to appear))
5. Beloglazov, A., Buyya, R., Lee, Y.C., Zomaya, A., et al.: A taxonomy and survey of energy-efficient data centers and cloud computing systems. Advances in computers 82(2), 47–111 (2011)
6. Bennani, M., Menascé, D.: Resource allocation for autonomic data centers using analytic performance models. In: Autonomic Computing. ICAC '05. pp. 229–240 (June 2005)
7. Castiglione, A., Gribaudo, M., Iacono, M., Palmieri, F.: Exploiting mean field analysis to model performances of big data architectures. Future Generation Computer Systems 37(0), 203–211 (2014), special Section: Innovative Methods and Algorithms for Advanced Data-Intensive Computing Special Section: Semantics, Intelligent processing and services for big data Special Section: Advances in Data-Intensive Modelling and Simulation Special Section: Hybrid Intelligence for Growing Internet and its Applications
8. Castiglione, A., Gribaudo, M., Iacono, M., Palmieri, F.: Modeling performances of concurrent big data applications. Software: Practice and Experience pp. n/a–n/a (2014), http://dx.doi.org/10.1002/spe.2269
9. Cerotti, D., Gribaudo, M., Piazzolla, P., Pinciroli, R., Serazzi, G.: Multi-class queuing networks models for energy optimization. In: Proceedings of the 8th International Conference Performance Evaluation Methodologies and Tools (2014)

10. Cerotti, D., Gribaudo, M., Piazzolla, P., Serazzi, G.: Matching performance objectives for open and closed workloads by consolidation and replication. Ann. Oper. Res. 1–24 (2014), http://dx.doi.org/10.1007/s10479-014-1591-9

11. Ciardo, G., III, R.J., Miner, A., Siminiceanu, R.: Logic and stochastic modeling with SMART. Perform. Eval. **63**(6), 578–608 (2006), http://www.sciencedirect.com/science/article/pii/S0166531605000726, modelling Techniques and Tools for Computer Performance Evaluation

12. Ciardo, G., Miner, A.S.: Smart: the stochastic model checking analyzer for reliability and timing. In: International Conference on Quantitative Evaluation of Systems, pp. 338–339 (2004)

13. Fan, X., Weber, W.D., Barroso, L.A.: Power provisioning for a warehouse-sized computer. In: Proceedings of the 34th International Symposium on Computer Architecture. pp. 13–23. ACM, New York (2007), http://doi.acm.org/10.1145/1250662.1250665

14. Ficco, M., Palmieri, F.: Introducing fraudulent energy consumption in cloud infrastructures: a new generation of denial-of-service attacks. Systems Journal, IEEE PP(99), 1–11 (2015)

15. Gandhi, A., Harchol-Balter, M., Das, R., Lefurgy, C.: Optimal power allocation in server farms. In: Proceedings of the 11th International Conference on Measurement and Modeling of Computer Systems. pp. 157–168. ACM, New York (2009), http://doi.acm.org/10.1145/1555349.1555368

16. Gribaudo, M., Iacono, M., Manini, D.: Improving reliability and performances in large scale distributed applications with erasure codes and replication. Future Generation Computer Systems (2015), http://www.sciencedirect.com/science/article/pii/S0167739X15002290

17. Gribaudo, M., Piazzolla, P., Serazzi, G.: Consolidation and replication of VMs matching performance objectives. In: Analytical and Stochastic Modeling Techniques and Applications, vol. 7314, pp. 106–120. Springer (2012), http://dx.doi.org/10.1007/978-3-642-30782-9_8

18. Kolodziej, J., Burczynski, T., Zomaya, A.Y.: A note on energy efficient data, services and memory management in big data information systems. Information Sciences 319, 69–70 (2015), energy Efficient Data, Services and Memory Management in Big Data Information Systems

19. Nathuji, R., Schwan, K.: Virtualpower: Coordinated power management in virtualized enterprise systems. SIGOPS Oper. Syst. Rev. **41**(6), 265–278 (Oct 2007), http://doi.acm.org/10.1145/1323293.1294287

20. Palmieri, F., Ricciardi, S., Fiore, U., Ficco, M., Castiglione, A.: Energy-oriented denial of service attacks: an emerging menace for large cloud infrastructures. J. Supercomput. **71**(5), 1620–1641 (2015)

21. Piazzolla, P., Ciardo, G., Miner, A.: Power consumption analysis of replicated virtual applications. In: Gribaudo, M., Manini, D., Remke, A. (eds.) Analytical and Stochastic Modelling Techniques and Applications, Lecture Notes in Computer Science, vol. 9081, pp. 188–202. Springer International Publishing (2015)

22. Pinheiro, E., Bianchini, R., Carrera, E.V., Heath, T.: Load balancing and unbalancing for power and performance in cluster-based systems. Available at http://www2.ic.uff.br/julius/stre/pinheiro01load.pdf (2001)

23. Raghavendra, R., Ranganathan, P., Talwar, V., et al.: No "power" struggles: Coordinated multi-level power management for the data center. SIGARCH Comput. Archit. News **36**(1), 48–59 (Mar 2008), http://doi.acm.org/10.1145/1353534.1346289

24. Sfrent, A., Pop, F.: Asymptotic scheduling for many task computing in big data platforms. Information Sciences 319, 71–91 (2015), energy Efficient Data, Services and Memory Management in Big Data Information Systems

25. Song, Y., Wang, H., Li, Y., et al.: Multi-tiered on-demand resource scheduling for VM-Based Data Center. In: Proceedings of the 9th Symposium on Cluster Computing and the Grid. pp. 148–155. IEEE (2009), http://dx.doi.org/10.1109/CCGRID.2009.11

26. Vasile, M.A., Pop, F., Tutueanu, R.I., Cristea, V., KoÅ,odziej, J.: Resource-aware hybrid scheduling algorithm in heterogeneous distributed computing. Future Generation Computer Systems 51, 61–71 (2015), special Section: A Note on New Trends in Data-Aware Scheduling and Resource Provisioning in Modern {HPC} Systems

27. Watson, B.J., Marwah, M., Gmach, D., et al.: Probabilistic performance modeling of virtualized resource allocation. In: Proceedings of the 7th International Conference on Autonomic computing,. pp. 99–108. ACM, New York (2010)
28. Xu, X., Hu, H., Hu, N., Ying, W.: Cloud task and virtual machine allocation strategy in cloud computing environment. In: Network Computing and Information Security, vol. 345, pp. 113–120. Springer (2012), 10.1007/978-3-642-35211-9_15

An Agent-Based Platform for Resource Configuration and Monitoring of Cloud Applications

Rocco Aversa, Luca Tasquier and Davide Fusco

Abstract Cloud monitoring is a task of paramount importance for both providers and consumers. On one side, it is a key feature for controlling and managing the infrastructures; on the other side, it provides information and Key Performance Indicators (KPIs) for both platforms and applications. In order to overcome conflict of interest coming from monitoring data collected by the same provider that is supplying the Cloud environment, a third-party monitoring infrastructure is desirable. However, even if this monitoring infrastructure is available to check performance indexes on a Cloud infrastructure, this framework remains unaware with respect to the specific application that is running on the environment, without any knowledge about its components' distribution.In this work we present an architecture and a prototypal implementation of an agent-based framework that allows the configuration of a monitoring infrastructure for Cloud applications, giving the possibility to customize both the application stressing tests and the analysis of the benchmarking data in order to shape the monitoring infrastructure to the specific application.

Keywords Cloud application monitoring · Mobile agents · Iaas cloud · Service level agreement

R. Aversa · L. Tasquier (✉) · D. Fusco
Department of Industrial and Information Engineering,
Second University of Naples, Aversa, Italy
e-mail: luca.tasquier@unina2.it

R. Aversa
e-mail: rocco.aversa@unina2.it

D. Fusco
e-mail: davide.fusco@studenti.unina2.it

© Springer International Publishing Switzerland 2016   299
L. Caporarello et al. (eds.), *Digitally Supported Innovation*,
Lecture Notes in Information Systems and Organisation 18,
DOI 10.1007/978-3-319-40265-9_22

1   Introduction

Monitoring of Cloud environments is one among the major challenges that nowadays is affecting this widely used computing paradigm. In order to ensure scalability and dependability, the user's applications are often distributed on several computational resources, such as Virtual Machines, storages and so on. For this reason, the customer is able to retrieve information about the Cloud infrastructure only by acquiring monitoring services provided by the same vendor that is offering the Cloud resources, thus being forced to trust the Cloud provider about the detected performance indexes. Different Cloud deployment models bring problems in accessing the data to monitor and in trusting the parameters agreed in the Service Level Agreements (SLAs). While in private Cloud all is available to the user, in a public Cloud customers can only access to monitoring information made available by the suppliers without having the possibility to counter-prove the measures; this fact leads to trust issues due to the conflict of interest that providers have in ensuring the guarantees on service levels they provide. However, even if a third-party monitoring infrastructure is available to check performance indexes on a Cloud infrastructure, this framework remains unaware with respect to the specific application that is running on the environment, without any knowledge about the components' distribution and thus without giving the possibility to implement an application centric configuration of the monitoring infrastructure and the analysis of the computed data driven by the weakness of the application's components. This kind of monitoring can be very useful in order to understand what the bottlenecks and the critical components of its application are and to discover oversizing of the runtime environment with respect to the specific application, thus allowing the developer to exploit the elasticity of Cloud Computing by adapting the infrastructure to the application's real requirements.

In this work we present an architecture and a prototypal implementation of an agent-based framework that allows an application driven configuration of a monitoring infrastructure, giving the possibility to customize both the application stressing tests and the analysis of the benchmarking data in order to automatic shape the monitoring infrastructure to the specific application. The paper is organized as follows: related work is presented in Sect. 2; in Sect. 3 the architecture addressing the application driven monitoring infrastructure configuration is detailed, while its agent-based implementation is described in Sect. 4; in Sect. 5 is explained an use-case exploited to validate the proposed architecture and its prototypal implementation, while in Sect. 6 conclusion is due.

2   Related Work

The increasing use of Cloud Computing to manage applications, services and resources puts even more emphasis on the necessity of monitoring the QoS parameters in order to have the desired performances: infrastructure level resource monitoring aims at the measurement and reporting of system parameters related to real or virtual infrastructure services offered to the user [8]. Monitoring of the Cloud infrastructures is a so relevant challenge that a new concept has been recently introduced within the contest of the service models: the Monitoring as a Service (MaaS) [10]. Having a monitoring service is an opportunity for both provider and user. First of all, the MaaS facilitates the monitoring by offering several functionalities and thus avoiding the development of ad hoc tools. Besides, through the implementation of the "pay-as-you-go" model, the possibility to choose the monitored parameters and the detail's level of the measurements is given to the customer by taking into account his/her needings, as well as his/her available funds. Furthermore this service encourages the providers to invest in the monitoring field in order to provide improvements of both QoS and performances.

There are many tools which provide Cloud monitoring facilities to retrieve information on the status of the virtual platform at the virtualized hardware layer (e.g., in terms of CPU, memory, workload, etc.), at the operating system layer and at the network layer [6, 16]. Most of them (e.g., CloudWatch [2], AzureWatch [12], CloudKick [15]) are commercial solutions provided by the Cloud vendors that are offering the services to the users, and so the customers have to trust the measures provided by the same entities that are supplying the Cloud services.

In [1] a survey about commercial and open-source platforms for monitoring of private and public Cloud infrastructure is presented: each solution addresses only few parameters (e.g. only some performance indexes and the Availability as QoS parameter) and it is not possible to extend the number of measurable parameters. Moreover, they aim at monitoring Cloud resources without being aware about the application that is running on them.

Our solution proposes a third-party, customizable and highly extensible monitoring infrastructure that is capable to configure itself autonomously in order to best fit the monitored parameters with the application and thus giving the possibility to the developer to properly size the Cloud infrastructure and to understand potential problems and bottlenecks within the application.

3 Application Driven Monitoring Architecture

The monitoring activities of a Cloud infrastructure are aimed at continuously checking the fulfillment of the requirements in order to avoid saturation or under-utilization of Cloud resources and to check the compliance of the signed SLAs with the real performance of the infrastructure. To do this, a complete monitoring architecture has been conceived (Fig. 1): it relies on a modular structure composed by three parts. The first one is the Infrastructure Definition Module, that accepts the resource configuration together with the performance constraints as input and allows the configuration of the monitoring infrastructure. The second module is the Setup & Management Module, which is in charge of initializing the monitoring facilities by taking the description of the monitoring infrastructure from

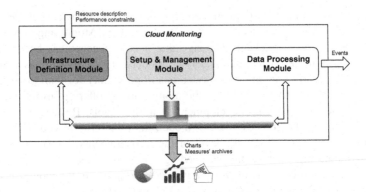

Fig. 1 Cloud monitoring architecture

the Infrastructure Definition Module: it installs the needed modules on the selected resources, manages the monitoring operations by starting, stopping and reconfiguring probes on the resources; moreover, it collects monitored data and allows the visualization of the monitoring results. The third module is the Data Processing Module that allows the configuration and the triggering of events based on some conditions that are occurring on the Cloud infrastructure: it implements a Complex Event Processing module (CEP) for the Cloud execution environment that can be used for both SLA fulfillment check and distributed attack detection.

Research activities about the Infrastructure Definition Module and on the Setup & Management Module have been described in previous works: in [4] a prototypal implementation of a module for the creation of the monitoring infrastructure has been proposed, while the architecture and an agent-based implementation of the Setup & Management Module is detailed in [3]: in particular, the proposed solution exploits the strength of the mobile agent's paradigm to address in-place and specialized monitoring, also in case of very restrictive firewall policies; moreover, the agents are trained in order to map measured performance indexes to QoS parameters and to react to environment changes, self-adapting the monitoring infrastructure to the new resources' configuration; measurements can be provided by using different algorithms and technologies without taking care about the agent's framework, thanks to a complete decoupling between the agent's execution and the measurement's module: for this reason, the Monitoring Framework is capable to take measure at different levels, thus allowing the SLA check at both resource parameters level (e.g. CPU speed, etc.) and QoS level (e.g. Availability, Throughput, etc.). Furthermore, studies about the automatic provisioning of the Cloud infrastructure and the generation of the resource description that feeds the monitoring architecture have been conducted in [19, 20, 17].

The proposed architecture allows the configuration of a monitoring infrastructure that provides measures about performance indexes and QoS parameters of the Cloud environment but it is "general-purpose": the monitoring framework is not aware about the application that is actually running on the Cloud infrastructure and thus it is not

Fig. 2 Benchmarking
Module

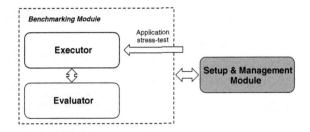

optimized to take under control the parameters which are really critical for the specific utilization of the environment. The modular design of the architecture allows a straightforward extension of the framework by giving the possibility to the user to adapt the monitoring infrastructure to the application distributed within the Cloud. To address this scope, it has been designed a new module that, even if external, inter-operate with the existing module by using their interfaces: the *Benchmarking Module*. This module allows the submission of application's benchmarks and the training of the monitoring framework according to the benchmarks' results. The application's benchmarks can be conceived as end-user programs that, invoking the application's services and following the specific application's workflow, are aimed at stressing all the components distributed within the environment in order to bring out the limits of these components and how the critical runtime conditions of one or more components affect the performance of the whole application. The Benchmarking Module (Fig. 2) is divided in two submodules:

1. *Executor*: this module prepares the monitoring infrastructure to collect data and allows the submission of the application's benchmarks.

2. *Evaluator*: it evaluates the monitoring results and decides, for each resource, which the critical parameters to be monitored are; it also evaluates and sets additional parameters' constraints, such as thresholds and measurement periods. As described in Sect. 4, the evaluation logic can be implemented according different algorithms which can be inserted into the Evaluator by using a plug-in approach. Furthermore, this module adapts and configures the monitoring infrastructure following the evaluated monitoring configuration.

The whole Benchmarking Module cooperates directly with the Setup & Management Module in order to perform its behaviours: in particular, the collaboration among the submodules and the external components of the system is depicted in Fig. 3. The developer is the only one that knows the application's behaviour and how it has been deployed within the Cloud infrastructure. For this reason, he/she has to write a specific benchmark for the application in order to invoke the application's services and to stress it (i.e. the application stress-test of Fig. 2). After that, it can submit the benchmark to the Benchmarking service: the Executor starts the measurement operations by invoking the Setup & Management Module and executes the benchmark. Once the benchmark is over, the Setup & Management Module sends the monitoring results to the Benchmarking Module: these data are received by the Evaluator that, for each resource, evaluates the results

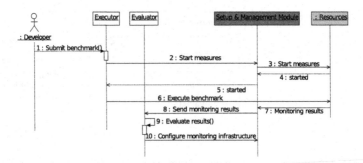

Fig. 3 Collaboration among Benchmarking submodules

and defines an optimal configuration for the infrastructure that best fits with the application. The Evaluator can also decides to repeat the benchmark by changing some parameter if the provided results are not exhaustive to reach an optimal configuration (e.g. the benchmark has not stressed the application too much, the Evaluator needs more parameters to analyze, etc.): in this case, it forwards back the request to the Executor which starts a new round of benchmark with the new parameters. If the Evaluator computes a result, it acts on the Setup & Management Module to implement the configuration and the provided policies on the monitoring infrastructure.

At the end of the operations, the Benchmarking Module provides an application driven monitoring infrastructure configuration that analyze, for each resource, the parameters that are critical for the application and that can lead to a performance degradation, bottlenecks, and so on. As a side effect of the benchmarking operations, the results of the elaboration are provided to the developer as a report that can be useful to resize the Cloud infrastructure in order to best fit the application's requirements. Future research activities could aim at exploiting these results to automatically tune the environment by implementing reconfiguration rules based on the benchmarking results.

4   Benchmarking Module Implementation

On the basis of the architecture described in Sect. 3, a prototypal implementation of the Benchmarking Module has been developed by using the agents' paradigm: the utilization of an agent-based model ensures high decoupling among the modules, thanks to its asynchronous communication methods; moreover, agents reactivity and proactivity allow a self-adaptation to environments that can rapidly change their configuration, such as a Cloud infrastructure.

For the implementation of the module's prototype, we select JADE [5, 18] as agent platform. JADE is fully written in Java, that is a widely-used technology with low impacts on computational resources, that is highly portable due to the fact that the whole execution environment is contained in a stand-alone Java archive (JAR). Moreover, JADE architecture and communication language are compliant with the ones released by FIPA [11]. The implementation of the Setup & Management Module taken into account to invoke the monitoring architecture services is the agent-based one described in [3]: in particular, on every resource is installed an agent that acts as probe and computes measures in place.

Each part of the Benchmarking Module has been mapped with an agent within the platform which addresses the tasks of the specific submodule. First of all, an *Executor Interface* has been designed in order to allow the submission of the benchmarks, decoupling the agent that executes the benchmark from the benchmark itself and allowing a straightforward communication between the agent and the benchmarking module without that the developer is aware about the agent's technology: the developer has only to implement the interface with a module that embeds the benchmark and that is loaded at runtime. The Executor agent will control the benchmark by invoking the operations overridden by the developer without being aware about the specific application: in this way it is possible to use the agent based architecture to manage the benchmark (written in whatever programming language) in a transparent way with respect to the upper layer. The interface is composed by actions (A) and notifications (N): the actions are the functionalities that are application-aware and have to be implemented by the developer in order to allow the management through the Executor agent; the notifications are events provided by the interface to the developer thanks to which the application can notify some events to the Executor agent. The Executor Interface description is provided in Table 1.

The Evaluator agent maps the corresponding Benchmarking submodule and is in charge of evaluating the data collected by the probes in order to fit the monitoring infrastructure with the application. The Evaluator can load two kind of evaluation module in order to perform its behaviour. The first one is an embedded module: the

Table 1 Executor Interface

Method	Type	Description
Start	A	This action has to be overridden by the developer in order to start the benchmark of the application. It is possible to customize the number of iterations for each process that is running within the benchmark, as well as to increase the level of parallelism of the benchmark by adding processes to the benchmark
Started	N	The developer uses this method to notify to the agent that the benchmark is started
Stop	A	The Executor can force the benchmark's interruption by using this action
Stopped	N	This method is used by the developer to notify the end of the benchmark
Cleanup	A	By overriding this action it is possible to implement the necessary operations to restore the application's components to the state before the benchmark's execution (e.g. cleaning temporary files, restoring databases, etc.)
Restored	N	At the end of the cleanup operations, the developer invokes this method

Evaluator is equipped with an embedded evaluation algorithm that analyze resources and computed measures to take decisions about parameters to monitor, measurement frequency, warning threshold and critical threshold; the module can also decide to run the benchmark another time by changing the number of iterations per process and/or the number of parallel processes. The second evaluation module is customized: it is given to the developer an *Evaluator Interface* by which he/she can customize the analysis of the benchmark's results and take decisions about the configuration of the monitoring framework. The first action of the interface is *analyze*: the Evaluator passes to the developer the resource's list with the monitoring results; each resource is accompanied with a detailed description of its configuration (operating system, memory amount, etc.) and the monitoring results are expressed in terms of measurement period, sequence number of the measurement, measures' list related to the specific sequence number; each measure's list is composed by the name of the measured parameter and the value, expressed in compliance with the SFlow standard [14]. By overriding the *analyze* method, the developer has all the information to take decision about the monitoring configuration of the single resource. While analyzing the results, it can set the monitoring parameters for a resource by using the *configure* notification: the developer has to specify the resource on which act, the chosen parameter, the measurement's period, an eventual warning threshold value, an alert threshold value. If the developer wants to add another rule for the same resource, it has only to re-invoke the *configure* method and to change the parameters for the same resource. At the end of the analysis, it is possible to use two notifications:

1. *Apply*: the utilization of this method allows the Evaluator to commit all the defined rules to the Setup & Management Module;

2. *Execute*: if the benchmark's results are evaluated as non-exhaustive, it is possible to request another benchmark's round; this method deletes the monitoring results and asks to the Executor for another benchmark's run, changing the benchmark's parameters.

The agents' deployment is depicted in Fig. 4: as it is possible to see, each part of the Monitoring Framework can be deployed in a different execution environment, giving to the whole infrastructure scalability properties.

Fig. 4 Agents' deployment

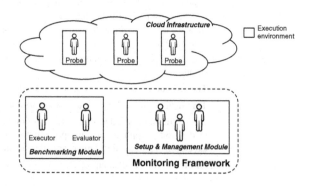

(a)

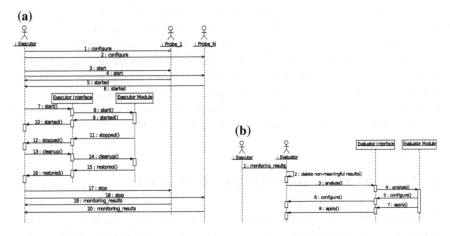

Fig. 5 Executor and Evaluator behaviours. **a** Executor behaviour. **b** Evaluator behaviour

The benchmarking protocol works as follows: at the beginning, the Executor configures the probes of the infrastructure to collect the measures at the maximum frequency in order to retrieve as much as possible data. The probes have two kind of operational modes: in *forward* mode, each probe computes a set of measures and sends it to a collector within the monitoring infrastructure, loosing it after the sending; in *local* mode, the probes stores all the measures locally and sends the whole packet of measures to the applicant at the end of the monitoring operations. In order to not affect the Cloud communication infrastructure with the traffic generated by the monitoring during the benchmark, the Executor sets all the probes in *local* mode. After these preliminary operations, it starts each probe and waits for the acknowledgement of the successful start coming from all the probes. At the reception of the last acknowledgement, it evaluates the time between the first start and the last stop in order to allow the Evaluator to skip the measures computed before the start of the benchmark. The Executor start the benchmark by acting on the *start* method of the interface, that calls the overridden implementation and starts the benchmark. At the end of the benchmark, the module uses the *stopped* notification to inform the Executor about the end of the operations; the Executor sends a *cleanup* request to "clean" the infrastructure and, after receiving the *restored* notification, it stops the probes and collects the monitoring results (Fig. 5a).

Once the Executor agent's operations finished, it sends the monitoring results to the Evaluator agent that starts elaborating the information. It exploits the delay between the beginning and the end of the probes start in order to delete non-meaningful data, that are the ones gathered when the benchmark was not actually started. After this cleaning operation, it evaluates the results by calling the *analyze* method on the Evaluator Interface, which is forwarded to the embedded or customized Evaluator Module. During the analysis, for each parameter that is considered critical, the *configure* notification is invoked, setting up the monitoring rule which might be implemented on the Setup & Management Module. At the end of the evaluation, if a large amount of data are considered to be not enough to exhaustively configure the monitoring infrastructure, the Evaluator Module developer can ask for another benchmarking round by using the *execute* callback; on the contrary, if the monitoring configuration ends exhaustively, the Evaluator Module commits the monitoring rules by invoking the *apply* notification through the Evaluator interface, using the Setup & Management Module services to implement the monitoring rules. The evaluation protocol is shown in Fig. 5b.

5   Usage Scenario and Prototype Evaluation

To validate the proposed architecture, its prototypal implementation has been applied to a testbed application: this one consists of on a secure file storage service where the user can upload and download his/her files by using a DES algorithm to encrypt and decrypt the data. The application has been distributed on a private Cloud environment based on OpenStack [13]: in particular, it has been used three Virtual Machines (VMs) to host the application components. On the first one has been installed the application frontend, where the file storage service is exposed; the second VM has been used to host a MySQL based relational DBMS [9], which takes care about the users' accounts. The third VM host represents the computational unit and hosts the encryption algorithm. Together with this infrastructure, it has been used an external MongoDB document oriented database as a Service (DBaaS) [7], which is suitable to store a large amount of data, as the encrypted files are. The user authenticates himself against the frontend that forwards the request to the VM hosting the relational database: after that, he/she submits the file and the encryption key to the frontend that provides them to the computation entity. The encrypted file is stored in the DBaaS service and an acknowledgement about the successful save is sent back to the frontend. On this environment has been installed the monitoring and benchmarking framework described in Sect. 3 and a benchmark has been developed to stress the application by continuously invoking the encryption service, thus understanding the best monitoring configuration and the application's bottlenecks.

As an example, in Fig. 6 are depicted the benchmarking results for what concerning the CPU usage of the resources. The Evaluator module has been implemented to consider exhaustive a benchmark on this parameter when the average CPU usage overcomes the 75 %: as it is possible to understand, after some benchmarking rounds, the threshold has been exceeded by the computation entity when the number of simulated parallel users increases, while this parameter does not affect other resources. On the contrary, the benchmark highlights that on the frontend the parameter that is more affected by the stress test is the network interface, where the average number of received packets per second increases with the parallelism of the users (after 25 users, it exceeds 6000 received packets per

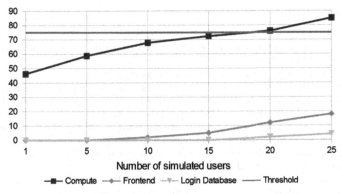

Fig. 6 Benchmark results on CPU usage

second). For these reasons, the Evaluator agent configures the Setup & Management Module in order to focus the monitoring on the CPU usage parameter for the computation entity and on the network interface for what concerning the frontend VM. These results also reveal that it could be useful to exploit the Cloud elasticity by adding a redundant VM hosting the encryption algorithm in order to scale the application on the users' growth by balancing the workload.

6 Conclusion

In this work we presented an architecture and a prototypal implementation of an agent-based framework that allows an application driven configuration of a monitoring infrastructure, giving the possibility to customize both the application stressing tests and the analysis of the benchmarking data in order to shape the monitoring infrastructure to the specific application. The proposed architecture gives the possibility to an application developer to implement benchmark in any programming language and to easily embed it into the Benchmarking module, allowing a self-adaptation of the monitoring facility to the specific application. The results obtained by using the prototype on a Cloud testbed validate the designed architecture and encourage us in going ahead on this research field. In particular, future research activities could aim at exploiting the proposed framework to automatically tune the Cloud environment by defining and implementing reconfiguration rules based on the benchmarking results.

Acknowledgments This work has been supported by CoSSMic (Collaborating Smart Solar-powered Micro-grids- FP7-ICT-608806).

References

1. Aceto, G., Botta, A., De Donato, W., Pescapè, A.: Cloud monitoring: a survey. Comput. Netw. **57**(9), 2093–2115 (2013)
2. Amazon: Cloud Watch, http://aws.amazon.com/cloudwatch/
3. Aversa, R., Panza, N., Tasquier, L.: An agent-based platform for cloud applications performance monitoring. In: 2015 Ninth International Conference on Complex, Intelligent, and Software Intensive Systems (CISIS), pp. 535–540. IEEE (2015)
4. Aversa, R., Tasquier, L., Venticinque, S.: Agents based monitoring of heterogeneous cloud infrastructures. In: 2013 IEEE 10th International Conference on Ubiquitous Intelligence and Computing, and 10th International Conference on Autonomic and Trusted Computing (UIC/ATC), pp. 527–532. IEEE (2013)
5. Bellifemine, F., Poggi, A., Rimassa, G.: JADE–A FIPA-compliant agent framework. In: Proceedings of PAAM, vol. 99, p. 33 (1999)
6. Caron, E., Rodero-Merino, L., Desprez, F., Muresan, A., et al.: Auto-scaling, load balancing and monitoring in commercial and open-source clouds. Cloud Comput. Methodol. Syst. Appl. (2012)
7. Chodorow, K.: Mongo, D.B.: The definitive guide. O'Reilly Media, Inc. (2013)
8. Clayman, S., Galis, A., Chapman, C., Toffetti, G., Rodero-Merino, L., Vaquero, L.M., Nagin, K., Rochwerger, B.: Monitoring service clouds in the future internet. In: Future Internet Assembly, pp. 115–126 (2010)
9. Du Bois, P.: MySQL. Pearson Italia Spa (2004)
10. Meng, S., Liu, L.: Enhanced monitoring-as-a-service for effective cloud management. IEEE Trans. Comput. **62**(9), 1705–1720 (2013)
11. O'Brien, P.D., Nicol, R.C.: FIPA—towards a standard for software agents. BT Technol. J. **16**(3), 51–59 (1998)
12. Paraleap Technologies: Azure Watch, http://www.paraleap.com/azurewatch
13. Pepple, K.: Deploying Openstack. O'Reilly Media, Inc. (2011)
14. Phaal, P., Panchen, S., McKee, N.: InMon corporation's sFlow: A method for monitoring traffic in switched and routed networks. Technical. report, RFC 3176 (2001)
15. Rackspace: Cloud Kick, http://www.rackspace.com/cloud/monitoring/
16. Spring, J.: Monitoring cloud computing by layer, part 1. Secur. Priv. IEEE **9**(2), 66–68 (2011)
17. Tasquier, L., Venticinque, S., Aversa, R., Di Martino, B.: Agent based application tools for cloud provisioning and management. In: Cloud Computing, pp. 32–42. Springer (2013)
18. Telecom Italia: Telecom Italia Lab, http://www.telecomitalia.com/tit/it/about-us/business/activities/telecom-italia-lab.html
19. Venticinque, S., Tasquier, L., Di Martino, B.: Agents based cloud computing interface for resource provisioning and management. In: 2012 Sixth International Conference on Complex, Intelligent and Software Intensive Systems (CISIS). pp. 249–256. IEEE (2012)
20. Venticinque, S., Tasquier, L., Di Martino, B.: A restfull interface for scalable agents based cloud services. Int. J. Ad Hoc Ubiquitous Comput. **16**(4), 219–231 (2014)

Author Index

© Springer International Publishing Switzerland 2016   311
L. Caporarello et al. (eds.), *Digitally Supported Innovation*,
Lecture Notes in Information Systems and Organisation 18,
DOI 10.1007/978-3-319-40265-9

Printed in the United States
By Bookmasters